A HISTORY OF SOVIET LITERATURE

1917–1964
FROM GORKY TO SOLZHENITSYN

VERA ALEXANDROVA

TRANSLATED BY MIRRA GINSBURG

ANCHOR BOOKS
Doubleday & Company, Inc.
Garden City, New York

10766

A History of Soviet Literature was originally published by Doubleday & Company, Inc., in 1963. The Anchor Books edition is published by arrangement with Doubleday.

Anchor Books edition: 1964

Library of Congress Catalog Card Number 64-16559
Copyright © 1963, 1964 by Vera Alexandrova-Schwarz
All Rights Reserved. Printed in the United States of America

CONTENTS

Introduction	vii
1. From Pre-Revolutionary to Soviet Literature	1
2. Literary Developments: From the Revolution to World War II (1917–39)	18
3. Vladimir Mayakovsky (1893–1930)	61
4. Sergey Yesenin (1895–1925)	80
5. Yevgeny Zamyatin (1884–1937)	97
6. Mikhail Zoshchenko (1895–1958)	112
7. Ilya Ehrenburg (1891–)	127
8. Isaac Babel (1894–1941)	143
9. Boris Pilnyak (1894– ?)	156
10. Boris Pasternak (1890–1960)	174
11. Yury Olesha (1899–1960)	188
12. Leonid Leonov (1899–)	203
13. Mikhail Prishvin (1873–1954)	222
14. Alexey Tolstoy (1883–1945)	236
15. Mikhail Sholokhov (1905–)	251
16. Literary Developments: World War II and After (1939–62)	271
17. Konstantin Paustovsky (1892–)	302
18. Vera Panova (1905–)	317
19. Alexander Tvardovsky (1910–)	331
20. Valentin Ovechkin (1904–)	344
21. Victor Nekrasov (1910–)	357
22. Vladimir Dudintsev (1918–)	370

	Contents
23. Three Young Writers: Yevgeny Yevtushenko, Yury Nagibin, Yury Kazakov	383
24. Epilogue	406
Bibliography	439
Index	451

INTRODUCTION

Russian literature of the nineteenth century may be generally considered to consist of the works of some fifty or sixty writers, poets, and critics. The average intelligent reader contents himself with familiarity with the works of twenty or thirty writers, beginning with Karamzin and ending with Gorky and Bunin. The actual number of writers who made their contribution to the literature of the nineteenth century was, of course, much larger, but many did not pass the test of time and are almost entirely forgotten.

According to the report of the Credentials Commission of the First All-Union Congress of Soviet Writers in August 1934, held fifteen-odd years after the appearance of the first literary works of the revolutionary period, the Congress was attended by 591 delegates, representing 1500 members of the Writers' Union. At the Third All-Union Congress of Soviet Writers in May 1959, the Credentials Commission reported a membership of *more than 4500*. In the attempt to write a history of Soviet literature, such an enormous increase makes all the more necessary a careful selection of writers whose names may be expected to survive in the memory of future generations. However, a true history of literature cannot confine itself to works of enduring literary value alone. In the present study of Soviet literature—or, to be more precise, of Russian Soviet literature—I shall deal, therefore, with a number of works which, though of merely passing literary significance, retain a measure of importance for the understanding of the development of this literature or the development of Soviet society.

In the choice of writers we are often helped by time itself. Many writers who attracted attention in the early 1920s, such as Sergey Klychkov, Vladimir Kirillov, and

Alexey Tveryak, are now forgotten. Others—such as N. Ognyov, author of *The Diary of Kostya Ryabtsev*, Semyon Podyachev, etc.—who seemed important to their contemporaries, can no longer be considered of any real historical or literary significance.

But in the course of literary development the opposite may also occur, and we encounter writers who, at the height of their powers (and sometimes until the end of their lives), met a cold or harsh critical reception—who were, indeed, barely permitted to exist even at the periphery of literary life—but who later became favorites with the reading public. Despite all his stubborn faith in happy miracles, Alexander Grin surely never dreamed, as he was writing his novel *Scarlet Sails* at the House of the Arts in famine-ridden Petersburg in 1920, that it would be used twenty-five years later as the basis for a ballet of the same name, to be produced with great success in the middle 1940s and to remain in the repertoire until the end of the '50s and perhaps longer.

The problem of the selection of writers and works which successfully reflected their epoch was touched upon by Marietta Shaginyan in her book *On Art and Literature* (1958). She wrote:

"Why is it, with the vast quantities of material accumulated during the thirty-six years of the socialist development of literature, that our literary criticism seems unable to cope with the task of tracing its general trends and establishing a convincing division into periods? The need for such generalization is acute. Several generations of readers have grown up, to whom our 1920s and '30s are virtually 'ancient history,' known only from hearsay. To them, even the years of the Great Patriotic War [World War II—V.A.] are dim memories, seen through the mist of early childhood, much as the revolution of 1905 and the Russo-Japanese War are to people of my generation. To these new generations, a great deal of Soviet literature is simply unknown, unread, and unfamiliar, and they are compelled to study it from textbooks which contain no breath of those inspired years when our young literature was being born, in the midst of stormy struggles and fervent searching. And because our young, and even our middle-aged readers . . . do not have available to them a truly generalizing work on the history of Soviet literature, they do not see it as an integrated, organic entity, and are therefore frequently unable to understand modern Soviet books as links in a developing whole. . . . How drily, for example, the history of Soviet literature of the early years of the revolution, the Civil War era, and the 1920s is presented in our textbooks—without any vivid, integral conception of the great practical demands facing the Soviet people of that time!"

Marietta Shaginyan merely touched upon the problem, but did not venture to develop it further. For in reality, the history of Soviet literature seems uninteresting because Soviet literary historians carefully conceal many of the problems and works which agitated readers in those years. The sad state of Soviet literary scholarship and criticism becomes painfully evident on the slightest acquaintance with Soviet textbooks. Thus, *Modern Soviet Literature*, by L. Timofeyev—the textbook most widely used in Soviet secondary schools—does not even mention in its edition of 1946 and in a number of subsequent editions the names of such poets as Boris Pasternak and Nikolay Kluyev, or such prose writers as Mikhail Zoshchenko, Yevgeny Zamyatin, Isaac Babel, Boris Pilnyak, and others. True, many writers who were damned and dishonored during the numerous "purges," and who ended their lives either in prison or in distant exile, were "rehabilitated" after Stalin's death. But in most cases, this rehabilitation involved only writers who were already dead. Of suppressed writers who survived the evil years and returned to literary activity, we may mention only a few isolated individuals, such as the once popular satirist Nikolay Erdman and the poet Boris Ruchyov. While these men have resumed writing, they seem to live as though with broken backbones. Moreover, the rehabilitation itself was conducted in a quiet, cautious manner, without any open statement in the press, but merely by renewed acknowledgment of literary existence through the reissue of one-volume (and occasionally two-volume) editions of "selected" works. Under these conditions some of the works of Isaac Babel, Ivan Katayev, Mikhail Koltsov, Artyom Vesyoly, and others have reappeared in recent years.

In studying the literary life of the early 1920s we often encounter a characteristic trait: the literary youth of those years, especially the members of the then influential Association of Proletarian Writers, were fond of parading their "internationalism" and "kinlessness." In essence, however, this was little more than an expression of social mimicry, of adaptation to the political and social fashion of the time. The true sources of Soviet literature lay elsewhere. In *Gorky Among Us* (1943–44), a still unfinished trilogy devoted to life in the early 1920s, Konstantin Fedin, himself one of the pioneers of the Soviet period in Russian literature, tells about an interesting conversation with Alexey Remizov, a writer known long before the revolution. Returning with Fedin from some literary evening, Remizov said: "And so, the young ones are emerging from their backwoods—their suburbs and hamlets. I have always said: wait, they will come, from unexpected corners, they will come to take over, and with full right. Not incubator babies, not homunculi, but born of a father and a mother, children equally of the Russian revolution and of Russian literature."

Remizov predicted correctly that the literary revival would come from the depths of the Russian provinces, and that this provincial youth would be the true pioneers of the Soviet period in Russian literature. In order to understand the atmosphere of those years, however, it must be noted that the provincialism of the pioneers was of secondary importance to their readers. To post-revolutionary readers, these writers were the spokesmen of the people, emissaries from the heart of the country, with a new and original message to match their own new lives and aspirations.

One should note, too, that the "cosmopolitanism" of the pioneers of the new literature, which at first received so much official encouragement, was later condemned. In

Introduction

the early 1930s Soviet critics began to devote a good deal of attention to the problem of the "forerunners" of Soviet literature. Maxim Gorky is usually spoken of as the "bridge" between pre-revolutionary and Soviet literature. But Gorky was not typical of the literature which sprang up during the first years of the revolution of 1917. The late Alexey Tolstoy treated this problem with considerable insight in his essay "A Quarter Century of Soviet Literature" (1942). He cited an excerpt from a letter written by his famous namesake Leo Tolstoy to the critic Nicolay Strakhov. I quote Leo Tolstoy's statement more fully than it is given by Alexey Tolstoy:

"Have you noticed in Russian poetry today a connection between two facts, which exist in reverse proportion to one another: the decline in poetic arts of every type—music, painting, poetry; and the trend toward the study of Russian folk poetry of every type—music, painting (and decorative arts), and poetry? It seems to me that it is not even a decline, but a death, with a promise of renascence in the folk. The last poetic wave reached its highest point in Pushkin's time; afterward came Lermontov, Gogol, we sinners—and then it went underground. Another current led to the study of the people, and will emerge to the surface, God willing. But the Pushkin period has died altogether, has petered out completely. You will probably understand what I am trying to say. Happy are those who will take part in the emergence. . . ." (Letter of March 3, 1872, *Complete Works*, Vol. 61.)

Historically and socially, Soviet literature may be regarded as the product of the "emergence" foretold by Tolstoy. However, this emergence has taken place under conditions that often lend a distorted character to the process itself. The makers of Soviet literary policy established from the very first something of a "coast guard," checking those who emerged, who swam up to the surface, making their own selection and silencing the voices of those who failed to meet their requirements. Thus, many of the "newly emerged" disappeared prematurely from Soviet literature. On the other hand, many writers came to the forefront not because of literary merit, but thanks to the "correct ideology" of both the authors and the heroes of their works. Among these we may name Dmitry Furmanov and Alexander Serafimovich.

This situation, naturally enough, often provoked feelings of bitterness. In 1921, in an essay, "I Am Afraid," commenting on the literary life of the first post-revolutionary years, Yevgeny Zamyatin, one of the older pioneers of Soviet literature, recalled a decree issued in France in 1794. The decree spoke of "a multitude of nimble writers who constantly watch the latest trend; they know the fashion and color of the season; they know when to don the red cap, and when to discard it." Zamyatin says bitterly: we offer the writings of such "masqueraders" to the people "as a literature worthy of the revolution." And he goes on to say: "These literary centaurs rush, kicking and crushing one another, in a mad race for the magnificent prize—the monopoly on the scribbling of odes, the monopoly on the knightly occupation of slinging mud at the intelligentsia. . . . This merely depraves and degrades art. And I am afraid, if this continues, that the entire recent period in Russian literature will become known in history as the nimble age, for those who are not nimble have been silent now for the past two years. . . ."

Among the silent "non-nimble," Zamyatin names Alexander Blok, who had written nothing for two years after his poem "The Twelve." Andrey Bely and others, he says, are also complaining of the "conditions of life." "The writer who cannot become nimble," continues Zamyatin, "is compelled to trudge to an office with a briefcase if he wants to stay alive. In our day Gogol would be running with a briefcase to the theater department; Turgenev would undoubtedly be translating Balzac and Flaubert at the offices of World Literature [a publishing house founded in 1918, but no longer in existence—V.A.]; Hertzen would lecture to the sailors of the Baltic Fleet; and Chekhov would be working in the Commissariat of Public Health. . . . And so the writer stands before a choice: either he becomes a Breshko-Breshkovsky [a vapid but extremely prolific writer—V.A.], or he is silent. To the genuine writer and poet, the choice is clear.

"But even this is not the main thing. Russian writers are accustomed to going hungry. The main reason for their silence lies neither in the lack of bread nor in the lack of paper; the reason is far weightier, far tougher, far more ironclad. It is that true literature can exist only where it is created, not by diligent, reliable officials, but by madmen, hermits, heretics, dreamers, rebels, and skeptics. And when a writer must be prudent, sensible, and rigidly orthodox, when he must be useful at the present moment, when he cannot lash out at everyone like Swift, or smile at everything like Anatole France, then there is no bronze literature, then there is only a flimsy paper literature, a newspaper literature, which is read today and used for wrapping soap tomorrow."

Zamyatin concludes his essay, permeated with pain and anxiety for the fate of the literature of his time, on a profoundly pessimistic note:

"I am afraid that we shall have no genuine literature until we cure ourselves of this new brand of Catholicism, which is as fearful as the old of every new, heretical word. And if the illness is incurable, then I fear that the only future possible to Russian literature is its past."

Fortunately for the country and its people, this prophecy has not been fulfilled. Despite all the monstrousness of the conditions under which Soviet writers have had to work and must still work today, they have created in the forty years of the Soviet period a literature of considerable literary value, and of even greater value as a source of social and political information. This informative value of Soviet literary works, which was at first disputed not only abroad, but also among Soviet readers, is gaining ever wider recognition on the part of the reading public, both here and in the Soviet Union.

As years go by, the conviction grows that Soviet literature will in time become one of the basic sources from which future generations will study the complex and frequently tragic paths of development of revolutionary Russia and its people. This, indeed, is why a history of Soviet literature is, even at this date, of such urgent significance. Of course, we must not close our eyes to the fact that the study of its materials is frequently impeded both by the literary weakness of many works, and by the effects of the rigid party control and censorship that have compelled writers to conformity and violation of their artistic conscience. However, these difficulties, which in the future may render the weaker works uninteresting or incomprehensible, are often of no decisive importance today. We, the contemporaries of the revolution, are still in possession of the "key" which helps us to discover the true meaning and intent of a given work and to understand what is written between the lines.

Soviet literary historians usually divide post-revolutionary Soviet literature into five periods: the period of the Civil War and War Communism (October 1917 to 1921); that of the New Economic Policy (NEP) and reconstruction (1921–28); that of the Five-Year Plans (1928–39); World War II (1939–45); and the postwar period.

I shall confine myself to a simpler division: from the beginning of the revolution to World War II (1917–39); and from the outbreak of the war to the present time. This is not only sufficient to the purposes of this study, but essential: World War II created significant and lasting socio-psychological changes in the Soviet Union. Wartime and postwar literature have acquired certain strikingly new characteristics and, even more importantly, have come to reflect many new features in the life and psyche of Soviet people.

The present study consists of two general surveys of the development of Soviet literature, each dealing with a period of some twenty-odd years, and each followed by a series of portraits of individual writers who embody in their works the most salient traits, ideas, and aspirations of their time. The number of these portraits is necessarily limited, and I have often been compelled to omit individual treatment of writers who, generally speaking, deserve more detailed examination. The choice of writers dealt

Introduction

with at greater length in a study such as the present is always, in a degree, arbitrary. At times the value of a writer's works as a source of information led me to choose him rather than another of possibly greater talent. At times I commented on a writer only in the general survey because of the smallness of his output or the small number of his works of which the reader need be made aware. Occasionally—and this refers primarily to the second part of the book—my choice was also in some measure determined by the desire to acquaint readers with writers who are almost or entirely unknown to them. Readers familiar with Soviet literature may criticize my failure to devote individual essays to such writers as Fedin, Fadeyev, Simonov, Panfyorov, or Gladkov, or to certain poets. I regret these omissions as much as my readers, but limitations upon the size of the present book have made them unavoidable.

1 FROM PRE-REVOLUTIONARY TO SOVIET LITERATURE

MAXIM GORKY (1868–1936)

The best-known Soviet histories of modern Russian literature speak of the work of Maxim Gorky as the transition or "bridge" between pre-revolutionary and contemporary Soviet literature. This appraisal has prompted Professor L. I. Timofeyev to include a detailed analysis of Gorky's life and work in his book *Russian Soviet Literature* (Moscow, 1950). He concludes his hundred-odd-page analysis by saying, "Every period of Soviet literature is marked by Gorky's influence and by living, creative ties with him."

However, Timofeyev's assertion is at variance with the facts. It is well known that Gorky's initial reaction to the victory of the October revolution was highly critical. This was expressed in a series of articles, "Untimely Thoughts," which appeared in 1917–18 in the Petrograd Social-Democratic newspaper *Novaya Zhizn* almost until its suppression in the summer of 1918. But even after the closing of *Novaya Zhizn*, Gorky continued to be critical of the new government. The relations between Gorky and the leaders of the Proletcult (the first literary organization formed after the October revolution) were equally inimical. Gorky early began to consider departure abroad. In 1921 he succeeded in leaving Russia. In Europe, Gorky lived for a time in Berlin, where he contributed to the magazine *Beseda* (founded at the end of 1922 and published under the imprint of the Epokha Publishing House). Later, Gorky went to Capri. He returned to Russia only in the late 1920s, after repeated hints and invitations from the literary powers that be. The nature of these hints may be judged from a poem by Mayakovsky, which is rarely quoted today. In this poem, "A Letter from the Writer Vladimir Mayakovsky to the Writer Alexey Maximovich Gorky" (Mayakovsky, *Collected Works*, Moscow, 1927, Vol. V, pp. 22–29), the poet speaks frankly to Gorky:

> I greatly regret, Comrade Gorky,
> That you aren't
>   seen
>   at the building of our days.
> Do you think—
>   from Capri,
>   from the hill,
> You see better than we?

It was not enough for Mayakovsky that Gorky, though living abroad, was closely following the development of the young Soviet literature and responding to many new works. He felt that it was bitter for "friends of the working class" to think "of Gorky the *émigré*":

> Justify yourself,
>   Come!
> I know—
>   you are prized
>   both by the government
>   and by the party,
> You would be given all—
>   from love
>   to apartments.
> Prose writers
>   would sit down
>   before you
>   on a school-bench:
>   —teach!
>   lead!

Mayakovsky refused to believe that Gorky could be content with life abroad, as Chaliapin was content—for their past, he felt, was very different. And, alluding to Gorky's famous poem about the proud falcon and the grass snake, Mayakovsky asked:

Alexey Maximovich,
           from behind your glasses
Can you
      still
          see
              the soaring falcon?
Or have the
           grass snakes
                     crawling in the garden
           made friends
                     with you?

It was only in 1928 that Gorky returned to Soviet Russia. But by that time many young writers had already published works which were later to pass the test of time and which showed no Gorky influence whatever.

There is still further, if indirect, evidence that Gorky's influence was by no means as great as Soviet literary scholars began to assert later.

Gorky's work, in contrast to that of the Russian classics, presents a rather motley picture. He came into Russian literature in the early 1890s on the crest of the wave which, rising from the depths of popular resentment, shook the old regime with the first labor strikes. Gorky's appearance in literature coincided with the revolutionary awakening of the working class. Gorky began to write in the provinces and was soon noticed by another important revolutionary-democratic writer, Vladimir Korolenko. It was Korolenko who brought Gorky into the field of major literature. Gorky came there, surrounded by his heroes—tramps, vagabonds, the dregs of society. Such heroes were by no means strangers to pre-revolutionary literature; many writers, and particularly Dostoyevsky, had long won for the "insulted and injured" admission tickets to Russian society. But, though not unfamiliar, Gorky's heroes immediately attracted attention, for they seemed to be returning these admission tickets with a bold, careless gesture. Independent, gay, and impudent, these tramps brought with them a stream of fresh air, a faith in the creative potential of the lowest of the low; and all that was young and revolutionary in Russian society of the late nineteenth and early twentieth centuries took them warmly to heart.

Gorky's literary biography is usually divided into three periods. The works of the early period, such as Gorky's first story, "Makar Chudra" (1891) and "Emelyan Pilyay," are predominantly romantic. Another work of the period is the prose-poem, "Song about a Falcon" (1895), to which Mayakovsky alluded in his "Letter" to Gorky. In his "Song" the author cries to the self-satisfied grass snake in the name of the proud falcon who had smashed himself to death: "Those who are born to crawl can never fly!" "The Old Woman Izergil" and "Chelkash" belong to the same period.

The second period embraces the late 1890s and early 1900s. It is characterized by Gorky's turning to new literary forms—the long story, the novel, and the play. To this period belongs the "Song of the Stormy Petrel" (1901), with its lines that became, as it were, the battle cry of the revolution:

"A storm! A storm is breaking! The bold petrel is proudly soaring among lightnings over the wrathful, roaring ocean; the harbinger of victory is crying:
Let the storm rage ever stronger!"

During this second period Gorky also wrote the poem "Man," in which the writer glorifies Man who preaches the idea of heroic deeds, undaunted in the face of death: "I go, to burn with the brightest flame, to light the deepest darkness of life. And death is my reward." These lines inevitably suggest a direct kinship with Danko in the story "The Old Woman Izergil." The legendary Danko, whose tribe has lost its way in the forest, decides to save his people. He plucks the heart from his breast and lifts it high over his head. The heart, aflame like a torch with his love for the people, lights up the surrounding darkness and helps them to escape from the forest.

Despite their element of grandiloquence, these works won Gorky wide popularity throughout the younger Russia, which longed for radical change. Gorky became the master of the thoughts and aspirations of this younger generation.

But Gorky, the romanticist inspired with revolutionary moods, also possessed another characteristic, which was to emerge more fully later, after the revolution of 1917. The writer's official biographers are fond of pointing out that in the works of his maturer years, and particularly in such novels as *Foma Gordeyev*, *The Life of Matvey Kozhemyakin*, and *The Artamonov Business*, Gorky exposed the "historic dull-wittedness and brutish class cruelty of the bourgeoisie." In reality Gorky's attitude toward the Russian bourgeoisie was always far more complex than the official legend would have it. And Gorky himself refutes the legend in his works. Already in *Foma Gordeyev*, which presented a gallery of portraits of Russian merchants, beginning with Foma's father, Ignat Gordeyev, it was clear that Gorky's attention was drawn to the Russian merchant class not only because of its "historic dull-wittedness" and "brutish cruelty."

In his *Reminiscences*, written in 1917 and devoted to his meetings with the millionaire merchant Bugrov, Gorky admits that encounters with such people had always aroused in him a complex reaction: along with dislike, he also felt "intense curiosity." And their response to Gorky was equally complex. One day Bugrov confessed to Gorky how much he liked the merchant Yakov Mayakin (in the novel *Foma Gordeyev*), because "he is Russian through and through, in heart, in mind, in political intelligence." And, with a broad smile, he added: "It's very instructive, the way you *prompt the merchant* how he should live and think. Ve-ry!" Another wealthy merchant, from Nizhny Novgorod, told Gorky about the arguments among his fellow merchants as to who had served as the prototype for Yakov Mayakin. Yakov Bashkirov, he said, had boasted: "Mayakin—that's me! It was from me that he was drawn. See how smart I am!"

Why Gorky the revolutionary was moved to "intense curiosity" in respect to the Russian merchants is best told by himself in his *Reminiscences*. Bugrov was in love with work, and said to Gorky on one occasion that, were he given power, he would "stir up" the whole nation: he would give medals and decorations not to the nobles, but "to carpenters, machinists, to obscure, laboring people." "You've done a good job?" Bugrov continued. "Then you get honor and glory. Go on competing!" In Bugrov's feeling for work, remarks Gorky, there was something "religious." "This coincided with my own attitude toward labor: to me work is a region where the imagination knows no bounds."

But at the time when *Foma Gordeyev* was published, in the early twentieth century, the minds of the youth were turned in quite a different direction, and it is small wonder that the greatest impression was produced not by *Foma Gordeyev*, but by another of Gorky's novels, *The Mother* (1906).

The Mother is based on events that took place in Nizhny Novgorod and its suburb of Sormov. Its central characters are the young worker Pavel Vlasov and his mother, Pelageya Nilovna (the prototypes for Gorky's characters, Pavel Zalomov and his mother, both lived to see the revolution of 1917). In the beginning of the novel Gorky depicts the life of a working-class family in a workers' district. Pelageya Nilovna is not yet an old woman, but her life has been so hard and joyless that it turned her into a frightened person, afraid of her husband's blows, afraid of want. But later, through her son, she finds herself surrounded by young workers, his friends. Gradually, she not only begins to help in her son's revolutionary activity, but begins to divest herself of the yoke of fear, meekness, and submission. Although the novel closes with the defeat of the revolutionaries, the reader is left inwardly convinced of the ultimate victory of the revolution.

One of the reasons for the novel's lasting success was its harmonious combination of realism and romanticism, rare in Gorky's work. And it was this that enabled the Soviet literary historians in the early 1930s to proclaim

The Mother the forebear of a new literary method—of so-called "socialist realism."

Gorky's pre-revolutionary works include two novels which appeared in 1909-10, *The Okurov Township* and *The Life of Matvey Kozhemyakin*. These books paint a gloomy picture of Russian provincial life. But despite his merciless view of the provinces, Gorky remained true to himself and his faith in the creative powers of the people. Yakov Tiunov, one of the characters in *The Okurov Township*, says: "And I'll tell you, from the heart, our Russian people is a fine people . . . fine, strong, gifted!" The same ideas are expressed by the former soldier Pushkar, who says he has walked the length and breadth of Russia, and is convinced that Russia has stored up for herself two hundred years of work; all that is necessary is to start and "put her in order."

Two autobiographical novels, *Childhood* (1913) and *Out among People* (1916), also belong to Gorky's pre-revolutionary period. The third part of this autobiographical trilogy, *My Universities*, was written in 1923. The novel *The Artamonov Business* appeared in 1925.

It is also important to note Gorky's work in the magazine *Letopis* (Annals), which he founded in 1915 and which opened its pages to a number of young writers who were just beginning their literary careers.

Despite his initially critical attitude toward the October revolution, Gorky maintained lively contact with young writers even after his departure abroad, helping them to find a place in literature. However, it is enough to name some of those who felt indebted to Gorky to see that this was not a matter of literary influence on their development, but rather of help in the most exact sense of the word. Gorky saved the life of Alexander Grin (author of the fantasy novel *Scarlet Sails*), who was dying of hunger. He helped the young Vsevolod Ivanov, who later became a prominent member of the Serapion Brotherhood, to make his way. He gave very considerable moral support to the young Isaac Babel, and so on.

The list of writers who may be said to have been influenced by Gorky in their work is relatively small. Perhaps the most important of these was the late Fyodor Gladkov, author of the first industrial novel, *Cement*. He first met Gorky in 1901. Gorky's stories, he later said, "turned over" his soul. According to Gladkov, he did not free himself of Gorky's influence until many years later. In reality, Gladkov never quite overcame the influence of the young Gorky, the romanticist, and its traces can easily be found even in Gladkov's autobiographical works (*The Story of My Childhood* and *Volnitsa*, 1951). Among the other writers of the older generation whom Gorky influenced were some lesser figures, such as Semyon Podyachev, Vladimir Bakhmetyev, Alexey Bibik, and the peasant writer Ivan Volnov.

Still longer is the list of writers whom Gorky helped by his words of encouragement to overcome the tormenting doubts that beset every beginning writer.

The many ways in which Gorky helped other writers in the early 1920s are movingly described by Korney Chukovsky in his book *Repin, Gorky, Mayakovsky, Bryusov*: "Gorky took the burden of all our needs upon his shoulders. When a child was born to one of us, he managed to secure a bottle for the newborn. When we were ill, he saw to it that we were admitted to the hospital." Even more significant, perhaps, is the testimony of Olga Forsh: After "his government," she wrote, had come into power, and "the leaders of the Jacobin revolution had set themselves to extirpating the remnants of the feudal class order, and the unbridled masses, abetted from above, began to attack the most precious growths of culture and art, Gorky lay down like a bridge between us and them. It is forgotten now, but all of us have walked across that bridge."

Gorky's concern for his fellow writers and the fate of the pre-revolutionary intelligentsia was not dictated by kindness alone. Few Russian writers were as infatuated with culture as Gorky. His initially negative reaction to the Bolshevik coup was prompted by the fear that the Jacobin turn of the revolution might destroy the new growth of Russian culture. This fear played a decisive part in Gorky's attitude toward the new regime. Living abroad, he closely followed developments in the life of the young Soviet society. With joy he watched the revolution bring forward tens of thousands of energetic young people, burning with the desire to build a new and better life. And gradually, Gorky's negative attitude toward the new government began to soften.

His return to live permanently in Soviet Russia coincided with his sixtieth birthday. The literary authorities and the government did not stint in organizing gala celebrations of this birthday. In the eyes of the older generation of Soviet writers, Gorky became the Ivan Kalita[1] of Russian literature of the Soviet period. And it was in this role that Gorky made his most generous contribution to the culture of the new post-revolutionary Russia.

ALEXANDER BLOK (1881–1921)

Quite different was the role played in the new literature by the greatest lyric poet of the early twentieth century, Alexander Blok. An intellectual, a member of the gentry, and an individualist, Blok came to Russian poetry as the bearer of the living tradition stemming from Pushkin and continued by Lermontov, Tyutchev, Vladimir Solovyov, and Fet. It was the poetic tradition of the highly-cultivated chamber style. But Blok made use of this self-contained, chamber lyricism, this fine musical style, which had been nurtured for decades by cool, shadowy old parks and melancholy Russian expanses, to sing of new themes, of a snowy, windy Petersburg evening, a shrill barrel-organ in a deserted alley, the hoarse din of a variety show, the dust of the summer suburb, the lazy boredom of the villa on the outskirts of town.

A similar transposition was made in his time by the German poet Heinrich Heine. But Heine invested this literary revolution with the fireworks of irony and sarcasm.

---

[1] Ivan Kalita was a famous Russian ruler of the fourteenth century, who unified the separate hereditary principalities into a single Muscovite state.

Blok's essentially religious temperament was entirely alien to irony. His revolution in lyric poetry consisted in the transfer of the rhythms of the classical lyric to permanent residence in the city. And so it happened that the poet, who was in his essence remote from the revolution and its problems, objectively participated in the revolution on the poetic "front," initiating the wide circles of urban and plebeian intelligentsia into the mysteries of poetic craftsmanship, giving them the musical key to the poetic heritage of Russian lyric poetry. And it is in this that we find the explanation not only for Blok's popularity among the pre-revolutionary democratic intelligentsia, but also for his marked influence on the rhythmic patterns of Soviet poetry as a whole.

As a poet, Blok was distinguished by a phenomenal gift of inner perception. He seemed to respond to all the events in the world somehow by ear, often identifying the world with music. By this inner ear Blok was the first to discern in the revolution of 1905 the beginning of the end not only of the old Russia, but also of an entire epoch in world history. Three motifs, now merging into one, now distinct, early began to dominate his work: the sense of doom, an aching tenderness toward Russia ("Oh, my beggared land, what do you mean to the heart?"), and the presentiment of a new revolution. Blok feared this impending revolution not so much for himself and those close to him, as for Russia itself. And yet he sensed with all his heart its inevitability and its justice in the highest sense of the word. The last of Russia's "penitent nobles," Blok felt that the "coming Bridegroom" of the revolution would not admit him to his chambers, although he had "saved the oil" in his lamp. Blok accepted this without rebellion, regarding it, in a way, as a historical "requital." There are many entries on this theme in his diary of 1919. Characteristic in this connection is the entry commenting on the obstacles which the new regime was raising to the publication of his books: "And if hands, dirtier than mine, throw out of the printing presses the books of such a writer as A. Blok, who may have earned some 'merit' with the revolution, *I dare not judge it*. It is not these hands that are doing it, or, perhaps, not only these hands, but also distant, unknown millions of poor hands; and looking on are millions of eyes which may not know what it's all about, but which have suffered hunger and pain, and which have seen the stately, well-fed gentleman prancing before them. . . . And the eyes are grinning: So, the gentleman has pranced, he's had his fun, and now the gentleman is *for us*? But *is* he for us?"

The entries in the *Diary* also help to decipher the long poem "The Twelve," with which Blok was the first to respond to the October revolution. In the light of the poet's moods, we begin to understand the closing strophe of the poem, in which Jesus appears at the head of the rowdy platoon of twelve Red Guards:

> Through the blizzard unseen,
> By the bullets untouched,
> Like a spray of pearly snow,
> In a crown of pure-white roses,
> On the storm with gentle tread
> Jesus Christ walks at their head.

Because of this poem, and particularly its ending, many of his former friends turned against Blok. Nor did the poem satisfy the official critics. But Blok was not excessively disturbed by these responses. Some three years after its appearance Blok said that although he could no longer write a poem like "The Twelve," he did not repudiate it, because it had been written "in accord with the elemental surge" (*Diary*, Vol. 2).

And in his own way Blok was right: he had been closer then to the masses, closer to that youth which, coming home from the front, believed that after the four years of war the world could no longer return to the past. These moods are strongly felt in Blok's "The Scythians," written soon after "The Twelve." Blok felt that the world was undergoing a radical crisis similar to that experienced by mankind during the transition from barbarism to Christianity. His feelings found clear expression in a personal letter written by Blok to the poetess Zinaida Gippius (the wife of Dmitry Merezhkovsky): "But don't you realize that 'Russia will cease to be' just as Rome had ceased to be—not in the Fifth Century A.D., but in the first year of the First Century? Nor will there be an England, a Germany, or a France. Don't you realize that the world has already been reshaped? That the 'old world' has already been melted down?"

Regarding the end of the First World War as a beginning of a new epoch, Blok felt that in such new epochs "the barbarian masses turn out to be the preservers of culture, possessing nothing but the spirit of music. . . ."

Seeing his time thus, as a great new eve, Blok was not frightened by the temporary decline of culture and the manifestations of popular "barbarism." But he continued in his passionate belief that, out of the stormy flood of events which swept away the wreckage of collapsing civilizations like bits of flotsam, there would arise a new epoch, with "a new role for the individual."

Alas, Blok not only did not live to see his prophecies realized, but the prophecies themselves were disproved by events both in their universal and their specifically Russian aspects. Life in Europe, following the upheavals of war and revolutions, began to return, if not entirely to its former state, then to norms which were certainly not radically new. And in Russia, despite the victory of the revolution, the new regime was unleashing forces and emotions which filled the poet with revulsion, plunging him into profound despair. Yet, with a face "darkened as by a harsh wind," he continued to serve the people, working intensively over the publication of European classics.

Extremely valuable information about the final year of Blok's life (he died on August 7, 1921) may be found in the first part of Konstantin Fedin's unfinished trilogy, *Gorky among Us*. Blok's every public appearance was a major event in those fabulous years. There were four such appearances in Leningrad: his lectures on the collapse of humanism (1919) and on the poet's mission (1921), his reading of his poem "Retribution" (1921), and his reading at the House of Writers of his last poem, "To the Pushkin House" (1921), which contained the now famous lines:

> Pushkin! Paeans to *secret freedom*[2]
> Sang we in your light!
> Give us your hand in this foul weather,
> Help us in the silent fight. . . .

Listening to Blok, the young Fedin felt that to Blok "art was an eternal battle, in which he was ready at every moment to give up his soul." To Gorky, a great deal in Blok remained alien. Above all, this was true of the entire tragic "climate" of Blok's spirit. But he watched the poet with admiration, and said to Fedin "quietly and earnestly": "This is a Man." And not only Gorky, but many of the young writers of the day felt this about Blok. It was not by chance that Blok's death, though it coincided with a period of the sharpest "revolutionary division in literature," for a moment united everyone in the feeling expressed by Fedin: "Blok died young, but there was a strange awareness in all of us that his going also meant the going of the old epoch, the epoch which, having lived to see the revolution, seemed to have made a step into its realm, as if to show the direction that must be taken, and fell exhausted with the travail of its long journey. It became clear that no one would ever again take such a step from *there*, and even if anyone should, it would never again be with such courage and such *longing for the truth of the future* as had been shown by Alexander Blok."

IVAN BUNIN (1870–1953)

There was a good deal of the dramatic in the history of the relations between the late Ivan Bunin and Soviet literature, especially his relations with the official critics. Bunin left Soviet Russia in 1921, and lived as an *émigré* until his death in 1953. In his *Cursed Days* (*Collected*

---

[2] The words *secret freedom* were derived by Blok from a poem by Pushkin, "Reply to a Challenge," written in 1818.

Works of I. A. Bunin, Vol. X, Petropolis, 1935), he expressed his intransigent rejection of "October." This book opens with the chapter "The Last Spring" (1916). The "cursed days" are dealt with in the fourth chapter, which begins with the following entry: "Moscow, January 1 [old style], 1918: This cursed year is over. But what next?" Until his very departure from Russia, the character of Bunin's entries never changes; they note only the darkest aspects of the life which had begun with the victory of "October." To the end of his days, Bunin never relaxed in his enmity to the October revolution. His *Recollections* (Vozrozhdenie, Paris, 1950) provide ample evidence of his persisting hostility. Whenever he returns to the fateful year, Bunin never misses the occasion to intensify his initial response. Describing a visit to an exhibition of the works of Finnish painters in 1917, he interrupts his recollections with this bitterly lyrical aside:

". . . Fate has given us all too many 'great historical events.' I was born too late. Were I born earlier, my memories as a writer would have been very different. I would not have had to experience the things so inalienably a part of them: 1905, the First World War, 1917 and its aftermath, Lenin, Stalin, Hitler. . . . How can one help envying our forebear Noah! Only *one* deluge was allotted to his lifetime. And what a solid, comfortable, warm ark he had, and what a wealth of provisions: seven pairs of clean, and two pairs of unclean, but still very edible, beasts. And that messenger of peace and prosperity, the dove with the olive branch in her mouth, did not deceive him—not to compare with the present doves (of 'comrade' Picasso). And he made an excellent landing on Ararat, and partook of a fine meal, and drank, and slept the sleep of the just, warmed by the bright sun in the pure primeval air of the new universal spring—cleansed of all the antediluvial filth and corruption—so unlike our world, which has returned to the antediluvial! True, Noah had some trouble with his son Ham. But then, that's what he was—a Ham![3] And most important of all, in the whole world at that time there was only one Ham. But now?" (pp. 55–56)

[3] This is an untranslatable play on the word. "Ham" (*kham*) in Russian means boor.

With all the glaring bias of the *Cursed Days* and the many unjust appraisals in some of the asides in his *Recollections,* Bunin was right when he wrote:

"Our bias, after all, will be of great value to the future historian. Is only the 'passion' of the 'revolutionary people' important? And what of us, aren't we people?"

Interestingly enough, despite his sharp repudiation of "October" and the systematic silence of the critics concerning his works, Bunin had his own circle of readers in the Soviet Union. And soon after his death a one-volume edition of his works was published there (1955). Articles began to appear, commenting favorably not only on the writer's pre-revolutionary works, but also on many of his books written as an *émigré*. In 1961 a five-volume edition of Bunin's collected works was nearing completion. And in July 1961 the magazine *Moskva* began serial publication of his novel *The Life of Arseniev*, which won him the Nobel Prize for literature in 1933. Most astonishing in all this is the fact that, despite the extremely hostile attitude of the official critics, Bunin has always had a large number of admirers, not only among the older writers, but also among the very youngest. "Sensational" as this posthumous fate of the writer appears to be, it is essentially quite logical.

In the eyes of many readers, both abroad and in the Soviet Union, Bunin was the last representative of that pre-revolutionary Russian literature which, more than anything else, assured the Russian people such an eminent place in the world's family of nations. The sense of his blood-kinship with the classical period of Russian literature awakened in Bunin very early, perhaps at the time when "the decision somehow happened" that he was to become a writer. The circumstances of his childhood encouraged this feeling. His earliest years were spent in places made famous by earlier writers: a short distance from the Bunin home was the estate once owned by Lermontov's father; also nearby were the places where Turgenev had lived and hunted; some hundred versts away was Tolstoy's Yasnaya Polyana; also in the vicinity was the home of the poet Fet. Bunin recalls that his first awareness of these writers was not in terms of their books; they were "an intrinsic part" of his life.

His love for Pushkin came to Bunin together with his deep love of the summer day, the orchard, Russia. His first knowledge of Gogol came from the stories of his tutor, who had had the good fortune to see Gogol in Moscow. Very young at the time, the tutor did not remember Gogol's conversation, but he recalled a single phrase: "One may write about an apple tree with golden apples, but not about pears on a willow tree."

Bunin's feelings toward Tolstoy are also recreated with remarkable vividness in his *Recollections*.

Bunin's posthumous "return" to Russian literature is due above all to the power of his talent. Despite all the intimidations and all the efforts of the official critics to vilify Bunin's name, warm appreciation of his work has not been limited to such writers of the older generation as Fedin, Paustovsky, Gorky, and others. He is equally admired by many of the younger writers, including Yefim Dorosh, who devoted to him a moving and impassioned article, "The Writer and Reality" (*Literary Gazette*, March 22, 1956).

A still higher appraisal of Bunin is found in the article "About Mood, Plot, and Language" (*Voprosy Literatury* [Problems of Literature], November 1959), by the very young writer Yury Bondarev. Discussing the problem of imagery and vividness of language, and speaking of writers who possessed "the conquering power of clairvoyance," Bondarev names Bunin side by side with Tolstoy and Chekhov, describing him as "a remarkable Russian writer with a marvelous command of 'magic'—the ability to find the single word which takes the place of an entire paragraph, an entire page. . . ."

Bunin's example demonstrates once more that these "returns" and "discoveries" of writers whose significance was at first denigrated by Soviet critics (such as Turgenev, Ostrovsky, Dostoyevsky, Leskov, and many others) proceed according to laws which are subject to no official authority. We cannot help recalling Tolstoy's epilogue to *The Kreutzer Sonata*: "To the man who swims along the shore, it could be said: 'Guide yourself by that hill, that promontory, that tower,' and so on. But a time comes when the swimmers have left the shore behind, and then their only guides are the unattainable celestial bodies and the compass, pointing the direction. . . ." The same thing is now happening to the contemporary Soviet readers: the farther they move away from the shores of pre-revolutionary Russia, the oftener their eyes turn to the writers and artists whose works embody the immutable values of the moral culture of the Russian people.

2 LITERARY DEVELOPMENTS: FROM THE REVOLUTION TO WORLD WAR II (1917–39)

Revolutions are seldom unexpected; the presentiment of revolution enters, in some measure, into the personal biographies of many of its contemporaries. This is especially true of the Russian revolution of 1917, which was foreseen both by younger and by older writers. The sense of impending change was vividly expressed in 1908 by Alexander Blok in an article, "Elemental Upheavals and Culture":

"We still do not know precisely what events to expect, but the seismograph needle has already swung in our hearts. We see ourselves, as it were, against the background of a glowing sky, in a light lacy airplane high over the land; below us is a rumbling mountain breathing flame, and down its sides, behind clouds of ash, creep liberated streams of molten lava."

"There is Russia," wrote Blok in another article ("Flame"), in 1913, "which, breaking away from one revolution, stares avidly into the eyes of another, perhaps a far more terrible one."

The revolution which flared up in March 1917 was received like a fulfillment of hope, a storm that clears the air. The coup that took place eight months later and the emergence of the Communist dictatorship brought confusion and consternation into literary circles. But gradually life settled somewhat and the new literary development began to assume shape.

The Bolsheviks came to power in a tragic moment: the war continued, but the front became increasingly exposed daily, thanks to the mass desertions and the virtual collapse of the entire military machine. Russia's "gray-coat blood," to use the graphic expression of Mikhail Sholokhov, streamed homeward, inundating cities, stations, and railway junctions. The threat of German occupation of Petersburg seemed imminent. In the cities, amid the "iron silence" of idle factories, there was a shortage of the most basic food products and fuel. And all this in an atmosphere of terror directed by the new government not only against the upper strata of the old regime, but also against all who did not want to, or in conscience could not, give it full support. In the tumultuous peasant mass, swept by its own elemental land rebellion, the cities no longer rose as beacons, but smoked faintly with barely flickering wicks. "Russia is perishing." This sense of doom was not confined to the conservative upper strata of the old society; it was widespread throughout the country. The sharp anxiety—"Russia is perishing"—pulsed in the minds of the greater part of the progressive young intelligentsia as well.

At this dramatic moment came the quiet words of Alexander Blok's long poem, "The Twelve":

> Black evening,
> White snow.
> Wind, wind!
> A man cannot stand on his feet.
> Wind, wind—
> Across God's world!

The poem lives to this day with the lonely life of a work of genius; its voice still excites us. And different emotions are aroused in readers by the image of Jesus, at the end of the poem, walking at the head of a Red Guard detachment.

"FROM STRONG HANDS": THE GROUPS EMERGE

In the first part of his trilogy *Gorky among Us*, Konstantin Fedin, speaking of the initial period of Soviet literature, remarked: "History invited the young to accept the heritage from strong hands." And there were many who were willing to "accept the heritage." There were the Futurists, led by Mayakovsky, the Imaginists, who were joined by the peasant poet Sergey Yesenin, the "proletarian" writers who had already in 1918 organized the Proletcult association. The Proletcult claimed "hegemony," creating a situation which made life difficult for nonproletarian writers, although the latter were in a preponderant majority. In this disturbed post-revolutionary atmosphere the literary scene also witnessed a good deal of socio-political mimicry, which left its imprint on literary development for years to come.

Externally, there was great animation in the literary world, with heated debates, declarations, and programs of every variety. But, with very few exceptions, and those mainly in the field of poetry (Blok, Yesenin, Mayakovsky), few works of more than passing value were written at the time.

A characteristic feature of literary life during the first decade of the Soviet regime was the urge among writers to belong to some literary group. There were also writers who belonged to no groups, but they were relatively few in number: Maxim Gorky, Alexey Tolstoy, Leonid Leonov, and several lesser figures (V. Veresayev, Boris Lavrenyov, Konstantin Trenyov, etc.). The vast majority, however, divided into various groups. Some of these groups dated from the pre-revolutionary period when they had existed in less organized form as literary trends. This was true of the Futurists, led by Vladimir Mayakovsky, who now created their own literary organ, the *LEF* (Left Front in Art). But most of the groups were new.

THE PROLETCULT

Among the organizations which were influential at that time and during the ensuing years, first mention must be given to the Proletcult. Its ideological foundations were laid before the revolution, by *émigrés* like A. Bogdanov (A. A. Malinovsky), an old Bolshevik belonging to the Vperyod (Forward) group. Bogdanov preached the idea of the triple character of the workers' movement: in its striving toward socialism, he said, the movement works through political organization (the party), economic organization (the trade-unions), and cultural organization. These three branches of the workers' movement constitute a single whole, but each is autonomous. In September 1917—that is, still before "October"—the foundations were laid, through Bogdanov's initiative, for an organization that was to provide an outlet for the striving of the working-class masses toward cultural activity. Such were the roots of the Proletcult, which expanded greatly during the early years of the Soviet regime.

Its principal activity was the establishment of workers' clubs, literary circles, dramatic studios, workers' "universities," "palaces of culture," etc. In August 1918 the Proletcult called a conference of proletarian writers in Moscow, which was attended by delegates from Petrograd, Moscow, Samara, Perm, Voronezh, and other cities. The conference resolved to establish an all-Russian union of writers "of working-class origin and point of view." Although this union was not established immediately, the Proletcult was connected with the first distinct organization of proletarian writers, the Kuznitsa (Smithy), and later, in 1923, to the Moscow Association of Proletarian Writers (MAPP), which subsequently developed into the RAPP and VOAPP (to be discussed later).

The characteristic feature of the Proletcult ideology was the *idea of a break with cultural tradition*. Later, Fedin (who rejected this idea) described it in *Gorky among Us*: "One historical stage is finished, and another has begun. Between them is dug a moat, and the deeper it is, the more secure. The Proletcult watched with enormous zeal lest the idea of cultural continuity should emerge to the surface anywhere." Proletcult spokesmen visualized the building of a socialist culture as the creation of a culture of the working class, radically different from the culture of other social classes, a distinguishing feature of this culture being its collectivist character and decisive condemnation of everything individual. Alexey Gastev, a metalworker who became one of the leaders of the Proletcult, wrote in *Proletarskaya Kultura* (Proletarian Culture) in 1919 about the anthology *Shock-work Poetry* (1918), the first book published by the Proletcult, that the connection between working-class psychology and machine production lent this psychology a "normalized" character:

"It is precisely this feature that lends proletarian psychology a remarkable anonymity, which permits the definition of the individual proletarian unit as A, B, C. . . . This normalized character of proletarian psychology and its dynamism hold the key to the elemental nature of proletarian thought. . . . This tendency imperceptibly leads to the *impossibility of individual thinking*, transforming itself into the objective psychology of a whole class. . . . This psychology reveals a new working-class collectivism, which may be described as *mechanized collectivism*. . . . The motion of these collective-complexes approaches the motion of objects, in which there is *no longer any human individual face*, but only regular, normalized steps, faces without expression, a *soul devoid of lyricism*, measured not by outcries, and not by laughter, but by a manometer and taxometer."

In short, the proletariat was to be transformed into *"an unprecedented social automaton"* and its art was to be based on "open, stupendous grandiosity, *without a trace of anything intimate or lyrical.*"

THE SERAPIONS

There is no need to prove that no literature could develop on the basis of such a conception. And it is not surprising that the first perceptible step in the development of Soviet prose literature was made in a distinctly different milieu—in that writers' "fraternity" founded in 1921 that called itself the Serapion Brotherhood (borrowing the name of the hermit Serapion from the German writer E. T. A. Hoffman). It is worth noting that this was the first literary grouping in the Soviet Union which, while not opposing the regime, set great value on its own independence. In *Literaturnye Zapiski* (Literary Notes), the journal of the Writers' House in Petersburg, Mikhail Slonimsky, a member of the Serapion Brotherhood, or a Serapion, as they called themselves, wrote in 1922: "Most of all, we were afraid of losing our independence, of suddenly finding ourselves a 'Society attached to the People's Commissariat of Education' or to some other institution." And Lev Lunts, the theoretician of the Serapions, wrote in the same magazine at the time, explaining "Why We Are the Serapion Brothers":

"We have chosen the name of Serapion Brothers because we do not want any coercion or boredom, we do not want everyone to write in the same way, even if it were in imitation of Hoffman. Each of us has his own face and his own literary tastes. In each of us can be found traces of the most diverse literary influences. Each has his own 'drum,' as Nikitin said at our first meeting. . . . Each of us has his own ideology and political convictions, and each paints his hut his own color. . . . But all together, we—the Brotherhood—demand one thing: that the voice should not ring false; that we should believe in the reality of a work, whatever its color might be. . . ."

In his book *The Writer, Art, and Time* (1958), Konstantin Fedin recalls how he had come to Petersburg in 1921 and joined the Serapion Brotherhood. At a meeting of the Brotherhood, Lunts thundered:

"Russian prose has ceased to 'move,' it 'lies inert,' nothing happens, nothing takes place in it; its characters either discuss or feel, but they do not act. . . . It must inevitably die of lack of blood circulation, of bedsores, or dropsy. It has become a mere appendage to ideologies and programs, a mirror of journalism, and has ceased to exist as art. It can be saved only by plot—the mechanism which will animate it, compel it to walk, to perform willed actions. The traditions of plot has its home in the West. We must bring this tradition here and fructify our supine prose. . . . Therefore, our motto is: 'To the West!' . . ."

A quarter of a century later, in 1946, during the first postwar purge, these statements of the Serapions were recalled by the late Secretary of the Central Committee of the Communist Party, Andrey Zhdanov, in his attack on the Serapions and, particularly, on Lunts and Zoshchenko, for "adulation of bourgeois culture" and "glorification of literature devoid of ideas, of art for art's sake, art without purpose or meaning."

The Serapion Brotherhood was not an organization in the strict sense of the word. It was a loose grouping which did not seek expansion and which, in fact, began to "scatter" after 1924.

From among the Serapions a number of writers emerged whose names became a part of the history of Russian literature. Closely linked with them was Evgeny Zamyatin, whom the Serapion Brothers regarded as their spiritual father, but who did not consider himself, and was not officially considered, a Serapion. Among the younger members of the group were Mikhail Zoshchenko, Vsevolod Ivanov, Venyamin Kaverin, Konstantin Fedin, Mikhail Slonimsky, Nikolay Tikhonov, and the literary critic Ilya Gruzdev. The ideologist of the fraternity—Lev Lunts—died in 1924.

PEREVAL

Another significant group of writers during the first decade of Soviet literature was Pereval (The Pass), which was closer to official ideology. However, it was not party spirit that characterized the members of this organization (although many of them were members of the Communist Party), but their common moods, which they had brought out of the recent Civil War. Pereval was founded in 1924, with the active participation of Alexander Voronsky, an old Bolshevik and editor of the magazine *Krasnaya Nov* (Red Virgin Soil), the first so-called "big" magazine of the Soviet period. The circumstances of the organization of this group, its existence, full of dramatic struggle, and its end are not only of historical interest, but help us even today to understand more deeply the nature of the problems which still agitate many Soviet writers, problems whose solution is blocked by insuperable obstacles within the framework of the existing regime.

The founding of the Pereval group is described by V. Nasedkin in 1926 in the fourth volume of the *Pereval* anthology. In 1923, he tells us, there were stirrings of ferment in the literary groups Molodaya Gvardia (Young Guard) and Oktyabr (October), the first consisting entirely, and the second in large part, of beginning writers who were members of the Comsomol. This literary youth wanted to take a deeper look into life around them and to show in their work not only the "pluses," but also the "minuses" of revolutionary life. Very soon, the "fathers" in the Oktyabr group discerned undesirable notes in the work of their younger colleagues. A polemic ensued, and accusations were made of "surrender of revolutionary positions," "defeatism," and lack of steadfastness before "the pressure of the petty-bourgeoisie." As an example of such lack of steadfastness, the guardians of revolutionary piety cited the attitude of the proletarian poets toward the Fellow Travelers (a term coined by Trotsky and subsequently widely used to designate non-Communist, but not anti-Soviet writers). These "rebels" not only did not disdain learning from the Fellow Travelers, but also published their works in the latter's organ, *Krasnaya Nov*. To the fathers of Oktyabr, such a liberal attitude toward the nonpartisan Fellow Travelers was intolerable. As a result of the conflict, a part of this youth left to join the magazine *Krasnaya Nov*.

Thus, the editorial offices of *Krasnaya Nov* witnessed the meeting between the Comsomol poets and prose writers and nonpartisan young writers, which gave rise to the literary association Pereval. To the members of Pereval, party membership or party spirit were of no importance. Their philosophy was based on the idea: we are all children of the people, eager to build a new life. And it was this feeling that distinguished Pereval not only from such groups as Molodaya Gvardia, Oktyabr, and the representatives of extreme revolutionary orthodoxy assembled in the Proletcult, but also from the Serapion Brothers.

There were other distinguishing features. Among the Serapions the tone was set by natives of the capital cities, who had united in common search for new forms of art which could encompass all the varied aspects of life. Pereval members were in the main the product of provincial Russia, less sophisticated in literary matters, content from the very first with "realism" and "learning from the classics." In 1927 they published a "declaration" in which they formulated their literary-political platform. In it they stressed that they all fought actively in the Civil War on the side of the revolution, and that they now intended to serve the revolution in the field of literature. They were profoundly convinced that artistic realism, humanism, sincerity, and the ability to see the world were the best guarantee of the creation of works worthy of the revolution. This declaration was violently attacked by the magazine *Na Postu* (On Guard).

PERSECUTION AND LIQUIDATION

Pereval enjoyed the sympathy of A. K. Voronsky, the editor-in-chief of *Krasnaya Nov*. (Later, Voronsky was removed from his post and charged with Trotskyism.) With his aid the Pereval group succeeded in obtaining permission to publish its anthologies, under the title of *Pereval*. The group's literary slogans soon resulted in the persecution of its anthologies and its members by the official critics. Pereval was liquidated in 1932, after the Central Committee of the All-Union Communist Party adopted a resolution "Concerning the Reconstruction of Literary and Artistic Organizations." But informal contacts among its members continued for some years, until the "great purge" and trials of the latter 1930s. During the first trial, in August 1936, *Pravda* published an article accusing the "Perevaltsy" of concealing their "direct ties with and assistance to bitter enemies of the party." Since then, and to this day, Pereval became a synonym for "anti-party" positions, and it was not by accident that it was mentioned at the meeting of the Presidium of the Soviet Writers'

Union in 1954, during the discussion of "the errors permitted by the editors of the magazine *Novy Mir*," who published V. Pomerantsev's article in defense of "sincerity in art."

"WE ARE FIGHTING FOR FUTURE GENERATIONS": KATAYEV

The moods of the Perevaltsy are seen with greatest clarity in the works of their most talented member, Ivan Katayev. Characteristic of his work is the story "Milk." Its hero loves human "warmth" and is convinced that without warm, honest, and good people "everything can go to ruin." Also striking is Katayev's feeling that the generation which had taken active part in the October revolution was doomed. The first writer to express this thought was Alexander Arosev, an old member of the Bolshevik Party. Arosev was the author of the short novel *Harvest Time* (1921), which was the first to sketch images of Soviet "superfluous people." (It was published under another title, *Notes of Terenty the Forgotten*, in Berlin in 1922.)

Katayev's sense of the inevitable doom of the active participants in the revolution was expressed in the short story "The Poet." It is voiced by the poet Gulevich, in whose name the story is told. "We are all bound to perish," he says, "if not today, then tomorrow, if not tomorrow, then in ten years. All of us! We are a doomed generation." His feeling is disputed, but Gulevich insists on his presentiment: "We are fighting for future generations, and they will enjoy the fruits of our struggle. But we must fearlessly sacrifice ourselves. You and I—we are only the sacrificial lambs."

The most significant of Ivan Katayev's critical statements is his article "The Art of the Socialist People," published in the spring of 1936 in Gorky's magazine, *Nashi Dostizheniya* (Our Achievements). In it, Katayev wrote:

"We must inwardly prepare ourselves for these changes. . . . Our art, our literature, must be democratic: in spirit, in tone, in ideals, sympathies, and ties—in the idea, the plot, the syntax, the vocabulary, in every movement of thought and feeling. And then we can be sure that everyone will find his expression in it: the miner, the cotton worker, the railway conductor, and the cook. But for that, it is essential that art should become 'the art of the great socialist democracy.'"

At the same time Katayev directed annihilating criticism at the creative practice of the majority of writers, for their "caste" segregation, their alienation from the life and interests of the working people, their "Buddhist indifference, and their ignorance of real life."

In 1937 Katayev was arrested and "disappeared." He was rehabilitated much later, after his death, although the exact year of his death is still unknown. In 1957 the Gosizdat (State Publishing House) published a volume of his short novels, stories, and sketches.

On the whole, Ivan Katayev, especially in his later statements, was considerably in advance of the Perevaltsy as they were in the 1920s and early '30s. In the earlier years many different writers had joined the Pereval group. Later, some of them flinched in the face of increasing persecution and left the group; others remained true to it until the end. But for all of them the years of common work in Pereval were fruitful ones. Among the Perevaltsy who left a significant trace in literature, we must name, in addition to Katayev, such writers as Dmitry Gorbov and Abram Lezhnev (the theoreticians of the group), Mikhail Prishvin, Alexander Malyshkin, Pyotr Pavlenko, Eduard Bagritsky, Anna Karavayeva, Rodion Akulshin, and Ivan Yevdokimov. The list could be extended considerably.

MAPP, RAPP, AND VOAPP: THE PARTY LINE

Antithetical to Pereval were the incomparably more influential Associations of Proletarian Writers, taking their roots from the Proletcult: the Moscow Association (MAPP, originating in 1923), then the Russian Association (RAPP, founded in 1925), the Associations of most of the other Union Republics, and finally, the All-Union Combined Associations of Proletarian Writers (VOAPP,

1928). The Associations of Proletarian Writers energetically presented themselves as the only true spokesmen of the working class in literature, and launched a bitter attack in their magazine *Na Postu* (On Guard)—renamed in 1926 *Na Literaturnom Postu* (On Literary Guard)—against all heterodox writers, and particularly against the Fellow Travelers. The resolution of the First All-Union Conference of Proletarian Writers in January 1925 openly declared—and what this meant under the conditions of the Communist dictatorship requires no explanation—that "the literary works of the Fellow Travelers are essentially works directed *against* the proletarian revolution," and that "the Fellow Traveler is predominantly a writer who distorts the image of the revolution in literature, who frequently maligns it, and who is imbued with the spirit of nationalism, great-power ideology, and mysticism."

To understand the atmosphere of the time—still far, especially in the early years, from total compulsory conformism—it must be noted that these sharp attacks did not remain unanswered. For example, at the conference on literary problems called in May 1924 by the Press Section of the Central Committee of the Communist Party, a cautious protest was advanced "against wholesale attacks" on writers who did not share the views of the Onguardists, "which they present, moreover, as the position of the Communist Party as a whole." The protest was signed by Valentin Katayev, Alexey Tolstoy, Isaac Babel, Sergey Yesenin, Vera Inber, Nikolay Tikhonov, Vsevolod Ivanov, Osip Mandelstam, Marietta Shaginyan, and others. Altogether there were thirty-six signers, most of them already quite well known.[1]

Predominant at all times among the Associations of Proletarian Writers was the RAPP, under the leadership of Leopold Averbakh, Vladimir Yermilov, and Yury Libedinsky. One should not be misled about the reasons for the

---

[1] The text of this protest, including all the signatures, may be found in *Istoriya Russkoy Sovetskoy Literatury* (*The History of Russian Soviet Literature*), published by the U.S.S.R. Academy of Sciences, Vol. 1, Moscow, 1958, p. 47.

RAPP's pre-eminence in Soviet literary life: the RAPP's power was not based on the literary achievements of its members, but came rather from its energetic support of the policy of the Communist Party known as the "general line." The essential aim of this policy was rapid industrialization of the country and collectivization of agriculture. Encountering resistance, especially among the peasantry, the "general line" was enforced by intensified terrorization of opponents, real or suspected, in all areas of life, including the so-called "literary front." It was in the service of this policy that the Associations of Proletarian Writers succeeded in achieving what the Onguardists had dreamed of in the early 1920s. At the 1924 conference on literary problems their spokesman, I. Vardin, had urged: "We need a Communist cell in literature. Those who expect to do without it have no real desire to win literature for the revolution." The RAPP became just such a "Communist cell" in the literature of the late 1920s, and retained this role until its liquidation in 1932.

The RAPP waged a struggle on many fronts indeed: against "neobourgeois" writers, as the RAPP leaders designated such men as Ilya Ehrenburg and Alexey Tolstoy; against the remnants of the already crushed Kuznitsa; against Pereval, and particularly two of its most active members, Ivan Katayev and Dmitry Gorbov. It also fought against *voronshchina*—Voronsky and his protégés, the Fellow Travelers; against the *LEF*, with its most brilliant spokesman, Vladimir Mayakovsky, and its theoretician, Sergey Tretyakov; and, finally, against peasant writers who sympathized with Populism. The RAPP's sharpest attack, however, was against the so-called "Pereverzev school," led by the eminent but extremely independent Marxist literary scholar Professor V. Pereverzev.

The leading RAPP spokesman, Averbakh, attacked all dissenters with such fury that he virtually terrorized the literary milieu. It was perhaps the fear of being declared an enemy of the working class and the Soviet republic that prompted the official membership in the RAPP of many prominent writers who were quite alien to its moods both in their temperament and in their writing—men like Mikhail Sholokhov, Alexander Fadeyev, and Dmitry Furmanov. The RAPP was hated not only by the majority of writers who did not belong to it, but also by many of its members, and its liquidation in 1932 was greeted by the literary world with a sigh of relief.

The liquidation of the RAPP is not devoid of paradox. Despite its energetic, demonstrative, and frequently noisy support of the "general line," the RAPP was sharply opposed in its organizational policy to the views then prevalent in the upper circles of the Communist Party. The Communist Party was striving in those years to prepare the soil for a broad consolidation of Soviet writers into a single writers' organization, to be controlled by the party. This aim was not realized until April 1932, when the Central Committee of the Communist Party adopted its resolution "On the Reconstruction of Literary and Artistic Organizations." This resolution decreed the "dissolution of the Associations of Proletarian Writers (VOAPP, RAPP)" (and, although this was not stated openly, of all other writers' organizations) and the "unification of all writers who support the platform of the Soviet regime and seek to participate in socialist construction, into *a single union of Soviet writers, with a Communist faction in it.*"

Since then, there have been no writers' organizations in the Soviet Union aside from the "single" Union of Soviet Writers.

Along with all the other groups, the resolution of April 23, 1932, also put an end to the large, but organizationally loose, grouping of peasant writers. Its best-known members included Alexander Neverov, who died quite young, Ivan Makarov, Fyodor Panfyorov, P. Zamoysky, and the poet Mikhail Isakovsky.

However brief, this account of the organizations and groupings of Soviet writers during the years just after the October revolution may serve to give some idea of the enormous tensions and difficulties with which the founders of Soviet literature—and their followers—had to live and work.

SOVIET PROSE OF THE 1920S

The theme of most of the works written during the years just after the October coup was the Civil War. Only a few, however, have stood the test of time. These are *The Iron Flood* by Alexander Serafimovich, *Chapayev* by Dmitry Furmanov, *Red Cavalry* by Isaac Babel, *Armored Train 14–69* by Vsevolod Ivanov, *The Rout* by Alexander Fadeyev, and *White Guard* by Mikhail Bulgakov.

SERAFIMOVICH: *The Iron Flood*

Alexander Serafimovich (1863–1949) was a native of the Don region. His real name was Popov. He began to write long before the October revolution. Best known among his pre-revolutionary works is the novel *A Town in the Steppe* (1907–10). Its central character is the well-to-do Cossack Zakharka Koroyedov, who becomes, through a series of shady operations, the boss of the town in the steppe. After the revolution Serafimovich, formerly a nonpartisan writer of liberal leanings, joined the Communist Party. His best-known post-revolutionary work is *The Iron Flood* (1924). Some Soviet critics regard this novel as the precursor of "Socialist realism." The novel is based on the historic campaign of the Taman army which, finding itself caught in a ring of anti-Bolshevik Cossacks, retreated from the Kuban in 1918 and started out across the Caucasus range to join the Red Army. In Serafimovich's novel the leader of the Taman army is the Bolshevik Kozhukh (his prototype was Epifan Kovtyukh, later also depicted by Furmanov). Kozhukh is a veteran of World War I; for his legendary courage, he was twice sent to officers' school during the war, but proved unable to master the studies. He was sent a third time and probably would have failed again if it were not for the acute shortage of officers in the latter stages of the war. As a result of this shortage, Kozhukh left the school as an officer. But his fellow officers were hostile toward the former peasant. The young officers said nothing openly, but Kozhukh read contempt in their eyes, and repaid it in kind. Nor did his officer's rank provide him with satisfaction anywhere else: on the one hand, he was not accepted by his fellow officers; on the other, the common soldiers, who had formerly loved him as "one of them," were now to some extent estranged. Then the revolution begins, and the pent-up hatred of the men for the officers breaks through to the surface. The soldiers, swept by anarchic moods, rebel against all authority and it is only because of his steadfastness and persistence that Kozhukh finally succeeds in controlling and molding this unruly mass into a disciplined fighting group.

All the Soviet textbooks on literature stress that Serafimovich's principal achievement in this novel is his success in showing "the guiding and directing role of the Communist Party" even at the very beginning of the October revolution.

FURMANOV: *Chapayev*

The critics stress the same qualities in *Chapayev* (1922), a novel written by Dmitry Furmanov (1891–1926) when he was twenty-seven. Furmanov's father was a peasant of the Ivanovo-Voznesensk Oblast, who later moved to the city and changed his legal status from peasant to *meshchanin* or "townsman." The writer had only fragmentary memories of his early childhood. His father kept a teashop; the boy began very early to feel oppressed by his surroundings and became an avid reader. His special favorites were Conan Doyle, Jules Verne, Mayne Reid, and Walter Scott. On graduation from the city school and the commercial school in Ivanovo-Voznesensk, he took examinations which made up for the years of subsequent schooling necessary for university matriculation, and left for Moscow, where he managed before the outbreak of the war to finish his studies at the Philology School of Moscow University.

During World War I, Furmanov worked as a male nurse on hospital trains. In 1916 he returned to Ivanovo-Voznesensk and became a teacher at courses for workers. In his youth he sympathized with the Left Socialist-Revolutionaries, later, with the anarchists. Soon after the October revolution he joined the Communist Party and became a deputy chairman of the Soviet of Workers' Deputies. During the Civil War he went to the front. Furmanov describes this period in two short novels, *Chapayev*, and the less known *Rebellion*. In 1918 Frunze, who had been appointed commander of the 4th Army, invited Furmanov to accompany him. The party committee permitted Furmanov to go. Soon after that Furmanov met Chapayev —a former peasant guerrilla leader who had become a revolutionary commander of legendary skill and courage—and was attached to his unit as a political commissar. Furmanov appears in his own novel as Fyodor Klychkov. But whereas Chapayev is a vivid and colorful figure in the novel, Furmanov-Klychkov is pale and unconvincing. The pious myth created by Soviet critics would have it that Klychkov represents the "directing and guiding hand" of the Communist Party; in reality Klychkov combines party leadership with the scarcely attractive role of a "snooper," assigned to keep an eye on Chapayev and his men.

The novel tells the story of Chapayev's activities and death. In the history of the Civil War, Chapayev was not an isolated phenomenon; in those years many such "people's commanders" emerged from the depths of peasant Russia (in the Ukraine, in Siberia, and in the Far East). Furmanov succeeds in showing Chapayev's character with particular vividness in an incident which takes place in Buzuluk, on the Samara river in 1919. Before going in to attack, Chapayev calls a meeting of the Red Army men and addresses the soldiers. He is not "one of the old generals," he says, who sat in the rear and issued orders for attack. He, Chapayev, is "always out in front" and his main job, as he sees it, is to choose the place of battle so as to make sure that all the men will come out alive, because "every living soul begs for life, and nobody wants to die." The meeting concludes with the gay strains of the

"Komarinskaya," and everyone, including Chapayev, joins in a merry dance.

Over the years Furmanov's novel was subjected to substantial posthumous editing. In the introduction to the second edition of *Chapayev* (1923), Furmanov himself said that the work was in the nature of a "sketch." The chaotic presentation, "and the occasional contradictions," he wrote, were "not so much the result of the author's inability to 'tie things up,' as a reflection of the chaos of the Civil War itself. A war is not a lecture—everything does not go smoothly in it." His "sketch," he added, made no claims to "artistic finish." This introduction was deleted from later editions.

FADEYEV

Two novels by Alexander Fadeyev, *The Rout* and *The Last of the Udege*, are still of interest today. Although Fadeyev (1901–56) was born in European Russia, his parents (both were *feldshers*, or "trained nurses") went to live in the Far East when he was still a child. Most of his childhood and youth was spent in the Southern-Ussuriysk region. Fadeyev attended commercial school at Vladivostok, but dropped out before graduating. He became an active member of the Communist Party at the early age of seventeen. As a boy he was a great admirer of Jack London, Mayne Reid, and Fenimore Cooper. In a letter to a friend Fadeyev admits that without *The Last of the Mohicans* he could not have conceived in his youth the plot of his novel *The Last of the Udege*. Also interesting is Fadeyev's admission that in his literary tastes he was something of an "Old Believer." He liked the "monumental form of the old realistic novel," where everything was "firmly and stably built, but all the more penetrating and profound, and the more lasting in the influence of the author's great humanist ideas upon the spirit of the reader."

Fadeyev conceived *The Rout* as early as 1921–22, but it was not completed until 1925. The novel's basic idea is the "selection of human material" which, the author feels, takes place in a revolution. Everything that is hostile to the revolution reveals itself in its true nature, as does the Socialist-Revolutionary Mechik in the novel. He is contrasted, on the one hand, with Morozko, a man who has gone through the stern school of pre-revolutionary life: Morozko has his faults; he can lie and can treat a woman rudely, but in decisive moments he instinctively takes the side of the revolution. On the other hand, the "politically conscious" element representing the "guiding principle" of the Communist Party is embodied in Levinson. From a literary point of view, he is one of the less successful characters in the novel.

IVANOV

Among the works of nonpartisan writers the most interesting is Vsevolod Ivanov's *Armored Train 14–69*. Ivanov was born in 1895 in the village of Lebyazhie, in the Semipalatinsk Oblast. Without completing the village school, he ran away with a circus, worked as a fakir, a salesman, a singer of couplets, a sailor, and a printer. He developed an early passion for reading and read everything available, "from Dumas to Spencer, and from dream books to Tolstoy." Maxim Gorky played an important role in Ivanov's literary life. Ivanov sent one of his first stories, "On the Irtysh," to Gorky for an opinion. The happiest day in his life, Ivanov said later, was the day when the postman came to the dirty, dark basement printing shop where he was working and handed him a letter from Gorky.

In contrast to Gorky, Ivanov had never been concerned with political or social problems. When the revolution broke out, he joined two parties at once—the Socialist-Revolutionaries and the Social Democrats. The revolution itself, however, quickly helped him to make up his mind. He abandoned literature and plunged into the revolution, defending Omsk against the Czechs and participating in the partisan movement against Kolchak. He was wounded, contracted typhoid fever, and narrowly escaped being shot. He went to Petrograd in 1920. There again he was helped by Gorky. In Petrograd, literature became Ivanov's prime occupation. His first important and lasting success came with the novel *Armored Train 14–69*. The novel was based on an actual event: a detachment of Siberian partisans, armed only with rifles, and headed by the peasant Vershinin, seized a White armored train with weapons and ammunition. In order to stop the train even for a moment, it was necessary for someone to lie across the rails and allow himself to be run over. One of the partisans, a Chinese, decided to sacrifice himself. He lay across the rails and was crushed by the armored train. This story was expanded in the narrative; Ivanov introduced into it many characters he had met when he was a partisan himself. He also changed the site of the action, transferring it from Western Siberia to the Far East. The novel was later made into a play, which was presented with great success for a number of years at the Moscow Art Theatre. The role of Vershinin in the play was acted by the late Kachalov.

An examination of the works of the early years of the revolutionary period soon reveals that the attention of the writers was centered not so much on the ordeals of the Civil War as such, as on the subjective participants in the revolutionary process, its living embodiments, in all the diversity and drama of their clashing interests and aspirations.

BULGAKOV

A vivid illustration of the conflicts within the victorious revolution is found in Mikhail Bulgakov's novel *White Guard*.

Mikhail Bulgakov was born in Kiev in 1891. He went to school in Kiev, where he graduated with distinction in 1916 from the College of Medicine. However, he did not use his medical title very long. One night, traveling in a ramshackle train, by the light of a candle stuck in a kerosene bottle he wrote his first story. He took the story to the editors of the newspaper in the city where the train had brought him. The editors published it. In 1920 Bulgakov abandoned his career as a doctor and began to write.

White Guard was autobiographical. Later, the author dramatized the novel into a play, *The Days of the Turbins*, which ran with consistent success for a decade at the Moscow Art Theatre.

The novel *White Guard* immediately arrests attention with its epigraph, taken from Pushkin's *The Captain's Daughter*: "A fine snow began to fall and suddenly pelted down in an avalanche of huge flakes. The wind howled; a snowstorm began. Within an instant the dark sky merged with the sea of snow. Everything disappeared. 'We are in trouble, *Barin*,' cried the coachman. 'A blizzard!'"

This blizzard engulfs the Turbin family. Only yesterday there was a comfortable dining room with a warm tile stove, there were books, accumulated since the children began to grow up; now suddenly everything disappears, whirled away in the terrible storm. The Turbin mother dies, and her place is taken by the older sister. "How can they live? How can they live? Their life was shattered at the very dawn." The Turbin brothers fight on the side of the White Army, then, in the ordeals of the struggle, one of them (or, to be more exact, the author himself) discovers the secret meaning of the revolutionary drama. The writer embodies this meaning in an unforgettably tragic image: ". . . Before death, preceding it, ran the gnarled peasant wrath. It ran through the frost and blizzard, in torn bast shoes, with hay in its tousled uncovered head, and howled. . . ." Later, the younger Turbin inwardly goes over to the Bolsheviks.

The success of the novel and the play boomeranged against the author. The censorship began to cause him endless difficulties, especially in regard to his talented satirical stories. In the end, Bulgakov was compelled to retire from literature for many years; he became a literary consultant, first with the Moscow Art Theatre, and later with the Bolshoy.

Perhaps the largest number of the works about the Civil War came from the pens of peasant writers. But only a few of the tales and stories devoted to rural life during the first post-revolutionary years will remain in literature. These include two tales of Alexander Neverov, who died in 1923, *Andron the Good for Nothing* and *Geese and Swans*; Lydia Seyfullina's *Manure* and *Virineya*; L. Leonov's *The Badgers*; Fyodor Panfyorov's *Bruski*; M. Sholokhov's *The Quiet Don*; and I. Babel's *Red Cavalry*.[2]

A NEW THEME: GLADKOV'S *Cement*

Gradually the theme of the Civil War, which occupied so large a place in the works of the early 1920s, began to give way to a new theme: the life of the new society that had begun to take shape within the framework of the victorious revolution. Among the new works dealing with this theme were two novels, B. Pilnyak's *The Naked Year*[3] and A. Neverov's *Tashkent, City of Bread*, both of which enjoyed great popularity. In the latter, Neverov painted a portrait of the peasant boy Misha Dodonov, who decided, in the year of the frightful famine on the Volga, to make his way to the distant, unknown city of Tashkent, rumored to be rich in bread. The story of this journey, with all its privations and disappointments, forms the content of the novel. Misha succeeds in returning home with some grain, but finds that his mother has died in the meantime.

The greatest popular success in the middle 1920s was won by Fyodor Gladkov's novel *Cement*. Gladkov (1883–1958) grew up in the large family of a poor peasant. His parents were Old Believers, adhering to stern traditions in their family relations. Gladkov was eight when his parents began to wander about in search of a livelihood. They worked in the fisheries on the Caspian Sea, then moved on to Kuban. At the age of twelve Gladkov was sent to work. He developed an early admiration for Gorky. In 1904 he

---

[2] *The Badgers* is discussed in Chapter 12, *The Quiet Don* in Chapter 15, and *Red Cavalry* in Chapter 8.
[3] *The Naked Year* is discussed in Chapter 9.

began to take part in the revolutionary movement, was arrested and exiled. Shortly before the revolution of 1917 he returned to Kuban and became a teacher. Gladkov began to write before the revolution, but none of his works attracted attention. *Cement* (1925), however, immediately brought him to the forefront of Soviet literature.

The action of the novel unfolds at the end of the Civil War, at the meeting point of two dramatic post-revolutionary epochs—War Communism and the NEP (New Economic Policy). After several years of fighting in the Civil War the worker Gleb Chumalov returns to his old factory. The immense, handsome plant stands idle. Its workers have turned to petty trading and making cigarette lighters. "The electricity went out in the factory and in the barracks; the factory whistles were choked with dust. The silence and idleness began to cluck and grunt, transformed into a village idyl. And the industrious husband and his parsimonious wife locked themselves sullenly inside their domicile."

Gleb Chumalov decides to undertake the rebuilding of the half-wrecked factory. Such is the plot of this work, which became the prototype of the Soviet industrial novel. Still greater, perhaps, was its importance in revealing what the revolution had given to the Russian woman. This theme is embodied in a lively, often dramatic manner in the person of Dasha Chumalova, Gleb's wife. Before the revolution Dasha was an ordinary woman, centered entirely on the care of her family—her husband, and her child. After Chumalov's departure for the front, the town is occupied by the Whites, and Dasha becomes involved in underground activities. When he returns from the Civil War, Chumalov finds a ruined factory and a ruined family. Despite Chumalov's fervent wish to see Dasha resume her former self, she refuses. One day, coming home from work, he finds a note from Dasha. She has left him to live her own independent life.

LIBEDINSKY: *The Commissars*

Less popular, but successful nevertheless, were the early works of the young writer Yury Libedinsky. Libedinsky (1898–1959) was born in Odessa, but spent his childhood and youth in the Urals, where his father worked as a factory doctor. He attended the Chelyabinsk secondary school. His literary tastes were influenced by Blok and Bely; his favorites among the classics were Turgenev and Tolstoy. At one time the young Libedinsky was attracted to Populism, but a deeper and more lasting mark on his development was left by anarcho-syndicalist ideas. In 1920 Libedinsky became a member of the Communist Party. At the same time he began to write. Literary fame was won easily in those days. His first book, *The Week* (1922), made Libedinsky a celebrity.

Young Libedinsky's work was characterized by his skill in grasping, amid the manifold and quick succession of events, the focal problems of his time. In the middle 1920s one of these "focal problems" was that of the peasantry, its political moods and aspirations. These are vividly portrayed in the novel *The Commissars* (1925).

The "thunder of the Civil War" is stilled, and the military commissars disperse to their homes: some marry daughters of priests and merchants, some simply give themselves to drink, others acquire some property of their own, losing "the proletarian spirit." To tighten up these scattered cadres, the chief of the military district decides to organize courses for former commissars. The novel turns into a review of the erstwhile command elements of the Red Army. Most of the ex-commissars are peasants. In his characterization of these war commissars of peasant origin, Libedinsky sometimes achieves the mastery of the true artist. At one of the lectures, the instructor, true to the letter of Marxist theory, explains to his audience that the peasantry is by its very nature a "petty-bourgeois" class. This assertion provokes the heated protest of the peasant Communist Gladkikh: "Now he tries to turn us into Socialist-Revolutionaries. . . . But if you really think about it—isn't it on us that the whole economy of the republic rests?" The director of the courses, who is present at the lecture, attempts to soften the harsh characterization of the peasantry offered by the instructor. But no matter how hard he tries, he sees "as he looks at those sullen, secretive faces, the stubbornly bowed peasant heads, concealing their eyes," that neither their days in the trenches on the Western Front, nor membership in the peasant sections of the Soviet, nor participation in the Civil War have as yet "budged the peasant nature of these fellows." The official explanations and theories do not penetrate their minds, but are like the "agile, long-legged mosquitoes" that skim over the surface of "dark stagnant waters."

SEMYONOV AND CHUMANDRIN

The most significant of the young working-class writers was Sergey Semyonov (1893–1943). The son of a Petersburg worker and himself a worker before the revolution, he became a Communist as early as 1917 and took part in the suppression of the Kronstadt rebellion in 1921. After that, however, he devoted himself entirely to literature. His best-known work is the novel *Natalya Tarpova* (in large measure autobiographical). In this novel the writer touched on a number of interesting problems, specifically those of the relations between the personal and the social. In the character of the engineer Gabrukh, Semyonov was one of the first to portray the "nonpartisan specialist" working with the Bolsheviks. Gabrukh feels that the Bolsheviks are doing in the economic field what he would have done in their place. He says to the Communist Ryabiev: "The path of Russia and your deeds—not your words, but your deeds—coincide. Do you hear?—coincide! The power of grim facts has turned out to be such that, without sparing life or limb, you are doing in Russia exactly what I would have done in your place."

Almost forgotten today is Mikhail Chumandrin, a young writer of working-class origin who died during the Finnish war in 1940. The only one of his works that is still of some interest today is his novel *The Rablé Factory*. It describes a privately owned factory and working conditions in it that are in certain respects better than those in state enterprises.

"WORKING-CLASS" POETS

Still slighter is the trace left in literature by working-class poets. Properly speaking, there were few genuine worker-poets among them; most of those who claimed the title of "working-class" or "proletarian" came, like A. Zharov, from villages. In their themes the "proletarian" poets may be divided into two groups: the members of one wrote about cosmic vistas and the remote, ideal future (Kirillov); the others specialized in what was known as *agitka*, or "propaganda verse." Most popular among the latter was Demyan Bedny. Making free use of the form of Krylov's fables, he responded to all the events of the day: "Steklov's daily editorials in *Izvestia* and Demyan Bedny's daily *feuilletons* in *Pravda* are the party's diary," wrote V. Lvov-Rogachevsky in his *Essays on Proletarian Literature*. The group also included A. Bezymensky (*The Smell of Life*), A. Zharov, and others.

A COMPROMISE

Disappointed in the writers and poets of working-class background, the official critics turned with carping zeal to watching the work of former provincial intellectuals and peasants. From the very outset, they denied the right of the latter to express the ideology of the "proletarian revolution." The position of the official critics was not an easy one: the writers of working-class origin proved unsatisfactory in their political temper; as for the Fellow Travelers, they distrusted them on principle.

Since there were no working-class writers expressing in their work the requisite emotions of "leaders of social progress," the official critics were obliged to compromise, and they hastened to award the "proletarian" accolade to those who, though stemming from other social classes, nevertheless created works full of the "social optimism" of the "victors." The honorary title of "proletarian" was withdrawn, however, as easily as it was awarded. This title was very soon withdrawn, for instance, from Alexander Tarasov-Rodionov, a member of the editorial staff of the magazine *Oktyabr* and a member of the Bolshevik Party since long before the October revolution. The reason for his disgrace was his novel *Chocolate* (1922), which anticipated in many details the mechanism of extracting "confessions" of guilt from the defendants at the dread Moscow trials of the latter 1930s. It was not by chance that during the Moscow trials, fifteen years later, the novel was branded a "malicious slander," and its author "an enemy of the people." Tarasov-Rodionov was arrested, and nothing is known about his subsequent fate. His name was not included among those rehabilitated after Stalin's death.

NEW HEROES

Despite the censorship and arbitrary interference, literature flourished during the NEP period. In the course of some six to eight years significant contributions were made to the new post-October literature, which attracted the attention of both European and American readers. Some of these works still developed Civil War themes; but the forefront was already occupied by fiction dealing with problems of the interrelations of social forces inside the victorious revolution.

This change in subject matter was attended by the appearance of several new heroes in the works of the latter 1920s. Prominent among these is the optimistic Communist economic functionary (Badyin in Gradkov's *Cement*, Andrey Babichev in Yury Olesha's novel *Envy*, the engineer Forst in Boris Pilnyak's novel *Machines and Wolves*, and others). In the novels devoted to life in the NEP-period village, the type of the optimistic functionary has its parallel in the prosperous peasant (Ilya Plakushchev in Panfyorov's *Bruski*, Svaaker in Konstantin Fedin's novelette *Transvaal*, the Gogin brothers in Yakov Korobov's novel *Dyoma Bayunov*, and others).

At the other pole the optimism of the "leading" heroes of the NEP is balanced by the attitudes of the "ex-heroes," the dreamers of the days of the Civil War and War Communism, who, under the NEP, have found themselves to be "superfluous men." Such are Mitka Vekshin in L. Leonov's novel *The Thief*, Mikhail Lykov in I. Ehrenburg's novel *The Grabber*, and Buzheninov in A. Tolstoy's *Azure Cities*.[4] Outside the city this army of the disenchanted is represented by poor peasants: Stepan Ognyov in Panfyorov's *Bruski* and Dyoma Bayunov in Yakov Korobov's novel of the same name.

The number of the disillusioned—asking themselves sadly or bitterly "What did we fight for?"—was, however, relatively small. The vast Russian semi-urban, semi-peasant population continued to believe, despite all the "punches in the jaw" from the official ideologists, that the "temporary breathing spell" proclaimed at the beginning of the NEP would be extended, so that ultimately "our side will win out!" This conviction, never openly formulated, seemed to be reinforced by the strong current of humor that characterized the first decade of Soviet literature. It found expression in the humorous stories of Panteleymon Romanov and Mikhail Bulgakov, in the early stories of Leonid Leonov, Ilya Ilf and Evgeny Petrov, and particularly in the entire work of Mikhail Zoshchenko.[5]

However, NEP society, especially by the end of the 1920s, was the scene of violent contradictions that sooner or later had to explode the temporary situation created by the New Economic Policy. Yet, the proclamation of the "general line," with its sweeping program of speeded-up industrialization and compulsory collectivization, struck

---

[4] *Envy* is discussed in Chapter 11, *Machines and Wolves* in Chapter 9, *The Grabber* in Chapter 7, and *Azure Cities* in Chapter 14.
[5] See Chapter 6.

many contemporaries like thunder out of a clear sky, or "a second offensive of the revolution." This was most vividly depicted in Panteleymon Romanov's novel *Comrade Kislyakov* (1930).

THE FICTION OF THE 1930S

ROMANOV

Panteleymon Romanov (1884–1938), of noble origin, was born in the village of Pokrovskoye in the Tula province. On completing his studies at Moscow University (he was a lawyer by training), he devoted himself to literature. After the October revolution he was popular not only for his humorous short stories, but also for his stories about the "excesses" in the life of the young society, and particularly the fashionable attitudes toward love, with their easy dismissal of traditional values (*Stories about Love*, *Without Cherry Blossoms*, etc.). Actually, Romanov was most interested in the social conduct of the intelligentsia in its relations with the new government. This problem is dealt with in two of Romanov's works, *The Right to Life* (1927) and *Comrade Kislyakov* (1930). In the latter, Romanov wrote that this "second offensive" was "more terrifying to many people than all the storms and tempests of the first: at that time it was somehow possible to jump aside and wait it out." Now there was no place to hide. *Comrade Kislyakov* was confiscated shortly after publication, and the doors of all magazines and publishing organizations were closed to its author. In 1936 the ban was lifted and several of Romanov's sketches appeared in magazines. He died of heart disease two years later.

"SHOCK WORKERS": HEROES OF THE '30S

The new political course of the early 1930s was marked in literature by the appearance of new heroes, members of the *déclassé* youth. Most notable among them are Sanka

Golod in Alexander Avdeyenko's *I Love* and "Captain" Kostya in the play *The Aristocrats*, by the young dramatist Nikolay Pogodin. Captain Kostya, the hero of the play, together with his fellow convicts in a northern labor camp, develops an overwhelming enthusiasm for the goals of construction, and with great zeal turns out fantastic norms, far in excess of official demand. In this way he and those like him make up for the various sins of their past.

Another kind of new hero—the young "shock worker"— appeared in works devoted to industrialization. Such is Kolka Rzhanov in Ilya Ehrenburg's *The Second Day*,[6] Korchagin in Boris Levin's *There Were Two Comrades*, the young engineer Morgulies in Valentin Katayev's novel *Time, Forward!*, and others. These young heroes are matched by an entire gallery of similarly energetic directors of gigantic industrial projects. Notable among them are Shor in Ehrenburg's novel, Uvadyev in Leonid Leonov's *Sot*, Kurilov in his *Road to the Ocean*, Vatagin in Fyodor Gladkov's *Energy* (devoted to the building of Dneprostroy), and Ignatov in Yakov Ilyin's *The Large Conveyor*.

Two characteristics strike the attention of the reader of this industrial fiction: the "enthusiasm" of the shock workers, who were soon to become the "aristocrats of the country," and the energy of the directors of the new projects. The construction of huge industrial complexes is described against a background of the gloomy moods and murmurings of the masses of rank-and-file workers. But while the "enthusiasm" of the directors of enterprises and of the young and successful shock workers is stressed in every possible way, both by the authors and by the official critics, the dissatisfaction and apathy of the working masses are relegated to a minor place in the narrative. A considerable proportion of this anonymous mass toiling for the greater glory of industrialization consists of peasants who either fled from collectivization or were dispossessed as kulaks. In his novel *Fate* (1935) the young writer Alexander Avdeyenko, author of the autobiographical *I Love*

[6] See Chapter 7.

(1932), imprudently spoke of the real builders of the period of Five-Year Plans as "a peasant army in bast shoes," for which he was severely reprimanded in the press.

NEGATIVE HEROES: AFINOGENOV'S *Fear*

In citing the works that met with the approval of the official literary critics, we cannot ignore those that provoked unfavorable comment. Among these a special place is held by the once sensational play *Fear*, by Alexander Afinogenov (b. 1904), who died on November 4, 1941, during a bombardment of Moscow. Afinogenov belonged to the small number of writers in this period who had an innate sense of the dramatic. Although he was a member of the Proletcult in his youth, and was later closely connected with the RAPP, Afinogenov's creative personality remains puzzling in many respects to this day.

The principal hero of the play *Fear* is Professor Borodin. A representative of the pre-revolutionary intelligentsia, he suffocates in the conditions created by the Soviet regime for nonpartisan scientists, and makes public the results of his study of the stimuli that lie at the root of the conduct of Soviet people of the most diverse social groups. It turns out that the main stimulus in the conduct of 80 per cent of those he investigated was *fear*: "We live in an age of great fear. Fear compels talented intellectuals to repudiate their mothers, to lie about their social origins, to worm themselves into high positions. Fear dogs a man's footsteps. . . . We are all rabbits. How, then, can anyone work creatively?"

Despite the play's flaws and its very dubious "happy ending," it became a sensation in the Soviet Union. The only thing that saved both the play and its author was the deliberately planted portrait of the old Bolshevik Clara. In reply to Borodin's talk she makes a speech about the fear that shackled the working people under the Czarist regime. However, says she, the working people succeeded in mastering this fear and forging within themselves the courage needed in the fight against their oppressors. But while the audience in the theaters listened to Borodin with bated breath, they closed their ears to the speech of the old Bolshevik, aware that this was the necessary tribute that the author was obliged to pay for his boldness. And members of the audience might well have repeated to themselves the words that summarized the entire inner meaning of the play: "Destroy fear, destroy everything that breeds fear, and you will see how rich, how creative, life will become in our country!"

Still more symptomatic of "negative" trends was another feature of the industrial literature. Side by side with the energetic, affirmative images of young builders, the reader encounters in almost all of these works the figure of a young man filled with doubts about the results of the construction work, and dreaming, in this atmosphere of compulsory "enthusiasm," of a different life and individual freedom. Such is Volodya Safonov in Ehrenburg's *The Second Day*, Debets and Budne in Boris Levin's *There Were Two Comrades*, and Dmitrievsky in Ilyin's *The Large Conveyor*. In Levin's story the young Communist Debets goes so far as to say to Korchagin: "We are building, standing up to our knees in mud, with frost blistering our skin. It would be better if we were warm, clean, and properly fed. And to shout, to boast about our conditions —that's altogether absurd." Ilyin's Dmitrievsky is even more intransigent. The author tells us that Dmitrievsky "hated this country, its air, its newspapers, its leaders; he compared the regime in the country with the days of Catherine."

The most significant fact about these disillusioned young people was that they were not "outsiders" or "alien elements." All of them had grown up under the Soviet regime, and had been enthusiastic supporters of the revolution in the past. Dmitrievsky had been a member of the Comsomol; Skutarevsky's son in Leonov's novel of the same name had taken part in the Civil War on the side of the Reds, but was later repelled by the lies and hypocrisy of the official ideologists of the regime. However, though the authors of these works carefully tried to disavow these "negative heroes" in order to avert the possible charge of secret sympathies for the "opposition," though they merely sketched their silhouettes in a few quick lines, these characters were memorable, and the critics soon began to brand such heroes as "Soviet Pechorins" (in reference to the central character of Lermontov's *A Hero of Our Times*).

THE CRITICS ANSWER: *How Steel Was Tempered*

To counterbalance these disenchanted young men of the 1930s, the critics launched, shortly after the assassination of Kirov in 1934, a propaganda campaign for the novel *How Steel Was Tempered*, by a hitherto unknown young Communist, Nikolay Ostrovsky. The novel was autobiographical in character. Nikolay Ostrovsky (1904–36) was born in the family of a poor worker in the Ukraine. He joined the Bolsheviks at an early age, performing, with his friends, a variety of tasks for the party. In 1919 he volunteered for the front without telling his family. A year later he was severely wounded and partially lost his vision. However, he refused to be defeated. In 1926 it was found that he was suffering from polyarthritis, a disease that kept him bedridden for the rest of his life. Three years later Ostrovsky became blind and partially paralyzed. Then he decided to become a writer. He invented a special device with raised lines, which made it possible for him to write, feeling the lines through the paper. He sent the first part of his novel to the magazine *Molodaya Gvardia* (Young Guard) in 1931. A year later he was notified that it had been accepted for publication. The novel was printed serially during 1932, but did not arouse much interest. Nor did the second part attract attention when it appeared in the same magazine from January to May, 1934. It was only after the assassination of Kirov by the young Communist Nikolayev and the discovery of the assassin's diary, voicing the moods of the disenchanted, that Ostrovsky's novel came to the center of attention of the literary world. Wide party and official circles became interested in Ostrovsky's fate; they surrounded him with solicitude and care and tried to save him. A whole brigade of writers was dispatched to help him with his second novel, *Born of the Storm*.

In the meantime his first novel was published in book form, in a considerably edited version. In the version that had earlier been published in *Molodaya Gvardia*, Ostrovsky had described the tense atmosphere of his home, his own suffering when he became an invalid, his relations with his wife, whose mother incited her against him, and their separation. All this disappeared in the later editions of the novel. In its final version the novel was in full conformity with all the rules of "Socialist realism."

COLLECTIVIZATION: A TRAGIC PERIOD

The destinies of the writers whose works reflected the life of the peasantry after the October revolution and, particularly, during the collectivization of agriculture followed tragic lines. The talented peasant poet Sergey Yesenin[7] committed suicide in 1925. Equally tragic was the fate of his "older brother" in poetry, Nikolay Kluyev (1887–1937). Like Yesenin, he experienced a brief period of enthusiasm for the October revolution (expressed in his cycle of poems *Red Roar*, 1917–18). But as early as the end of 1918, realizing the antipeasant nature of the revolution, Kluyev began to turn away from it, openly expressing his feelings. As a result, he soon became the target of violent attacks by the critics. By the end of the NEP period the poet's life had become especially difficult. In 1927 the January issue of the Leningrad *Zvezda* (Star) published his poem "The Village." The same year saw the publication of his "Lament for Yesenin." Soon after that he wrote a long poem, "The Burnt-Out Land," but it never appeared in the Soviet Union; after the late 1920s none of his work was admitted into print. In 1933 he was arrested and

[7] See Chapter 4.

sent into penal exile, from which he never returned. He died in 1937, and was never rehabilitated. A two-volume collection of his poems (including "The Burnt-Out Land") was published in New York in 1954 by the Chekhov Publishing House.

The fate of the peasant writers was particularly difficult during the period of collectivization. Even Communist writers were placed under suspicion; they were frequently accused of having become "muzhik mouthpieces," and various obstacles were put in their way. Suspicion fell, for instance, on the peasant Communist writer Ivan Makarov after the appearance of his short story "The Island" in the magazine *Novy Mir*, in 1929. The hero of the story, the peasant Fyodor Mikhailovich, is an individualist and an opponent of collectivization. Feeling that the times are against him (even his son abandons him), he commits suicide. Makarov could not, and indeed would not, conceal his compassion for Fyodor Mikhailovich—for which he was accused of "surviving sympathies for property-owning elements" in the villages. Makarov himself admitted at the time: "It is difficult for me to write today, and getting more difficult from hour to hour." The "difficulties" he hinted at were the same as those of the majority of writers in those years; they were political. The almost total absence of new writers of peasant origin who could give direct testimony concerning rural life during the era of collectivization put a special stamp of artificiality on all the works on peasant life written in those years (N. Bogdanov's *The Challenge*, V. Stavsky's *Stanitsa*, P. Zamoysky's *Bast Shoes*, M. Karpov's *The Unsubmissive*, and others).

SHOLOKHOV: *Virgin Soil Upturned*[8]

This tragic period is described most vividly in Mikhail Sholokhov's novel, *Virgin Soil Upturned*, the first part of which appeared as early as 1932. More boldly than any

[8] See Chapter 15.

other writer, Sholokhov recorded the tragic flow of events as they occurred in the Cossack village, Gremyachy Log. In the still turbulent life of the village, which had not yet assumed stable new forms, two groups emerge: the adherents and the opponents of collectivization. The former include the representatives of the local government: the chairman of the local Soviet, Andrey Razmetnov; the secretary of the party cell, Makar Nagulnov; and Semyon Davydov, sent from the city to help the local authorities (one of the "twenty-five-thousanders" mobilized by the party to implement the collectivization). The Cossacks themselves, even those with little land, are at best in a "wait-and-see" mood: "I want to see what kind of life it's going to be, in the kolkhoz. If it's good, I'll join, if not—why go there?" argues the poor Cossack Lyushnya at a village meeting. In the opinion of the middling peasant Kuzma, the government is "a bit wide of the mark" in setting up the kolkhozes, in which all sorts of people are included. According to him, people should be brought together under a different principle: "the diligent men, in one kolkhoz—the poor, in another—the prosperous, by themselves—and the loafers, outside the village—let the G.P.U. teach them to work."

The impact of collectivization on the life of the village is shown most dramatically in the episode in which Makar Nagulnov's old friend, Titok Borodin, is dispossessed and arrested. Shaking his bound hands as he is taken to prison, Titok cries to Nagulnov: "*Makar!* Remember! . . . Our paths will cross! You've trampled me down, but my turn will come. Whatever happens, I'll get you! Our friendship's dead!"

THE SEARCH FOR MURAVIA

Despite obvious attempts on the part of the writers to mitigate the picture of village life during the collectivization, the reader is constantly aware of the fundamental fact that the mainstay of the village—the prosperous diligent peasant—has been shaken; he senses sharply that all further struggle is doomed to defeat. Especially dramatic is the picture of the collectivization in the third volume of Panfyorov's novel *Bruski*. The active opponent of collectivization, Nikita Guryanov, finally leaves his native village, Shiroky Buyerak, and sets out across the land in search of the legendary peasant country of Muravia, where there is no collectivization. On the way he meets other "involuntary travelers" like himself. In his wanderings he goes all the way to Novy Afon, but never finds his Muravia. Weary, and longing for his accustomed work on the land, Guryanov returns to Shiroky Buyerak.

Some years later Alexander Tvardovsky, then just beginning his literary career, devoted a poem, *The Land of Muravia*, to the same theme. The title was admittedly borrowed from Panfyorov's story of Nikita Guryanov's search.

But who, under those circumstances, was in favor of collectivization? A large percentage of the adherents (or, rather, accomplices) of collectivization consisted of the village youth. And here it is important to note a fact that throws interesting light on the dynamics of the agrarian revolution: a significant proportion of these accomplices and aides was made up of *children of former prosperous peasants*. Most astonishing, perhaps, is that this is pointed out by the most diverse writers (V. Stavsky, *Stanitsa*; V. Katayev, *Time, Forward!*; D. Vityazev, *An Ocean of Flax*), which suggests that the phenomenon was not accidental. However, the reader is not entirely unprepared if he has previously read the works about village life during the NEP period, which showed that the village Comsomol attracted not only the children of poor peasants, but also many children of prosperous peasants; it was precisely the latter who played the most prominent role in it.

THE ARTICULATE KULAK: *Mountains* AND *Loneliness*

It is impossible, however, to ignore another feature of the works dealing with village life in that period: as the years went on, and it became obvious that the peasantry

Literary Developments: Revolution to World War II

had not been strong enough to resist compulsory collectivization effectively, more and more novels and stories began to show strong, prosperous peasants—*articulate kulaks*—with unmistakable sympathy. Among the first of these characters was the rich peasant Plakushchev in Panfyorov's *Bruski*. A similar peasant, Agapov, appeared in Zarubin's novel *Mountains*. Agapov escaped from the collectivization to Altai, where he devoted himself to beekeeping. The Communist Bezugly, who had known Agapov during the war (Agapov had saved his life on one occasion), meets him again in Altai. Over a glass of tea with homemade honey Agapov decides to have a "heart-to-heart" talk with Bezugly: "Vanya, why do you hobble Russia's feet? You know that 160 million men are sitting around with folded hands." Agapov would like Bezugly to come out at the All-Russian Congress and say: "We've had enough, Comrades, of playing cat and mouse with the peasant. It's time to let him strike some roots into the lands. . . ."

A full-length tragic portrait of the kulak appears in the novel *Loneliness*, by the young writer Nikolay Virta. The action of the novel takes place in the early years after the October revolution, during the Civil War period, in the province of Tambov. But the "historic" character of the novel is very tenuous, and the readers of the 1930s thought of the principal hero of the novel, the peasant Storozhev, as a contemporary. Storozhev is involved with the leader of an uprising against the Soviet regime, Antonov, but despises him and dreams of freeing himself of the tie as soon as the rebels manage to overcome the Bolsheviks. There is great inner strength in Virta's picture of Storozhev's life after the advent of the NEP, when the chances of a successful overthrow of the Soviet regime dwindle. Separated from his family and land, Storozhev hides out in the woods, living like a beast at bay. His longing for his loved ones, for work on the land, drives him from place to place, and he haunts and circles other people's fields.

The novel provoked lively discussion. The critics felt that the writer's chief success was in the "vividness of the image of the class enemy." But a great deal must be read between the lines of such writing. Much more important was the fact that, even after the main resistance of the peasantry to the collectivization was broken, the figure of the "prosperous, efficient peasant," with his rugged, single-minded strength, continued to appeal to writers and to hold their imagination.

THE SECOND FIVE-YEAR PLAN: FALSE RESPITE

For a short time, during the early part of the Second Five-Year Plan (it began in 1933), it seemed that a period was about to begin when Soviet society would be able to live more peacefully and at a somewhat more relaxed "pace." This hope was soon shattered by the Moscow trials of 1936–38.

The first trial of the "Trotskyite-Zinovievite terrorist group" in August 1936 struck the writers like a moral and political earthquake. The Presidium of the Writers' Union made a hasty attempt to bring its—by then already traditional—tribute of "indignation" against the "enemies," publishing a statement that the court's verdict in the Trotsky-Zinoviev case is "our verdict." But this tribute did not appease the literary authorities. The final crushing of the Pereval group also took place at this time. There was a wave of arrests of writers in both capital and provincial cities, ferreting out not only "Trotskyites" but also those who "abetted" them. Added to the terror and brutality of the "retributions" were the fear and uncertainty of when and where the blow would fall. Some conception, however inadequate, of life in those bitter years may be gained from certain of the poems that appeared in the latter 1950s, especially from Margarita Aliger's "Rightness" (*Oktyabr*, November 1956), which describes a meeting with a friend of her youth who was arrested on false charges and has finally returned home after seventeen years in a concentration camp. A similar meeting occurs in a chapter of

Alexander Tvardovsky's poem *Vista beyond Vista*.[9] References to such encounters can also be found in many prose works of the most recent, post-Stalin period.

Along with the persecution of writers guilty of contacts with those arrested or implicated in the Moscow trials, there was a wholesale campaign against editors, critics, and everyone suspected of secret sympathies toward the Right or Left opposition (the list of those arrested at the time included the playwright Afinogenov, the editor of the magazine *Novy Mir* (New World), Gronsky, former leaders of the RAPP, and many others). Only a few of the victims managed to return alive, years later, after Stalin's death and their consequent rehabilitation.

IDEOLOGICAL CONSOLIDATION: MAKARENKO'S *Book for Parents*

But apart from terror, there were other phenomena that deserve attention and attest to the process of consolidation taking place in the upper strata of Soviet society. This process went on very cautiously, manifesting itself in a number of small details. Among those who contributed to this ideological consolidation and crystallization was the late Alexey Tolstoy[10]—in his historical novel *Peter I*, and in his trilogy (still uncompleted at the time) *The Road to Calvary*. A. S. Makarenko (1888–1939) also helped to articulate this process. A pedagogue by profession, he combined his teaching activities with literary work. His novel *A Pedagogical Epic* (1934), which related in fictional form his experiences with *besprizorniki* (stray children) in a children's commune, enjoyed wide popularity. Most revealing of the new trends in the development of the upper stratum of Soviet society, however, is his *Book for Parents*, which appeared in the magazine *Krasnaya Nov* (Red Virgin Soil) in 1937.

Makarenko's *Book for Parents* was the first attempt at a "heart-to-heart talk" with representatives of the top levels

[9] See Chapter 19.
[10] See Chapter 14.

of the new society on the raising and education of their children. The author proceeds from the pious assumption that Soviet society is "classless." The facts he cites, however, eloquently disprove this assumption. He sketches a great variety of children and adolescents, from those who hate their parents, especially their fathers, to the point of running away from home and joining the strays, to their opposites. One of the latter, Alyosha, fourteen years old, is the son of a prominent Soviet dignitary; when he learns about the family's forthcoming journey to the Crimea for the summer vacation, he is indignant because they will travel in an ordinary railway car. The year before, his parents made the vacation journey in an "international" car. He attributes this "demotion" to the fact that they are taking him along; they evidently feel, he thinks, that he can travel "any old way." Such demands for privilege on the part of children of leading officials were by no means infrequent, and Makarenko discussed the problem with many parents. The parents seemed quite bewildered: "But what am I to do? If I take my family along to a resort, do you think I should travel in one car, and they in another?" Makarenko patiently explained to such fathers that it was their task to teach their children that "great" and serious demands could be made only by those who earned privilege, and that such privilege required the "sanction of society." The children of such dignitaries, however, were less flexible "dialecticians": born in the social upper strata, and judging from their own personal experience and standards, they felt that their right to privilege was assured by the existing order of things, and demanded to live "as they properly should."

Makarenko gives another typical example: a young girl, a student and a member of the Comsomol. Her father is a senior economist, her mother, a director of a library. The father has a mistress, and the mother compensates for her frustrations by excessive solicitude toward the daughter, Tamarochka. Her daughter's life, she feels, must exemplify the unalloyed "radiant progress of womanhood." Tamara does not have brown shoes to match her brown dress, and she makes a violent scene. When the mother timidly suggests that she had suffered greater deprivations in her youth, Tamara replies: "Oh, she's harping on that again? How do I know what you had or didn't have, or why you went hungry? That was under Czarism, what do I care? Today it's different." Such arguments are still being raised today, in the postwar years —as, for instance, by the grandson of the old Bolshevik Tyoma Kirpichev, in the play *Guests* (1954), by Leonid Zorin.

STABILIZATION

Against the background of a widely felt need, both at the upper levels of society and among its broader strata, for some stabilization of existence, the subject matter of fiction began to change. There was a perceptible turn to the depiction of personal life, of intimate relationships and experiences—and, concurrently, a greater need to report on the unsatisfactory living conditions that continued to exist—as in the novel *Provincial People* (1938) by A. Malyshkin, A. Losev's *A Young Man*, and F. Gladkov's *Energy*.

Even more significant was the shift of literary attention to the provinces. This increasing interest in the provinces was stimulated by the many new provincial centers and cities during the years of industrialization. At first many of the engineers and specialists sent to the provinces retained their apartments in the capital, secretly dreaming of returning to Moscow. But as the years went by and new factories were built everywhere, provincial cities grew and acquired their own universities and theaters; their life began to assume definite shape, and their residents, particularly the local technical intelligentsia, developed a sense of belonging and of local pride. Moreover, the economic and cultural policy-makers sought to stimulate the growth of such provincial cultural centers. All of which brought about an increase of interest in this provincial life among writers. This is graphically illustrated in the story "In a Small Town" (1938), by the young writer Alexander Pismenny. The wife of the engineer Turnayev scolds the engineer Muraviev, a "swell-head from the capital," for his supercilious attitude toward the provinces: "The Stakhanov movement," she says, "began in the provinces. Mikhail Sholokhov lives and works in the provinces. All our coal is in the provinces, and our oil, and our metal. And what tremendous numbers of remarkable people! The provinces are the whole country, with the sole exception of the capital."

Soviet literature had taken its original source in the provinces; however, the shift of emphasis that occurred in the late 1930s was not a mechanical "turn of the wheel." The provinces of the early days of the October revolution were hostile, to use Pilnyak's vivid expression, to the "proletarian romanticism of October." The new, industrialized province, less bound by its past history with the ideology of the October revolution as a "proletarian" revolution, proclaimed its candidacy, as it were, to an active role in the completion of that revolution. Here, in these industrialized provinces, the anonymous ideologists of the tendency seeking to "finish October," to put an end to the persistent atmosphere of crisis, hoped to find the requisite dynamism and the requisite people—strong men, heroes averse to "sentimentalizing" and "whining." And indeed there were many signs that seemed to confirm the prognosis that history was at last about to grant Soviet society an opportunity for more peaceful and orderly development, an opportunity to bring the ship of Russia, which had wandered so long over the ocean of socio-revolutionary utopia, into a safer harbor—the harbor of a mighty industrialized power.

In fiction all the aspirations of these years found their expression in a flowering of the novel and of epic poetry.

The Second World War disrupted all calculations and hopes, temporarily putting a halt to the emerging tendencies toward normalization.

3 VLADIMIR MAYAKOVSKY (1893–1930)

The Russian revolution was unlucky with its poets. Alexander Blok, the most eminent lyric poet of the early twentieth century, author of the long poem "The Twelve," glorifying the October revolution, died in August 1921. And although he had died a natural death, rumor, which grew into a legend with the passing years, insisted that the true cause of his death had not been heart disease, but the "lack of air" of which he had increasingly complained during his final years. Sergey Yesenin, that most melodious peasant poet of the revolution, committed suicide in December 1925. And Vladimir Mayakovsky, the "agitator and bawling ringleader," shot himself in April 1930, at the height of the first Five-Year Plan.

But if it was possible, with a certain stretch of logic, to say that Blok and Yesenin had chosen to die because they remained emotionally and socially alien to the Bolshevik revolution, this explanation certainly could not be applied to Mayakovsky's case. There was no poet closer to the October revolution in spirit, sweep, and temperament than Mayakovsky. And it is small wonder that his death spread consternation among party and literary circles.

Boris Pasternak, one of the most reflective and profound poets of our time, wrote in his poem "On the Poet's Death":

> Your shot was like an Aetna
> Among the foothills of cowards. . . .

And Bukharin, one of the leading party theoreticians, dissatisfied with the hasty assurances of the official press that an inquiry into the circumstances of the suicide had established that "its motives were purely personal," cried out, "Vladimir Vladimirovich, why, why did you do it?"

The young Mayakovsky came to literature with the stream of artistic Bohemia that shortly after 1910 launched its rebellion against the traditional tastes dominant in the art of the time. His first poem, "Night" (1912), appeared in the Futurist anthology *A Slap in the Face of Public Taste*. The title piece, written by Mayakovsky jointly with his friend David Burlyuk, was received by the public as the manifesto of the young Futurists, who had borrowed their name from their Italian confreres. In his book *Literature and Revolution* (1922) Trotsky characterized Futurism as "the presentiment in art of the impending blasts that were to discharge the social electricity accumulated in the air of the old, pre-revolutionary society." The most colorful figure among the young Futurists was Mayakovsky.

"Large, rumpled, bristling all over with the quills of stinging words, as though he were indeed the very embodiment of the revolution, with its bristling bayonets, this unruly, rebellious giant flung the boulders of his massive phrases at established idols. He was the revolution's trumpet of Jericho, its roaring lion, huge, self-confident, blasting out as fearlessly as thunder," wrote Bukharin under the fresh impact of Mayakovsky's suicide (in his article "Sketches").

While many poets and writers who later came to play a prominent role in Soviet literature were still searching their souls, debating whether they should accept the revolution, withdraw in silence to the sidelines, or perhaps emigrate, Mayakovsky was never troubled by such doubts. In his autobiographical diary, *I Myself*, there is an entry dated October 1917: "Accept or not accept? This question has never existed for me (or for any of the other Moscow Futurists). This was my revolution. I went to Smolny. I worked. I did anything that came to hand. . . ."

Mayakovsky burst into literature headlong, shouting his challenge, girt like a soldier with ribbons of machine-gun bullets, the spokesman of the "tongueless street." And because this street had "nothing to speak or shout with," he broke the traditional meters and banished lyrical themes, bringing taverns and brothels into his verse, saturating it with the air of scandal. His loud poetic voice had even managed to outshout the din of war, compelling readers to listen to the approaching thunder of the revolution:

> I,
> Laughed at by the present tribe
> Like a long
> Smutty anecdote,
> I see approaching over the mountains of time
> What no one sees.
> Where men's short vision stops,
> There, at the head of hungry hordes,
> In the thorny crown of revolutions,
> I see the advent of the sixteenth year.
> (*The Cloud in Trousers*, 1915)

In *I Myself*, Mayakovsky tells us the basic facts of his literary biography: "I am a poet. This is the interesting fact about me. This is what I write about. And about the rest, only as it settles down into the sediment of words."

Mayakovsky was born in 1893 in the village of Bagdady, in the Kutais Province of Georgia. His father, a forester, died of blood poisoning when the poet was only thirteen. The family was left in great want. They had no relatives to turn to. Vladimir was the youngest of three children, and the only son. His older sister was studying in Moscow, and the family hastily sold its belongings and moved to Moscow to join her.

The first book that the future poet read as a child was *The Poultry Maid Agafya*, by Klavdia Lukashevich, a writer of saccharine tearjerkers for adolescents. In this book the poultry maid Agafya talks with honeyed adulation of the kindly countess who is her mistress. Mayakovsky remarked later that if he had encountered a few other stories like it, he would have given up reading altogether. "Fortunately," he said, the second book he read was *Don Quixote*. "What a book! The man made himself a wooden sword and armor, and struck out at his environment."

The future writer was taught to read and write by his mother and older sisters. When Vladimir was old enough to go to school, the family moved to Kutais. At first Mayakovsky was an excellent student. He read a great deal, was held spellbound by Jules Verne, and generally loved everything "fantastic." A friend of the family noticed that the boy had artistic ability and taught him to draw. In 1904 his older sister brought some revolutionary poems from Moscow and showed them to her brother. After that, "poems and revolution became linked in my mind." When the revolution of 1905 broke out, Mayakovsky could no longer pay any attention to his studies. He ran about to demonstrations and, as he puts it, experienced all events "pictorially." He joined a Marxist circle which studied Socialist literature (at the age of twelve!); his favorite revolutionary figure was Lassalle, whom he preferred to Marx.

In Moscow the family had great difficulty in getting along on the mother's pension of ten rubles a month. Mayakovsky began to supplement the family income by drawing and burning designs on wood. He also dyed Easter eggs and sold them to a craft shop. It was during this period, too, that he began to write poetry. In 1908 he joined the Bolshevik Party. Soon afterward he was arrested, but was released after a short imprisonment. Later that year he was arrested again, but was freed on bail. A year later he was arrested once more, this time to be sent to prison for a year. There he read a great deal and returned to writing poetry. He read Byron, Shakespeare, and Tolstoy. In 1910 he was released. He describes his state of mind at the time in the following words:

"I came out greatly perturbed. Those whom I have read, I thought, are the so-called great. But how easy it is to write better than they did! I have already developed a correct approach to the world. All I need is experience in art. But where am I to find it? I am ignorant. I must have some serious schooling, yet I haven't finished even secondary school. . . . If I remain in the party, I must go underground. But being an 'illegal,' I cannot study. The only perspective then would be to write leaflets all my life, to express ideas taken from books—correct enough, but someone else's. If what I've read is shaken out of me, what will remain? The Marxist method. But hasn't this weapon fallen into childish hands? It is wielded easily enough when you deal only with the ideas of your own people. But what happens when you meet enemies? I cannot write better than Bely, no matter what I do. He speaks of his joy—'I flung a pineapple into the sky!'; but I keep whining about my 'hundreds of weary days.' It's all right for other party members. They have university training. (And as for higher education—I did not know as yet what it was—I respected it then!)

"What can I set against the aesthetics of the past bearing down on me? Would not the revolution demand serious schooling of me? I went to see Medvedev, still a party comrade at that time. I want to create socialist art, I told him. Seryozha had a long laugh: 'Your gut's too soft.' Nevertheless, I think he underestimated my guts. I interrupted party work and set myself to studying."

Mayakovsky enrolled in the School of Painting, Sculpture, and Architecture (where, incidentally, Boris Pasternak's father was teaching). At this school he formed a friendship with David Burlyuk, later his fellow Futurist. Mayakovsky himself explained the reasons for this friendship: "David's was the anger of an artist in advance of his time; mine, the passionate enthusiasm of a socialist who knew the old was doomed to die. And so Russian Futurism was born."

Mayakovsky once more began to write poetry. He showed a poem to Burlyuk, but, fearful of his friend's judgment, he said it was by someone else. Burlyuk listened to the poem, looked up at him, and suddenly "barked out": "But it is yours! But you're a genius!" His praise stirred Mayakovsky deeply. "That evening I unexpectedly became a poet." This creative period was attended by noisy scandals, often provoked by the poets themselves in their attempt to "rouse the public out of apathy" by their deliberately clamorous antics. The press began to take notice of them, and finally Mayakovsky and Burlyuk were expelled from the art school.

At that time (1913) Mayakovsky was working on his first tragedy, *Vladimir Mayakovsky*. It grew out of a short cycle of poems, *I*, published as a small booklet earlier in the year. The very first lines of this cycle announce the main theme—the inner contradictions of contemporary society. As the theme gathers force, we hear more and more clearly the poet's despair and hatred of the world of property, which mutilates the human being. This is not enmity of a personal nature, but grief for all mankind. Mayakovsky succeeded in presenting his tragedy on the stage of the Luna Park Theatre. Its principal character —the Poet—was played by the author himself, and Mayakovsky's remarkable voice and passionate temperament carried away the audience, overcoming its initial wary skepticism. Blok, who attended the performance, was impressed by Mayakovsky.

Early in 1914 Mayakovsky began to write *The Cloud in Trousers*. This poem, which occupies a central place in the poet's pre-revolutionary work, reflects his protest against current tastes. The struggle against banality and philistinism found in Mayakovsky a rabid spokesman and an even more intransigent fighter than the early Gorky. The hero of his poem is a "simple," ordinary man who feels the entire hopelessness of his position in the surrounding world. The personal tragedy of the principal hero broadens into the social tragedy of a man thrown into the streets of a big city. And yet, the hero has faith in the strength of the popular masses, in the richness of their spirit:

> Are we to beg for bounties from time?
> We—
> Each—
> Hold in our fists
> The driving belts of worlds!

Loud as they are, however, these declarations carry little conviction. Fortunately, along with its revolutionary theme and its indictments of the old, the poem glows here and there with the author's exciting sense of youth:

> I've not a single gray hair in my soul,
> And none of senile mildness!
> My thundering voice shakes the world,
> I walk—handsome,
> Twentytwoyearold.

The war of 1914 broke out while Mayakovsky was at work on *The Cloud in Trousers*. He responded to it with great agitation and wrote the poem "War Is Declared":

> The newsboys shouted hoarsely, 'Evening paper!
> Italy! Germany! Austria!'
> And in the night, starkly outlined in black,
> Crimson blood poured and poured in a stream.

So great was the poet's agitation that in August 1914 he decided to volunteer for army service. He was not accepted because he could not produce a certificate of political reliability.

As the war went on, Mayakovsky was more and more deeply disturbed over it. His moods were reflected in such poems as "Mamma and the Evening Murdered by the Germans" and the longer poem *War and Peace*, in which he openly expressed his hatred of the war and showed the tragedy of the masses of people drawn into it.

Mayakovsky's last long work of the pre-revolutionary period was "Man." In this poem he concretized on a personal plane the theme developed in his *War and Peace*—the liberation of man from the enslaving power of capitalism.

As we review Mayakovsky's pre-revolutionary work, we find that, by the time the revolution broke out, he was already a mature poet, and one familiar with foreign poets and writers as well. In his poems he mentions in passing the names of Edgar Allan Poe, Walt Whitman, and Jack London; he was obviously well acquainted also with the work of François Villon, Baudelaire, Francis Jammes, Verlaine, and Rimbaud. Mayakovsky himself did not shun lyrical themes in his early writings. In 1914 he wrote the well-known lines:

> But listen!
> If the stars
> Are lighted—
> It means that someone needs them?
> It means—it is imperative
> That every evening
> At least one star
> Should kindle over roofs?!

Victor Pertsov, the author of a three-volume study, *Mayakovsky, His Life and Work* (Moscow, 1957), has offered the interesting conjecture that this poem was written under the influence of the Catholic poet Francis Jammes (1868–1938), and particularly of his "Prayer for a Star."

> God, give me a single golden star,
> Perhaps I'll find in it salvation for my soul. . . .

Also popular, even after the revolution, was Mayakovsky's "Bargain Sale" (1916). Enumerating the riches of his soul, the poet offers to give them all away "for a single word—a tender, human word":

> "One human word—
> Cheap, don't you think?
> But go
> And try—
> How will you find it?"

Typical of Mayakovsky's youthful efforts in literary criticism is his short article "The Two Chekhovs" (1914). In this article the author hails Chekhov as "one of the dynasty of 'Kings of the Word.'" Before Chekhov, he says, literature was made by men "from rich and quiet country estates," and their words obeyed "the inviolate rules of decorum and propriety"; they flowed "judiciously and comfortably like a barouche." And suddenly all that old beauty "began to creak like the corset of a ten-pood[1] daughter of a village priest": literature was invaded by Chekhov, "spokesman of the *raznochintsy*," the newly emerged urban intellectuals of motley origin. The article concludes with the generalization: "From behind the figure familiar to the common reader—the figure of Chekhov the disgruntled complainer, the defender of 'funny people,' the 'twilight singer'—emerge the lineaments of another Chekhov—the strong and gay artist of the word."

Many writers and poets sensed the approach and inevitability of the revolution. But none among them awaited it with so much almost-jubilant impatience as Mayakovsky, who passionately believed that "the revolution, the holy washerwoman, will wash away all filth from the face of the earth with her soap." This was why, when it finally came, and particularly after October, Mayakovsky plunged himself totally into the revolution, reserving nothing and never worrying about lowering his poetic dignity by applying his talents to "the rough language of the placard" or trenchant propaganda couplets.

Mayakovsky and the revolutionary street at that tumultuous time seemed to be completely at one, to understand each other almost without need of speech. The general flow of literature had been checked by the cataclysm; most of the pre-revolutionary writers were silent, the new had not yet emerged. This vacuum was filled by a handful of young poets and innovators, and among these Mayakovsky assumed the leading place. This period might be called the period of *revolutionary folklore*: Mayakovsky and the poets around him spoke with the voice of their roused contemporaries, embodying in their verse the thoughts and feelings of the people in revolt.

With all that, Mayakovsky never talked down to his public, never tried to accommodate himself to the tastes of the street. In his recollections about the early days of the October revolution, published in January 1928, in the

[1] A Russian weight, equivalent to approximately 36 pounds.

magazine *Novy LEF*, he described his visits to plants and factories during the October days, when he read to the workers his most "difficult" poems—*War and Peace, The Cloud in Trousers*. At that time, he says with a touch of irony, "there were no Polonskys between us, everyone understood everything." (Polonsky was the well-known critic and editor of the magazine *Novy Mir* who attacked Mayakovsky for writing poems that were "difficult" for the masses.)

The most vivid expression of Mayakovsky's political moods of that period is found in his "Ode to the Revolution":

> To thee,
>   hooted down,
>   mocked by batteries,
> To thee,
>   lacerated by the evil tongues of bayonets,
> I rapturously lift
> over the floating currents of abuse
>   My ode's solemn
> "O!"
>   O, bestial!
>   O, childlike!
>   O, penny-cheap!
>   O, great!
> . . . .
> To thee the philistine's—
>   O, be thou thrice accursed!
> And mine—
>   The poet's—
>   O, be thou four times gloried, blessed one!

In addition to his arduous work for Rosta (Russian Telegraph Agency) and for newspapers, Mayakovsky also managed in those days to write the poem, *150,000,000* and a *Mystery-Bouffe*, which he described as "a heroic, epic, and satirical picture of our epoch."

150,000,000 is a heroic poem about the revolution: the "hundred and fifty million" are simultaneously the poem's heroes and its creators. The central fact of our modern life, says Mayakovsky, is that "all middles" have been destroyed; all colors and shades are gone, except two—red and white. These colors are embodied in the two main heroes of the poem: the 150-million-headed Ivan and the President of the United States, Woodrow Wilson. The two heroes are at each other's throats. Mayakovsky intended the poem to become the *Iliad* of the October revolution.

The impact of the theme—the conflict between the capitalist and socialist systems—is considerably weakened by the grotesquely satirical manner of the poem. In the images of the principal heroes—the 150-million-headed Ivan and President Woodrow Wilson—there are no human qualities that involve the reader's emotions. However, two features of the poem deserve special note. The first has to do with its general anti-Americanism, an attitude typical of the majority of Soviet writers who had been to the United States, from Yesenin on through Boris Pilnyak (his *O.K.*), Ilf and Petrov (*One-Storey America*), and others. But Mayakovsky wrote his 150,000,000 before he visited the United States. And his anti-Americanism, in contrast to that of his colleagues, was considerably mellowed as a result of his later visit.

Secondly, the use of folk motifs in 150,000,000 indicates a trend in the poet's development. While Mayakovsky's pre-revolutionary work abounded in urban motifs borrowed from Western poets, affecting the very language and character of his images, his poems of the revolutionary period gradually freed themselves of extraneous elements and made more and more frequent use of Russian folklore.

The *Mystery-Bouffe* is a play written throughout in a solemn mood. Its principal hero is the mass of people awakened by the revolution and demanding radical changes in its way of life. Mayakovsky's many efforts to have the play produced were for a long time frustrated by the opposition both of those who controlled theatrical policy and of theater people themselves. Its production was undertaken by Meyerhold and it had its premiere on

May 1, 1921. Mayakovsky's clashes with the directors of literary policy and with critics were not confined to this instance; they continued throughout the poet's short but stormy literary life.

There were grounds enough for conflict. A lifelong captive of the moods of revolutionary exaltation that filled the air of the early post-October months, Mayakovsky refused to the very end to reconcile himself to the decline of that initial fervor. He hated the NEP, which he blamed for the revival of the old social standards and for the triumph of philistine elements in the life of the new society. He also detested the revolutionary bureaucracy that helped to consolidate this triumph of the old in new forms.

With deep sorrow he expressed his feelings about the changes taking place under the aegis of the NEP in his poem, "About Scum" (1921):

> The storms of revolutionary depths are stilled.
> The Soviet brew is overgrown with slime.
> And from behind the back of R.S.F.S.R.
> Peers out
> The snout
> Of the philistine.

Mayakovsky threw all his rebellious passion into the fight against this renascent philistinism. "How he sent them spinning under his blows—the canaries, geranium pots, double beds, and all the other attributes of paltry philistine happiness," recalled Bukharin in his article "Sketches."

But Mayakovsky did not confine himself to fighting the anonymous philistine. He also raised his hand against a more potent adversary, the bureaucracy which was consolidating itself during the NEP years. This bureaucracy, in turn, did not remain in debt to the poet and avenged itself at every opportunity—often in cowardly, underhand ways, through subservient literary critics who labeled Mayakovsky a "petty-bourgeois malcontent" alien to the interests of the working people. But Mayakovsky continued to fight, bitterly lampooning the Communist philistines who occupied first-row seats in life while speaking with great aplomb in the name of "workers and peasants." After the poet's death, all this was carefully hidden from the readers, particularly by the authors of officially sanctioned textbooks on the history of Soviet literature.

A special and rather large place in Mayakovsky's work is held by the poems which deal with his life abroad. Beginning in 1922, and almost to the end of his life (1930), Mayakovsky made frequent trips abroad. He visited Germany and France six times, made a journey to Spain, and came to the United States in 1925. He observed foreign life carefully, weighing his impressions in terms of possible usefulness to Soviet citizens. The scope of his observations was far wider than that of many of his fellow writers and poets who traveled abroad. He made no effort to conceal his excitement over the beauty of Paris; New York impressed him greatly, and in Mexico he was moved both by the country and by the warmth, hospitality, and direct simplicity of its people.

Mayakovsky felt that it was the task of every Soviet citizen who came to America to "assimilate American technology." He spoke of this in "My Discovery of America" (1925). Other works of the period include the poems, "Spain," "The Atlantic Ocean," "Havana," "Mexico," and "America." The best-known poems of the so-called American cycle are "Black and White," "Skyscraper in Cross-Section," "Brooklyn Bridge," and "Broadway." The poet attempts to camouflage the profound impression America made upon him by stressing its social inequality. And yet, he writes:

There's something here to look at for our Moscow
    brethren.
Not in a day
    can they walk end to end.
This is New York.
    This, Broadway.
How do you do!

I am entranced
> With New York City.
But I'll not pull my cap
> From off my head.

And the reason the poet refuses to pull his cap from off his head is that "Soviet people" have "their own pride"; it is not fitting for them to defer to the "bourgeois."

It was also during the NEP years that the elements of satire and angry exposé began to come to the fore in the poet's work. These find their most complete expression in two of his plays, the "magical comedy" *The Bedbug* (1928) and the drama *The Bathhouse* (1930).

The hero of *The Bedbug* is the former worker, former party member, and "currently fiancé," Ivan Prisypkin, who changes his unimpressive name to Pierre Skripkin. As a representative of "the young, victorious class," Pierre Skripkin proclaims as his motto the right "to live beautifully." Hence, he breaks with the working girl Zoya Berezkina in order to propose to the daughter of a barbershop owner, Elzevira Renaissance. Zoya commits suicide, but this leaves Prisypkin entirely unmoved. The future mother-in-law is delighted with the bridegroom: he is a proletarian and therefore will bring into her home a valuable "dowry"—a trade-union card and a party card. However, Prisypkin's wedding comes to a sad end. A fire breaks out and all the participants in the celebration perish.

While the first part of the comedy is laid in the early revolutionary period, the second part comes much later when communism had already been achieved. Prisypkin's corpse, which has been accidentally discovered, is brought to the research institute concerned with the problem of vanquishing mortality. Prisypkin is revived, and so is the Bedbug in his clothing—his symbol—which had died with him. The resurrected Prisypkin brings back with him all his old qualities—toadying, ignorance, bragging, and vanity—and their contagion spreads to the virtuous people of the Communist era. In order to protect the Communist society from this contamination, Prisypkin and his companion, the Bedbug, are placed in a metal cage, tagged "*Philistinus vulgaris*." The public assembles before the cage to stare at Prisypkin as he strums his guitar and sings, "On Lunacharsky Street, I remember an old house. . . ."

The satirical sting of *The Bathhouse* (1930) is considerably sharper. Its action unfolds in the large Soviet government department, the Coordination Administration. The Administration director, Pobedonosikov, is "an official of major importance." He is always busy: now his mind is on "the current moment," now on "a speech, a report, a resolution, socialism." He recommends himself as a faultless worker: "I carry out directives, file resolutions, set up liaison, pay party dues, receive the party maximum, sign documents, affix rubber stamps . . . in short—a living bit of socialism." Pobedonosikov's closest aides—his secretary Optimistenko and his "liaison man" Momentalnikov—are creatures of the same breed. Momentalnikov's motto is:

> Excellency, at your orders,
> We're a modest lot,
> Merely give us an ass-sign-ment,
> And it's ready on the dot.

Like every Soviet institution, the Coordination Administration also employs a "private secretary," Madam Mezaliansova, and an embezzling bookkeeper, Nochkin.

All these bureaucrats, big and small, are contrasted in the play with ordinary Soviet citizens—the Comsomol member Velosipedkin, the modest typist Underton, the inventor Chudakov, several workers and, finally, the "phosphorescent woman," a delegate from the future Communist society of the year 2030.[2]

---

[2] Translator's note: the names of the characters here are meaningful in themselves. "Pobedonosikov" is a contemptuous play on the Russian word for "victory"; "Momentalnikov" is derived from "instantly"; "Mezaliansova," from "misalliance"; "Nochkin," from "night" or "nocturnal"; "Velosipedkin," from "bicycle," and "Chudakov," from "eccentric."

Plot is secondary in both *The Bedbug* and *The Bathhouse;* the poet's meanings depend on caricature and on parody understandable only to contemporaries. The inventor Chudakov succeeds in building a Time Machine. On this machine the phosphorescent woman prepares to fly into the future, inviting the Soviet people to fly with her to her homeland, Integral Communism. Her first impressions of life in the Soviet state please her, but she soon learns from private conversations about the less attractive side of Soviet reality. Her early impressions are dispelled. Pobedonosikov's wife, Polya, tells her that she has been abandoned by her husband but that he keeps the break secret for fear of being charged with "licentiousness." The manner in which a Soviet institution is run is described to the phosphorescent woman by the dismissed typist, Underton. But the phosphorescent woman chooses to conceal her knowledge of the facts until the proper moment. She proposes the election of delegates to accompany her to her homeland. Pobedonosikov promptly appears with his valise, briefcases, and private secretary. He is excited and happy "for himself and for his apparatus," and demands a separate compartment for himself. The Time Machine soars up into the sky, and then something astonishing happens: the delegates who are traveling in it are an altogether different group—Velosipedkin, the typist Underton, and several workers. As for Pobedonosikov, the machine pitches suddenly and throws him overboard. The stunned Pobedonosikov turns to the author and the audience, asking: "What did you mean to say by this? That communism does not need me and my kind?"

The real Pobedonosikovs never forgave the author for his boldness. All the textbooks on the history of Soviet literature dwell at length on the poet's pre-revolutionary work, and discuss in even greater details his writings of the revolutionary period, but they draw a line at *The Bedbug* and *The Bathhouse.* Mayakovsky's two long poems *Vladimir Ilyich Lenin* (1924) and *It's Good* (1927), both of them inferior works, have long been dismembered into quotations. The latter poem was dedicated to the tenth anniversary of the October revolution. It is interesting that, a year later, Mayakovsky mentioned in his autobiography that he intended to write a long poem, "It's Bad." This poem, begun in 1928, was never published. All the studies of his work devote considerable space to analysis of the preface to his poem *At the Top of My Voice* (1930):

> Respected
> comrades of posterity!
> Rummaging
> in today's
> petrified dung,
> studying the darkness of our times,
> you may,
> perhaps,
> ask also about me. . . .

Recent critical studies have included comments on the two poems "I Love" (1922) and "About This" (1923), which were severely condemned during the poet's lifetime for their strongly personal flavor. The official critics seemed to be irked by the poet's excessively lyrical approach to love, his insistence that loving meant giving, rather than taking.

Sympathetically, but briefly, these latter studies also discuss Mayakovsky's satirical works, with the exception of *The Bedbug* and *The Bathhouse*. The critics are apparently even now unable to accept Mayakovsky's sincerity and fearlessness.

But if Mayakovsky's relations with the literary bureaucracy are quite clear, his relationship with the Soviet regime as a whole is much more complex. In a sense it is reminiscent of the relationship between the Czarist government and Pushkin. Through its spokesmen, the government of Nicholas I had always sought to instill in the public an image of Pushkin as a loyal subject, frequently citing his ode, "No, I am not a sycophant when I sing free praises of the Czar." The modern Soviet press emulates this stratagem with Mayakovsky, endlessly quoting these lines from his poem *At the Top of My Voice:*

> We shall not quarrel to apportion fame—
>   We are all men of a kind—
> Then let our
>   common monument be
> Socialism
>   built
>   in battles.

And yet, the official appraisal of Mayakovsky contained a certain measure of truth. Despite all his intransigence toward the Soviet bureaucracy, Mayakovsky, in the course of the revolutionary years, had in fact developed a "civil soul." This was sensed correctly by Boris Pasternak, who wrote in his *Safe Conduct* that "the bond between them [the Soviet government and Mayakovsky] was so striking that they might have been twins." And when he was about to sum up his life with a bullet, Mayakovsky addressed himself to the government as to a friend or close relation, as though he were trying to lighten the burden of cares that would inevitably be imposed on it by his suicide:

> Comrade government,
> Have pity on my mother,
> Take care of my lily-sister.
> In the desk there are two thousand,
> Let the tax collector take his due,
> And I shall quietly die.

Mayakovsky's fate was similar to Pushkin's in another respect as well. Along with the official popularization of Pushkin, many of his poems seeped down among the people and were transformed into songs. Pushkin's "Black Shawl," "The Blizzard Veils the Sky in Darkness," and other poems became widely diffused as folk songs, their true authorship often unknown to the singers. The same thing has happened to some of Mayakovsky's poems. In his book *In Search of Optimism*, Victor Shklovsky relates that Mayakovsky's farewell note, "Comrade Government," was widely sung by the *besprizorniki,* or homeless waifs, to the tune of a popular ballad.

In Mayakovsky's untimely death, Russia lost a matchless artist and poet of the revolutionary street, who made rich use of its verbal wealth. As a true poet, Mayakovsky never shunned the use of trite expressions. But the most shopworn words, eroded like kopeks that had passed through millions of hands, gleamed under his pen like burnished gold. He disdained neither the popular limerick, nor the stately phrase of an ode, nor the caustic jibe of an irascible old scold in order to convey the fundamental thing—his passionate impulse to rebuild human life.

4 SERGEY YESENIN (1895–1925)

The career of no other Soviet poet evoked such wide and often passionate discussion as that of Yesenin, who committed suicide in 1925, at the age of thirty.

Yesenin's entire literary output consists of four small volumes of poems, but their popularity has never dimmed. Even at the height of the first Five-Year Plan, long after Yesenin had been officially "explained away" as the "father of hooliganism" and his poems withdrawn from libraries and reading rooms, his little books, tattered and read virtually to shreds, could still be found, together with the inevitable tin kettle and spoon, in the canvas bags of *letuny*—migrant workers traveling from job to job in defiance of the authorities—and in the trunks of Red Army soldiers. The poet's popularity has survived the passing of decades. In 1955 we find a correspondent to the *Literary Gazette* reporting that he came upon a little volume of Yesenin's poems among the books belonging to a worker in a young people's dormitory.

Readers have loved Yesenin for the deep lyricism, the lilting freshness of his poems, for their sincerity, melancholy, and fire. They have loved him also because, although he had been among the first to cry "My mother, homeland, I am a Bolshevik!," soon afterward, "afraid of no one's fist," he spoke out in protest against the government. Anarchic protest is inevitable wherever lies become the official religion of a state; as the poet says of Hamlet himself, "were he alive today, he'd be a brigand and a thief."

Yesenin is a peasant poet through and through. This is expressed in the entire vocabulary of his poetry. The horse, the most important factor in the simple peasant economy, is Yesenin's favorite image. Even in ears of wheat this great artist found a resemblance to horses' manes. As if in presentiment of his early death, he wrote these melancholy lines in his poem, "I Am the Last of Village Poets" (1919):

> And only ears of wheat, like steeds,
> Will for their master grieve. . . .

In "A Hooligan's Confession" (1920) the poet says:

> And as he meets a cabby in the square,
> Recalling the manure smells of his native fields,
> He wants to carry every horse's tail
> Like the train of a wedding dress.

In one of his best poems, "Sorokoust" (1920), Yesenin looks with sadness at a foal trying to race a train, and asks tenderly:

> The dear, the funny little fool,
> Where is he racing, and what for?
> Does he not know the living horse
> Was vanquished by steel cavalry?

Yesenin's peasant nature flares up in his work continually, and permeates all his writings. In "A Hooligan's Confession" he replies to his critics:

> And then I am happy to remember
> . . . .
> That somewhere I've a father and a mother
> Who do not give a damn for all my verse,
> Who love me as they do a field, as their own flesh.
> . . . .
> They'd come at you with pitchforks
> For every insult you have hurled at me. . . .

In this connection it is interesting to recall the remark of Yesenin's friend and fellow Imaginist, Anatoly Mariengof (in his *Novel Without Lies*, 1928), that Yesenin "regarded the peasant in himself with affection and pride." During his lifetime Yesenin wrote several short autobiographies as introductions to his books of verse. The most complete of these, the fourth, was reprinted in "New Facts about Sergey Yesenin" (in the anthology *Poetry Day*, Moscow, 1956). From this autobiographical essay, written by Yesenin a year and a half before his suicide, we learn that he was born in 1895, of a peasant family in the province of Ryazan. His father soon moved to the city, and Yesenin was brought up in his native village by his grandparents. His first memories go back to the age of three or four: "I remember the forest, the wide, deeply rutted road. I am with my grandmother, on the way to Radovetsky Monastery, some forty versts away." The boy was tired. Clutching at his grandmother's cane, he was barely able to keep up with her, while she kept saying: "Come along, come along, my little berry, God grant you happiness." Their house was often visited by blind old men who wandered from village to village, singing sacred chants about the glories of paradise, Lazarus, the Saints Mikola and Menikh, and "the bright guest from the unknown city." Yesenin's grandfather also sang to him—"old, slow, mournful songs"—and on Saturdays and Sundays recited chapters from the Bible and "Sacred Chronicles," evoking images that the poet remembered all his life. The boy's street life was entirely unlike his life at home. The village boys were full of high spirits and mischief. Together with them he climbed fences into neighbors' gardens and disappeared in the fields for days at a time, undeterred by the inevitable punishment on his return.

He learned to read at the age of five. When he was nine, he began to write poems. From the very first his poems showed the influence of *chastushki*—a popular form of folk verse widely sung throughout the Russian countryside. He attended the village school until the age of twelve, when he was sent to a teachers' training school by his family, who wanted him to become a rural teacher.

At eighteen Yesenin went to Moscow, living at first with his father, who was working in a butcher shop. Soon he joined the Surikov Circle, a group of writers and poets of working-class and peasant origin. The Circle decided to publish a magazine, *A Populist Family*. Shortly after the outbreak of World War I its members prepared the first issue of this magazine, to which Yesenin contributed a poem, "Jackdaws." But the issue was censored and confiscated while still in proof.

Yesenin's new friends found him work as a mailing clerk at Sytin's printing plant. He also registered as a nonmatriculated student at the Shanyavsky People's University, where he attended lectures on literature, history, philosophy, and economics. He wrote a great deal and sent some of his poems to Petersburg magazines, but received no replies. Then he went to Petersburg himself. There he made the acquaintance of the senior peasant poet Nikolay Kluyev, who recommended Yesenin to the publisher M. V. Averianov. At the end of 1915 Averianov published Yesenin's first book of poems, *Radunitsa*.

An interesting portrait of Yesenin was sketched by the Leningrad poet Vsevolod Rozhdestvensky (*Zvezda*, January 1946), who met Yesenin in the spring of 1915 in the editorial offices of a magazine where both had come to try their luck. Rozhdestvensky was immediately struck by the young man in the peasant's sheepskin coat. Many of the people in the waiting room mistook him for a messenger. Noticing Rozhdestvensky's shabby coat, Yesenin sat down next to him. Within a few minutes he told him all about himself and even recited one of his poems, "My native land, fields like a church calendar. . . ." Rozhdestvensky thought the poem "fresh," but "too much in the style of ikon painting." He spoke of Blok's poem on the same theme, which is far more masculine and simple. Yesenin exclaimed: "But that is Blok! He is a Father Superior compared to me. And who am I? A novice—an unfrocked one at that!"

Later, in 1923, at the zenith of his fame, Yesenin told Rozhdestvensky about his first visit to Blok. When he arrived in Petersburg, he decided to go to Blok directly from the station. He obtained the address at a bookstore. Approaching the older poet's apartment, Yesenin became so panic-stricken that, "with a hammering heart and wet with perspiration," he went down the stairs and back into the street. Then he climbed up again by the back stairs. Blok was friendly and gave him a letter to the editors of a magazine. "When I left Blok, I did not feel the ground under my feet."

Yesenin welcomed the revolution of 1917 with fervent sympathy, but, in his own words, "more emotionally than intellectually." In 1917 he married an actress of the Kamerny Theatre, Zinaida Reich. In 1918 they separated. After that he began "a life of wanderings, like all Russians." He went to Turkestan, the Caucasus, Crimea, Bessarabia, the Orenburg steppes, the Murmansk shore. . . . In 1921 he married Isadora Duncan and left with her for America. America repelled him. He wrote: "The general course today may be toward America but I would rather have our own gray sky and landscape: a peasant hut, half sunk into the earth, a hayrack with a tall shaft rising from it, and, in the distance, a peasant's lean horse, swishing its tail in the wind. No skyscrapers, which have given the world nothing as yet except Rockefellers and McCormicks, but the very things which have nurtured our Tolstoy, our Pushkin, Dostoyevsky, Lermontov, and so many others."

The poet concludes his autobiographical sketch with some reflections on the nature of art. He repudiates Imaginism as a separate school in Russian poetry. At first, together with the poets Vadim Shershenevich and Anatoly Mariengof, he was himself the soul of this movement, but later he came to feel that "a poet should not adhere to any specific school. This binds him hand and foot. Only a free artist can speak free words."

A colorful representative of Russian Imaginism during the revolution, Yesenin himself traced his literary origin to the mid-nineteenth-century poet Alexey Koltsov (cf., "O Russia, spread thy wings"). The revolution of 1917 was a turning point in Yesenin's life, sweeping out of his poetry the religious and mystical motifs and images characteristic of his first phase, and giving him a new impetus. The poet entered a period of intense productiveness and activity. He traveled widely over the country, reading his poems before large, admiring audiences. According to the unanimous testimony of his contemporaries, Yesenin read with remarkable artistry. His unique blend of dashing recklessness, mischief, and melancholy tenderness conquered his listeners.

In "Pantocrator" (1919) he exclaims to God:

> For thy curly gray locks,
> For the coins from the gold aspen tree,
> I cry out—To hell with the old!—
> Thy disobedient, brigand son!

Elsewhere, in 1920, he mourns:

> The owl hoots autumnally
> Over the endless morning road,
> Fall bares my head,
> My bush of gold hair fades.

In the spontaneity of his lyrical talent Yesenin is reminiscent of one of the greatest poets of fifteenth-century France—François Villon, who spent the greater part of his life wandering the land, whose friends were vagrants and thieves, but who left behind imperishable poems ("Petit Testament" and "Grand Testament"). The resemblance to Villon becomes even more pronounced in the poems Yesenin wrote during the last two years of his life, when he plunged into wild extremes of drinking and brawling. In one of his autobiographies Yesenin wrote that his most complete biography is contained in his verse. Among the poems of his last years we find such titles as "Verses of a Brawler," "Songs of a Drunk," "The Hooligan," "Tavern Moscow," "Son of a Bitch," and "Black Man" (1925).

In 1923, in a poem written at the Polyanka Hospital in Moscow, the poet says:

> The evening scowls with raven brows,
> Someone's horses are out by the gate,
> Was it but yesterday I drank away my youth?
> . . . .
> What have you brought me to,
> My reckless head?

In the poem "I Have One Amusement Left" Yesenin says:

> The evil fame has spread
> That I'm a brawler and a debauchee. . . .

Glancing back at his life, the poet confesses:

> I am ashamed that I believed in God.
> I bitterly regret I don't believe today.

And yet, despite all his sins, he would like "to be laid out under the ikons in a Russian shirt to die."

Yesenin's poetry of nature is full of melancholy loveliness. In a single image he evokes a complete picture in the reader's mind. Speaking to a bare and ice-encrusted maple, he compares it to a drunken watchman who has come out upon the road in winter, sunk into a snowdrift, and frozen his feet. The maple reminds Yesenin of himself; he, too, has "become unsteady on his feet" and cannot make his way home from a drinking bout with friends; now he stops to stare at a willow, now at a pine, and finally, "losing all modesty, losing all sense," he embraces a wayside birch "like another man's wife."

But Yesenin's muse is by no means devoted only to love of his native land and landscape. Very early, before the revolution, Yesenin also wrote poems dedicated to animals: "The Cow"—"Senile, toothless . . ."; and "Song about a Dog"—"Early in the morning, in the corn bin," a bitch bears seven pups, and all day long till evening she caresses them and combs them with her tongue. And in the evening her sullen master comes, puts the seven pups into a sack and drowns them. The bitch runs after him and can do nothing to save her young. But when she drags herself slowly back, "licking the sweat off her flanks, it seems to her the moon over the hut is one of her lost pups."

Yesenin's poetry is marked by deep tenderness for every beast—a village dog, cats, sheep. He calls them all his "younger brothers." But love of animals is only a part of the poet's spiritual equipment. Still more characteristic is his sympathy with humbled man; he has a quick sense of kinship with the thief, the bandit, and the homeless waif. One of Yesenin's best poems, "Homeless Russia" (1924), is devoted to the *besprizorny*—the homeless children of the early years of the revolution, who spent their nights in idle factories or even in "privies":

> Let them, at least,
> Read in a poem
> That there are some
> Who grieve about them in the world.

During Yesenin's lifetime the critics did not take the trouble to look deeply into his work; they were too preoccupied with his "hooliganism." Even Mariengof, one of Yesenin's closest friends, severely condemned the poet for his rowdy outbursts. But in his book on Yesenin he put the blame for Yesenin's hooliganism chiefly upon "the critics and the public." It was they, he said, "who prompted Yesenin to create a scandalous reputation for himself" to win quick fame. Mariengof's view was later shared by many of the poet's contemporaries. Yesenin, he went on, was a self-taught peasant poet, and the proletarian October revolution remained essentially alien to him, creating stresses he was unable to cope with. Mariengof also spoke of Yesenin's vanity, his desire to become "a second Pushkin." And Yesenin himself, in his well-known poem "To Pushkin" (1924), appears to confirm this. In his day, says the poet, Pushkin had also been a "scapegrace," but this had not dimmed his genius or prevented his being immortalized in bronze monuments; he, Yesenin, would die of happiness at such a fate.

Mariengof's attribution of Yesenin's suicide to his peasant character was closely akin to Gorky's view. When Gorky heard of Yesenin's death, he recalled a story by the Polish writer Stefan Zeromski about a peasant boy who came to Cracow. For hours the boy ran frantically about the city, looking for a way out. But the more he ran, the more hopelessly he became lost in the unfamiliar, stony streets. When he finally came to a bridge, he threw himself into the river, hoping that it might carry him to his native fields.

This interpretation of Yesenin's suicide as a result of his "lack of consonance" with the revolution should not be taken too literally. The flowering of the poet's creative talent coincided with the first stormy years of the revolution. The "climate" of the revolution not only did not hamper his talent, but, on the contrary, unleashed in him that great, socially tinged, emotional rebellion that Yesenin had brought to the revolutionary city from the village. He had fervent sympathy for his oppressed brothers —from the downtrodden Kalmuck to the nameless workmen on whose bones the sumptuous "Peter's-burgh" had risen—and a special, visceral, understanding of the right of the oppressed to vengeance and rebellion, again reminiscent of François Villon. He won the reader's admiration by these qualities, as much as by his tender and warm lyricism, which found such poignant expression in poems like "I Am the Last of Village Poets" (1919), "Letter to My Mother" ("You are still alive, my old one?"), and "The Golden Woods Have Spoken" (1924).

The poet's keenly emotional social awareness was vividly expressed in *The Song about the Great Campaign* and the unfinished poem, *Pugachev*. The image of Peter the Great in the former is as monumental as it is in Alexey Tolstoy's novel *Peter I*, but Yesenin's attitude toward him is diametrically opposed to Tolstoy's. The nameless workmen of Peter's day, brought to life under Yesenin's pen, warn the Czar that he must be ready to die with dignity, should he fall into their hands. Neither these workmen nor the poet can forgive Peter for "favoring the nobles and ministers," and building a capital for them "upon the blood" of the homeless poor. The stones of the city remember this blood, and the builders cry to every house in it that they will yet return:

> "We shall yet come,
> We'll come, we'll come!"

The poet offers a new interpretation of the role of Petersburg in the Russian revolution:

> This is why
> Only working men
> Can live here. . . .

Still more characteristic of Yesenin is the unfinished poem, *Pugachev*. A large section of the poem was written as early as 1921. Its hero is the Cossack Emelyan Pugachev, leader of a peasant rebellion in the 1770s, during the reign of Catherine II. In rallying the rebellion Pugachev made use of the rumors that Czar Peter III, Catherine's husband, had not really been killed, but had managed to escape. Pugachev himself claimed to be Peter III, challenging Catherine's right to be Empress.

Yesenin's Pugachev is not historically true, but there is, perhaps, more social truth in Yesenin's interpretation than in Pushkin's tale *The Captain's Daughter*. There, because of Pushkin's ambivalent attitude toward Pugachev, the reader must guess this truth between the lines. Yesenin, however, not only justifies Pugachev's pretensions to the throne, he not only passionately sympathizes with the enslaved peasants, but he shares inwardly the lives of all the homeless and dispossessed who are gathering "great wrath" within their hearts. In graphic passages, Yesenin describes the flight of the Kalmucks from the intolerable oppression and arbitrary rule of the Czarist officials. When the Cossack ataman, ordered to catch the fugitives at any cost, tries to appeal to the "national" feelings of the Cossacks and says that the Kalmucks intend to go over to China, one of the supporters of the rebellion, Kirpichnikov, exclaims "Wait, ataman, enough/Of rattling your tongue in the wind! . . ."

Kirpichnikov explains to the ataman that, of course, the men are sad for Russia, because Russia is their "mother," but it does not dismay them that some people have chosen to leave their fields. "The Kalmuck is not a yellow hare that you can shoot for food." Kirpichnikov concludes his speech by wishing the "dark-skinned Mongols" luck on their way, and adds: "If our huts were on wheels, we'd also pull away."

Equally moving is the monologue of the ex-convict Khlopusha, Pugachev's comrade-in-arms, who remained faithful to him to the end and who was hanged by the Czarist authorities after the rebellion was suppressed. When Gorky heard Yesenin read this fragment, he confessed: "It moved me to the point of a spasm in the throat. I wanted to sob. I remember, I was unable to speak any words of praise, but I think he did not need any."

The concluding section—"Pugachev's End"—is especially powerful. Some of Pugachev's followers, exhausted by the struggle with the overpowering government, plot to surrender him to the authorities, and thus win Catherine's favor and forgiveness. Pugachev senses that his closest comrades are faltering, but he still cannot bring himself to believe it. And suddenly, as he looks at the autumn landscape, acrid with dampness and decay, the terrible truth about the two death-bringing crones, autumn and the old queen, flashes upon him:

> It is she!
> It is she who has bribed you,
> The evil, foul, bedraggled crone,
> It is she, she, she,
> Hair scattered in the quivering dawn,
> Who wants her native land to die
> Under her cold and joyless smile.

Realizing the inevitability of the end, Pugachev once more lets his mind roam over the many roads of his childhood and youth, asking:

> My God! Is this indeed my hour?
> Does a man fall under the soul's weight
>   as under a heavy burden?

Then, growing quiet, he whispers:

> And yet it seemed . . . why, only yesterday it seemed . . .
> My dear ones . . . my dear . . . friends . . .

Of course, these words were never spoken by the real Pugachev, who laid down his unrepentant head on the executioner's block. These are the words and emotions of the mortally weary poet himself.

Yesenin's feelings of disillusionment with the course of events in Soviet Russia were not a secret to his friends and other writers who knew him. These feelings deepened the personal conflict that tormented the poet during the last years of his life, and were expressed in all his works of that period. Yesenin was the first poet of the revolution who repudiated, not the revolution, but its regime, and who broke with it. A great deal of what he had written was never included in his published works. Many of his poems were passed from hand to hand in manuscript. Since Yesenin's moods were close to those of many of his literary contemporaries, poems appeared here and there that were also attributed to him (such as the "Letter to the Poet Demyan"). Future literary historians may, perhaps, be able to avail themselves of this apocryphal Yesenin, who will provide rich material for a clearer understanding of the character of that early disillusionment with the Soviet regime that was already making itself felt in the first half of the 1920s.

As he prepared the edition of his collected works, Yesenin himself decided against the inclusion of some of his poems. This edition did not appear until after his death, in 1926. It was published in four volumes with an introduction by A. K. Voronsky, the editor of the magazine *Krasnaya Nov*, where Yesenin's work appeared most frequently. But even the poems contained in these four volumes reveal the full force and profound justice of Yesenin's protest.

This outcry found still sharper expression in the unfinished play *The Land of Scoundrels*, published posthumously. (It was included, under this title, in the third volume of Yesenin's *Collected Works*, 1926). Under another title, *Nomakh*, fragments of the play appeared in *Krasnaya Nov* (March and April, 1926).

In a book of recollections about Yesenin (*Gosizdat*,

Moscow and Leningrad, 1926), Ivan Yevdokimov, one of the contributors, writes that Yesenin had thought at first of changing the title of the play to "Nomakh" (a thinly disguised version of the name Makhno[1]). Later, however, the original title was restored.

The lyrical hero of the play, Nomakh, exclaims:

> Bands! Bands!
> Throughout the land,
> Wherever you turn or look,
> You see, in its expanses,
> On horses
>   and without horses,
> Riding and walking, bone-hardened bandits.

The leader of these bands, Nomakh himself, declares that his banditism is "of a special brand." There was a time, he says, when he was filled with fiery faith, when he went along with the revolution, when he felt that "brotherhood was not an idle dream, that everything would flow together into a single ocean, all the hosts of people, tribes, and races." But now he has come to understand: those who have taken power are masquerading in "sheep's clothing." And this is why Nomakh-Yesenin leaves it to those "who are meaner and smaller in mind, those who have not stood, poor and naked, under the winds of fate" to sing the praises of "cities and women"; as for himself, he will henceforth "sing eulogies to criminals and tramps."

What compelled Yesenin to turn away from the regime and withdraw into individualistic rebellion developed in the poet's mind slowly, but its beginnings were already evident in 1922. ("All that is living, by a special mark/ Is branded from the first.") Yesenin's disillusionment is ultimately expressed in Nomakh's words: "Your equality is a deception and a lie. This world of noble words and

---

[1] Makhno was the leader of the Ukrainian peasant guerrillas of "anarchist" sympathies in the Civil War of 1918–21. With his men, known as the "Greens," he fought against both the Whites and the Reds.

deeds is nothing but an odious old barrel-organ tune. Good bait for fools; for scoundrels—a good catch."

It was precisely this that the official critics could not and will not forgive Yesenin. The climate of the revolution aroused great exaltation in the poet. But the lies and hypocrisy of the government, taking cover behind the façade of its revolutionary origin, repelled and angered him. Emotion knows of no compromise; the climate of compromise destroys it. And so he exclaims ("Stanzas," 1924):

> I am not your tame canary!
> I am a poet!
> And not one of your Demyans.[2]
> I may be drunk at times,
> But in my eyes
> There is the light of glorious illuminations.

And this is the reason why the present Soviet literary authorities refuse to "rehabilitate" the true Yesenin. Yesenin never learned to restrain, to "subdue himself" by "stepping upon the throat of his own song," as even such an essentially sincere poet as Mayakovsky had done. Yesenin could not, and refused to, dose out his feelings in approved portions. He preferred to "subdue" himself with a scarf, after slashing his veins.

Today, after twenty-five years of official neglect, Yesenin is again accorded partial and grudging recognition. In a textbook on Soviet literature published in 1950, L. I. Timofeyev reduces the achievements of Yesenin's lyric talent to "a moving depiction of Russian nature, and delicate love poetry" (although both Yesenin himself and many of his contemporaries spoke of the paucity of love motifs in his work). However, Timofeyev continues, Yesenin "proved unable to resist hostile influences, which kept him from a true understanding of the new life. . . . This alienation from the people had the gravest effect both upon his life and work. . . . He was unfaithful to

[2] The reference is to Demyan Bedny, a prolific writer of Communist propaganda verse.

himself, his talent, and his love for his homeland when he withdrew to 'Tavern Moscow,' as he titled the cycle of his most decadent poems."

Even more characteristic, perhaps, is the treatment of Yesenin's work in the *History of Russian Soviet Literature* (Vol. I, U.S.S.R. Academy of Sciences, Moscow, 1958). The essay on Yesenin, written by Kornely Zelinsky (pp. 374–96), is not based on the first, four-volume, edition of the *Collected Works*, published in 1926, but on the two-volume edition published in Moscow in 1956. In other words, the author of the essay deliberately used a carefully winnowed edition of selected works, which included neither the play *The Land of Scoundrels* (or *Nomakh*) nor many of Yesenin's poems. One of the notable omissions, for example, is "Homeless Russia" (1924), devoted to the *besprizorny* or homeless children of the early years of the revolution, which was quoted above.

Yesenin's contemporaries had very different feelings toward the poet, as may be seen from the numerous recollections about him and the response to his death. One of the first to respond was Vladimir Mayakovsky, who dedicated a poem to Yesenin (*Novy Mir*, May 1926, pp. 111–15):

> You have gone
> as people say,
> into another world.
> Emptiness . . .
> Fly,
> Plow into stars.
> No advances here,
> No taverns.
> . . . .
> No, Yesenin,
> This
> Is not a taunt,
> In the throat
> there is the lump of grief,
> Not laughter.
> . . . .

> It is painful
> and improper
> to play at mysteries.
> The people,
> the maker of language,
> Has lost
> Its bell-voiced
> Scamp of an apprentice. . . .

And Nikolay Kluyev, a fellow peasant-poet whom Yesenin had called his "older brother," wrote "A Lament for Yesenin."

In her book *The Crazy Ship* (1931) the novelist Olga Forsh vividly describes the "civil mass" held for Yesenin by fellow writers and admirers. The central place in this account, which provides an interesting sidelight on the period, is given to Kluyev's unorthodox "memorial service," expressing both love and grief over the younger poet's disintegration and death. In the first part of this "service" he told about his early meeting with Yesenin; in the second he spoke of the youth's betrayal of his "importunate older brother" and of himself. Gently and tenderly, Kluyev read his poem about the coming of the "sweet-voiced acolyte from the fields of Ryazan" (the poem was written in 1918). Then, relates Olga Forsh, "Kluyev suddenly stepped to the footlights like a tiger preparing to spring, hissing out his lines with angry passion; and then, before the audience was aware of what he was doing, he began to recite Yesenin's own poems, ending with the broken, drunken words:

> Russia . . . my Russia,
> My Asiatic land."

When someone in the shocked audience protested against *such* a memorial, Kluyev said: "But I am weeping for him. . . . At our last meeting I knew it was the hour of parting. . . . I looked, and saw the blackness cling all around him."

In heartfelt words the poet V. Kirillov describes Yesenin's "return" from Leningrad to Moscow in his coffin:

"A huge crowd gathered at the Nikolaevsky Station on December 30, 1925. . . . It was a gray winter evening. The locomotive suddenly loomed out of the mist. The air was strangely quiet and solemn. . . . Seryozha. . . . I looked at the approaching train, tears welling up in my eyes, thinking sadly: and so Seryozha is returning to Moscow. . . . The train rolled to a stop at the platform. To the sounds of a funeral march, friends carried Yesenin's coffin from the last car. Someone was sobbing loudly. . . ."

5 YEVGENY ZAMYATIN (1884–1937)

Yevgeny Zamyatin was the most brilliant representative of the contingent of Russian writers who began their literary careers before the revolution of 1917, but who quickly found contact with the revolutionary reality of the day.

The victory of the revolution brought with it a complete break with the old way of life. Russia was swept by a great flood-tide of ideas and emotions; everything was in flux and motion. Confusion and disarray reigned among the writers as they did throughout the land. Pre-revolutionary standards and authorities were cast aside, while new ones had not yet emerged. Life lay shattered before the eyes of men in all the unique details of a period of sharp transition. The literary artist was passionately eager to become a part of the new world, to capture it in his work. But events stunned him, and he searched agonizingly for some solid points of departure in the torrent of change.

Among the literary groups active at the time was the association of young writers called the Serapion Brotherhood. What united them was not a common literary program, but the very material of the revolutionary epoch and the method of reflecting it, the sudden realization that the starting point they had all so passionately sought was already there—outside the window, in the street, everywhere. That starting point was the revolution. And so, without theorizing, without any ready-made perspectives or all-embracing concepts, they began to write, setting themselves a modest goal: to express their vision of the time. This approach determined the literary form they chose—the short story, in which the characters and the action were merely sketched in rapidly, in a few telling strokes.

The Serapion Brothers, who generally disliked literary authorities, nevertheless chose Yevgeny Zamyatin as their guide and teacher, and his influence may indeed be felt in their early works. Zamyatin himself mentioned this influence in an article on "The New Russian Prose" (1923), but he was also one of the first to deny their "brotherhood," describing the group as "a meeting of chance fellow travelers in a railway car, whose journey together away from literary traditions can last only to the first junction. . . ." In this, as in many of his other judgments, Zamyatin proved to be a prophet.

Zamyatin's personal biography is extremely interesting. He was born in 1884 and grew up "among the fields of the Tambov province, in Lebedyan, famed for its card sharpers, gypsies, horse fairs, and the raciest of Russian speech—the Lebedyan that both Tolstoy and Turgenev had described." He grew up alone, without childhood friends, for these were early replaced by books. In his short autobiography[1] Zamyatin wrote: "I can still remember how I shivered reading Dostoyevsky's *Netochka Nezvanova* and Turgenev's "First Love." These writers were my elders, and they were, perhaps, a bit terrifying. But Gogol was a friend."

When he completed his studies at the *gimnaziya* (secondary school), Zamyatin entered the Polytechnical Institute in Petersburg. As a student, he took part in the revolutionary movement. "I was a Bolshevik," he writes, and adds in parentheses, "Today I am not." In the winter he studied in Petersburg, in the summer he worked in factories and made several journeys. The trip from Odessa to Alexandria was especially memorable. His visit to Odessa coincided with the sailors' mutiny on the battleship *Potemkin*, and his stay in Helsingfors, with the rebellion in Sveaborg. He graduated from the Polytechnicum in

[1] In the anthology *Writers. Autobiographies and Portraits of Contemporary Russian Writers*, sixth edition. (Moscow V. Lidin, ed. 1928).

1908 and was retained on the faculty of the Department of Naval Architecture.

His literary work began later, in 1911. The magazine *Zavety* published his first short novel, *The Provincial*. At that time the editorial board of the magazine included Alexey Remizov, Mikhail Prishvin, and Ivanov-Razumnik. These were writers who had continued, after the suppression of the revolution of 1905, to pay close attention to what went on below the surface, at the heart of the country. Hence, they all shared a common interest in provincial urban Russia, as well as a sense of kinship with the nineteenth-century writer Nikolay Leskov.

Zamyatin's gift of merciless analysis was first manifested in the short novel *At the World's End*, which unfolds in the remote province in Siberia, and satirizes the life of the local officers. After it appeared in 1913 Zamyatin was brought to trial for it, but was acquitted. The story is remarkable for its profound psychological insight into the minds of its characters—people forced, for one reason or another, to lead a stultifying existence "at the world's end."

The following passage from this story, describing one of the main characters, is a good example of the flavor and style of Zamyatin's writing:

"Each man has something that epitomizes him at a glance, that makes him immediately recognizable among a thousand others. In Andrey Ivanovich it was his forehead—the length and breadth of the steppes. And next to it—the nose, a typical Russian button nose, and a little flaxen mustache. When the Lord was making him, he drew a single wide stroke, and there was the forehead! And then He yawned, He suddenly felt bored, and finished with a smear here and there, anyhow. It'll do! And so Andrey Ivanovich went out into life—by the grace of God's yawn."

In 1915 Zamyatin was sent to England, to work on the construction of Russian ice-breakers. "One of our largest ice-breakers," says Zamyatin, "the *Lenin* (formerly *Alexander Nevsky*), is my work." In England, Zamyatin first tried his hand at satire. In *The Islanders* and *The Fisher of Men* the writer ridiculed the hypocrisy and cant of

English society. The bent and taste for satire were intrinsic to Zamyatin's talent. No wonder he regarded Gogol as a friend when he was a boy. But what is interesting is that Zamyatin's satire is almost always tinged with lyricism. Hence the duality of the final impression, as if the first draft had been written by a satirical pen but the finishing touches applied with soft water-colors.

While he was living and working in England, Zamyatin learned about the outbreak of the revolution in Russia. And then, as he says, "it became intolerable" to remain abroad. In September 1917 Zamyatin returned to Russia. Awaiting him at home was "the merry and grim winter of 1917–18": "Trolleyless streets, long lines of people carrying sacks, dozens of miles trudged daily on foot, improvised stoves, herring, oats ground up in the coffee-mill. And, along with the oats, all sorts of world-shaking plans, such as the publication of all the classics of world literature of every period. . . ."

Zamyatin's best account of this time may be found in his "Reminiscences about Blok," published in the magazine *Russky Sovremennik* in 1924:

"For three years after that we were all locked together inside a steel projectile—and, cooped up in darkness, whistled through space, no one knew where. In those dying years we had to do something, to settle down to some sort of a life in the hurtling missile. And so extravagant plans were hatched inside the missile—the publication of 'World Literature,' the Union of Literary Workers, the Writers' Union, a Theatre. . . . We did not know as yet that we were holding our meetings riveted inside a speeding shell. . . ."

Blok's influence was also germinal in Zamyatin's development. Spiritually, Zamyatin was both younger and healthier than Blok. At that time, in 1917–18, he did not yet envisage clearly where the "steel projectile" was rushing. With an earnestness typical of both Blok and Zamyatin, they participated in all the literary enterprises of the period. "In frozen, hungry, typhus-ridden Petersburg," wrote Zamyatin in the same "Reminiscences," "there raged a veritable cultural-educational epidemic. Since literature is not education, all the writers and poets became lecturers." During that first post-revolutionary year Blok still had faith in the renewal of life that was to be brought by the revolution. When he realized he was mistaken, he fell into mortal despair, complaining to Zamyatin that there was "no air," and bitterly denouncing the atmosphere of "deadness and lies." Nevertheless, he once said to Zamyatin: "And yet, there is a gold mine of very genuine truth in all of this. A hating love—this is, perhaps, the most exact description of my attitude toward Russia."

Together with Blok, Zamyatin early came to feel that "Bolshevism and revolution are not to be found either in Moscow or in Petersburg. True Bolshevism, Russian, pious, lives somewhere in the heart of Russia, perhaps in the villages. . . ."

Both intellectually and emotionally, Zamyatin accepted the revolution. But he, too, soon came to be repelled by the official legend claiming that a "social revolution" had taken place in the country. Zamyatin began to paint the revolution as he saw it, in stories that attracted the attention not only of a narrow circle of young writers, but also of the wide reading public.

In a characteristic story of that period, "The Dragon," Zamyatin sketches the following scene: A trolley rushes screeching across the ice-locked city. On the platform stands a man, "a dragon with a gun": "The cap was down on his nose, and would have swallowed the dragon's head if not for the protruding ears, on which it came to rest. The army greatcoat hung down to the floor; the sleeves flapped loosely; the toes of his shoes were turned up—obviously empty. And in the darkness under the cap—a gaping hole—the mouth."

The "dragon" is telling one of the passengers about a prisoner he escorted the day before: "So I take him along. An intellectual mug, makes you sick just to look at it. And it talks, the scum! What do you think of that, it talks!" Then the passenger asks: "Well, and then? Did you bring him in?" And the "dragon" answers: "I sure did—nonstop to the heavenly kingdom. With my bayonet!" Yet a moment later the same "dragon," alighting at the corner, worries over a freezing sparrow, tries to revive it with his breath. The cap slips back on his head, opening two chinks "from the nightmare world into the human." The sparrow revives and flutters off to an unknown destination, and the "guide to the heavenly kingdom" raises his gun to his shoulder, pulls his cap down once more, covering the "chinks into the human world," and disappears into the fog.

In the unbearably poignant, but wholly credible contradiction between the lyrical end of the story and the terrifying image of the "dragon" who sends the "intellectual mug" nonstop to "the heavenly kingdom," we see the essence of Zamyatin's talent.

Zamyatin never confined himself to mirroring facts. He sought to comprehend them as an artist. In this connection "A Story about the Most Important Thing" is especially interesting.

In a tiny world—on a leaf of an apple tree—a pink-and-yellow caterpillar is about to die, about to turn into a chrysalis, and its body, racked with pain, is arched into a "quivering bridge." On the same day, in the vast world around it, on either side of the narrow creek, two groups of peasants—the "Reds" of Orlov and the "Whites" of Kelbuy—have come out to fight each other. The Orlov peasants are in favor of the Soviet government, the Kelbuy peasants are against it, because this government has set up one of the poorest men as the head of the village. The "Reds" are led by the Bolshevik Dorda; the "Whites" also are led by a revolutionary, Kukoverov. In Czarist times Dorda and Kukoverov spent a year together in a prison cell and became close friends. Now they are deadly enemies. The "Reds" win. Kukoverov is captured and faces execution by a firing squad. The girl Talya, who loves Kukoverov, comes to Dorda to plead for mercy. But Dorda is powerless. The best he can do is to allow Talya to spend with Kukoverov the last night before his execution.

At the end of the story Zamyatin returns to the underlying theme, embodied in the image of the caterpillar suffering on the eve of a new life: the peasants of Kelbuy and Orlov rise and rush at each other, and the earth in the meantime opens her womb to conceive and give birth "to new fiery creatures in the crimson light."

This story echoes Zamyatin's vision of the revolution, as formulated in his recollections of Blok: the vast country, he felt, had broken away from its former axis, and was rushing in an unknown direction; and its intentions were still unclear to the actors in the revolutionary drama.

In his *Fairy Tales for Adults* the writer criticized the falsehood and hypocrisy of revolutionary philistines. Still sharper and more merciless were the judgments Zamyatin the journalist expressed in his articles. Zamyatin lived in Petersburg, where the wind that was sowing lies and hypocrisy grew stronger daily, where the terror against anyone who dared to have opinions of his own was mounting from month to month.

Outspoken and sincere, Zamyatin irritated many people. At first the official critics did not dare attack him openly, but very soon they began to reproach him for his "elemental" picture of the revolution, and later, for his "bourgeois" approach. But Zamyatin refused to yield to pressure. He took an active part in literary life, lectured, was elected a member of the executive committee of the first Writers' Union, wrote criticism, and was one of the editors of the journal *Russky Sovremennik*. In an article, "About the Day and the Age" (1924), published in that journal, he reproached his fellow writers for giving "the day" pre-eminence over "the age." He wrote: "That which is merely of the day is greedily clutching at life, indiscriminate in its choice of means: it must hurry, it must live for the moment, before tomorrow comes. And hence, what we see in this life of the day is shifty nimbleness, servility, triviality, the fear of seeing the naked truth. That which is of the age is *above* the current day . . . it is far-sighted, it looks ahead. That which lives by the day alone takes from the epoch nothing but its coloration, its skin; it exists by the law of mimicry. But that which is of the age takes its head and its heart from the epoch—it lives by the law of inheritance."

If we examine the new literature, he continued—and it must be remembered that this was written in 1924—if we look at "everything that is parading today with the passport of belles-lettres, it will unfortunately become quite clear that there is far more in it of the day than of the age. And it would be well if this proportion, this ratio of the day to the age, did not grow—as does the philistine we see sprouting before our eyes like weeds out of every crack, choking out *man*." But the real substance, the body of our truth, says Zamyatin, will be discovered by our descendants not from the works that reflect the transitory "today," but from those which "breathe the spirit of the age," "with everything it holds of the repulsive and the beautiful."

In the middle 1920s Zamyatin became actively interested in the theater and wrote a play, *The Flea*, based on the folk story about Master Levsha, the left-handed smith, and on Nikolay Leskov's story on the same theme. *The Flea* was, once again, an expression of his views on the objectives of art, which, he felt, should serve the age, and not the interests of the passing day.

A great popular revolution had taken place in the country, but the theaters languished for lack of plays, while only anemic pseudo-revolutionary plays by nimble hacks were produced. On the stage they were even more obviously false than in the pages of the magazines. Zamyatin decided to extract from the past that Russia which, like the legendary city of Kitezh, had been submerged in the centuries of the country's history—plebeian, working Russia, "with its very human soul." The image of the famed Tula master craftsman, Levsha, who, with his comrades, outdid the English smiths and shod their "nimphosoria"—their marvelous steel flea—was an integral part of the treasury of Russian folklore. For four seasons *The Flea* enjoyed enormous success. After that it was withdrawn from the repertory.

At about the same time Zamyatin wrote his play *The*

Fires of Saint Dominic. Its theme was taken from the history of the Spanish Inquisition, the essence of which he embodied in the character of the ruthless inquisitor Munebrahi. His next dramatic work was the tragedy *Attila*. Zamyatin worked on it for three years, producing several versions. The principal character of the tragedy is Attila, ruler of the great land of Scythia. The dramatic crux of the play is formed by Attila's love for his captive, Ildegonde, a daughter of the King of Burgundy. But Ildegonde loves another, and kills Attila when he attempts to make her his mistress. (This play was later published in *Novy Zhurnal*, No. XXIV, 1950, New York).

Attila was approved by the Artistic Council of the Bolshoy Dramatic Theatre in Leningrad and accepted for production. It was already in rehearsal and was announced in posters, when it was banned at the insistence of the Leningrad District Literary Office, not for any subversive elements in the play, but because the authorities were increasingly displeased with Zamyatin's work generally.

Among Zamyatin's rich and varied literary output we must single out the short story "Comrade Churygin Has the Floor" (Anthology *Krug*, No. 6, 1927), which shows with remarkable subtlety by what untrodden paths the revolution sometimes reached the most remote and out-of-the-way corners of the land.

At an evening devoted to recollections of the October revolution, the young peasant Churygin, tells how the revolution took place in his native village of Kuyman. Despite its distance from urban centers, the whole village, in 1917, smoldered with subdued excitement in expectation of important events. And the events occurred after the arrival of the cooper's son, who had lost his legs in the war, and who had brought the news that, at long last, there was now "one of our own" at the Czar's court—the peasant Grigory Rasputin. The village was overjoyed. Now life would surely become easier, now there would be "an end and finish both to the war and to the landlords." And then, long after the event, another bit of news reached the village: Rasputin had been murdered. Enraged over the murder of "one of their own," the residents of Kuyman reply by killing "the former spider"—the landowner Tarataev. And this was how the village avenged itself for its "lost dream": this was how, in its own way, it joined in the dramatic epic of the people's revolution. . . . Soviet critics saw nothing in the story but a caricature of the October revolution.

Mounting frictions between the official critics and Zamyatin led him finally to break with the Soviet government. The occasion for this break was the publication abroad of Zamyatin's satirical novel *We*. Imbued with passionate protest against conformism and the suppression of freedom, it was written in 1920, and, though unpublished, it was widely read in manuscript in the literary circles of Leningrad and Moscow. In 1924 the novel appeared in English translation in the United States (published by E. P. Dutton, New York); later, it was published in abridged form in French and—in the journal *Volya Rossii*, in Prague—in Russian.

In many respects this novel anticipates George Orwell's *1984*. It takes place in the twenty-third century, in a country called "The Single State." The life, laws, and customs of this state are described in the diary of one of its citizens. The Single State is engaged in a colossal construction project: it is building the "Integral," an interplanetary flying machine, with the aid of which it plans to impose its own brand of "happiness" on other planets. The project is possible only because the entire life of the citizens, including their hours of rest, is controlled by the state. The author of the diary compares this general "unfreedom" with a dance, the "profound meaning" of which consists in "absolute, ecstatic subordination" and "ideal unfreedom." The state apparatus embraces all aspects of life. Even art in the Single State serves practical objectives, formulated by the appropriate officials. "Today," says the diarist, "poetry is not an irresponsible nightingale song; poetry is civil service, poetry is useful."

The head of the Single State is elected annually, on the holiday in honor of Unanimity of Thought. The election proceedings—quite unlike those of the long-forgotten democracies—last only five minutes: they consist of the invariable and "unanimous" re-election of the universally recognized leader known as "The Benefactor." But sedition rears its head in this harmonious state: a woman rebels against the ubiquitous state regimentation; she wants to love the man she is really attracted to, not the one assigned to her; she wants freedom to admire, not the Integral, but the buildings of the era when the world was still sunk in the morass of "anarchy." She raises the banner of rebellion. Others are found who think as she does. The author of the diary also yields for a time to the temptation of this mutiny. However, he is frightened at his own boldness. In the end, after a brain operation, in which the center governing imagination is removed from his brain, he becomes once again an obedient servant of The Benefactor.

Portents of his defection appear when the woman rebel confides in him her plan to seize the Integral. The author of the diary recoils in horror: "To seize the Integral! But that means . . ." And the woman completes the sentence for him: "It means revolution!" But that is what the diarist fears most. He was brought up with the idea that the revolution which led to the triumph of the Single State was "the last revolution, and there can be no others." After this "last revolution" there can only be "counterrevolution," in which he does not want to participate. At this point the paths of the diarist and the woman rebel diverge. She attempts to convince him that his very conception of the revolution as "the last one" is childish nonsense. Children are afraid of infinity. There can be no such thing as a last revolution, just as there can be no last number. . . .

The Single State, with its apparatus, suppresses the rebellion, and the woman rebel is executed.

In the image of the woman rebel, Zamyatin embodied all his longing for creative and political freedom, all his protest against the frightful octopus state. In Zamyatin's literary biography, the novel *We* played an almost fatal role. After the withdrawal of his play *Attila* from the

Soviet repertory, the critics recalled the novel (although it was never published in the Soviet Union) and launched a campaign of persecution against the author. This concerted onslaught was so vicious that Zamyatin was finally driven, in the summer of 1931, to write a letter to Stalin. The letter contained the following paragraphs:

"I know that I have a most inconvenient habit of speaking what I consider to be the truth, rather than saying what may be expedient at the moment. Specifically, I have never concealed my attitude toward literary servility, cringing, and chameleon changes of color. I have felt, and I feel today, that this degrades both the writer and the revolution. I raised this problem in one of my articles (in the journal *Dom Iskusstv*, No. 1, 1921), in a form that many people found sharp and offensive, and it served at the time as a signal for the launching of a newspaper and magazine campaign against me.

"The death of my tragedy *Attila* was a genuine tragedy for me. It made entirely clear to me the futility of any effort at changing my situation, especially in view of the well-known affair involving my novel *We*, which followed soon after. . . . The manhunt organized at the time was unprecedented in Soviet literature, and was remarked on even in the foreign press. Everything was done to close to me all avenues for further work. I became an object of fear to my erstwhile friends, publishers, and theaters. My books were banned from the libraries. My play (*The Flea*), presented with unvarying success by the Second Moscow Art Theatre for four seasons, was withdrawn from the repertory. The publication of my collected works by the Federation [Federatsiya] Publishing House was halted. Any publishing organization that attempted to publish my works was immediately placed under fire—including Federation, Land and Factory [Zemlya i Fabrika] and, particularly, the Publishing House of Leningrad Writers. This latter organization took the risk of retaining me on its board for an entire year, and ventured to make use of my literary experience, entrusting me with the stylistic editing of the works of young writers, including Communists.

"Last spring the Leningrad branch of the RAPP forced

my resignation from the executive board and the discontinuance of my work. The *Literary Gazette* triumphantly announced this victory, adding quite unequivocally: '. . . the publishing house must be preserved, but not for the Zamyatins.' The last door to the reading public was closed to Zamyatin. The writer's death sentence was pronounced and published."

Zamyatin appealed to Stalin with a request that is difficult to imagine today, in the light of subsequent events, but not yet unthinkable at that time. He asked permission to go abroad with his wife, with the right to return when, as he put it, "there is at least a partial change in the prevailing view concerning the role of the literary artist. And this time, I am confident, is near, for the successful establishment of a material foundation will inevitably be followed by the need to create the superstructure—an art and a literature truly worthy of the revolution. . . ."

Zamyatin was energetically supported by Gorky, and a year later he was given an opportunity to leave. The last story he published in the Soviet Union was "The Flood," which appeared in 1930. He settled in Paris, where he continued his literary work.

The most important of the longer works Zamyatin wrote in Paris was the novel *The Scourge of God*. This novel grew out of his play *Attila*. When the play was finished, Zamyatin felt that his entire work on it was, in essence, a preparation for a novel. Because of his untimely death on March 10, 1937, the novel was never completed: only its first part appeared (in Paris, in 1938).

The introduction to *The Scourge of God*, unsigned, but evidently written by someone who knew the late author very well, summarizes some of Zamyatin's ideas, which served as the basis for the novel. "Over the course of human history there are parallel epochs which seem to sound a similar theme. Such a parallel to our time is that of the 'migration of peoples,' of the greatest world wars, of the clash between an aging Western culture and the wave of fresh, barbarian peoples—the Goths and the Slavs."

Zamyatin himself wrote in a footnote to *The Scourge of God* that "Attila was by no means the savage, senseless destroyer depicted by Roman historians. He was unquestionably a man of tremendous will power and temperament, well educated for his time (as a youth, he had been a hostage in Rome and had studied there). He was a clever politician, whose policies are highly reminiscent of modern tactics: he instigated rebellions against Rome in Gaul, he acted against Rome in collaboration with Roman colonists. He was an irreconcilable enemy of Rome, who had set himself the objective of destroying the empire. . . ."

Zamyatin was not only a great literary artist, but also a gifted literary critic. While he was still living in the Soviet Union, he prepared a collection of his articles and literary portraits, which did not appear until 1955 (in New York).[2] I have already mentioned several of the articles included in the collection ("I Am Afraid," "Reminiscences about Blok," "About the Day and the Age," "A Letter to Stalin"). American and English readers may, perhaps, best judge Zamyatin's talents as a critic from his literary portraits of H. G. Wells and O. Henry.

In the introduction to the portrait of Wells, Zamyatin wrote:

"The laciest Gothic cathedrals are, after all, made of stone. The most marvelous, most fantastic fairy tales are, after all, made of the earth, the trees, the animals of a land. . . . But imagine a land where the only fertile soil is asphalt, where nothing grows but dense forests of factory chimneys, where the herds are of a single breed—automobiles, and the only fragrance in the spring is that of gasoline. This land of stone, asphalt, iron, and gasoline is twentieth-century London, and, naturally, it was bound to produce its own iron, automobile goblins, its own mechanical, chemical fairy tales. Such tales exist: they are told by H. G. Wells."

This introduction is followed by a brilliant analysis of the entire literary output of H. G. Wells.

[2] *Litsa*, Chekhov Publishing House, N.Y.

In his portrait of O. Henry, Zamyatin contrasts him with Jack London: "Jack London is the writer of the American steppes, snowy plains, oceans, and tropical islands. In O. Henry we see the American cities. True, Jack London is the author of *Martin Eden*, and O. Henry wrote a book of the steppes, *Heart of the West*, and a short-story collection, *Cabbages and Kings*, depicting the life of some southern province in America. Still, Jack London is the Klondike, and O. Henry is New York."

Zamyatin feels that O. Henry has something in common with motion pictures. The reader emerges from O. Henry's cinema "refreshed by laughter." O. Henry, he says, is unfailingly witty, amusing, youthfully gay—"very much like A. Chekhonte, who had not yet matured into Anton Chekhov."

Yevgeny Zamyatin was not only one of the pioneers of the Soviet period of Russian literature, but one of the most interesting and original Russian writers of the twentieth century, one who—like Blok—loved his land with a "hating love." He will transmit to future generations of readers a living image of his profoundly tragic epoch.

6 MIKHAIL ZOSHCHENKO (1895-1958)

In Soviet literature there is only one name that invariably evokes in the reader's mind the image of a "gay writer," a "king of laughter": Mikhail Zoshchenko. As is so frequently the case with famous humorists, he was in reality almost a hypochondriac, and his "gay" contribution to literature has already become an important source for the study of the life and psychology of men on the boundary separating two major epochs.

Zoshchenko was not only a pioneer of Soviet literature and a member of its first nonpartisan literary group, the Serapion Brothers, he was also the only Soviet writer who never experienced a crisis in his relations with the readers; they flocked to him in droves from the very first. "My sentence is short and easily accessible to the poor. Perhaps this is why I have many readers," he explained modestly in his article "About Myself, about Critics, and about My Work" (1927).

Zoshchenko was born in 1895. His father, a Ukrainian landowner, was a member of the group of artists known as *Peredvizhniki* and sympathized with the socialists. His mother, a Russian, was a former actress. Zoshchenko grew up in Petersburg. He was a poor student, and Russian was his worst subject. In the final examinations he received a failing mark for his Russian composition on "The Young Women in Turgenev's Works," and tried to commit suicide.

Early in 1914, after a year at the law school of the University of Petersburg, he was expelled for nonpayment of tuition and went to work as a ticket agent for a railroad. The outbreak of World War I ended this career. Zoshchenko volunteered for the army and was sent to the front. He began as an ensign and was later promoted to battalion commander. He was wounded and suffered from gas poisoning. Soon after the March revolution of 1917 Zoshchenko was appointed commandant of the main post office in Petersburg. Before devoting himself to literature he managed to go through a number of occupations: he was a border guard, a Red Army soldier, an agent for the criminal-investigation office, an instructor in rabbit- and poultry-raising, a militiaman, a carpenter, shoemaker, and clerk. He told about it in his long story *Youth Recaptured* (1933). Like most of the writers of the first post-revolutionary literary contingent, Zoshchenko came to literature from the very thick of the revolution-permeated life.

He won his first success with *The Stories of Nazar Ilyich, Mister Sinebryukhov* (1922). Nazar Ilyich, a former peasant, was later a soldier in the world war, a deserter, and finally a gadabout over the world. His stories about his experiences during the war and after his "life's course" was shaken up, are muddled and incoherent: the events he had witnessed were "so to speak, of an entirely pacific order," but Nazar Ilyich Sinebryukhov is obviously "not enlightened" as to their meaning. However, despite the narrator's incoherence and the triviality of his personal experiences, the stories hold the reader spellbound. The secret of their success lies in *the storyteller's language itself*—a hilariously absurd mixture of popular idiom and hastily acquired and undigested literary turns of phrase. Nazar Ilyich is a peasant by passport designation only (the peasant theme was generally alien to Zoshchenko, and his few stories from peasant life are weak). To the very marrow of his bones, Sinebryukhov is a representative of the urban lower-middle class—the *meshchane*. Before the revolution this group led a drab existence on the outskirts of town and the outskirts of life. When the revolution came, it felt that here at last was its opportunity for a more meaningful life.

From the very beginning of his literary activity Zoshchenko was interested in the masses of these urban "little people." Before the revolution, to use his expression, they lived like "walking vegetables." The revolution came, and they took an active part in it. However, for a number of complex reasons, it was difficult for them to utilize the victory of the revolution in their interests, even in the sense of cultural development. And nowhere did this fact express itself as clearly as in literature and journalism. The country's intellectual energies flowed into these fields, but —as so often happens in backward nations—those who progressed into the ranks of the intelligentsia became in certain measure alienated from the life of the lower social strata. While the young writers of the early revolutionary years were absorbed in cultivating the most fashionable and refined Western European literary forms (exemplified in the work of such writers as Verlaine and Whitman), the plain people had not yet mastered elementary literate speech. And then these simple people turned to a "crash program" of "self-education": greedily acquiring new words, they also gave them new twists and used them in their own special way. Zoshchenko was the first to sense this hunger of the masses for culture, and to respond to it as an artist.

Zoshchenko succeeded in creating his own unique literary style. His heroes speak of the trivial facts of contemporary life in the language of the man in the street, both simple-minded and with a touch of cunning. But through the ironic words of his heroes the writer gives expression to their pent-up bitterness. And it was this style that won the hearts of the readers, who sensed in it the writer's sincere concern with the destinies of the little, ordinary man.

In the same mocking, but lyrical manner Zoshchenko was able to discuss the fate of the Soviet writer. In 1922 in his article "About Myself, about Ideology, and a Few Other Things," he wrote:

"Generally, it is rather difficult to be a writer. Take, for example, ideology. Nowadays, a writer is expected to have an ideology. . . . But tell me, what kind of a 'precise ideology' can I have when no party attracts me in its entirety? From the point of view of party people I am a man without principles. All right! But what I will say about myself is that I am not a Communist, not a Socialist-Revolutionary, and not a monarchist. I am simply a Russian. . . . Honestly, I don't know to this day. . . . Well, take Guchkov. What party does he belong to? The devil alone can tell. I know he is not a Bolshevik. Is he a Socialist-Revolutionary or a Cadet? I don't know and I don't care, and even if I should find out, I'd go on loving Pushkin as I always have. Many people will take offense at me for saying this ('Look at that innocence,' they'll say, 'preserved after three revolutions!'). But it is so. And, in any case, this ignorance is a joy to me. I hate no one—and that is my 'precise ideology.' . . . But I am not a Communist (not a Marxist, to put it more exactly), and I think that I never shall be one. . . ."

With all the resources of his talent Zoschenko came forward as the spokesman of the masses of plain, insignificant people. "Of course, there's no argument about it—the personages here are small fry. Not leaders, certainly. Simply, in a manner of speaking, *etcetera citizens*, with their everyday actions and anxieties" ("Lilacs in Bloom"). But the writer is not in the least apologetic about his unimportant heroes. "Somebody has to respond to the lives of the other people, too, of the average men—those, so to speak, who are not registered in the velvet book of life" ("M. P. Sinyagin").

This was how Zoshchenko's stories were written. Later they were collected in a number of volumes (*Humorous Stories*, 1923; *The Lady* and *A Merry Life*, 1924; *Humorous Stories*, 1925; *Hard Times, Palefaced Brothers, Nervous People*, 1920–25). In essence, these stories have no heroes, and the events that constitute the plots are in themselves, to quote Zoshchenko, "unquestionably petty." Yet every story is like an opened window through which we hear the inimitable sounds of life in the revolutionary street of those years.

"What can an unemployed man live on in our needy times? I'll tell you plainly, nothing at all. You're lucky if a bicycle knocks you over and you can grab a ruble from the careless rider."

These are the opening lines of Zoshchenko's story "A Profitable Enterprise," which tells of an unemployed man who decides to tease some NEP-man's[1] dog into tearing his trousers. But the dog seems to sense his purpose and will have nothing to do with his trousers. Nevertheless, the jobless man manages to engage the dog's owner in a "serious talk" which ends with the latter slapping him. Seeing that the general sympathy of the street is on his side, the unemployed man hopes to earn at least forty rubles from the affair. In view of this "sure prospect" his neighbors even lend him some money. But in the end, the judge sentences the dog owner to six months' imprisonment for insulting a fellow citizen!

Another story tells "just a little fact from our Leningrad life": an elderly woman, absolutely devoid of "proletarian ideology," lives quietly in her room. Noticing a rough spot on the wall, she broods on it until she concludes that one of the former residents must have hidden a treasure in the wall. She calls a workman of her acquaintance and they begin to "dig down to the people's bricks." It turns out that there is no treasure, merely a sag in the main wall. In the meantime the man living in the next room hears the suspicious noises and also begins to break down his wall. The author remarks with mild irony: at any rate "one may draw a generalization from this trivial little fact: the petty-bourgeois element has begun to stir. It is digging into walls. Looking for buried treasure. And it hopes in this way to mend its shaken affairs. Now everything appears to be in order" ("Buried Treasure").

Or take the anonymous speaker who says, as he reviews "our achievements" on the tenth anniversary of the revolution, that, indeed, achievements are evident at every step. Consider, for example, transportation: in 1919 people traveled with constant interruptions, trains kept stopping all the time. What happened? The machinist ran out of fuel. The passengers would run into the woods, chop down

[1] The new type of businessman who emerged as a result of the New Economic Policy (NEP), 1921–28, which temporarily eased the early economic restrictions on private enterprise.

some trees, cut them up, and the train would resume its journey. But raw wood did not burn properly, and so there was more difficulty. And then, "before you count five," the train stopped again because the wind blew off the machinist's cap. The passengers gave him a hand. They broke up into teams and went out to search in "organized" fashion. At last the cap was found and delivered to the machinist, "someone made a speech on the uses of hats," and on they went. Today, the narrator concludes with a touch of nostalgia, "not only a cap, a passenger may be blown off —but the stop will not last more than a minute. Because time is precious. The train must go on" ("1927").

Out of the aggregate of these innumerable short stories there rises before us the city of the early years of the revolution. The revolution is over. But its breath still fills the air. The dire poverty of the city and country stares one in the eye. Of course, poverty also existed before, but then it was hidden; today it is all out in the open. The revolution has divested it of an attribute that attends it throughout the world—oppressive secret shame. The poverty shown by Zoshchenko is not only unashamed, it is even a bit brash, as if the poor were saying: "It's not our fault that we are poor!" In exposing it, Zoshchenko seems to be saying to the powers that be: "Hey there, you, up above! Don't get so carried away by your grandiose plans! Pay a bit more attention to what's right under your feet!"

The little people in Zoshchenko's revolutionary city are still living on the outskirts of life, but the demarcation line that formerly divided the rich from the poor no longer exists, or, perhaps, *does not yet* exist. Hence, Zoshchenko's poor have no feeling of being socially oppressed. Theirs is an almost cheerful, optimistic poverty. Only a very young or a potentially very rich people can bear its poverty so lightly.

In addition to his short stories Zoshchenko is the author of a number of longer stories, which must be dealt with separately. True, Zoshchenko himself resented any attempt to distinguish between his longer and shorter works: "Both my tales and my stories are written with the same hand.

And I do not make the fine distinction: I do not say, now I shall write a bit of nonsense, but the next work is a serious one, a work for posterity" ("About Myself, about Critics, and about My Work"). Nevertheless, separate examination of the longer works is justified, since they seem to form a closed cycle, especially interesting because each of them contains a fragment of Zoshchenko's continuing dialogue with his time.

Perhaps no Soviet writer, with the sole exception of Alexey Tolstoy, has pondered as much and as seriously as Zoshchenko over the new reader and the new directions in literature. The ideas of these two writers were in many respects antithetical from the very first. The course of development of the revolution led to the victory of Tolstoy's position. But Zoshchenko's defeat in this literary disagreement will introduce the reader better than any abstract discourse to the living complex of socio-psychological problems inherent in Soviet life during the first twenty post-revolutionary years.

"Damn, how difficult it is to work in literature! You sweat yourself to exhaustion before you push your way through the impassable jungle," Zoshchenko sighs, in the words of the luckless writer in "What the Nightingale Sang About."

"It is difficult to work in literature" because, on the one hand, there is no peace from the official critics who demand dazzling heroes and "hurricane ideology." On the other hand, there is the equally difficult "new reader." Zoshchenko alone was not afraid to speak out openly about a situation true then and, to some extent, still true today: with few exceptions the literature of the NEP and the first Five-Year Plan periods was not popular with the readers. And Zoshchenko, for his part, sympathizes with these readers (in "A Gay Adventure"):

"No, the author cannot lightheartedly stretch out in bed with a book by a Russian writer! To find some peace of mind, he must pick up a book by a foreign writer. . . . How pleasantly these foreigners write! Nothing but happiness, success, and unalloyed prosperity. All their characters are handsome. The women go about in silk dresses and the men wear pale-blue shorts. They bathe daily in their bathtubs. But best of all is the general cheer and gaiety and nonsense. . . . And now, take our dear Russian literature. The weather is mostly nasty—a blizzard, or a storm, or a wind blowing right into the hero's face. And the heroes seem chosen just for their unpleasantness. They swear all the time. They're badly dressed. Instead of gay and jolly adventures, you're fed descriptions of bloody clashes in the Civil War. Or else you get a story that puts you to sleep altogether. . . ."

But the main reason for the lack of popularity of this literature is that the reader wants to find in a work "some headlong flight of fantasy, some wild devilish plot. But where can you find it? Where can you find this headlong flight of the imagination when Russian reality is different?" Zoshchenko does not deny that Russian reality contains "large themes," such as the revolution. But this is precisely where the chief difficulty lurks, and "again you're stumped": "The headlong flight is here. And grandiose fantasy. But try to show it, and you'll be told it isn't so. It's incorrect, they'll say; it lacks a scientific approach to the question. The ideology, they'll say, is limping. . . . Oh, my dear esteemed reader! It's hard to be a Russian writer!" ("A Terrible Night.")

A good deal of what Zoshchenko observed was also seen by Alexey Tolstoy. And yet the two writers often drew diametrically opposed conclusions from the same facts. According to Tolstoy (see his preface to the story "Black Friday"[2]), the new reader "is the man who has lost his

[2] This preface to "Black Friday" (*Stories*, published by Ateney, Leningrad, 1924) was later deleted and was not included in any of the subsequent collections containing the story. It appeared, however, as a separate article, "About the Reader," in the thirteenth volume of the *Collected Works of Alexey Tolstoy* (Moscow: State Publishing House of Fine Literature [GIKhL], 1949), on page 275, in a somewhat revised version. Interestingly, Tolstoy said in this article that the reason why the writers had not yet succeeded in creating the image of the "new man" was "the fear

old standards and is searching for new ones. . . . He is the man who does not yet know any culture." Therefore the writer's task in relation to this reader, in Tolstoy's view, must consist in guidance—but, of course, skilled and careful guidance. "What we need is a hero of our time. Heroic novels. We should not be afraid of wide gestures and big words." Tolstoy spoke in this article for a literature of "monumental realism."

Zoshchenko, profoundly democratic in his entire outlook, disagreed with this approach. The writer, to him, is not a leader and not an interpreter, but an intermediary who helps the popular masses to become participants in cultural life. This is why, from the very beginning of his literary activity, he expended so much labor in creating a language understandable to the very broadest masses of readers. By this labor Zoshchenko sought to consolidate the victory of these masses in the revolution.

According to Zoshchenko's own classification, he belonged to the "naturalist" school. In his view this school was the "only honest one," to which "the entire future of Russian literature" belonged. These statements held the kernel of the reasons for Zoshchenko's long conflict with the official critics. Armed to the teeth with Marxism-Leninism, they flatly rejected artistic realism. The portrayal of *living man* seemed dangerous to them, for it exposed the insubstantiality of their "hurricane ideology" concerning the "supreme proletariat." And this was probably why they so early began to hound Zoshchenko, classifying him as a member of the host of suspicious Fellow Travelers of the revolution and accusing him of excessive fondness for "petty-bourgeois" subject matter. But, with the intuition of a great artist, Zoshchenko sensed the inherently democratic, *plebeian spirit* of the revolution, and fervently believed in the value of this democratic aspiration of the popular masses.

---

of the grandiose, which originated back in the time of Chekhov and the decadents." Tolstoy himself was not afraid of the grandiose; he was in favor of the "heroic novel."

"The proletarian revolution has brought up to the surface a whole vast layer of new 'indescribable' people. Before the revolution these people lived like walking vegetables. But today—whether they do it poorly or well—they can write and even compose poems. And this is the greatest and most solemn achievement of our epoch. This I have never doubted." (*Letters to the Writer*, 1930.)

Continuing his polemic with the official critics, Zoshchenko wrote in the same *Letters*:

"I distort virtually nothing. I write in the language in which the street speaks and thinks today. I have done this not for the sake of amusement, and not in order to draw a more accurate picture of our life. I have done this in order to fill, at least temporarily, that *enormous breach* which has occurred between literature and the street. . . . And whatever the future destiny of our country, the revision of language in the direction of the easy, popular speech is here to stay. No one will ever again write or speak in that unbearably stilted, 'intellectual' language to which many writers still cling, using it to the very last, as if nothing has happened in our country."

Zoshchenko's language, then, is the product of the artist's effort to create a living bridge to the mass of the "etcetera citizens." And it must be said that these "etcetera citizens" did not remain unresponsive, as is attested by the collection *Letters to the Writer*.

These *Letters* make up one of the most interesting books of the early 1930s. "I have collected the materials in this book," wrote Zoshchenko in the introduction, "to show the real and unvarnished life of real, living people, with their desires, tastes, and ideas." The letters from readers are accompanied by the writer's comments. The correspondents are chiefly workers, employees, and provincial maidens eager to start a "romance" with a famous writer. But there are also letters that are the first timid declarations of budding literary talents. Other letters complain of broken lives. The book truly carries a "breath of life," but a breath that is very different from that which so widely permeates contemporary Soviet fiction.

Youth Recaptured (1933) is a short work reflecting Zoshchenko's preoccupation with his ill-health. The story is accompanied by extensive comments and footnotes. Its plot is simple: the elderly professor of astronomy Volosatov feels daily the inevitable approach of old age. He seems to have reconciled himself to its inevitability, but in reality there is a mounting fear and rebellion against it in his heart.

Zoshchenko's comments on the story are very illuminating. In popular form and in great detail the writer presents the most complex problems of *autotherapy*, to which he has obviously devoted much thought. His personal interest in the material is clear at every step. But at the same time, Zoshchenko does not forget his prime task—literature. The whole development of contemporary fiction, according to his view, is proceeding along the wrong channels: because all of Soviet literature is preoccupied with two or three themes related to the revolution, the people's real life and needs remain outside the field of vision. Hence, many contemporary works remind Zoshchenko of "those drawings of cave dwellers," which depict "a profile with two eyes."

The range of Zoshchenko's topics in the early '30s was very remote from the things that interested the official critics and the upper strata of the newly emerging intelligentsia, technical and general. This intelligentsia, bound by many threads to the Communist Party, went along with the stream of official moods and exerted great influence on the development of literary tastes. For the first time in his literary life Zoshchenko found himself facing a creative crisis. Coiner of the expression which made a whole generation laugh—"inconsonant with the epoch"—he was himself becoming "inconsonant." His *Azure Book* (1935), a collection of stories about human love, failures, and baseness, with excursions into remote history, is weaker than his earlier works. The satirical sting is gone. Bowing politely, à la Chaplin, to "our magnificent reality," the writer adds that such "lamentable incidents" as those he describes are becoming "fewer and fewer."

The reasons for Zoshchenko's inconsonance with the

new epoch are not difficult to guess. It will suffice to recall his article "About Myself, about Critics, and about My Work," in which he wrote: "It is said that an order has gone out for a Red Leo Tolstoy. This order must have been issued by some careless publishing house. The demand of the life, the society, and the entire milieu in which a writer lives today is certainly not for a Red Tolstoy. . . . What is called for today is something in that humble, minor form which—at least in the past—was associated with inferior literary productions. I have contracted to supply this order. . . ."

Alas, this "careless publishing house" which Zoshchenko was ridiculing in 1927 turned out to be more far-sighted than the writer. The "order" of the early 1930s was for broad canvases glorifying the men of the new ruling strata. Zoshchenko's subjects and language did not please the parvenus and "aristocrats" of the Five-Year Plans; they were even slightly shocked by the writer's "vulgarity." For a time, this was not mentioned, but Zoshchenko was the first to sense it, to his keen dismay.

Among his works of the late 1930s and early '40s we may note his comedy *Dangerous Connections* (1940). True to his theme, Zoshchenko exposes in it the stagnant philistinism of men like Ivan Petrovich Bessonov, a petty party functionary. One of the wittiest scenes in the play occurs at Bessonov's birthday party, in which the guests —most of them his subordinates—are treated to an exhibition of snapshots of their chief. "Here, if you please, is Ivan Petrovich as a youth, completing his higher education at the four-year trade school. And here is Ivan Petrovich at the age of three, like Pushkin, in the arms of his nurse. . . ." Amusing, too, are the verses composed in Bessonov's honor by "an insignificant employee who has the good fortune of working under the direction of Ivan Petrovich. . . ." This play, which at first won critical approval, was soon censored. Even the fact that Ivan Petrovich was exposed in the end as "a former agent of the *Okhrana*," the Czarist secret police, was not enough to save the play.

Zoshchenko's "inconsonance," however, was not publicly denounced until the period of the Second World War. In an article on "A Quarter Century of Soviet Literature" (*Novy Mir*, Nos. 11–12, 1942) Alexey Tolstoy, after giving due recognition to Zoshchenko's "sly, clever, delightful prose," wrote: "Only yesterday we still saw Zoshchenko's hero in the kitchens, in the streetcars. Today he no longer exists. History advances with giant steps, and the sting of satire should be aimed today at other phenomena in our life." To Zoshchenko, this was the portent of his imminent end.

Despite the gathering storm, the June–July issue of the magazine *Oktyabr* (1943) still published the beginning of Zoshchenko's long autobiographical work *Before Sunrise*. This work is an attempt to embody in artistic form the ideas and spirit of the generation that received its baptism of battle in the First World War. The background picture of the eve of the revolution of 1917, with its collapse of the front, is brilliantly evoked. There are remarkable descriptions of the abandonment of the front by army units. Here is a tall, gray regimental commander. His cap is in his hands. "His gray side-whiskers fly in the wind. . . . He stands in the field, trying to halt the retreating soldiers. . . . The commander runs up to each man, shouting and pleading. . . ." Remarkable also are the pictures of pre-revolutionary and revolutionary Petersburg, of meeting with Gorky, Zamyatin, Mayakovsky, Blok, and Yesenin.

This work contains further fragments of the author's long and earnest conversation with his time, begun almost twenty years earlier, when Zoshchenko first came to realize that "the old Russia is gone," that he was facing "a new world, a new people, a new speech." The reader also finds many new autobiographical details on the early days when Zoshchenko worked as a census-taker, an agent for the criminal-investigation office, and so on. He had taken the job as census-taker "to see how people live. I believe only my own eyes. Like Haroun al-Rashid, I visit other people's homes. I walk along corridors, kitchens, look into rooms. I see dim lights, torn wallpaper, wash drying on lines, terrible crowding, refuse, rags. Yes, of course, we have just recently emerged from difficult years, hunger, ruin. . . . And yet, I did not expect to see what I did."

Before Sunrise was violently attacked by the critics, and its concluding parts never appeared in the magazine. Especially sharp criticism came from the magazine *Bolshevik* (No. 2, 1944). Nevertheless, Zoshchenko's writings still appeared occasionally in Soviet journals until the end of the war. The *Literary Gazette* of July 13, 1946, even reported that he had been elected a member of the editorial board of the journal *Zvezda*. The resolution of the Central Committee of the Communist Party of August 14, 1946, put an end to Zoshchenko's literary activity. With other writers he was charged with "adulation of the West" and was expelled from the Writers' Union and from literary life—erased as if he had never lived!

The immediate pretext for the attack was Zoshchenko's story "The Adventures of a Monkey." In plot it is a story for children rather than adults, and it first appeared in a children's magazine. Its action takes place during the war. In a certain southern city a bomb hits the zoo. A monkey succeeds in escaping. After a series of amusing misadventures, written in Zoshchenko's early style, the monkey thinks to herself: "Too bad I ran away! Life is so much easier in a cage. I must return to the zoo at the first opportunity." In the end, however, the monkey finds a home with the boy Alyosha Popov. The story ends with the author meeting the monkey. Entering Alyosha's room, the author finds both at the table. The monkey sits "importantly, like a lady cashier in a movie," eating rice with a spoon. Alyosha says: "I brought her up like a human being, and now all the children and even, to some extent, adults may follow her example. . . ."

This simple story provoked the wrath of the Central Committee of the Communist Party! The resolution of August 14, 1946, states: "Zoshchenko's latest published story, 'The Adventures of a Monkey,' is a vulgar lampoon, a repulsive caricature of Soviet life and Soviet people, slanderously showing Soviet people as primitive, uncultured, stupid, with philistine tastes and customs. Zoshchenko's malicious picture of our life is full of anti-Soviet attacks."

There followed a merciless campaign of persecution. In the course of this campaign the late Andrey Zhdanov, secretary of the Central Committee of the Communist Party and supreme authority on problems of literature and art, recalled to Zoshchenko all his past "sins," including *Before Sunrise,* and his statements of the early 1920s, quoted above. After that, Zoshchenko's name disappeared for almost ten years, not only from magazines, but also from textbooks on the history of modern literature.

After Stalin's death Zoshchenko's situation improved slightly. The magazine of humor *Krokodil* opened its pages to him. But it was no longer the old Zoshchenko; it was a man with a broken backbone. And yet, he remained essentially true to the credo he expressed when first entering upon the difficult road of a Russian writer: he remained inwardly independent.

"Many people complain about our writers," Zoshchenko wrote in a *feuilleton,* "Literary Everydays" (*Krokodil,* 1954). "Their writing is dry, they say. And they take such petty, niggling themes for their plump works. Or, still worse, they prettify reality, by who knows what right. . . ." All this is true, says Zoshchenko, "But the writers did not pluck their faults out of the blue, as the saying goes. One should keep in mind all the complexities of our profession, which often lead to these results. . . . Yes, literature is a complex business! Especially so in comparison with other, neighboring professions. . . ."

Anyone who reads these melancholy reflections can easily hear an echo of Zoshchenko's exclamation of more than a quarter of a century ago:

"Oh, my esteemed reader! It is hard to be a Russian writer!"

Zoshchenko died in 1958 from a heart ailment he contracted, as a result of gas poisoning, during the First World

7 ILYA EHRENBURG (1891–)

It may safely be predicted that most of the writers represented in this book by individual literary portraits will retain their place in the history of Russian literature. The future place of Ilya Ehrenburg is not as clear. Today he enjoys great fame as a writer who has participated actively in Soviet literature at its various stages of development. As he himself says in his autobiography (1958), he has always been involved with the "present."

This absorption in the events of the day was particularly evident during World War II. Ehrenburg was fully aware that the works devoted to the war were "not immortal tomes, not marble, but rather wax" (cf. his article "The Word as Weapon," in the magazine *Novy Mir*, January–February 1944). "The great books about the great war," he said, "will come later." But while "the lines written today may be forgotten in a day or a year, that which prompted their writing shall not be forgotten." And yet, much of what Ehrenburg produced, even before the war, is now forgotten. Who remembers such books of his as *The Love of Jeanne Ney*, *The Life and Death of Nikolay Kurbov*, and many others?

Ehrenburg's personal biography is as complex and tortuous as his literary career. He was born in 1891, in a well-to-do Jewish family in Kiev. When he was five, his parents moved to Moscow, where his father managed a beer brewery. The future writer received his secondary education at the Moscow Gymnasium. At first he was an excellent student, but soon, as he wrote in an early autobiography (1928), he "got out of hand," "escaped into the revolutionary movement," and was even arrested. After six months in prison he was released on bail, and left for Paris in 1908. There the young Ehrenburg shared in the enthusiasms prevailing among many of the younger European intellectuals on the eve of World War I. These included medievalism, Catholicism, mysticism, and the works of the famous fifteenth-century French poet François Villon (Ehrenburg translated many of his poems).

The traces of Ehrenburg's many enthusiasms are easily discernible in his first book of verse (*Poems*, Paris, 1910), published when the writer was only nineteen. The poems are not original either in form or content, but they show an undeniable poetic flair. As he wrote recently in his recollections (*People, Years, Life*, 1960), Ehrenburg was drawn to poetry because he understood that "in verse you can say things that cannot be expressed in prose." One rather interesting example of his early verse is a poem about Russia. The poet feels guilt because he fled from Russia, because he had not been able to live by her "holiness"; but he believes that, if his destiny should ever bring him to his homeland:

I shall know how small and poor I am before Thee,
How much I've lost in all these years.
And then perhaps I'll gather up again
What still remains of childhood, of my own,
And give Thee what is left of former powers,
What by some chance was hidden and preserved.

The war of 1914 put an end to Ehrenburg's restless spiritual quest. He became a war correspondent for the large Petersburg newspaper *Birzhevye Vedomosti* (Stock Exchange News). When the revolution broke out, he was irresistibly drawn back home and returned to Russia in July 1917, during the days of the first Bolshevik attempt to seize power. But he was not at that time with the Bolsheviks; nor was he with them after the October coup. It is scarcely necessary to dwell at length on his well-known "Prayer for Russia" (1917), which was copied and circulated from hand to hand, and which he later repudiated. The character of this "Prayer" was such that the Whites published it in Kiev during the Civil War. He rejected the "Prayer," but it is difficult to ignore the fact that recantations have always come somewhat too easily to Ehrenburg.

After wandering over the land, torn by Civil War, Ehrenburg arrived in Moscow from Georgia in late 1920 or early 1921. But he stayed there very briefly, leaving again soon for his beloved Paris, where he began his first novel, *The Extraordinary Adventures of Julio Jurenito and His Disciples* (1922). In his first autobiography (1928) Ehrenburg confesses that this was his "only book in earnest." In *Julio Jurenito*, he says further, "neither the critics, nor the readers, nor I myself can determine exactly where the wry grin ends."

The initially reserved or even negative response to the October revolution was not limited to Ehrenburg alone. It was characteristic of a large number of young writers who had begun to write on the eve of World War I. Ehrenburg, however, was the first to discern the *national* elements in the revolution. As early as 1920, living in the Crimea, which was then under White occupation, Ehrenburg wrote in a poem dedicated to Russia and the revolution that those who saw death in Russia's "delirium of travail" were wrong. The writer's favorite hero, Julio in *Julio Jurenito*, echoes this idea: "No, Russia is not dying. Her banners are imperial scarlet, and, with her thousand hands, she is laying the foundations of a new world."

The novel's action unfolds in Paris, Mexico, Rome, Moscow, and the provincial Russian town of Kineshma, during the war and the early years of the revolution. Julio Jurenito is a Mexican and, in the author's conception, a Mephistophelian character. But he might, perhaps, more properly be regarded as a representative of the international artistic Bohemia that is found in all the capitals of the world. Ehrenburg himself appears in the novel as one of the seven disciples of Julio, who has come into the world in order to destroy it by his own powers. Julio, "The Teacher," "indigent and great, did not possess even the ordinary man's meager capital: he was a man without convictions." The hidden paradox of the book is that this Teacher, who flaunts his lack of convictions, is in reality fanatically in love with the future, while his disciple, Ehrenburg, who pretends devoted allegiance to his Teacher, believes in nothing and proudly parades the philosophy of a renegade.

Enamored of the idea of destroying the old world, Julio welcomes the world war "as the first day of typhoid fever, from which a man will either come out regenerated, or will die." In the same spirit he welcomes the Russian revolution. The ideas about the revolution are, in fact, the most interesting element in the book. Underneath the chaff of the anecdotes and absurdities, the book contains a number of serious appraisals and prognoses. Julio is convinced that the outbreak of the revolution has initiated a period when the land must go through "the blackest, the sweatiest purgatory." Finding himself in the Cheka, Julio lectures the Chekists: "You have a great and difficult mission—to train man to such an acceptance of shackles that he will come to think of them as the tender embraces of his mother. . . . You must create a new mystique for a new slavery."

With this appraisal of the implacable tasks of the national revolution, neither Julio himself nor his disciple Ehrenburg are especially tempted to take part in its work. Julio is murdered in the street by thieves who take his boots, and Ehrenburg, his disciple and creator, leaves Moscow in 1921 for the cafés of Paris.

Julio Jurenito is still interesting, not only as testimony of the moods of a certain portion of the young Russian intelligentsia of the early revolutionary period, but also as an aid to the understanding of Ehrenburg the writer. In the preface to his book of poems *Eves* (*Kanuny*, 1915–21, Berlin, 1921), Ehrenburg anticipated the reader's reproach for his "inner dissonance" by openly admitting that, "like all the children of our fateful age," he had "two faces, two loves, two sorrows." This self-characterization is helpful in understanding Ehrenburg; the unsuccessful effort to overcome this duality runs through *Julio Jurenito* and through a number of subsequent works. In a certain sense Ehrenburg's books are not novels in the old meaning of the word, but lyrical reportage about the writer's time.

It was Ehrenburg's fundamental approach to the October revolution as a national revolution and his acute sense of being *déclassé* that gave birth to the sudden "left-ness" that marks almost all of his works of the NEP period. The writer's own sense of being *déclassé* seeks and finds expression in *déclassé* heroes. The Chekist Nikolay Kurbov (*The Life and Death of Nikolay Kurbov*, 1923) is the son of a "saintly" prostitute; Mikhail Lykov (*The Grabber*, [*Rvach*] 1926) is the son of a waiter; Sakharov (*Protochny Lane*, 1927) is *déclassé* through his marriage to an aristocrat. Of course, the prototypes of these characters existed in reality; wounded from childhood by their social "alienation," they frequently "escaped into the revolution." But Ehrenburg's tendency to overcrowd his works with such misfits lends his books an unhealthy, feverish glow and seems to verge on affectation, making the reader somewhat wary of the writer's observations and appraisals. Thus, for example, Nikolay Kurbov, an entirely unconvincing character, is interesting only as the first attempt in Soviet literature to create the image of the "saintly Chekist."

More convincingly motivated is Mikhail Lykov, whom the author invested with some features of his own childhood. Muddled, unstable, enamored of success, with eyes that are "deep, almost angelic in their sorrowful goodness" and hands that at times seem touching in their helplessness and "inertness," and at other times become "strong, prehensile, and desperate," Mikhail starts with sincere enthusiasm for the revolution, then plunges into speculation and ends his days in prison. Yet, Ehrenburg is fond of him until his last breath: "We love our hero. Let us, too, be judged for this."

Ehrenburg is also fond of Olga, Mikhail's wife. While he lent Mikhail certain incidents from his own childhood, he gave Olga a number of details of his own life abroad. Olga is the daughter of the owner of a match factory; the revolution has not only taken her wealth; it has freed her of the need for spiritual questing—of "aestheticism, urbanism, Catholicism, Nietzscheanism, Montparnasse, Sicily," and so on. Now she is "carried away" by the revolution. "Sympathy with the revolution has become her current camping ground. And the revolution attracted Olga precisely because it had no room for her."

More important than these central figures is the background of the novel. Ehrenburg's observations are keen, with a trace of ironic melancholy. And he is right when he says that "neither Wells, nor any other known writer of utopian novels has ever invented anything more unreal than the life of any Russian city" during the revolution. "As in the best of utopias, everyone lived by rations and endurance.... Sometimes the Cheka arrested men born without a shirt for speculation in benzine or kinship with a Left Socialist-Revolutionary. The Cheka shot people. But the Chekists called their prisoners 'Comrade.'" It was "an astonishing time, and what we want to do now, looking back upon it, is not to laugh, but to honor its magnificent absurdity." The pages of *The Grabber* abound in such lyrico-political digressions, glorifying the harsh, hungry days of the revolution when people lived and breathed "catastrophically," showing unexpected heroism, frequently studying, greedily and chaotically, and, of course, starving.

In *The Stormy Life of Lazik Roitschwantz* (1928) Ehrenburg painted a picture of this "magnificent absurdity" as seen through the eyes of a meek little "gentlemen's tailor" from Gomel. This tailor is able to discern in Soviet reality both the arrogance of those in power, and the shocking abrogation of rights and justice for the individual. Lazik is the Soviet Soldier Schweik. He knows that "when history stalks the streets, the ordinary man has nothing left to do but die with total ecstasy in his eyes." He attempts to protest against such a "Chinese two-times-two," but his timid efforts lead only to failures and imprisonment. Unable to transform his heart into "a thundering speech," Lazik wanders from city to city, from prison to prison, from country to country in search of the small but eternal truth—man's right to happiness—and ultimately comes to the conclusion that happiness is "only an antiquated word in a mighty language."

It is significant that Ehrenburg not only tends to choose

his heroes from among the *déclassé*, but that these *déclassé* are frequently the carriers of genuine social truth. In *Protochny Lane* (1927), a novel that depicts the lower depths of the NEP period, the bearers of social truth are the former Latin teacher who has become a beggar, the little Jewish musician Yuzik, and the homeless waifs. They all wander the dark byways of life, where "only the snow creaks underfoot, the snow of fields and steppes, reminding the heart how great our land is, how rich, how poor, and how terrible."

The basic idea of the novel is that the revolution is over, and the upper hand has been won not by anything new that came out of it, but by the old, brutal right of the strong, the right of the former merchant Pankratov, who knows that "the policeman on the corner of Protochny Lane is not standing guard over the world revolution. . . . He is standing guard over the ten bundles of rubles" which he, Pankratov, has accumulated by selling groceries in the Smolensky market. In this new life that is now entrenching itself, there is no trace of the things of which Olga had dreamed in the novel *The Grabber*. The country is now likened to a gang of homeless children:

"And it seems to me it is our own Russia walking there —just as childish and homeless, dreamy and embittered, without a corner of her own, without anyone to give her love or care, an infant country, but one that has already experienced everything—walking . . . down a parched empty road, amid other people's fields, other people's wealth. . . . And the heart goes numb, and does not dare to ask: will she reach it, will she reach her goal?"

The picture of the October revolution as it was synthesized by Ehrenburg's creative vision out of his immediate impressions of the early revolutionary years was shaken by the realities of the NEP period. Seeing the triumph of the "old" amid the ruins of heroic yesterdays, Ehrenburg nostalgically gave himself up to tenderly ironic reminiscences of the "magnificent absurdity" of the first years. The official critics dealt harshly with him for this "weakness."

They barely tolerated his patronizing affection for the days of War Communism, but his revelation of the "renascence" of the manners and customs of the old regime was entirely unforgivable.

Constant critical attacks compelled Ehrenburg, as they did many other Fellow Travelers, to abandon contemporary themes. Ehrenburg could do this easily, since he had already written historical fiction (the stories in *Thirteen Pipes*) and novels of adventure. At this moment of crisis he turned once more to historical subjects, producing the novel *The Conspiracy of Equals* (1928), devoted to Babeuf. Into this story of the French revolution, Ehrenburg transposed the atmosphere of another great revolution in its expiring days. His intimate contemporary knowledge helped the writer to reveal in simple and moving words the tragic solitude of Babeuf, the Left-wing revolutionary, amid the weariness and indifference of the Paris of his time.

It is difficult to assess the direction that Ehrenburg's political and artistic development might have taken. His lively sympathy with Babeuf might well have led him into the camp of the Left Opposition. He was saved by the new world crisis which began in Europe and America in 1929, and by the first Five-Year Plan in the Soviet Union. Ehrenburg summed up the hopelessness of the crisis in the destinies of a group of residents of Mont Blanc, a small Paris hotel, with its tiny musty rooms, and its water closet —"ancient and brutal like the human conscience," in which life "stinks without shame" (*Moscow Does Not Believe in Tears*, 1930). The only vital and optimistic person in this hotel is the Russian artist Mey. The secret of his optimism is his feeling that he has behind him a large, young country lying outside the sphere of the deadly crisis. The novel concludes with his departure for Russia.

Since the end of the 1920s, this theme of the final and hopeless crisis of the West has been assiduously preached by Ehrenburg the publicist (*White Coal, or the Tears of Werther*, 1928; *Ten Horsepower*, 1929; and other works). He has thus been squarely in the mainstream of that Left-wing European fellow-traveling intelligentsia whose radicalism is confined to the painting of constant gloomy images of a dying Europe and eulogizing the Soviet Union and its economic achievements.

In fiction Ehrenburg's acceptance of the policy of Five-Year Plans and the official line of the Soviet government found expression in two novels, *The Second Day* (1932) and *Without Pausing for a Breath* (1935). The former deals with the construction projects in the Kuznetsk Basin. Ehrenburg, who lived in Paris, came to the Soviet Union for a visit to collect material for his novel. *The Second Day* contains more reportage than the writer's other novels, especially in its background picture of the construction work. Amid the cold and hunger of a remote Siberian wasteland, a vast construction project is being launched by human will. Animals retreat before the bitter climate; even rats cannot endure the grim conditions. Only insects "remain true" to man. "They went along with him underground, where the coal seams glimmered faintly. They went with him into the taiga. Lice marched in dense hordes, fleas galloped, slow businesslike bedbugs crawled along." But the people endured: "They knew how to live in silence." Much later, in 1958, Ehrenburg wrote in his autobiography that, working on this novel, he came to realize "the necessity for truth in art," adding in elucidation: "Truth is frightening only to the decrepit old; and if it sometimes frightens adolescents, that is mostly because of their insufficient understanding."

Among the many lesser characters sketched in the novel, several claim particular attention. They are the director of the project, the Bolshevik Shor, and the foreign experts who marvel at "the enthusiasm, the lice, and the frosts." The foreigners live apart from the rest of the construction personnel; they have their own housing, they eat in separate dining rooms, and their salaries are paid in dollars. The central figures in the novel are the shock worker Kolka Rzhanov, who starts as a backward, ignorant country lad and wins local fame for his high output, and his antithesis, the student Volodya Safonov, a young man of intellectual parentage who is presented as the negative hero.

Ehrenburg's ideological reorientation had brought about a change of attitude toward the "negative hero" as well. Formerly, Ehrenburg preferred Mikhail Lykov to his "Correct" brother Artemy; he was fond of the shiftless musician Yuzik and the other "superfluous people" who found no place in the revolution. But now he treats Volodya Safonov like a disliked stepson; he fears Volodya, and it seems at times that the thing he fears in him is his own former voice and self. Unable to reply convincingly to Safonov's criticism, Ehrenburg hastens to blacken him morally. Safonov is outraged most of all by the enforced *conformism*, the standardized falsehoods, the official optimism and obligatory "enthusiasm" which are imposed upon the people. "Of course," Volodya agrees, "the Kuznetsk plant is a miracle of technology, and so on, and so forth. But it is being built as the pyramids were. They have driven a herd of peasants to the site and settled down to rest on their laurels: the peasant will do his job. There are excavators, derricks, graders, but the peasant carries the earth on his own back. He mixes the clay by treading it with his own feet. On the one hand, we have Morgan cranes, and on the other, not even Peter the Great, but the Russia of pre-Petrine days. And yet it could be done differently too." To Kolka Rzhanov these arguments are profoundly alien. He is even prepared to agree that the project might have been constructed differently, but then it would have been built without him, by the forces of capitalism.

Safonov dreams of standing up at a meeting one day and saying publicly all that he thinks: "Some people are silent because you have intimidated them; others, because you have bought them. Simple truths demand affirmation. As in the days of Galileo, they can be uttered only from a bonfire. You want to discuss the problem of culture. But it is unlikely that any of you understand what culture is. You have eliminated all the heretics, dreamers, philosophers, and poets. You have established universal literacy, and equally universal ignorance." Dreaming of this speech,

Safonov even becomes "more animated and younger-looking." But when he gets the floor at the meeting, he loses his nerve. In the end he commits suicide.

The second novel of this period, *Without Pausing for a Breath*, contains nothing essentially new. After its publication Ehrenburg seemed to become subdued, and wrote no fiction of any length for several years. He did write two books about Spain; the second, dealing with the Spanish Civil War, appeared in 1937. The latter 1930s were a period of the "great purge" and the subsequent triumph of conformism, brought to its ultimate degree and particularly dangerous to people of Ehrenburg's psychological make-up. Ehrenburg successfully weathered these dangers while living in Paris, until the Second World War opened before him new opportunities to expand.

In Ehrenburg's life the Second World War, especially after Hitler's invasion of the Soviet Union, was a period of extremely fertile literary activity in many forms. In 1940 he returned to live in the Soviet Union, where he soon wrote his novel *The Fall of Paris*. The first part of the novel had already appeared in the magazine *Znamya* when Hitler attacked the Soviet Union. Ehrenburg quickly shifted positions and transformed the French Communists, who had asserted in the early pages of the novel that this "is not our war," into virtually the only genuine French patriots. Nevertheless, there is something in the novel that leaves a lasting impression. This "something" is Ehrenburg's sense of history: the nineteenth century, he says, ended throughout the world with the outbreak of the First World War; it "died a timely death," and only in France, and particularly in Paris, "it overstayed its day." As one of the characters in the novel explains, "in our country generally the old are in no hurry to die." The occupation of Paris in 1940, and the entire situation under which it took place, signaled the end of nineteenth-century France. But at the moment when he realized this, Ehrenburg, the skeptic dabbling in radicalism, was moved momentarily by sincere regret for the old, dying France: "Like the knick-knacks on the table of one newly dead, the monuments of Paris moved one to tears. Its poets clutched their silent lyres. Its marshals galloped on dead horses. Its bronze orators conversed with the pigeons." Men recalled their city's past. But Paris lay "like a patient on the operating table, no longer capable of throwing off the chloroform mask."

Ehrenburg gained great prominence during the war as a publicist. He wrote widely for newspapers, and in 1943 his articles were collected in a book, *The War* (April 1942– March 1943). Of his numerous articles of that period it is important to mention "We and Europe." In it he wrote: "But we never drew any line between European culture and ours. We are linked with Europe not by rails or wires, but by our very bloodstream and the convolutions of our brains. We have been both the diligent pupils and the teachers of Europe. . . . Throughout the last century the leading minds of Russia shared Europe's passions, hopes, and griefs. They brought into the European consciousness Russia's passionate temperament, her truthfulness and humanity. . . . We do not look at Europe's tragedy from the sidelines. . . ."

The sincerity of these lines is beyond question. But we must also note, not only that such feelings were attacked by many official Soviet journalists, especially after the war, but that Ehrenburg himself was often disloyal to them.

More sparingly, but with greater conviction, Ehrenburg came forward again at the end of the war as a poet. Poetry occupies a special place in Ehrenburg's literary biography: he turns to it when he tires of his own grandiloquence. Characteristic among the poems he published soon after the end of the war (*Novy Mir*, October 1945) is the one dedicated to Paris. As if replying to the words of an unknown friend, the poet writes:

> With jealousy and with reproach
> You say I've fallen silent. . . .

But, almost apologetically, he speaks of his continuing love for Paris, which he likens to a "forest of stone":

Forgive that I lived in that forest,
That I experienced everything, and yet survived,
That I will carry to my dying day
The looming Paris twilight.

But on the whole, the poems deal with the theme of victory. In his autobiography of 1958 Ehrenburg admits that "the victory has turned out differently from what we dreamed of in dugouts and shelters." In a poem dedicated to victory the poet speaks of meeting her: "We did not recognize each other." She wore a "faded tunic" and knocked at the house where a mother waited for a son killed in the war. While the hundred capitals of the world were loudly applauding victory, "in a quiet Russian town two women kept a solemn silent vigil. . . ."

Of Ehrenburg's postwar works written before Stalin's death, two must be mentioned: they are his novels *The Storm* (1947) and *The Ninth Wave* (1951–52). When he began the serial publication of the latter, Ehrenburg wrote that these two novels were parts of a trilogy which began with *The Fall of Paris*.

The Storm is a summing up of Ehrenburg's impressions of World War II. Its action begins in Paris and is later carried into the Soviet Union. The opening chapters, describing the Paris of 1938–39, have many elements in common with *The Fall of Paris*: the "atmosphere" of Paris is the same in both, as is the underlying feeling of doom. This feeling is expressed most deeply by the uncrowned king of France—the financier Desser. He is convinced that the "climate" of the world has changed and that nothing can save the old-fashioned provincial France, "with its anglers, village dances, and Radical Socialists." The same feeling is voiced in *The Storm* by the Soviet engineer Sergey Vlakhov, who comes to Paris on an official mission at the end of 1938. Sergey, the son of old *émigrés* who left Russia before the First World War, was born in Paris, but returned with his parents to Russia soon after the beginning of the revolution. Coming back to Paris as an adult, Sergey feels that the city casts a spell upon him. He falls in love with the wan, mysterious Seine, the cool narrow streets.

But *The Storm* also contains some new notes: in *The Fall of Paris* Ehrenburg was silent about the reaction of the various French social circles to the Soviet-German pact of 1939. When he was writing *The Storm*, a spurious official myth was already firmly established, and Ehrenburg manipulated his picture of events to fit the myth: naturally, "the bourgeois and philistines" are indignant over "Moscow's betrayal," as is the manufacturer Lancier, whose daughter Madeau loves Sergey and longs to go to Russia. She hastens to the Communist sympathizer Lejean to speak to him of her anxiety. For a moment, he too was shaken by the pact, but he has rapidly oriented himself to the "situation" and now explains to Madeau: "Our Russian comrades have done the right thing—they are gathering strength. If Moscow holds out, France will also live." But generally, he intimates that the pact is a payment "for the sins of others"—"for Munich."

Another feature of *The Storm* is its continual stressing of the idea that a wide gulf separates Soviet life from life abroad. These are "two worlds" which have no common language. This idea is illustrated in the destinies of the Alper family. The tailor Naum Alper, a native of Kiev, has long dreamed of emigrating abroad. Shortly before the war of 1914 he realizes his dream. He goes to France and settles in Paris with his older son, Leo; his wife and younger boy, Osya, temporarily remain in Kiev. The outbreak of war prevents their departure. Naum Alper is killed in the war (he enlisted in the French army); Leo makes his way in the world, becoming an engineer. Shortly before World War II he succeeds in visiting the Soviet Union and searching out his relatives. Osya has become a Communist and treats Leo as if the latter were a Rothschild or a Deterding.

All the positive and negative qualities of Ehrenburg's work may also be found in the third part of his trilogy, *The Ninth Wave*. This novel is linked with *The Storm* by the presence of many of the same characters, but most of them are there merely to serve as mouthpieces for the author's ideas. The artist Samba, whom the reader knows from *The Fall of Paris*, is worth mentioning here. During the war and the first two postwar years Samba painted a number of Paris landscapes. One of his friends, examining his works, tells Samba: "How strange, you have virtually no people here, and yet I see the Paris of those August days. . . ." This remark may in a sense apply to Ehrenburg's novel as well. It often seems that all its journalistic welter is used by the writer merely as a pretext for returning in imagination to the old Paris which has been his lifelong love.

Among the new notes sounded in *The Ninth Wave* is its clearly expressed anti-Americanism, which infects most of its French characters. The keenly observant Ehrenburg was one of the first writers to discern the anti-American feelings which were just then emerging in many European countries.

As a literary work, the trilogy is one of Ehrenburg's artistic failures, and it is not by chance that it lacks a unifying title. The novels are unified only by the feeling that the old world is ending—a feeling first voiced by the writer in *Julio Jurenito* almost forty years ago. The sense of the old world's doom has haunted Ehrenburg throughout most of his life, although at different stages of his literary biography it was given different expression. Its clearest statement may be found in the collection of essays *White Coal, or the Tears of Werther*, which the author prefaced with the remarkable lines from Osip Mandelstam's poem "Tristia": "Those who have hearts must hear, Time, how thy ship is going down."

However, the "new world" did not turn out to be as new as the young dreamers of the great "eves" had expected. And although he was slow to see it, Ehrenburg, too, had finally come to face this truth. Hence the role he assumed soon after Stalin's death, taking up the defense of creative freedom in his article "About the Writer's Work" (*Znamya*, October 1953). This new direction found its sensational continuation in the novel *The Thaw* (*Znamya*,

April 1954) and its sequel *The Spring* (*Znamya*, April 1956).

Late, in "the deep autumn of his life," Ehrenburg has found strength to face many of the fatal errors of his earlier literary activity. Perhaps he has not said all that he might have, and has not spoken with the full voice of his talent, but on many occasions during the post-Stalin years Ehrenburg has championed creative freedom. During this period Ehrenburg has for the first time in his life taken up a position not only as an individual writer, but as a man exerting an influence on the formation of social moods among the literary milieu, and thus affecting in some measure the development of literature as a whole. This will be treated in greater detail in the chapter on "Literary Developments: World War II and After: 1939–62." Now we shall limit ourselves to mentioning Ehrenburg's brilliant essay "The Lessons of Stendhal" (in the magazine *Foreign Literature*, June 1957). In this essay the writer confesses that for him these "lessons" are contained above all in Stendhal's "absolute veracity": "This is perhaps the most important thing to us—not only to writers, but to all men of mid-twentieth century: the more passionate the attractions and revulsions of our time, the more insistently our conscience and our reason demand the truth."

8 ISAAC BABEL (1894–1941)

Isaac Babel, one of the most brilliant pioneers of Soviet Russian literature, was hounded by tragedy both in his personal and his literary life. During the 1920s he was eulogized as one of the most talented young writers; during the '30s his work appeared more and more infrequently in the literary journals. In 1939 he was arrested, and until 1956 his very name disappeared from even textbooks on the history of Soviet literature. It was not until 1957 that the reader learned (from the preface to his *Selected Works*), that Babel had died in 1941.[1]

Three of Babel's achievements assure him a firm place in the history of the new Russian literature. He was the first writer to discern in the scattered episodes of the Civil War the elemental surge of an essentially peasant revolution, in which exalted moral fervor existed side by side with unsurpassed brutality, and to embody his vision in unforgettable images. He was the author of the never completed epic cycle dealing with the adventures of the Odessa gangster, the "King" of the Moldavanka, Benya Krik, that Russian-Jewish version of the legendary twelfth-century English robber, Robin Hood, the terror of the rich and benefactor of the poor. Finally, Babel was the originator and great master of the miniature short story, or "novella," which became so popular during the early years of the revolution.

From the autobiography written by Babel for the collection of literary self-portraits, *Writers* (1926), the

[1] The arrest of Babel is mentioned by Ehrenburg, and A. A. Surkov in the new edition of the *Shorter Literary Encyclopedia* (Moscow: 1962), vol. I, p. 388. Surkov writes: "In 1937, Babel was illegally repressed [This is incorrect, according to Ehrenburg and other sources: Babel was repressed in 1939.—V.A.] He was rehabilitated posthumously."

reader learns that he was born in Odessa in 1894, in the family of a petty Jewish merchant in the Moldavanka district. Until the age of sixteen he diligently studied the Bible and the Talmud. His only hours of rest were at school. He attended the commercial high school, "a jolly, undisciplined, noisy, and multilingual institution" with a student body consisting of "children of Jewish brokers, titled Poles, Old Believers, and a number of overgrown billiard players," that is, young men with little interest in study and great devotion to billiards. During recess the students liked to run off to the harbor, to see the frequently arriving ships from distant places which teased the imagination—from Newcastle, Cardiff, Marseilles, and Port Said. Or else these students would take refuge in the coffeehouses of the Moldavanka (which later came to play such an important part in Babel's stories); there they drank cheap Bessarabian wine and amused themselves with games of billiards.

The school left a profound impression in the writer's memory, thanks especially to its French teacher, a Monsieur Vadon, a native of Brittany and a man of some literary talent. Under his tutelage the young Babel learned French so well that at the age of fifteen he began to write stories in that language. "My characters and my own comments and reflections," writes Babel in his autobiography, "turned out flat and colorless. I succeeded only with the dialogue" (indeed, Babel's brilliant mastery of dialogue was one of the most remarkable features of his talent).

In 1915 the young Babel went to Petersburg, where he endured great hardships. As a Jew without a permit to reside in the capital, he was obliged to hide from the police and found shelter with a drunken waiter. He resumed his writing, now in Russian, and tried to sell his stories to various magazines. No editors accepted them, and Babel finally brought them to *Letopis*, a magazine published by Gorky. Gorky was the first writer to recognize the young man's talent, and accepted two of his stories, "Mamma, Rimma, and Alla" and "Ilya Isaakovich and Margarita Prokofievna." The former is an immature work.

It deals with the Moscow family of a circuit judge who is working in Kamchatka. The mother and the two daughters, one eighteen years old, the other seventeen, live on the edge of poverty and rent out rooms to students. The mother finds herself deeper and deeper in debt, and the girls become involved in rather primitive affairs with the students. The story shows some sparks of Babel's talents, but the author is insufficiently familiar with the life he attempts to describe. But in the second story, "Ilya Isaakovich and Margarita Prokofievna," we clearly see the future master.

Ilya Isaakovich, the hero of the story, is a petty Jewish merchant from Odessa who comes to Oryol on business. He has no residence permit for this city, which is outside the Pale of Jewish Settlement; he is summoned by the police and ordered to leave at once under threat of deportation with a police escort. But his business demands that he remain in Oryol for a day or two. In the street he is hailed by an aging prostitute and, after settling on the price, he goes to her for the night. The next evening Ilya Isaakovich comes again, bringing some food for supper. They converse quietly as any two people who have met by chance and tell each other, in a friendly yet somehow epic manner, about their troubles.

After supper he sits down at a corner table to write business letters. Margarita washes her hair, and the room is pervaded by an atmosphere of domesticity (the writer does not say this, but the reader feels it). On the following day Ilya Isaakovich leaves Oryol. Unexpectedly, Margarita comes to see him off at the station, bringing a few homemade pastries. "Good-by, Ilya Isaakovich." "Good-by, Margarita Prokofievna." And this is all. The entire story is only four short pages!

In "The Beginning" (first published in 1938) Babel describes his first impressions of Gorky. The reception hours at the editorial office of *Letopis* began at six o'clock in the evening. Exactly at six the door opened and Gorky entered the room. Babel was struck by "his height, his leanness, the strength and size of his huge frame, the intense blue of his small, firm eyes, and the foreign suit which fitted him somewhat loosely but elegantly."

The visitors consisted of two groups: those who had previously submitted their manuscripts and now came for an answer, and those who were just bringing their works. This was on a Tuesday, and Gorky asked Babel to return for a reply on Friday. The speed with which his stories were to be considered astonished the young writer. He was even more astonished when he came back on Friday. Gorky did not call him until he had spoken to everyone else, and then invited him into his office. The words which the older writer addressed to the young man decided Babel's fate:

" 'There are small nails,' said Gorky, 'and there are large ones, as large as my finger.' And he raised to my eyes a long, powerful and delicately modeled finger. 'A writer's path is studded with nails, mostly of the large variety. You will have to walk on them barefoot, and you will bleed profusely, more profusely every year. . . . If you are weak, you will be bought and sold, you will be shaken and harassed and put to sleep, and you will wilt away, pretending that you are a tree in bloom. . . . But for an honest man, for an honest writer and revolutionary, traveling along this road is a great honor; to which arduous undertaking, my dear sir, I now bless you. . . .' "

It is unlikely that either Gorky or Babel suspected at that moment how prophetic this description of a writer's path would prove to be in Babel's case. Nevertheless, the young writer was sufficiently impressed by the significance of this initiation into the ranks of Russian literature. It was not by chance that he wrote that "the hours I spent at the editorial offices of *Letopis* were among the most important in my life."

After the interview Babel "completely lost the physical sensation" of his own being. In a thirty-degree frost he "ran deliriously through the vast corridors of the capital." He did not return to the room he had just rented at the home of a young engineer until late at night.

Babel's autobiographical "Story of My Dovecote," is dedicated to Gorky. As a child, the little Babel dreamed of owning pigeons, and his father had promised to buy him some if he passed the entrance examinations at the *gimnaziya*. "I was only nine," relates Babel, "and I was afraid of the examinations. In both subjects, Russian and arithmetic, I had to win top marks. The quota at the school was very stiff—only five per cent. Out of forty boys, only two Jews would be admitted to the preparatory grade. The teachers examined us cunningly; no one else was asked such confusing questions. Therefore, when my father promised to buy me pigeons, he demanded marks of five plus in the two subjects. He tormented me until I sank into an endless waking nightmare, a long childish dream of despair. I went to the examinations in this state of nightmare, and yet I passed better than anyone else. . . ."

After Gorky had approved his first literary efforts, Babel began to write almost a story a day, but Gorky rejected all his work and finally pronounced a stern verdict: "It is obvious, my dear sir, that you have no proper knowledge of anything, although you guess at much. . . . Therefore, you must go among the people."

This "assignment" lasted seven years. During that time, says Babel, "I traveled many roads and witnessed many battles. Seven years later, after I was demobilized, I made another effort to publish my work and received a note from him (Gorky): 'You may now begin.'"

Babel concluded his account of Gorky's role in his literary development with a characterization of his teacher: "He was possessed by an unrelenting, boundless, inexhaustible passion for human creativity. He suffered when a person from whom he had expected much proved to be sterile. And he rubbed his hands and winked happily at the world, the sky, and the earth when a spark flared into flame. . . ."

"The Letter," the first story in the future series to be known as *Red Cavalry*, appeared in the *Izvestia of the Odessa Province Executive Committee* in February 1923. It is so typical of Babel's entire manner of writing that it deserves closer attention. The story is told in the name of the author, who is asked by a Red Army soldier, Vasily Kurdyukov, to write a letter to his mother for him. The first part of the letter consists of the traditional greetings to all the village relatives, godparents, and kinsmen. This is followed by a request that his mother kill the speckled hog and send a parcel to him, at "Comrade Budenny's Political Section," for he suffers greatly without sufficient food and warm clothing: "Every day I lie down to rest without eating and without any clothing, so that it's mighty cold." He also reports to his mother that his unit is at the moment in poor country, that the peasants are hiding out in the woods with their horses from the "Red eagles," that there is not much wheat in the region, and what there is "is scrawny, and we laugh at it."

In the second part of the letter the son describes to his mother how his father, who had been a policeman before the revolution and who fought on the side of the Whites, had killed his son Fyodor, captured in battle. Vasily himself had not witnessed it, but was told about it by men who had: the father kept cutting away at his son until dark, repeating, "brute, Red dog, son of a bitch." Vasily and his other brother, Semyon, had both decided to avenge Fyodor's death. It had been difficult to catch the father, who had dyed his red beard black and had gone into hiding in the city of Maykop. But their kinsman Nikon Vasilyich had met him by chance and revealed his hiding place to Semyon. Vasily and Semyon then caught their father by surprise in Maykop. Vasily describes in detail how the sons avenged themselves upon the father for Fyodor's death.

After the letter is written, Vasily shows the author a family photograph: in the foreground, says Babel, sat the father, "a broad-shouldered village policeman in a uniform cap. . . . Next to him, in a little bamboo armchair, was a tiny peasant woman in a loose jacket, with a thin, faded, timid face." And against the wall, against the provincial photographer's background landscape, with its inevitable doves and flowers, towered two village lads, "broad-faced, goggle-eyed, standing petrified as on parade—the brothers Fyodor and Semyon Kurdyukov."

The close proximity of kindness and brutality at the height of the revolutionary tide of unleashed passions is shown in such stories as "Salt," "My First Goose," and "The Two Ivans." "Salt," only a few pages long, is also in the form of a letter; this letter is written to a newspaper editor by Nikita Balmashov, "a soldier of the revolution." He describes an outrageous incident which occurred near the Fastov Railway Station. Balmashov's platoon was in a hurry to get to Berdichev, but in Fastov the train was delayed by hordes of black marketeers who swarmed all over the cars, hanging on to the hand rails and climbing onto the roofs. The soldiers scramble out of the freight cars to help the station officials to disperse the black marketeers. A woman with an infant in her arms approaches Balmashov's car. She is traveling to join her husband, she says, and begs to be allowed into the car. Balmashov consults the other men of his platoon, and the soldiers agree to let her in, hinting that after them she "wouldn't want her husband any more." "'No,' I say to the fellows quite civilly," writes Balmashov, "'all my respect to you, men of the platoon, but I'm surprised to hear such coarseness from you. Remember your own lives, men, and how you were babies in your mothers' arms, and then you'll see it isn't right to speak like this.'" The Cossacks talk it over among themselves and, repenting their intentions, settle the woman comfortably in a quiet corner of the car.

By morning, however, the men notice that Balmashov is "sorely troubled." He finally approaches the woman, picks up her "infant," tears off its swaddling clothes, and discovers that it is not a baby, but a bag of salt. The woman begs forgiveness, but Balmashov replies that, for his own part, he could forgive her easily enough, but what of the two other women who were raped in the car during the night while she was spared? What of Russia, crushed with misery? And in a burst of anger he pushes the woman from the car while the train is in full motion. Then, seeing her getting up to her feet, he takes a rifle from the wall and wipes "this blot from the face of the workers' land of the republic."

The bearers of true humanity in these stories are often the peaceful residents of the small towns engulfed in the tide of civil war. In the story "Gedali" the little owner of a shop in the Zhitomir market revives the memory of Dickens. In his shop one may find gilt slippers, ship's cables, an ancient compass, a stuffed eagle, and a broken saucepan. . . . On Sabbath Eve, Gedali prepares to go to the synagogue. The author comes into the shop when the proprietor is about to close up and launches into a long discussion with him. Gedali is by no means opposed to the revolution; with his whole being he longs for the moral renewal of the world. But God, the things that go on all around! First the Poles were masters of the town and oppressed the peaceful inhabitants, then the Reds liberated the town. And then one of the liberators came to Gedali's shop and demanded his phonograph. When Gedali objected, the soldier threatened to shoot him, asserting that he was "the revolution." "The Pole shot us, my kind sir," Gedali answered, "because he is the counterrevolution. You shoot us because you are the revolution. . . . Good deeds are done by good men. The revolution is the good deed of good men. But good men don't kill."

Before he leaves for the synagogue Gedali begs his visitor: "Mister Comrade, bring some good men to Zhitomir. . . . Bring some good men, and we shall give them all our phonographs." Gedali has heard about the "International," but his own dream is of an "International of good men." Gedali is certain that his visitor knows "what the real International is eaten with." But the latter assures him that "it is eaten with gunpowder and spiced with the best blood. . . ."

The very first stories of the *Red Cavalry* cycle provoked lively controversy. Although there were many favorable comments, Dmitry Furmanov, the author of the highly successful novel *Chapayev*, reproached Babel severely for his "failure to stress the organizing, purposeful role of the Communist Party in the Civil War."

Displeasure was also expressed by Semyon Budenny, commander of the First Horse Army on which Babel drew for materials for his stories. Budenny reproached him for creating an untrue and "distorted" picture of "the life, customs, and traditions of the First Horse Army."

One of Babel's most energetic defenders at that time (1928) was Gorky. Highest praise for the stories came from the editor-in-chief of *Novy Mir*, the late Vyacheslav Polonsky. In his book *On Contemporary Literature* (1929) he wrote: "I read and reread *Red Cavalry*. It is a marvelous book, perhaps the most brilliant of the past decade. It will lose none of its luster when placed alongside the most outstanding works of our time, so beautiful are some of its pages."

Almost simultaneously with the appearance of the *Red Cavalry* cycle, Babel began to publish the stories known under the general title of *Odessa Tales*, and miscellaneous stories, later collected into a volume of *Stories*. The hero of the *Odessa Tales* is frequently the gangster Benya Krik ("The King," "How It Was Done in Odessa," "The Father"). Related to this series is also the play *Sunset*, published in 1928 and showing how the Krick brothers —Levka the hussar and Benya—married off their elderly maiden sister, Dvoira. In the originality of its language and its milieu, the play is reminiscent of John Gay's famous eighteenth-century play *The Beggar's Opera* and Bertolt Brecht's *Die Dreigroschenoper*.

In the collection *Stories* the scene is not always Odessa. In the best of its stories, however, such as "The Story of My Dovecote," "Di Grasso," and "In the Basement," the action is laid in Odessa. "Dante Street," "The Trial," and others deal with episodes of life in Paris, and "Guy de Maupassant" is laid in Petersburg. By the end of the 1920s Babel's name appeared more and more infrequently in Soviet periodicals and anthologies. There were increasing rumors in literary circles about the "crisis" that Babel was undergoing.

Among Babel's last works in the early '30s it is important to mention "Gapa Guzhva," the first chapter of a novel, *Velikaya Krinitsa*, which Babel was then beginning to write (this was in 1931—the novel was never finished). Its action takes place in the village of Velikaya Krinitsa during the period of collectivization. One of the inhabitants of the village is the woman Gapa Guzhva, who is said to have "damaged" all the local young men. One night Gapa comes knocking at the door of the visiting official with a question: "How will whores live under the collectivization?" The judge replies that they will live, but not in the way they've been accustomed to.

Perhaps the most striking passage comes at the end of the chapter: "The raging, lacerating night assaulted her. Thickets of clouds, hunchbacked ice floes glinting black. The sky, now turbid, now opalescent, rushed overhead. Silence was spread over Velikaya Krinitsa, over the flat, sepulchral, icy desert of the rustic night."

At the First All-Union Congress of Writers in August 1934, Babel took part in the discussion on Gorky's speech. He commented on the first generation of revolutionary writers: "My generation, which entered the literary field some twenty years ago . . . will bear witness to the hardships that attended our beginnings. We were not welcomed by ranks of philistines with fame and music. We toiled for many years to earn the name of a writer, always remembering that this name repays all the adversities encountered on our way. Those who win this name easily do not retain it long."

Babel was also a delegate to the Congress in Defense of Culture, held in Paris in 1935. His speech at this Congress is described by Ilya Ehrenburg in his introduction to Babel's *Selected Works* (Moscow, 1957). Ehrenburg recalls "the enthusiastic reception accorded Babel by Henri Barbusse and Heinrich Mann, Jean-Richard Bloch and Waldo Frank." He writes: "Babel did not read his speech, he spoke French fluently, gaily, and with complete mastery. For fifteen minutes he entertained the audience with several unwritten stories. The listeners laughed, but at the same time they understood that, under the guise of amusing stories, the speaker was dealing with the essential nature of our people and our culture. . . . Babel was an extraordinary storyteller, and it is a pity no one wrote down his stories. In the winter of 1938 in Moscow he often came to visit me and spoke, and spoke. . . . At that time I had hoped he would be able to write it all down. . . ."

Extremely valuable reminiscences about Babel as a young man are found in K. Paustovsky's book *The Time of Great Expectations* (1959). Paustovsky met Babel in Odessa during the period of 1920–21, when the former was secretary of the editorial office of the newspaper *Moryak* (Seaman). Babel, he says, was a raconteur of genius. His oral stories "were even stronger and more perfect than the written ones." From Babel, Paustovsky heard wonderful Cossack songs. Two lines remained in his memory:

> Star of the fields above my father's house,
> My mother's grieving hand . . .

Paustovsky and Babel came to know each other well during the summer when they lived in neighboring villas on the outskirts of Odessa. When Babel approached a manuscript of his story lying on the desk, says Paustovsky, he stroked it "like a half-tamed beast." He ruthlessly polished every story he wrote, saying: "Clarity and force of language are not in the phrase to which nothing more can be added, but in the phrase from which nothing more can be deleted."

Paustovsky was especially moved by Babel's description of how he wrote his stories:

"I cannot invent. I must know everything to the last dot, otherwise I shall not be able to write anything. The device engraved on my shield is 'authenticity.' This is why I write so little and so slowly. It is very difficult for me. After each story I age by several years. Where the devil is that vaunted Mozartian lightness, joy over the manuscript, and the easy flow of imagination? . . . Even when I am writing the tiniest story, I work over it like a ditchdigger, like a laborer who must single-handedly level Mount Everest to its foundations. . . ."

As illustration, Babel showed Paustovsky a plump manuscript of some two hundred pages. On the first sheet Paustovsky read the title, "Lyubka the Cossack." He had read the story and, recalling that it was very short, he now asked whether Babel had expanded it into a novel. With some embarrassment Babel replied that it was the same story. It was not more than fifteen pages long, but the manuscript contained the twenty-two versions he had written before arriving at the final one. The story tells about Lyubka Shneiveis, queen of the Odessa smugglers, whose enterprise and schemes were every bit as bold and striking as those of Benya Krick.

Babel's last work, the play *Maria*, appeared in the magazine *Theatre and Dramaturgy* in 1935. Its plot is based on life in Petersburg during the first years of the revolution. The action unfolds in a hotel on the Nevsky, the residence of the speculator Dymshits, who has organized a system of smuggling food products to the capital with the aid of a group of war invalids, who are usually allowed to pass the roadblock units without being closely searched. Dymshits is earning substantial profits from this scheme. He becomes involved with Ludmila, the daughter of a former general, Mukovnin, who hopes that he will marry her. A girl of easy morals, dislocated by the revolution, she ends in prison. Her arrest finally undermines the health of her father, who is suffering from a weak heart. His other daughter, Maria, has left home, joined the Bolsheviks, and is working for the Political Department of the Red Army. The old Mukovnin dies, and the apartment is taken over by new tenants—a worker and his wife. The play conveys memorably the atmosphere of the early revolutionary years in Petersburg.

Babel's last appearance in the Soviet press during his lifetime was in the *Literary Gazette* of December 31, 1938. On New Year's Eve the *Literary Gazette* usually publishes articles by prominent writers, expressing their wishes for the new year. At that time Babel wrote:

"I would wish that our bookstores were stocked in 1939 with the works of Lev Tolstoy in inexpensive editions. They are almost unobtainable, and the deprivation to readers is self-evident. I judge by myself: with the passing of years, my admiration of the beauty and truth of these books grows irresistibly. . . ."

In his introduction to the small volume of Babel's selected works published in 1957, Ehrenburg writes: "He loved quiet, but he lived a restless life; he fought, he traveled much, he shared in all the hopes and all the suffering of his time. He welcomed the revolution as the fulfillment of everything he held dear, and preserved to his dying day the high ideals of justice, internationalism, and humanity." Babel revealed most fully the essence of humanism in his story "Gedali." But, says Ehrenburg, in contrast to Gedali, Babel not only believed in "an International of good men," he also knew how to fight for it.

And so, throughout his literary life, Isaac Babel proved worthy indeed of that high honor to which he had been pledged by Gorky at the beginning of his writing career.

9 BORIS PILNYAK (1894– ?)

Difficult as the road of the Russian writer was in old Russia, it became still more difficult in the new, post-revolutionary society. The fate of Boris Pilnyak, one of the pioneers of Soviet Russian literature, may well serve as an illustration of this. Twice the official critics excommunicated him. Both times, after Pilnyak confessed his "errors," and after Gorky and other prominent Communists intervened in his behalf, he was forgiven. In 1937, during the period of the Moscow trials, he was expelled a third time—now irrevocably—for his "ties with enemies of the people." Since then his name has disappeared from print.

Pilnyak (whose real name was Vogau) was born in 1894 in Mozhaisk (Moscow province). His father was a district physician, descended from the German colonists of the Volga region. His mother belonged to an old merchant family of Saratov. Pilnyak's parents were interested in social questions. The populist movement, long since abandoned in the capitals, was still alive in the provinces in the '80s and '90s of the last century. Certain features of this movement were maliciously, but sharply captured by Gorky in his last, unfinished novel, *Klim Samgin*.

In his autobiography Pilnyak describes the evening when the writer's instinct had first awakened in him, at the age of nine. He recalled this moment again in his novel *The Third Capital*:

"This happened in childhood, in Russia, in Mozhaye, and it must have been in September, or early October. I sat on the window sill. Across the street was a house—a gray merchant's house, the home of the Shishkins. To the right was a square, and beyond it, a church, where Napoleon had spent a night. Opposite the Shishkin house, on the corner, there was a street lamp, which the fire station supplied with hemp oil, but which gave no light. The wind was so violent that it knocked down our fence, tore off a shutter and some iron roofing from the Shishkin house, and rocked the street lamp. The wind was visible —it was gray, it rushed in, it burst out from behind the corner, sweeping gray clouds, gray air, strips of paper, a broken sieve. It rattled the gates, the hinges, the shutters in the street—all at once. The earth was frozen, coated with a gray crust of ice. People's clothes tossed and swirled in the air, flew up over their heads. People walked with all their limbs splayed out, and, as they passed the lamp, all had a single thought: unbalanced by the wind, they made a vain attempt to grasp the post, but their feet shot out at grotesque angles, and they flew helplessly after the rolling sieve. . . . The earth was icy, the wind was terrifying, like Gorynich in the fairy tale, and everything was gray and steely—the earth, the sky, the wind, the buildings, the air, and the street lamp. And, besides all this, the wind was *free*. . . . It must have been then that I wrote the poem which I still preserve from out my ancient childhood—'The Wind Blows Past the Window.' . . ."

The contrast which first awakened the writer in the little Pilnyak—the contrast between the free, mighty, rushing element of the wind and the poor, helpless life of human beings, the polarity between the conscious and the unconscious, between will and reason—forms the leitmotiv of his whole creative work. The October revolution, full of contrasts and clashes between impulse and the realities of Russian life, between the idea and its embodiment, found its inspired voice in Pilnyak.

Pilnyak came to literature almost on the eve of the revolution. He came to it with a good knowledge of provincial Russia. He found in it Andrey Bely, another writer who was primarily cerebral, and whose experiments in Russian prose especially appealed to Pilnyak. In the field of Russian prose Pilnyak attained greater results than the "chamber-scale" Bely; his experiments, his style soon became the common property of a whole bevy of young writers of the early years of the revolution: N. Ognyov, A. Malyshkin, A. Vesyoly, and others.

The revolution in Russian prose, begun by the leader of the Symbolists, Andrey Bely, and his early comrades-in-arms, Alexey Remizov and Yevgeny Zamyatin, found in Pilnyak its most significant popularizer. The first quest for new ways in prose expressed itself in a shift to *provincial-urban subject matter*. This provincial-urban theme had long wound its way as a timid rivulet through the wide field of Russian literature, often disappearing, only to reappear again. It first emerged in Pushkin's *Belkin's Tales*, and was later continued by Gogol. But it was difficult for the provincial-urban theme to compete with the larger theme of landowner and peasant life, and it soon ran dry. Of the writers dealing with small-town provincial Russia in the latter half of the nineteenth century, only Leskov has retained his place in literature.

When they began to write about small-town life, Bely (*Silver Dove*), Remizov (*The Fifth Wound*), and Zamyatin (*The Provincial* and *At the World's End*) could not, of course, write in the language of Turgenev; too much had to be told about the life of the provinces during the decades when they had been almost entirely absent from literature. Hence, the very phrase of Bely and his followers was invested with multiple meaning; it became more encompassing.

But Pilnyak might not have succeeded in popularizing the small-town theme if the revolution had not intervened. The revolution determined the course of this significant theme, awakening wide circles of readers to a keen interest in the people who had emerged from the unknown backwoods to such a prominent place in the revolutionary deeds and days.

Pilnyak's first large work, the novel *The Naked Year* (1922), which he built by combining and revising a number of stories first published in the collection *Bygone Days*, represents the first attempt to synthesize the broad material of the Russian province into a general picture of the revolution. As in most of Pilnyak's works, the novel has no plot in the narrow sense of the word. It is not centered on the fate of one or several heroes, but on the revolution itself, in all its contradictions. The character of the plot made it necessary to break down traditional narrative forms. The country is seen, as it were, swept by a great wind. Storms and blizzards blow through every page of the novel, tearing off old signs, scattering the old life. And it is not by chance that the first new Soviet word formations are heard through the wild play of these elemental forces:

"Do you hear the revolution howling like a witch in a snowstorm? Listen: Gviiu, gviioo! Shoya. . . . Gau! And the wood goblin is drumming: Glavbum, glavbum! . . ." ("Gviu" were the initials for the Chief Engineering Administration: "Glavbum" was the Chief Administration for the Affairs of the Paper Industry.)

The action of the novel was set in the small town of Ordynin: "The last time this town was alive was seventy years ago. There was a period in Russia—the devil alone knows what it might be called!—when there was, properly speaking, no Russia at all, only an interminable, parched expanse punctuated by striped mileposts, past which officials dashed posthaste to Petersburg" in order to report that everything was well in the regions entrusted to them. This "well-being" rested on the old, stable way of life, in which eccentric, irresponsible tyranny, cruelty, and feeble-mindedness competed with each other. Donat, the son of one of the pillars of this "order," who had run away from his father, a leading merchant of the town, before the war, returns to Ordynin in October 1917. Donat's role in the novel is small: it merely provides the writer with a pretext for a quick characterization of the old merchant way of life, now being swept away by the revolution.

But not only the old merchant life is breaking up. The entire former class structure of society is being shattered. The house of the old Prince Ordynin, "assembled through centuries until it had become a triple-thick foundation, resting on three whales, had faded, crumbled, and collapsed within a single year." Under the impact of events the old Prince turns to mysticism. His eldest son, Boris, shoots himself when he learns that he is ill with congenital syphilis. The second, Yegor, becomes an alcoholic. And the youngest, Gleb, turns his back on all worldly concerns. The only healthy member of the family, Natalya, becomes a Bolshevik.

The Bolsheviks in the novel are the builders of the new: "leather people in leather coats—Bolsheviks! Every one of them picked to match, handsome, stalwart, thick curls breaking out from under the cap, pushed far back upon the head; each one, above all, a man of will—will in the tight cheekbones, the folds of the lips, the bold, steady movements."

Despite such an enthusiastic endorsement, Pilnyak was inwardly little concerned with the "Bolsheviks." What interested him most was the response of the ordinary Russian people to the revolution, the ideas and feelings of merchants and saintly halfwits, of intellectuals, workers, artisans, and peasants, who lived it, thought about it, and cursed it. These feelings and ideas were presented by the writer together with the living piece of flesh from which they had been wrung. And because of this, Pilnyak succeeded in showing us a segment of that great Russia which had thrown the whole mass of herself into "making her own history."

Pilnyak was the first writer to sense the beginnings of a great *popular* revolution in the events of October 1917. Today this seems self-evident, a truism, but in 1922 it was a great heresy. And the official Soviet critics missed no opportunity of reminding Pilnyak of his "petty-bourgeois" origins, which prevented him from understanding the "proletarian" character of October.

Pilnyak's basic thesis, his point of departure, was that the October revolution was a popular and peasant revolution. The intelligentsia, he felt, recoiled from October because, in its very origins, it was not even an organic phenomenon. It was a product of the policies of Peter the Great, who had pulled Russia up by the scruff of the neck, while the people itself continued its immemorial existence. And this, indeed, was why now, when the people was making its own revolution, the country had "gone back to the seventeenth century," even in its external way of life. These ideas, expressed by the intellectual Gleb, find their counterpart in the thoughts of the anarchistic peasant Yegorka: "There's no International. There's only a popular Russian revolution, a mutiny, nothing else."

The same thesis is developed in even sharper outline in the novel *Mother-Stepmother* (the first title of this novel was *The Third Capital*). It appeared with the following dedication: "This novel, by no means a realistic one, is dedicated to Alexey Mikhailovich Remizov, the master with whom I served as an apprentice." The novel was written under the direct impression of a journey to postwar Europe, and was conceived "somewhere near Sebezh, on the boundary of two worlds—the old, 'dying' cultural world of Europe and the new, which is being born in anguish." The author's acceptance of the October revolution, the entire philosophy of this acceptance, is expressed in one of the asides:

"However terrible the drunken Peter may have been, the days of his era remain in Russian history as a poem, and the chapters of this poem, which tell how bells were melted down for cannon (church bells, ancient ones), are good chapters of Russian history as a poem." Pilnyak was a contemporary of a new chapter in Russian history, and the "price" paid by the country often caused him consternation: "I have just seen the janitor who had eaten his wife; he could not but go insane," he says, but adds immediately: "But this does not frighten me—I saw something else, too. I measured things with another yardstick. I know: all that is alive, like the earth, like the earth in springtime, renews itself, dying, again and again."

Pilnyak embodies all his frequently tormenting doubts in the image of Emelyan Razin, "Russian Candidate of Philosophical Sciences," who is the secretary of the District Office of Education. For five years this modest secretary toiled devotedly, in poverty and want. Then he went abroad. And when he returned home, he suddenly saw "how poor, how infinitely wretched Russia was. He heard all the Russian disorder and saw the blanket in the window (the glass was broken, and the hole was stuffed with an old blanket years ago). He could not forgive the world for his wife's worn shoes. Not everyone has the gift of sight; but those who see, go mad."

Henceforth, the image of Emelyan Razin, the modest, inconspicuous Russian who uncomplainingly endures his own privations in the great "poem" of Russian history, but who gathers in his heart damning testimony against this "poem," becomes a constant presence in Pilnyak's works. Between the two grandiose schemes—the acceptance and the rejection of the October revolution—there seeps in, almost imperceptibly, a living force, coming from the depths of provincial, small-town Russia. Its specific gravity in Pilnyak's consciousness is not great, and yet, he is perhaps the only writer who sensed that the testimony and the judgment of this Russia might come to play a deciding part in the future.

The idea that the October revolution was a people's revolution—Pilnyak's point of departure in *The Naked Year*—became considerably more complex in *The Third Capital*. Here the revolution appears in three aspects: the "will to will," the "will to see," and the "will not to see." Three factors meet in the vast expanses of the country: the elemental force of the revolution, the government produced by it, and the reality of the country itself, following the revolution, but resisting its regime.

"The Tale of the Unextinguished Moon" (1926) almost destroyed Pilnyak. In contrast to most of his works, written in a difficult style, the plot of this story is simple: at the demand of the Central Committee of the Communist Party, the army commander Gavrilov comes to Moscow from the Caucasus, where he was on furlough because of illness. He is told that the Central Committee wants him to undergo an operation. Gavrilov himself fears this operation, and the doctors at the health resort were unanimous in the opinion that the operation could be avoided. But the mysterious "center" insists on it. One of its most prominent leaders, "the man who never stoops," virtually orders Gavrilov to lie down on the operating table. Gavrilov obeys and submits to the surgeon's knife. But his organism resists chloroform; it must be administered in large doses, and Gavrilov dies without regaining consciousness. From the conversation of the doctors, called in for a consultation, it becomes clear that the Moscow doctors had also opposed the operation. . . .

Pilnyak's tale had its parallel in history. In 1925 the Red Army Commander, Frunze, died on the operating table. Soon after his death, it began to be rumored that the operation had been "ordered" by Stalin himself, as a convenient means of eliminating Frunze, whose sympathies in the intramural party struggle were with Zinoviev. It was under the influence of these rumors that Pilnyak wrote "The Tale of the Unextinguished Moon," which appeared in the May 1926 issue of the journal *Novy Mir*. After a number of copies had already been mailed to subscribers, the edition was suddenly withdrawn and replaced by a new "May issue" containing a story by another writer in place of Pilnyak's "Tale." Several issues of the initial edition have been preserved, but the story remains relatively unknown. There is all the more reason, therefore, to dwell on it in greater detail.

It opens on a gray autumn morning in Moscow. The train, to which the car of the Army Commander Gavrilov is coupled, rolls smoothly into the deserted station. A silent guard lines up at the entrance to the Commander's car. An inconspicuous-looking man suddenly appears near the car and asks someone to tell the Commander that Popov, Alyosha Popov, wants to see him. One of the guards goes in to announce him, and a few moments later invites Alyosha Popov to follow him. Popov turns out to be an old friend of Gavrilov. In their distant youth both had been weavers in Orekhovo-Zuevo; both had early joined the revolutionary movement; they sat in prison and went into penal exile together. Later, both succeeded in escaping and making their way abroad, to Paris. Both rose to important, if unequal, positions during the days of the

October revolution: one became Chief of Staff of the Red Guard, and the other became chairman of a Province Executive Committee. But despite the difference in position, they had always retained a deep loyalty to each other and to the cause to which they had devoted their lives.

Gavrilov is delighted at the meeting with Alyosha, who inquires after his health. Gavrilov answers reluctantly: "My health is fine, it's quite restored—but who knows, you may yet have to stand honor guard at my coffin." And it is not clear whether Gavrilov is jesting or serious. The writer adds that Gavrilov's remark sounded, "at any rate, like a mirthless jest."

At this moment an orderly enters and reports that a car "from House No. 1" has come for the Army Commander; he is "invited to come there." The mail has also come. Gavrilov opens a newspaper and finds, on the third page, a curious report of his arrival in Moscow for "an operation for stomach ulcer." "Comrade Gavrilov's health," he reads, "gives cause for alarm, but the specialists vouch for the successful outcome of the operation." This report sharpens Gavrilov's joyless forebodings, and he says to his friend: "Do you hear, Alyosha? There's something behind it!"

The scene shifts to "House No. 1." In the study, on a wooden chair behind a large desk, sits "the man who never stoops." At times Pilnyak calls him "Number One." The following strange dialogue ensues between Number One and Gavrilov:

"Gavrilov, there is no need between us to talk about the millstone of the revolution. Unfortunately, I guess, the wheel of history is turned in great measure by death and blood—especially the wheel of revolution. It is not for us to talk about death and blood. Do you remember how you and I had led the ragged Red Army troops against Yekaterinoslav? You had a rifle, and I had a rifle. A shell killed your horse, and you went ahead on foot. The Red Army men turned to flight, and you shot one of them with your revolver to stop the rest. Commander, you would have shot me too, if I had shown fear. And, I suppose, you would have been right."

In reply to this curious tirade, Gavrilov suddenly asks, "sternly and quickly": "Talk without preambles: why was I called here? There's no need for diplomacy. Talk straight."

"The man who never stoops" answers: "I called you because you must undergo the operation. The revolution needs you. I called in the specialists, and they said that you'll be on your feet within a month. The revolution demands this. The specialists are waiting, they'll examine you. They'll understand everything. I have already issued orders. Even a German doctor has come."

Gavrilov makes one final attempt to escape this strange operation, which had been ordered, not only without the consent of the patient, but even before the doctors had been able to examine him. Gavrilov says to Number One: "My doctors have told me there is no need for an operation, the ulcer will heal by itself. I feel entirely well. There is no need for an operation, and I don't want it."

After a short silence Number One answers: "Comrade Commander, do you remember the time when we discussed whether four thousand men were to be sent to certain death? You ordered them sent. And you did the right thing. In three weeks you will be on your feet, I have given orders. . . . Excuse me, there's nothing more to be said, Comrade Gavrilov." Gavrilov finished his cigarette, rose, said "Good-by" to Number One, and heard the answer: "For the time being. . . ."

"The Tale of the Unextinguished Moon" elicited another unexpected consequence. The June issue of *Novy Mir* printed a "Letter to the Editors" by A. Voronsky, editor-in-chief of the journal *Krasnaya Nov*, to whom Pilnyak dedicated his "Tale." This astonishing document deserves to be quoted in full:

"The fifth issue of the journal *Novy Mir* carried Boris Pilnyak's 'Tale of the Unextinguished Moon.' Although the preface to the tale states that its contents have no connection with the death of Comrade Frunze, its entire setting, some of its details, and so on, point to the contrary. The tale persuades the reader that the circumstances of the death of its hero, the Army Commander, coincide with the actual circumstances and facts attending the death of Comrade Frunze. Such a representation of an unfortunate and deeply tragic event is not only the cruelest distortion, insulting to the very memory of Comrade Frunze, but also a malicious slander of our party, the All-Russian Communist Party. The tale is dedicated to me. Because such a dedication is the greatest insult to me as a Communist, and might cast a shadow on my reputation as a party member, I indignantly reject it. With comradely greetings, A. Voronsky."

How great must have been the confusion at the top levels to permit the appearance of such a reminder of the "published" and deleted tale!

In "The Tale of the Unextinguished Moon" Pilnyak touched upon the conflicts which had arisen within the social group that had been victorious in the revolution. But already in his novel *Machines and Wolves* the writer had sought to find the sources of these conflicts.

Machines and Wolves attests to Pilnyak's intuitive insight into the internal collisions of the revolution. It is, perhaps, even less of a formal novel than *The Naked Year*, although the novelistic elements here are more fully developed and independent. Such elements or fragments of a novel are contained in the story of the destinies of the large Roschislavsky family, of the Russian gentry. The elder son of the family ends his days in an insane asylum: imagining himself a "wolf," he clutches at the throat of another patient, and is killed by a third inmate; his brother, an engineer, suffers a mental breakdown as a result of overwork and throws himself under the flywheel of a machine; and, finally, the third, Dimitry, seeks and finds a compromise with the revolution.

The crux of the work is suggested in the beginning of the novel: it is a gray, early morning over the wide Russian expanses, crisscrossed by roads and highways. Wandering over these roads, on foot and by cart, are "Russian gypsies," covering thousands of miles, lost in these endless miles, suffering cold and hunger, "for who will give them shelter, and where?" Another traveler, but this one riding in an old, ramshackle car which the people have nicknamed a "furufuz," is a man whom the writer describes as "a condensation of Communist will, all of him covered with the factory soot of the revolution, all of him centered on building a world with a ruler and steel." Halted by a decayed wooden bridge, he encounters face to face the group of wandering "Russian gypsies." The circumstances of this quiet encounter, so unlike the atmosphere of meeting halls, awaken in him the need "to think and speak quietly and truly."

The basic conflict within the revolution, according to Pilnyak, lay in the fact that Russia had to make a leap of more than a thousand miles from the starting point of October 1917. The capital cities quickly managed this task. But while the romanticism of the "proletarian, machine revolution" was being forged in the cities, the rest of Russia went its own way, proceeded with its own "peasant mutiny," alien and hostile to the cities and factories. And then "the curtain went up on Russian tragedies." Two truths clashed head on—"the truth of the machine" and that of "peasant, muzhik Russia." In this duel, "wolfish," peasant Russia fought with "figures,"[1] which were "bloodless," but terrible. As the statistician Nepomnyashchy ("Unremembering") says in the novel, this Russia replied to wars and to revolution "like me—with figures, with the year 1920, with the famine on the Volga." She did it because "you can't make legs grow out of armpits, they grow from the proper place . . . and I am for Russia." The provincial district statistician Nepomnyashchy (who remembers everything very well!) condemns the socialist revolution, the "machine" revolution, because its demands upon Russia are beyond her strength. And somewhere in the depths of his heart, Pilnyak does not accept it either.

Quite different is the approach to "the proletarian revolution" of the former nobleman Dimitry Roschislavsky,

[1] An allusion to the frightful famine of 1921, which carried away millions of lives.

an early forerunner of the future "nonparty Bolsheviks" of the type of Alexey Tolstoy. He is attracted to "the metaphysic of the proletarian": "A country (like an individual) has its weekdays and its drunken days—and that's revolution. Russia has been on a drunken spree for five years—magnificent years! Now it is settling down to everyday life. The revolution is ending, and I say: it is not revolution, and not revolutionary policemen who bring happiness"—work alone brings happiness to man.

These thoughts of the dispossessed nobleman Roschislavsky about the future sway of work under the direction of the technical intelligentsia coincide with the ideas of the engineer Forst: "Only work, only the accumulation of values, will save Russia." This is why the nonpartisan specialist Forst extends his hand to the worker Lebedukha, saying, "We're fellow travelers on the same road," and anticipating the alliance of "the nonpartisan with the Communists" that was proclaimed by Stalin ten years later. In Forst's view it had already become clear during the NEP period that there were only two real forces: the philistine man in the street, and the Communist. "If the philistine wins, Russia is lost." But at the same time, Russia will also be lost if she refuses to realize that "you can't make legs grow out of armpits." What is needed is a realistic assessment of the two forces, and their synthesis. And this means that the "proletarian romanticism" must be set aside and everyone must get down to hard work. For Russia is still "illiterate and hungry." "Power in Russia is a terrible thing, and to wield power in Russia is terrible. In snapshot perspective there is no picture more frightful than Russia. But Russia does not live either by the present or by the past. Russia lives by the future."

It was thus, in his own ways, that Pilnyak overcame the contradiction between the authoritarian regime and the people's revolution, and approached a synthesis—the acceptance of a super-class (and super-revolutionary) government which is destined to conquer both "machines and wolves." He embodied this synthesis in two works, *The Volga Flows into the Caspian Sea* (1930) and *The*

Ripening of Fruits (1935). But he did not achieve the synthesis without anguished vacillations and doubts, the traces of which are so clearly visible in *Machines and Wolves*.

This novel sees two Russias. One is backward, wolfish, anarchic, and stateless. In 1917 this Russia threw itself into the making of its own history. But without outside help, the country would not have been able to cope with its task; its anarchic, elemental surge would have led it to disintegration. "The Russian national soul—a frightful blizzard over Russia! It will scatter everything if . . . someone's black hand, cruel and steely, like a machine, a governing hand," does not intervene "in this sweeping blizzard—gnarled, bloody, flashing with lightnings, reckless, brigand-wild, and anarchic." And this governing hand became a fact. It closed on "Russia, the Russian blizzard, and the peasant, squeezing them to suffocation. It wanted to build, to build—do you hear?—to build!" Here we find the formula for the entire philosophy of the future industrialization, to which the Soviet technical intelligentsia came later.

The Volga Flows into the Caspian Sea is a novel without a philosophy, a novel of illustration. But before he wrote it, Pilnyak suffered another disaster. He had written a short novel, *Mahogany*, which was accepted for publication by the magazine *Krasnaya Nov*. Simultaneously, Pilnyak sent the manuscript to his Berlin publishing house (Petropolis, Berlin-Moscow, which published many works by Soviet writers at that time). The book appeared in Germany, but by then *Krasnaya Nov* had decided against printing it. The times were harsh; the first Five-Year Plan was just beginning, and terror against the Left opposition was in full swing. For reasons of party policy, rank-and-file party members were not permitted to know too much about this struggle.

Mahogany touched only in passing on the question of Left-wing Communists. The story concerns itself with life in Uglich in the late 1920s, but at the same time it contains a warm sketch of a group of "Lefts" who had been expelled from the party for their position back in 1921. Consistent and intransigent, these Communists turn into a Soviet variety of *fools in Christ*, a new version of the traditional Russian *yurodivy*. Repudiated by their wives, they find shelter under the kilns of a crumbling brick factory. Pilnyak's picture of these oppositionists was condemned as an "idealization," and the door to further literary activity was again shut to him for this "gross political error." The vicious hounding of Pilnyak continued for more than six months, until Gorky intervened in his behalf in his article "A Waste of Energy" (*Izvestia*, September 13, 1929).

After receiving his pardon Pilnyak rewrote *Mahogany* into the novel *The Volga Flows into the Caspian Sea*, devoted to the construction of a "monolith," which is to divert the flow of the Oka and transform the Moscow River into a navigable waterway. In writing the novel he made use of numerous plans, already drafted at that time, for the construction of the Volga-Don Canal. The originator of the project in the novel is the academician Pimen Sergeyevich Paletika. In Paletika, Pilnyak has drawn a portrait of a scientist of pre-revolutionary training. Although Paletika is an old Bolshevik, he bears little resemblance, either in his way of life or his habits, to the younger Soviet scientists. "Very few names," remarks Pilnyak, "not more than twenty or thirty throughout Russia, have succeeded in remaining the same in 1924 as they were in 1914."

After the harsh punishment for *Mahogany*, Pilnyak carefully purged his approach to the Five-Year Plan of any tormenting doubts or questions. Pilnyak knows that Moscow and the rest of Russia are living the difficult life of a "military camp" during the Five-Year Plan. From under the "glacier wills" of the men bent on transforming the country creep "dampness, mold, discontent, disbelief, ignorance, treason, filth, and stench." But the writer is no longer troubled by it: "This is precisely how histories should be built when they are built. . . . The rubble of history must be buried into geology, like the rubble of construction."

During the first half of the 1930s Pilnyak seemed full of optimism and faith that the major difficulties of construction were already behind, and the discontent of the masses was safely in "geology." But the writer himself is not too adept at burying his intimate knowledge of life "into geology." Even in *The Ripening of Fruits* (1935), a seemingly irreproachable work from the political point of view, this knowledge breaks through into the pages of the book. *The Ripening of Fruits* deals with the famous Russian village of Palekh, whose residents have for centuries combined agricultural work with art of a high order. The ikons painted by the Palekh artists have brought down to our own day the traditions of the famed seventeenth-century religious painter Andrey Rublev. After the October revolution the village went into a decline. But thanks to the resourcefulness of the artists themselves and the protection of certain influential party members, the Palekh artists "switched" from religious to more currently acceptable subjects. Among their newer works are the illustrations to the ancient Russian epic *The Tale of Igor's Host*.

Along with his enthusiastic description of the life of Palekh artists under the Soviet regime, Pilnyak gives us a highly interesting portrait of "an internal *émigré*" in the character of the young artist-restorer Pavel Pavlovich Kalashnikov. The son of a Moscow house-painter, Pavel was eight years old when the revolution broke out. He completed the seven-year school already under the Soviet regime. But he is remote from his time, in love with the past, and feels that "the seventeenth century was far better than ours." Although these views of the young restorer partially coincide with Pilnyak's own ideas in the early days of the revolution, the writer now condemns them. Kalashnikov seems to him "an absurdity." And yet, the very fact that a Kalashnikov exists prompts the idea that "somewhere in Moscow, in the narrow Moscow side streets, a social milieu survives, and social forces gather which pull people backward, to the seventeenth century."

The Ripening of Fruits turned out to be Pilnyak's last published work. When the Moscow trials of 1936–38 began, Pilnyak was charged with "Trotskyism" and declared "an enemy of the people." In reality he was not a member of the Communist Party, but was closely acquainted both with Radek and with Eideman (shot in connection with the Tukhachevsky trial). At that time Pilnyak disappeared from both literature and life. The exact date of his death is still unknown. And his name also disappeared for many years even from textbooks on the history of Soviet literature. He is not mentioned either in the first edition of the *Large Soviet Encyclopedia* (1940), or in the new edition, or even in the supplementary fifty-first volume, sent to press on April 28, 1958. Pilnyak's name may be found only in the *Literary Encyclopedia* (Vol. 8, 1934), which says that, in his early works, the writer "expressed the moods of the Russian bourgeois intelligentsia." The article stresses, however, that "Pilnyak did not belong in the camp of the militant bourgeoisie," and this determined his attitude toward the October revolution. Although he "welcomed the revolution," the article continues, "he welcomed it as a promise of national renascence, and later stressed the growth of the country's productive forces, ignoring the social content of the revolution." As for *Mahogany*, the article says that it was essentially "a pasquinade on Soviet life."

After almost twenty years of silence Pilnyak's name has recently reappeared in two texts, the *History of Russian Soviet Literature* (Vol. 1, published by the U.S.S.R. Academy of Sciences, Moscow, 1958) and the *History of Russian Soviet Literature* (Vol. 1, Moscow University Press, 1958). In the former the writer's work is evaluated only on the basis of his earliest books, *Ivan and Marya* and *The Naked Year*. The latter also mentions *The Third Capital* and *Machines and Wolves*. But the general appraisal (based on these works) remains the same: "Both the poetization of 'the Russia of peasant huts,' and the affirmation of a Russia which is 'strict as a Diesel' reflect the writer's reactionary moods, profoundly alien to the ideals of socialism."

Judging from these comments, Pilnyak's rehabilitation is still remote.

It may well be that the true reason for the silence about Pilnyak is his penetrating insight into the inner mechanism of the revolutionary epoch. And it was precisely this insight which caused the downfall of the writer—one of the most original and paradoxical artist-philosophers who had attempted to ponder the destinies of "all of Russia."

10 BORIS PASTERNAK (1890–1960)

The photographs of Boris Pasternak's funeral and the procession that followed the poet to the cemetery insistently suggest something elusively familiar: the lofty skies of early summer, the stretching chain of people, the peculiar self-absorption of each participant in the procession. And suddenly, as in a flash of illumination, one recognizes it: why, these are people on a pilgrimage! The cortege was, perhaps, smaller than those seen at the funerals of officially approved celebrities, but it bore the unmistakable imprint of folk participation. And if we recall the special circumstances of the last period of Pasternak's life, following his selection for the Nobel Prize, it will become still clearer that the poet was escorted on his last journey by representatives of that Russia which the regime has failed to break or intimidate.

From the very beginning of his literary career Boris Pasternak became known as a "difficult" poet. In a certain sense this reputation is justified. To understand Pasternak, to enrich ourselves by the generosity of his poetic gift, we must read him with an open heart and an active mind. As reward, we shall receive, not an abstract idea, but some facet of reality, a particular detail still quivering with inimitable life:

> The moon laid baulks, not shadows,
> Or absented herself entirely.
> And softly-softly flowed the night,
> Padding from cloud to cloud.

Or:

> From dream, it seemed, more than from roofs,
> Forgetful, more than timid,
> The light rain shuffled at the door,
> And smell of wine-corks filled the air.
>
> (Both from "Summer")

Pasternak's "difficulty" results from the immense stores of lyricism in his talent. It is not by chance that the poet says in his autobiographical essay, *Safe Conduct* (1929–31), that he had always seen the principal aim of art as the transposition of the image "from cold axles to hot." His talent is remarkable for its sense of detail; in this he is akin to the great French poet Paul Valéry. Characteristically, he says:

> I don't know if the riddle of the dark
> Beyond the grave is solved,
> But life—like autumn
> Silence—is detailed.

Two godmothers—silence and mystery—stand over the cradle of the poet's creative work: "Silence, you are the best of all I've heard." And here is Pasternak's definition of the task of poetry:

Poetry, do not abandon breadth,
Preserve living exactness—the exactness of mysteries.

Pasternak was the son of the well-known portrait painter Leonid Pasternak. His mother, born Rosa Kaufman, was a talented musician. In his childhood and early youth Pasternak intended to devote his life to music, with the encouragement of his teacher, the composer Alexander Scriabin.

In *Safe Conduct* Pasternak wrote: "More than anything in the world, I loved music; and more than anyone in it, Scriabin." It is almost impossible to convey the quality of this adoring love: "To love selflessly and without reserve, with a strength equal to the square of distance, is the task of our hearts while we are children." But when Scriabin, then newly returned from abroad, listened to the boy's composition and blessed him warmly to a life in music, the sixteen-year-old Pasternak felt suddenly, illogically, but with some scarcely acknowledged prophetic sense that he was not meant to be a musician.

During the difficult period that followed, the young man turned once more to his favorite poet, Rilke, whose books he had discovered in his father's library some six years earlier. The poet had instantly captured the boy's attention, but it was not until much later that Pasternak recalled the scene which he described in *Safe Conduct*:

"On a hot summer morning in 1900, the express train was leaving the Kursk station. Just before its departure, someone in a black Tyrolean cape appeared at our window. With him was a tall woman, perhaps his mother or elder sister. . . ."

This stranger was the famous poet Rainer Maria Rilke, and the woman with him was the German writer Salome, who had come to Russia to visit Tolstoy at Yasnaya Polyana. On that early occasion Rilke traveled a part of the way with the Pasternak family, on its way south. The train halted for a moment at a tiny junction where no stops were scheduled, permitting Rilke to disembark at a point nearest the Tolstoy estate, to which he was to proceed by carriage.

This wayside junction is marvelously described in the opening pages of *Safe Conduct*: "The silence of this junction, which knew nothing of us, was momentarily disturbing, like a shot. We were not to remain there. The others waved their handkerchiefs in farewell. We waved back. We could still see the coachman helping them up. He gave the lady the dust apron, then raised himself a little, red-sleeved, to adjust his belt and tuck the long tails of his coat beneath him. Now he would start. But at this moment we were caught up by a curve and, slowly turning like a page just read, the junction disappeared from view, the face and the incident to be forgotten."

But neither the face nor the incident were forgotten: "Rilke came to my hand at a most difficult time in my life," a time when the poet was saying his "farewell to music." Yet, after relating this childhood episode, Pasternak hastens to make it clear that he is not writing his own biography, but merely turns to it when another's biography demands it. The ideas suggested to him by the memory of Rilke are remarkable:

"The poet gives his whole life such a voluntarily steep

incline that it cannot be encompassed in the vertical of biography, where we expect to meet it. It cannot be found under his own name, but must be sought under the names of others, in the biographical columns of his followers. The more self-contained the creative individuality, the more collective, without any figurative speech, is its story. . . . It is composed of all that happens to his readers and which he does not know. I am not presenting my recollections to Rilke. On the contrary, I myself have received them as a gift from him."

The transition from music to poetry did not occur at once. There was an interlude when Pasternak's infatuation with the philosophy of Hermann Cohen took him to Marburg, where Cohen was lecturing. The poet's account of his journey across the Harz and his description of Marburg, where Lomonosov had studied two hundred years before, are unmatched in their graphic artistry. Pasternak sensed vividly the scars left in this part of Germany by the Thirty Years War, the entire "somnolent rather than exciting landscape of a historic calamity when it is measured by decades and not by hours. Winters, winters, and winters, and then, after the passage of a century barren as a cannibal's yawn, the first appearance of new settlements under the vagrant skies, somewhere deep in the wild-grown Harz, with names black as charred ruins, such as Elend, Sorge [Misery, Care] and the like. . . ." Of Marburg itself Pasternak says that, just as in the days of Lomonosov, "in its first sum, the town, scattered at one's feet with its gray-blue swarm of slate roofs, resembled a flock of pigeons, enchanted in mid-flight to a new feeding place."

But Cohen's lectures disappointed Pasternak. After a journey to Italy, he returned to Moscow. In 1914 he published his first book of poems, *The Twin in the Clouds*. That year Pasternak met Mayakovsky, who greatly impressed him; he was especially moved by the tragedy *Vladimir Mayakovsky*, as read by the author himself, and by his "Backbone Flute" and "Man." The latter was recited by Mayakovsky at a poetry evening at which many famous poets, including Konstantin Balmont, Andrey Bely, Vladislav Khodasevich, and Marina Tsvetaeva, read their works. Most of them listened to Mayakovsky, says Pasternak, without transcending "the limits of enviable self-esteem." They all remembered that they were "names," poets. Bely alone "listened with utter self-oblivion, carried far, far away by the joy which grudges nothing, because at the heights where it knows itself at home nothing exists but sacrifices and eternal readiness for them. . . ." In this description of Bely, Pasternak probably formulated for the first time his idea of the artist as one who lives in a world where nothing exists but self-immolation and the unfailing readiness for it.

The young poet was a member of a circle of writers and poets connected with the Musaguet Publishing House.[1] One evening Pasternak delivered a talk before the circle on "Symbolism and Immortality." On the way home he learned of Leo Tolstoy's death; he attended Tolstoy's funeral with his father, who had been summoned to Astapovo, the little wayside station where Tolstoy had died.

Shortly before the outbreak of World War I, Pasternak was translating *The Broken Jug*, a comedy by the German poet Heinrich Kleist, intended for production at the newly-formed Kamerny Theatre.

At the same time he continued to write poetry. His second collection, *Above Barriers*, appeared in 1917. But his fame as a poet began with the publication of his third collection, *My Sister, Life*. The poems in this collection were written in 1917, during the same period as those of *Above Barriers*, but the book did not appear until 1922. In 1923 came another book of poems, *Themes and Variations*.

The first half of the 1920s was especially productive in Pasternak's literary biography. It was then, too, that he

[1] Pasternak wrote about this in his short *Autobiography*, which was published only abroad, in 1958. This small book was first conceived as an introduction to a new edition of the poet's selected verse, announced in the Soviet press at approximately the same time as the forthcoming publication of *Doctor Zhivago*. The projected collection suffered the same fate as the novel.

made his first efforts in prose. In 1925 he published a small book of stories, containing among others "The Childhood of Luvers," "Aerial Ways," and "Letters from Tula." Pasternak's prose bears the imprint of his poetry, but it is more accessible to the general reader and gradually introduces him to the author's poetic world.

One juxtaposition will illustrate this. "The Childhood of Luvers," the story of an adolescent girl, contains a rapidly sketched picture of a snowstorm which is almost as vividly powerful as the description of the blizzard in Pushkin's *The Captain's Daughter*:

"It was already snowing in earnest. The sky shook, and white kingdoms and territories tumbled from it—countless, mysterious, and awesome. It was obvious that these lands, falling from no one knew where, had never heard of life or of the earth; blind and midnight-born, they engulfed the earth without sight or knowledge of its existence."

Another description of a snowstorm occurs in Pasternak's *1905* (1926):

> We throw snowballs,
> We knead them of the down-tumbling
> Failing marks
> And snowflakes
> And talk belonging to the time.
> This avalanche
> Of kingdoms,
> This drunken fall of snow—
> The school yard
> On the corner of Povarskaya
> In January.

The most characteristic of Pasternak's early stories is "Letters from Tula" (1918), written in the form of a poet's letters to his beloved, with whom he has just parted. The story is almost without plot. The poet shares his dinner table at the hotel with a group of motion-picture actors who come to Tula to film *The Troubled Times*. They behave in typical Bohemian fashion, conversing loudly across the table, throwing down their napkins. The poet is irked by this; he suffers from the knowledge that he is also essentially of the Bohemian world. He is disturbed and cannot fall asleep. Suddenly the true reason for his restlessness flashes upon him: "But this is Tula! This is night—a night in Tula. A night in place, associated with Tolstoy's biography. No wonder the magnetic needles begin to dance! What is happening is in the nature of the place. It is an event on the territory of conscience, on its gravitating, ore-bearing region." The poet grieves because life has taken such a turn that "now there are no places on earth where a man could warm his soul with the fire of shame; shame has been dampened down everywhere and will not burn." That night, for the first time since his distant childhood, the poet "burned," thinking passionately "about his art, and about finding the true road."

Almost all of Pasternak's works are rich in autobiographic details. In 1926 he published his long poem *Spektorsky*, and somewhat later, the story "The Tale." The author himself spoke of the autobiographical character of both works in his note on "The Tale":

"There will be no contradiction between the novel in verse called *Spektorsky*, begun later, and the prose offered here: both deal with the same life."

"The Tale" is a story about an adolescent boy, Seryozha, and his journey to his sister in Solikamsk. In *Safe Conduct* there are two references to a journey to the Urals before the February revolution. But it was not until the appearance of *Doctor Zhivago* that the reader learned of the wealth of impressions which this journey had left in the mind of the young Pasternak.

Among Pasternak's major works of the '30s, we must mention the book of verse *Second Birth* (1934), inspired by his friendship with several leading Georgian poets (especially Paolo Yashvili and Titsian Tabidze), whom he had visited during his trip to the Caucasus. He translated their works, as well as those of N. Baratashvili, into Russian. Pasternak wrote about this in his short *Autobiog-*

raphy, mentioned earlier. With Paolo Yashvili, who later committed suicide, Pasternak was bound by old ties of friendship, dating back to the years before World War I, and it was Yashvili who introduced him to Titsian Tabidze during his visit to the Caucasus. The character of the land, with its ancient peasant culture, is captured with remarkable sensitivity in Pasternak's poem "We Were in Georgia":

> We were in Georgia. Multiply
> Want by tenderness, and hell by paradise,
> Then set a hothouse on a pedestal of ice,
> And you will have this land.

Pasternak did not name his friends in *Second Birth*. Nor can the names of Yashvili and Tabidze be found in any of the Soviet textbooks on modern literature or the literatures of the Soviet national republics. They are mentioned, however, in Toroshelidze's address at the First All-Union Congress of Writers in 1934 as poets "who still have difficulty in reorienting their creative world, and remain in the position of literary Fellow Travelers." Translated from official jargon into general terms, this meant that the two poets remained true to their own creative individuality. Pasternak was equally true to himself and he retained his fierce integrity to the end. Already in his poem "A Noble Malady" (1923–28), he said of himself and those who felt as he did:

> We were the music in the ice.
> I am speaking of the whole milieu
> With which I had it in my mind
> To leave the stage, as yet I'll do.
> Here shame can have no place.
>
> I was not born in order thrice
> To look men differently in the eyes. . . .

Official recognition came to Pasternak late and did not last long. N. I. Bukharin, in his speech on modern Soviet poetry at the First All-Union Congress of Writers in 1934, spoke of him as one of the most eminent contemporary poets. But even after that the critics remained cool to the poet, reproaching him for "inconsonance with the time," "individualism," and the "chamber character" of his work. They relented somewhat only during the years of World War II, when Pasternak published two small books of poems, *Early Trains* (1941) and *Spacious Earth* (1945). But the old distrust of the poet persisted.

An important place in Pasternak's literary work is occupied by his translations from German, English, and Georgian. Besides Kleist's comedy *The Broken Jug*, he translated his drama *Prince of Homburg*. He also made a new translation of *Faust* (1953). But most of his translations were from English. In 1942, soon after he completed translation of *Romeo and Juliet*, he published a short article, "My New Translations" (*Ogonyok*, November 22), in which he said:

"Shakespeare will always be a favorite of generations that have suffered much and are historically mature. Ordeals teach men to value the voice of facts, genuine insight, and the rich and serious art of realism. Shakespeare remains the ideal and the crowning point of this school. No one has spoken of man with such truth, and no one has given this truth such willful expression. At first glance these are contradictory qualities. But they are directly interdependent. In the first place, we see a miracle of objectivity. His famous characters are a gallery of types, ages, and temperaments—with all their distinct actions and language. And Shakespeare is never troubled because their speech is interwoven with the outpourings of his own genius. His aesthetics rest on the succession of self-oblivion and attention, the alternation of the lofty and the ridiculous, of prose and verse. His presence is felt in his works not only in the aspect of their originality. Whenever they raise the question of good and evil, truth and falsehood, we see before us a figure unimaginable in an atmosphere of cringing and servility. We hear the voice of a genius, a king among kings and a judge over gods—the voice of later Western democracies, founded on the proud dignity of the toiler and fighter. . . ."

Pasternak spent most of the early years of the war in a small town on the Kama River, working on a translation of *Antony and Cleopatra*, intended for production at the Moscow Art Theatre.

In addition to the above statement Pasternak also wrote two articles on his translation from the English. One appeared in the magazine *Znamya* in 1944; the other, "Notes on Translation of Shakespeare's Tragedies," was published in the anthology *Literary Moscow* (No. 1, 1956).

These "Notes" are especially significant, as well as characteristic of Pasternak's literary personality. Pasternak translated nine of Shakespeare's tragedies, including *Hamlet*, *Romeo and Juliet*, *Antony and Cleopatra*, *Othello*, both parts of *Henry IV*, *King Lear*, and *Macbeth*. I shall cite here only a few excerpts from his comments on these tragedies. *Hamlet*, in Pasternak's view, is "not a drama of weakness and indecision. It is a drama of duty and self-denial. When it becomes manifest that appearance and reality do not coincide, that there is a wide gulf between them, it is not important that the reminder of the falseness of the world comes in supernatural form, and that the ghost demands vengeance of Hamlet. What is far more important is that Hamlet is elected by the will of chance to be the judge of his time and the servant of a time still looming in the future. *Hamlet* is a drama of high destiny, of a commandment to heroism entrusted to one foreordained."

Pasternak's comment on *Romeo and Juliet* is profoundly poetic. Outside the window there is a clashing of swords as Montagues and Capulets fight one another, while the servants quarrel in the kitchen. And to the accompaniment of these rude sounds, "as to the thundering blasts of a brass band, the tragedy of gentle feelings runs its course, written throughout its major part in the soundless whisper of the conspirators. . . ."

Discussing Shakespeare's poetic style, Pasternak speaks of the essential meaning of the metaphor: "The metaphor is the natural consequence of the brevity of man's life and the long-range vastness of his problems. He is obliged to look at things with an eagle's sharpness and to express himself in instantaneous and immediately understandable illuminations. . . . The metaphor is the great individual's shorthand, the speedwriting of his spirit."

Like so many of Pasternak's utterances on Shakespeare, these words are equally applicable to himself.

Before examining Boris Pasternak's last work, his novel *Doctor Zhivago*, for which the Swedish Academy awarded him the Nobel Prize, it is necessary to mark one of his dominant traits, which clearly manifested itself in his two autobiographical essays, *Safe Conduct* and *Autobiography*: Pasternak is always extremely reticent when writing about himself. But his short portraits of contemporaries—Blok, L. Tolstoy, Mayakovsky, Yesenin, Bely, Fadeyev—are striking both in brilliance of form and in depth of insight. These portraits give the reader an intimate sense of the life of Russian writers during the unique transitional period of their country's existence. In this respect *Doctor Zhivago* is especially revealing.

In its essence *Doctor Zhivago* is the confession of the generation of intellectuals who did not take any active part either in the revolution of 1905, or in that of 1917. Our attention is immediately drawn to Pasternak's remark that Doctor Zhivago dreamed from his earliest years of writing a book about life, about all the dynamic explosive elements constantly emerging in it, and occupying his reflections. At the time when the wish first came to him, he was still too young to realize it, and he began to write poetry. But as he did so, he thought of himself as an artist making sketches for a large canvas that was already alive within him.

Russian readers, especially those of the spiritual world to which Pasternak assigned the central place in his novel, will find in it many features of their own internal biography; they will find in it those "things past" which were not reflected either by Gorky in his *Life of Klim Samgin* (English title: *Bystander*, 1926-36), representing the history of forty years of Russian life, or by Alexey Tolstoy in his trilogy *The Road to Calvary* (1918–41).

The first mention of the forthcoming publication of *Doctor Zhivago* appeared in the April issue of the magazine *Znamya* in 1954, in Pasternak's preface to the poems from the novel:

"The novel will probably be completed this summer. It embraces the years between 1903 and 1929, with an epilogue related to the Great Patriotic War.

"Its hero, Yury Andreevich Zhivago, a doctor, is a man of a reflective and questing turn of mind, creative and artistic in temperament. He dies in 1929, leaving his notes and, among other papers, a number of finished poems, written in his youth. Some of these poems are offered below. The entire group will comprise the last, concluding chapter of the novel."

Doctor Zhivago has not yet appeared in the Soviet Union. It was published only abroad, both in Russian and in translation into many other languages. This was the third time in the history of Soviet literature when a Russian writer's novel made its first appearance abroad, in the original and in numerous translations. The other two works were Yevgeny Zamyatin's satirical novel *We* and Boris Pilnyak's *Mahogany*. However, in distinction to these works, Pasternak's novel is devoid not only of sensational political content, but of "politics" generally, in the common usage of this word.

From the very first pages the reader is carried away by the sweeping, breathless "vista of the novel," to borrow Pushkin's phrase. It opens with a description of the funeral of Marya Nikolaevna, the mother of the future Doctor Zhivago. Against the background of the history of several families, bound by kinship, old friendship, or acquaintance with the family of the late Marya Nikolaevna, we see the story of three generations. But the core of the novel is the history of the generation whose adolescence witnessed the revolution of 1905, and whose youth coincided with the First World War and the revolution of 1917.

Yura Zhivago and his contemporaries and friends—Misha Gordon, Nika Dudorov, Tonya Gromeko, Lara Gishar, and Pasha Antipov—sympathize with the revolution of 1905 in their early youth. Later, in 1917, their paths diverge, and some of them, like Yusupka Galiullin, find themselves in the camp of the Whites.

But regardless of the camp in which they later found themselves, their spiritual world was formed outside the mainstream of social development. This is especially true of the two principal characters of the novel, the future Doctor Zhivago and Lara Gishar, whose life, broken and mutilated from her earliest years, forms one of the most moving threads in the plot of the novel. It was probably with her in mind that Doctor Zhivago wrote these lines in his poem "Parting":

> In years of tribulation, in the days
> Of unimaginable life
> The wave of fate had swept her from the depths
> Onto his shore.

In the course of the narrative it transpires that the barrister Komarovsky, who played such a fatal part in young Lara's life, had also been the evil genius of Yura Zhivago's father, who had committed suicide.

An important influence on the development of Yura Zhivago was exerted by his maternal uncle Kolya—the writer and philosopher Nikolay Vedenyapin. Vedenyapin detested everything that smacked of the "herd," which he called "the refuge of mediocrity," and it made no difference to him whether people swore "by the name of Vladimir Solovyov, Kant, or Marx." To him, the most important thing in modern man was "the idea of the free personality, and the idea of life as sacrifice."

Much later, already after Zhivago's marriage to Tonya Gromeko, came his meetings with Lara at the front during the First World War, and in a small town in the Urals. They were drawn together by the sense of a "community of spirit," which gave them even greater joy than their mutual love: "they were united by the abyss which separated them from the rest of the world; they were both equally repelled by the fatally typical in modern man, his enthusiasms learned by rote, his shrill excitement, and the deadly mediocrity so assiduously cultivated by innumerable workers in the fields of science and art in order that genius should remain a great rarity."

Along with its living picture of three generations of Russian intelligentsia, *Doctor Zhivago*, more than any other work by Pasternak, is also a rich source for the understanding of the spiritual world of the poet himself. Pasternak's was a religious nature, and, like Blok, he ceaselessly listened to the "music" of his time. This listening brought him to the optimistic conclusion that, although the liberation and the brighter life that people had expected to follow the end of the war had failed to materialize after the victory, "the augury of freedom was in the air throughout the postwar years, forming their sole historic content."

Pasternak's death brought to a close a great lyric tradition in Russian poetry, graced by the names of Fyodor Tyutchev, Vladimir Solovyov, and Pasternak's older contemporary, Alexander Blok.

The spiritual life of Blok was permeated by the profound conviction that true art demands sacrifice from the artist. Pasternak's Hamlet (in the poem of that name, found among Doctor Zhivago's papers) prays to fate to carry the cup of suffering past him. But he knows that destiny will not alter its design:

> . . . the order of the acts is planned,
> And unavoidable the end. . . .

And the poet himself courageously traveled his road to the very end.

11 YURY OLESHA (1899–1960)

The literary legacy of Yury Olesha, who died on May 10, 1960, is quite small: the novel *Envy* (1927), the adventure novel *Three Fat Men* (1928), a collection of short stories, *The Cherry Stone* (1930), the play *A List of Blessings* (1931), the long story "From the Secret Notebooks of the Fellow Traveler Zand" (1932), the play *The Black Man* (1932), and the play *A Stern Youth* (1934). Soon after Olesha's speech at the First All-Union Congress of Writers in 1934, a speech which was both a confession and an affirmation of individual belief, his name disappeared from Soviet literature for many years. It began to appear again in the early 1950s, but his works since then consisted mainly of articles, essays, and reminiscences. One of these essays, "From my Literary Notebooks," was published in the anthology *Literary Moscow* (Vol. 2, 1956).

Despite the modest volume of his literary output, Olesha will be remembered in the history of contemporary Soviet literature as one of the small band of gifted writers who remained faithful to the end to the ideas for which they had fought when they first entered upon their literary paths. He won wide fame with his first novel, *Envy*. The article on Olesha in the *Literary Encyclopedia* is accurate in saying that, after the publication of *Envy*, Olesha was immediately lifted out of the ranks of the unknown contributors to the magazine *Gudok* (The Whistle), for which he had been writing verse *feuilletons* under the pen name of Zubilo (Chisel), into the forefront of Soviet literature.

In the short autobiographical sketch "A Writer's Notes" (in the collection *The Cherry Stone*) Olesha relates that he was born in Elisavetgrad, in the former Kherson Province. When he was three, his parents moved to Odessa, and it was this city that he invested with "all the lyrical emotions connected with one's birthplace." In this sketch Olesha says little about his working methods; the only interesting fact he mentions is that he never made any preliminary plans or outlines for the work at hand, even when he wrote his adventure novel, *Three Fat Men*.

He speaks at somewhat greater length about his literary work in his "Reminiscences about Eduard Bagritsky" (1934). Olesha belonged to the group of young writers and poets which Victor Shklovsky gave the name of "Southwest." Other members were Eduard Bagritsky, Valentin Katayev, Zinaida Shishova, Adelaida Adalis, and later Semyon Kirsanov. Olesha's closest ties were with Bagritsky. Although all the members were approximately of the same age, Bagritsky was by far the best educated among them in the field of literature. He taught his friends to appreciate good poetry, and introduced them to the work of Innokenty Annensky, Boris Pasternak, Anna Akhmatova, Nikolay Gumilyov, Osip Mandelstam, Nikolay Kluyev, and Vyacheslav Ivanov.

The novel *Envy* impresses the reader with its multifaceted theme: it deals with the conflict between the moral values of the old, vanished world and those of the new, born of the victory of the revolution. The values of the past are defended by a young man of indefinite occupation, Nikolay Kavalerov, and the ex-engineer Ivan Babichev, a derelict wallowing in the depths of alcoholism. The world of the new men and ideas is represented by Andrey Babichev, Ivan's brother, Andrey's protégé Volodya Makarov, and Ivan's daughter Valya.

Andrey Babichev is an old Bolshevik, a member of the Society of Former Political Prisoners (of Czarist days), and the director of a food-industry trust. Fulfilling his party assignment, he has become "a great sausage maker, confectioner, and chef," and the creator of the giant cafeteria "The Quarter," where a two-course meal will cost only a quarter.

The novel's action centers on three characters: Nikolay Kavalerov, Andrey Babichev, and his brother Ivan. Kavalerov's acquaintance with Andrey Babichev occurs by accident: returning home one night, Andrey finds Kavalerov lying drunk in the street and brings him home, where he puts him up temporarily in the room of Volodya Makarov, who is away visiting his parents in Murom.

From the very first day of his stay with Andrey Babichev, Nikolay begins a close and prejudiced observation of his "benefactor," toward whom he harbors a secret envy. Kavalerov is educated, well-bred, but deeply unhappy. His principal misfortune is that he would like to enter into the new life, but does not know how to do it. He is incapable of closing his eyes, as so many of his contemporaries do, to the contradictions of this life and the frequent crudity of the new moral concepts. Feeling that the reason for his failure lies not only in his own ineptness, but in the profound conflicts existing in reality, he is continuously preoccupied with the effort to justify himself and to convince himself that the heroes of the age are mediocrities who have gained prominence merely by chance. Kavalerov's envy is intense and corrosive. And yet, despite his occasionally repellent traits, Nikolay Kavalerov is defending genuine values. Many of his observations are entirely just, even when his insights are prompted by personal frustrations.

Nikolay Kavalerov does not conceal that he not only envies Andrey, but literally hates him for his zest in living, his unquenchable energy and health. "In the morning he sings in the toilet." This is the first line of the novel and the beginnings of Kavalerov's comments on Andrey's life. Kavalerov considers himself more intelligent than Andrey and makes no attempt to hide his feelings: "In our country the roads to fame are barred. . . . A gifted man must either lose his luster or venture, at the cost of great scandal, to lift the bars." He confesses to Andrey that he wishes he had been born somewhere in Europe, in some small town in France, where one might grow up with ambitious dreams and one fine day set out for the capital, there to work tirelessly, and ultimately to "achieve the goal." Unfortunately, he was not born in the West. Moreover, in his own country he is now being told that not only he, but even the most remarkable individual, is "nothing at all." Sometimes he is filled with the urge to "commit some act of dazzling mischief," so that afterward he might come out into the public square, take his bow, and cry out: "I have lived! I have done what I wanted to do!" At times his restless tirades end in the confession that he would like to hang himself in the doorway of the house where Andrey Babichev lives. But Babichev is totally unimpressed by all these outpourings. He merely advises Kavalerov that it would be better to hang himself in the doorway of the Supreme Soviet building: "There, it would look more effective."

The only attentive listener Kavalerov can find is Andrey's brother, Ivan Babichev. Ivan calls himself "the last dreamer on earth." He immediately senses a kinship between himself and Kavalerov. The latter's animosity toward Andrey is steadily growing. He decides to leave him and writes a farewell letter in which he openly confesses all his feelings: "I hate you, Comrade Babichev. . . . From the very first days of my life with you I began to feel afraid. You crushed me. You weighed me down. . . ." Kavalerov protests that Babichev has no right to "crush" him. Andrey, he says, is certainly neither more intelligent, nor richer spiritually, nor more important than he, Kavalerov. His observations of Babichev in the course of a month have brought him to the conclusion that Babichev is a dull bureaucrat, a pompous "dignitary," and a "capricious tyrant." In an attempt to wound him most cruelly, Kavalerov says that Babichev is really nothing but a *barin*, a wealthy gentleman of the old school, and that his feelings toward Volodya Makarov are not in the least paternal, but those of a wealthy squire toward a poor dependent. Moreover, Andrey is accustomed to flattery and hates the truth. Kavalerov concludes his letter with the cry that, while "the lickspittles were singing hymns of praise to you . . . a man lived next to you whom no one took into account and whose opinion no one troubled to ask." Yet this same man has come to the conclusion that Andrey Babichev is "a mediocrity raised to enviable heights thanks solely to external conditions. . . ." He, Kavalerov, intends to "wage war" against him and his ilk for the sake of Ivan Babichev, for Ivan's daughter Valya, "for tenderness, for emotion, for individuality, for names which stir the imagination, like the name of Ophelia, for everything that is suppressed by you, the remarkable man."

Equally full of belligerent spirit is Andrey's brother, Ivan Babichev. He urges Kavalerov to take part in his cherished plan for a "conspiracy of feelings." "My dear friend," he argues, "a man must either submit or make a scandal. Or else he must exit with a bang. Slam the door, as they say. This is the main thing: exit with a bang. Leave a scar on the face of history. Make a grand flourish, the devil take you! They won't let you into their world anyway. Don't give up without battle. . . ."

Ivan Babichev is the inventor of a fantastic machine which can destroy all the new twentieth-century machines. He has given his machine the tenderest of names, "Ophelia," and has invested it with "the most banal human emotions." Ivan's invention is his "revenge upon his age." It is a "dazzling fig which the dying age will hold up to the nose of the age now being born." But the plans hatched by Ivan and Kavalerov, their "conspiracy of feelings," and their miraculous machine all come to naught. These two rebels against the new world end up finding refuge in a dirty rooming house, in the ample embraces of an aging, untidy woman, Anechka Prokopovich.

The success of *Envy* is understandable. Apart from its literary merit, the novel impressed Soviet readers with the immediacy and relevance of the problems it raised. *Envy* was the first work about the Soviet "superfluous man" who had emerged among the younger intellectuals, the man who felt alien and ill at ease in the new, post-revolutionary world. Despite his personal unattractiveness, Kavalerov cannot be denied either intelligence or education. This is even more true of Ivan Babichev. Readers sense that the personal faults of Kavalerov and Ivan were the price the author paid for the right to bring to discussion urgent questions of moral values, questions which he felt should not be relegated to the archives of history.

So vivid and meaningful was this image of the Soviet "superfluous man" in the 1920s that, in comparison, Volodya Makarov, who aspired to the career of a Soviet Edison, seemed a schematic, lifeless puppet. Reluctantly, even Soviet critics had to admit the failure of the positive hero, Volodya Makarov, to come alive. This admission cost Olesha a great deal: the critics accused him of sympathy toward individualism, of "Nietzscheanism" and "banal triteness" in his ideals. The writer was placed under suspicion as a spokesman for "petty-bourgeois individualism."

The struggle between two worlds and two cultures remained the principal theme in virtually all of Olesha's subsequent works. The only exception was the novel *Three Fat Men* (1928), which was later presented in play form and was also made into a successful ballet. The plot of this fantasy novel transports us into a world of adventure. In some distant fairy-tale land, in a castle outside the city, protected by moats and guards, live Three Fat Men who oppress the people.

The Three Fat Men have no heirs of their own. They separate two orphan children—the brother and sister Tutti and Suok, and take Tutti into the castle to be brought up as their heir. They summon the scientist Toub and order him to construct a mechanical doll—a copy of Suok. Then they give the real Suok away to an itinerant circus and leave the doll with Tutti, pretending that she is his sister. They also order Toub to take out Tutti's living heart and replace it by an iron one, but Toub refuses, saying that "a man must not be robbed of his human heart": "no other heart—neither of iron, nor of ice, nor of gold—may be given a man instead of his ordinary, real human heart." For his refusal to obey the order of the Three Fat Men, the learned Toub is placed in a cage, in which he sits for eight years, until the people, with the aid of the gunsmith Prospero and the gymnast Tibul, defeat the Three

Fat Men. The little dancer Suok proves to be of great help to Prospero and Tibul in their fight.

Apart from the play *The Conspiracy of Feelings*, the works which most characteristically embody Olesha's basic theme of the struggle between two worlds are the stories in the collection *The Cherry Stone*, the play *A List of Blessings*, the story "From the Secret Notebooks of the Fellow Traveler Zand," and the short play *The Black Man*.

Olesha's preoccupation with this conflict within the individual mind between opposing worlds, and the resulting alienation, originated long ago, while the "old world" was still alive. This is revealed in "I Look into the Past" (in the collection *The Cherry Stone*). The little boy, hero of the story and the author's alter ego, loves to read. Among his greatest experiences is his first acquaintance with *Don Quixote* (interestingly enough, *Don Quixote* also made a great impression on the child Mayakovsky). The image of Don Quixote opens the boy's mind for the first time to the concept of "a man created by another man," of "immortality in the only form in which it is possible on earth." And yet, instead of curing the boy's sense of loneliness, reading intensifies it. In "I Look into the Past" the author tells us that he possesses the secret of "transforming sadness into joy." Nevertheless, he adds, "it is pleasant to be sad." Sadness evokes the need to dream, and so, gradually, leads to "solitude—a destiny of lifelong loneliness, a man's destiny of remaining solitary everywhere and in everything."

A List of Blessings (1931) opens with a presentation of *Hamlet* by the talented actress Elena Goncharova. The play begins with the final curtain on the performance. Goncharova herself takes part in the audience discussion about the staging of *Hamlet*. In spite of her talent and fame, Goncharova is unhappy and longs to leave the Soviet Union. She keeps a diary, which is divided into two parts: in one, she writes down "the crimes of the revolution"; in the other, she lists its "blessings." Goncharova suffers keenly from loneliness, realizing that "the struggle between two worlds" is taking place within her own heart, and that, in essence, she is engaged in an argument with herself. Goncharova's tragedy is the tragedy of the entire Russian intelligentsia, which is bound in all its thoughts and feelings to the past. Her tragedy is the tragedy of Olesha himself. Neither of them is a counterrevolutionary, and their "list of crimes" is not a list of "philistine" complaints against discomforts and privations of day-to-day living, but a record of what frightens them most in the Soviet state—its crimes against human individuality.

At the discussion which takes place at the opening of the play, Goncharova succeeds in expressing three important ideas: contemporary Soviet plays are schematic and false, and it is difficult to act in them; one should not be daunted by the fact that the duty of an artist—even in an epoch of rapidly moving events—is to "think slowly"; and, most important of all, the proletariat and the party violate the artist, but he should reply to them in Hamlet's words that, though the government would like to "pluck out" of him the very heart of his mystery, it "cannot play upon" him.

After repeated attempts Goncharova succeeds in leaving Soviet Russia on an assignment abroad. In Paris she feels at first how close "the ancient stones of Europe" are to her heart. At this point the spectator seems to witness the climactic moment of the play. Yet it is precisely at this moment that the tragic element in it is sharply reduced: Goncharova suddenly "recovers her sight." From the "beautiful distance" the Soviet world appears to her virtually as the kingdom of light, and she begins to long for it. In the end she perishes absurdly during a clash between Paris strikers and the police, shielding a French Communist from the bullet of a Russian *émigré*, a *provocateur* in the pay of the Paris police.

The theme of loneliness also appears in the story "From the Secret Notebooks of the Fellow Traveler Zand." The hero of these notebooks, the writer Modest Zand, is fond of looking at a painting which depicts Schiller receiving a public ovation after the première of *Love and Intrigue*. Zand dreams vainly of creating a work that would be welcomed by the "new class" with as much enthusiasm as Schiller's drama elicited among the representatives of "young Germany." In his notebooks he says that his feeling toward many writers, including Jack London, Balzac, and Pushkin, the creator of *Boris Godunov*, is "noble envy." But he believes that he could equal their achievements if he were allowed creative freedom. The only exception, he admits, is Tolstoy, whose greatness is a natural phenomenon of the same order as "stars and waterfalls," and, therefore, cannot be an object of envy.

Modest Zand has a friend, the Communist Kolotilov, a man of action and will, who does not understand Zand's "quibbles." But Zand cannot write "to order"; he can write only after he has himself experienced the emotions which he seeks to embody in his heroes. In the end Zand meets another friend, an editor of a party newspaper, and talks to him about his problems. Again he fails to elicit any sympathy or understanding. The editor responds to all the questions raised by Zand with the stock formula: "You must become one with the masses."

The theme of the "Secret Notebooks" is continued in the short play *The Black Man* (published in the magazine *Thirty Days*, in June 1932.) Its hero is the same Modest Zand. In the preface to the play, Olesha puts the following rather interesting reflections into the mouth of Zand: ". . . In order to become a writer who is consonant with the epoch, one must renounce a large number of themes. There are themes which may be quite remarkable, but they are unnecessary to our time. And not only unnecessary, but harmful and reactionary, if only because they are pessimistic. They 'de-magnetize' the reader who is engaged in building. These themes, it is said, should be stricken from our notebooks. But is this a valid solution—striking out a theme? Will it also disappear from the mind? After it is thrown out of the notebook, will it not remain in the brain?" And here Olesha adds his own comment. "Even if the writer Zand," he says, "should devote himself to a new, great, vital, optimistic, 'sunny' theme, the black theme, like a noxious lizard, will push its evil-smelling tail or venomous head through Zand's new work. . . . What is to be done? How can this theme be extirpated? The present play is devoted to the struggle of the writer Zand with the 'Black Man,' the struggle between the idea of death in art and the idea of reconstruction of the world through creative work."

The extent to which Olesha was preoccupied with this theme can be seen from an interview with him which appeared in the *Literary Gazette* (No. 25, 1935.) In this interview Olesha confessed: "'I never worked as hard as I have during the past two years. In two years I have published two stories and two plays. . . . It is difficult for me to continue, and even more difficult to complete work begun, because in my mind one theme devours another, because . . .' he laughed with joy at finding an apt image, 'because I am consumed by a veritable cancer of an imagination! *Envy* was the product of all I had seen throughout my conscious life until the age of twenty-seven. There are colors in it which entered my awareness in early youth. . . . My creative work is moved by the sincere desire for a true understanding of all the stages of our development. *The Conspiracy of Feelings* was the product of the transition from the world of property to a new world. . . .'" But, Olesha added at this point, it was impossible for him to write a work in which he was not represented by one of the characters.

With moving sincerity Olesha spoke about all the doubts that troubled him as a writer and about his literary "Credo" in his speech at the First All-Union Congress of Writers in 1934. Many of the confessions contained in this speech still agitate the minds of Soviet writers today:

"An artist's relations with what is good or bad are extremely complex. When you depict a negative hero, you become negative yourself. You raise from the bottom of your soul things that are evil and unclean, and so you learn that this evil and uncleanness exists in you, and hence you take upon your consciousness a very heavy psychological burden. . . . Six years ago I wrote *Envy*. The central character in the book was Nikolay Kavalerov. I was told that there was a great deal of myself in Kavalerov, that he was autobiographical, that Kavalerov was I myself. Yes, it was true that Kavalerov looked at the world with my eyes. Kavalerov's images, colors, similes, metaphors, and conclusions were mine. And those were the most vivid colors I saw. Many of them had come to me from childhood, were drawn from the most cherished corners, from the secret drawers of unique and unrepeatable memories and observations. As an artist, I manifested in Kavalerov the purest power, the power of a first work, of first impressions. And then I was told that Kavalerov was a cheap, banal nonentity. . . . Knowing how much of myself there was in Kavalerov, I felt that this accusation of banality and insignificance was directed at me, and I was deeply shaken. . . ."

After that, according to his own confession, Olesha "withdrew into himself," but deep within his heart he felt the accusation to be unjust. He said to himself: "A man endowed with fresh powers of observation and the ability to see the world in his own way cannot possibly be a banal nonentity." Then he decided to write a new novel, to be called "The Pauper."

Olesha's account of the initial stages of an artist's work on a new book is very interesting. When he conceived the idea of this novel, his first act was to imagine himself such a "pauper." "I imagined myself leading a life full of hardship and suffering—the life of a man deprived of everything." To do this, it was necessary to sink, as it were, "to the very bottom." He visualized himself barefoot, in a shabby quilted jacket, trudging across the land: "I saw myself walking at night over construction sites. Scaffoldings, fires . . . and myself, walking barefoot." But once, during these imaginary wanderings, "in the pure fresh air of a certain morning," he saw himself coming to a wall in a field. Such half-ruined walls are sometimes encountered near towns and cities. He walked along the wall and came to an archway, a narrow entrance, "such as you see in Renaissance paintings." He approached it, ascended a staircase, stepped across a threshold, and seemed to turn around for a look at himself. And at that moment he felt as if he had unexpectedly regained his youth. He sensed it even physically, noticing how young the skin of his hands had become. He was again sixteen. And suddenly he understood that "there was no need for any of this pain. All my doubts, all sufferings were gone. I was young, with my whole life before me...."

At this point, says Olesha, "I understood that my central intention, my main dream was to preserve the *rightness of youth*, to defend my freshness of response against the charge that freshness is banal and worthless. It was not my fault that my youth had been spent under conditions when the surrounding world was frightful." However, Olesha never wrote this novel, and it was only later that he understood the reasons why. . . . He was frequently advised by acquaintances to choose some topic reflecting the life of the country during the first Five-Year Plan, but Olesha felt that, as an artist, he could not identify himself with such a topic: "I would have to lie and invent, I would feel nothing of that which is known as inspiration. It is difficult for me to understand the worker, the heroic revolutionary. I cannot be one...." Toward the end of his remarkable speech, Olesha said: "The most terrible thing is to abase oneself, to say that one is nothing in comparison with a worker or a Comsomol member. . . . No, I have enough pride to say that, although I was born in the old world, there is a great deal in me, in my soul and my imagination that places me on a level of equality both with the worker and the Comsomol member."

Very remarkable, too, is the conclusion of Olesha's speech, in which he spoke of his creative plans: "I shall write about our youth." And he would ask this new youth: "What are your feelings, what do you dream of, do you know how to cry? Are you tender?"

The delegates to the congress were tremendously moved by Olesha's courageous and eloquent confession and declaration of faith. Years later, in the first public response to his sudden death (Olesha died of a heart attack in 1960),

Lev Nikulin, writing in *Literature and Life* (May 13, 1960), recalled his speech as "profound and brilliant in form." According to Nikulin, it was highly praised at the time by Gorky and by many other writers "who are no longer with us." Among these were the late Lydia Seyfulina and Alexander Arosev, who were deeply impressed with Olesha's speech.

However, the wide praise of Olesha's speech at the Writers' Congress did not alter the attitude of the official critics, who persisted in their attacks. This was especially apparent in the response to his play *A Stern Youth* (1934). The plot of this play, which was intended as a film script, is simple: Doctor Stepanov, an eminent surgeon, saves the life of the Comsomol member Olga, a friend of the young Communist Diskobol. Stepanov's friend Tsitronov is in love with the former's wife, Masha. But Masha loves the obscure Comsomol member Grisha Fokin. Thus, the play, like the novel *Envy*, has six characters, and is, in essence, another attempt to deal with the same theme. The old world represented in the play by Stepanov, Masha, and Tsitronov, none of them as gifted as Kavalerov and Ivan Babichev. Unlike the latter, who longed for lost moral values, Tsitronov is negative and cynical. He gloats because inequality continues to exist in the new world. Dr. Stepanov, who has adjusted himself and seems to be in sympathy with the new world, nevertheless shares many of the attitudes of people of the old, and not necessarily those of progressive views. Like Olesha himself, Stepanov tends to think that "only misfortune, only suffering can be the ferment activating the movement and development of personality." Opposed to such "decadent" reasoning is the "moral code" evolved by the Comsomol member Grisha Fokin: a socially conscious young Communist, in his view, must seek to equal the best, give due admiration to talent, and develop within himself the qualities of modesty, nobility, loyalty, and altruism. At the end of the play Tsitronov is unmasked and turned out by Stepanov. But Stepanov himself must also step aside to make way for the new. He is jealous of Grisha.

Grisha tries to master his feeling for Masha, but she takes the initiative and leaves her husband for him, thus leaving the old world for the new.

The first response to the play, an article by Victor Pertsov, "A Conspiracy of Noble Minds," published in the *Literary Gazette* on September 28, 1934, was generally favorable. The critic remarked that the play was in many respects "*Envy* reversed." However, Pertsov felt that the entire philosophy on which the play was based was erroneous. Its message, urging emulation of the best, meant —in plain paraphrase—"pay due tribute of admiration to noble minds." This, in turn, was not too far from an exhortation to humility. Olesha, he felt, had also erred in ignoring "the extraordinary collective body of our land." Instead of adopting humility, asserts Pertsov, our people collectively have raised the slogan: "Dare! And then no conspiracies will hold any terrors for you!"

Other comments were far more harsh. Some critics even found "elements of Fascist ideology" in Olesha's play! In reality, *A Stern Youth* was an unwitting illustration of Olesha's idea that a theme thrown out of a writer's notebook must, once it was born in his mind, ultimately reappear in another form in one of his future works.

A Stern Youth was never produced; it was Olesha's last major work. Some two years after its publication (in 1934) his name disappeared from Soviet literary journals. It did not reappear until after the war, in the early 1950s, and then mostly over articles, essays, and memoirs. His "Literary Diaries" and the excerpts from his notebooks reveal that, although doomed to silence, Olesha continued to work stubbornly, systematically, and intensively on perfecting his literary form. In a short story, "In the World," Olesha mentions that he had preserved in his old folders three hundred pages of a manuscript, each marked with the numeral "1." They were the three hundred versions of the first page of his novel, *Envy*, none of which was used in the final text.

A vivid intimation of Olesha's great skill as a writer is found in the short essay "Not a Day without a Line." The writer recalls how, as a child, he was walking down the street one day, when someone called "Boy!" He did not know to whom this was addressed, but he turned around. Olesha wonders:

"Would I turn around now if someone called, 'Old man!'? Perhaps I wouldn't. Why? Because I would not want to? No, it seems to me that it would be chiefly because of disbelief, astonishment that it has come so soon. . . . Has it really come?

"'Old man! Hey, there old man!'
"No, this is not addressed to me, it cannot be.
"'Old man!'
"No, I will not look around. It cannot have happened so soon.
"'Old man! The fool, he doesn't turn around! This is I—death!'"

And indeed, death stole upon the writer so suddenly that he did not have time to "turn around." He died correcting the proofs of an article which was published in the same issue of the *Literary Gazette* that carried L. Nikulin's short obituary. The article Olesha was correcting was on Hemingway. Analyzing Hemingway's work, Olesha wrote: "A great writer does not imitate. But somewhere at the bottom of one work or another by an author who has paid particular attention at the beginning of his literary life to some writer of the past, you can always discern the light of the earlier one. And so, you can sometimes see at the bottom of Hemingway's work the light of Tolstoy—of *The Cossacks*, the *Sevastopol Stories*, *War and Peace*. . . . To put it more exactly, this is the light of Hemingway's love for Tolstoy."

The one-volume edition of Olesha's selected works, published while he was still alive (Moscow, 1956), offers the reader a vivid picture of the late writer's mastery of his art and an intimation of how many unrealized and uncompleted ideas for further work were lost with him. Everything he wrote was permeated with love of that which was the cherished ideal of Russia's entire pre-revolutionary literature—love of freedom and man's creative spirit.

12 LEONID LEONOV (1899–   )

Many young writers begin their literary careers with a work they call a novel. On closer acquaintance it quickly becomes obvious that their book can scarcely be called a novel by the standards normally set for this literary form. "In order to construct a novel," said Chekhov,[1] "it is necessary to have a good knowledge of the law of symmetry and the balance of masses. A novel is an entire palace, and the reader should feel free in it, neither astonished nor bored as in a museum. Sometimes he must be given a rest both from the hero and the author. This can be accomplished with a landscape, or something amusing, or a new twist in the plot, new characters. . . ."

Leonid Leonov is one of the relatively small company of genuine novelists who know "the law of symmetry and the balance of masses."

Leonov was born in 1899 in Moscow, the son of a self-educated peasant poet who was at one time the chairman of the Surikov Literary and Musical Circle (the poet Surikov was also of peasant origin). Later, Leonov's father joined the literary group which called itself "Sreda" (Wednesday) and which attracted at the turn of the century many young men who subsequently became famous writers, including Bunin, Leonid Andreyev, and others. Leonov's grandfather owned a grocery store in Zaryadye, the market district in the old section of Moscow. A stern manner and great kindness were the most striking characteristics of this unusually colorful man, whom Leonov later used as the model for Bykhalov in his novel *The Badgers.*

Leonov's earliest memories were of 1905, when the ter-

[1] Quoted by A. Serebrov (Tikhonov) in *Chekhov in the Recollections of Contemporaries* (Moscow: State Publishing House for Fine Literature [GIKhL], 1952), pp. 474–75.

rorist Kalyaev assassinated the Grand Duke Sergey Alexandrovich. During the same year the future writer's father was arrested for publishing two pamphlets. The boy was twice taken by his grandmother to visit his father in prison. After twenty months in prison his father was released, but was exiled soon afterward to Arkhangelsk, where he remained even after the expiration of his term of exile. Leonov visited his father in Arkhangelsk several times, and the north made a great impression upon him, later reflected in a number of his works (particularly *Sot*).

Leonov received his elementary education at the city school in Moscow. His favorite teacher was Mitrofan Platonovich Kulkov. In 1925, when the young writer's works were first translated into German, he wanted to present a copy of the German edition to his old teacher, but the old man was no longer alive: both he and his wife (also a teacher) had died in the early part of the Civil War. Leonov later gave the name of Kulkov to the teacher of General Litovchenko, one of the characters in the novel *The Taking of Velikoshumsk* (1944).

During the Civil War, Leonov joined the Red Army as a volunteer, but was freed in 1921 in order to continue his education. At that time Leonov planned to study painting. When he returned to Moscow, he found none of his relatives or acquaintances there, except his mother's cousin, the locksmith Vasiliev, who readily accepted the young man into his home. But Leonov insisted on repaying his uncle's hospitality by helping in his locksmith's shop. For a long time afterward, he "toiled over the smoky forge." Later, the famous Russian graphic artist Falileyev took an interest in the young writer, and it was while living in his studio that Leonov wrote *The Petushikhino Breakthrough* and *The End of a Little Man*. Falileyev introduced Leonov to some well-known artists and literary figures of the mid-1920s. These included two publishers—Koppelman (of the Shipovnik Publishing House) and Sabashnikov. On hearing several of the young writer's stories, both of them offered to publish a volume of the pieces. This initiated a new phase in Leonov's life—the beginning of professional literary activity.[2]

Leonov's first stories—"Buryga," "The Wooden Queen," and the longer tale *The Petushikhino Breakthrough*—were merely gropings for a theme, merely attempts to relieve the pressure of ideas and images that filled his mind. "Buryga" is an imp who, after a complicated series of adventures, finds himself far from his native woods, in distant Spain, with the cook of a "Spanish count," and his only friend, an old dog. "The Wooden Queen" is a little poem in prose, inspired by a long December evening and the flute song of a blizzard. The most interesting of these first "trials of the pen" is *The Petushikhino Breakthrough*. It is a tale of village life on the eve and in the early days of the revolution. Amid a tangle of human destinies the writer singles out the warm image of the quiet boy Alyosha, filled with a tender love of the world, living like a fragile azure flower somewhere at the edge of a forest.

In this tale we find Leonov's first use of lyrical digression, reflecting on the meaning of the large events of the time. These digressions were later to be given a firm place in Leonov's works. In this story Leonov devotes his lyrical digression to the distant future: "The troubled days will pass, we shall put on velvet trousers, sit down around electric samovars, and recall, and recall the dance of frantic rainless winds . . . when our guiltless Mitkas, Nikitkas, and Vasyatkas went without shrouds or coffins to public, crossless graveyards. . . . We shall recall how we fought for our right to be Red. . . ."

Fame came to Leonov early, with *Kovyakin's Journal*. This *Journal* is kept in the name of an old resident of Gogulev, a decaying hamlet forgotten by the powers that be. There is a humbled quality in Kovyakin, reminiscent of Gogol's Akaky Akakievich, but in contrast to Akaky, Kovyakin is a man well pleased with himself.

[2] Cf. *Sovetskiye Pisateli*, Vol. 1 (Moscow: State Publishing House for Fine Literature [GIKhL], 1959), pp. 660–66.

But neither *Kovyakin's Journal* nor *The End of a Little Man* marked Leonov's emergence as a major literary figure. This was accomplished by his first novel, *The Badgers* (1925), reflecting the early years of the revolution, which "reshuffled the cards" in such a way that the "game" proceeded according to new, unheard-of rules, under which "non-trump yokels beat true-born kings."

The novel is built on two planes: the village and the city. The poor peasant Savelin sends his two sons, Pavel and Semyon, to the city to learn new ways of earning a livelihood. They go to live with a former neighbor who had moved to Moscow and now owns a stall in the Zaryadye district, where the wretchedly poor village has long been disposing of its human "surpluses." The enterprising ones among these "surpluses" survive the harsh ordeal and "make their way in the world." Others, the seekers after "justice," remain at the bottom.

Leonov knew Zaryadye very well from frequent childhood visits to his grandfather. It was like a second home to him, and his novel captures the very air of the bustling market district in pre-revolutionary days. We see Zaryadye both on "a crisp December morning," and on a quiet evening in April, filled with the festive ringing of Lenten churchbells, its odors floating steadily along—"solid and slow, like a procession of well-fed Zaryadye tomcats."

Fate early separates the Savelin brothers. The elder, Pavel, lame, unlucky, and disgruntled, goes to work in a factory. Semyon, thoughtful and more even-tempered, adjusts himself to Zaryadye. Here he falls in love with a merchant's daughter, Nastya, but the merchant refuses the poor suitor, and Semyon harbors a deep grievance against him for this refusal.

With the outbreak of the revolution the brothers' paths diverge still further. Semyon is drawn back home. Their village, called Vory ("Thieves"), has long been engaged in litigation with a neighboring village, Gusaki ("Ganders"), over Zinkin meadow. The revolutionary government resolves this old dispute in favor of Gusaki. Its decision gives a new turn to the ancient quarrel: the Vory peasants, who feel wronged by the new authorities, become enemies of the Soviets, secretly hoping that "all this smashing business may make the city crumble into dust."

The pretext for an open rising against the new government is provided by the searches and requisitioning of grain. Semyon becomes the leader of the rebellious villagers. The peasants leave the village, intending to withdraw into the woods. A procession of carts loaded with the wretched peasant belongings heads for the forest, but on the way one of the ringleaders breaks down and exclaims: "Brothers, peasants . . . there's really no place for us to go!" And this cry from the depth of his heart serves as a signal for retreat. Most of the peasants turn back. But Semyon, with a group of other intransigents, becomes a partisan. They make their headquarters in the woods, living in dugouts like badgers (hence the title of the novel). They are joined by Nastya, Semyon's old love. She puts on trousers, and lives and fights together with the partisans.

Supported by the local peasantry, the partisans make flying raids against the representatives of the government, terrorizing them. The center sends army units to fight the rebels. With them comes Semyon's brother, Pavel, who became a Communist in the early days of the revolution. When he learns that Semyon leads the "badgers," Pavel arranges a meeting with him, at which, without revealing his present mission, he tries to convince his brother that, "historically," the village must follow the "Soviets," and that "there is no future for it without the Communists." But even without this naïve propaganda, the "badgers" are shaken with the coming of spring: their longing for the land becomes too strong.

Leonov was one of the first writers to depict the "Green" village—the village which rebelled against the Reds, but did not accept the Whites. He also sought to show the socio-political development of the peasant masses, awakened by the revolution.

The reader will encounter many of the characters of *The Badgers* in the writer's later works. The quiet, inwardly illuminated hatmaker Katushin will reappear in *The Thief* as the master mechanic Pchkhov. In the same novel Manka Vyuga (also Masha Dolomanova) is reminiscent of Nastya, of *The Badgers*. But there is one quality in *The Badgers* which makes it difficult for the reader to become involved in the novel's narrative flow: the writer does not seem to be genuinely interested in the destinies of his heroes. Leonov attempted to overcome this flaw in *The Thief* (1927).

In this novel, against the broad background of the outskirts of Moscow during the NEP period—a period of officially acknowledged retrenchment from revolutionary policies in the face of the country's backward economy—Leonov gives us the first picture of the socio-political conflict which has arisen within the revolution. The hero of the novel is Mitka Vekshin, the son of a railroad watchman at a small, out-of-the-way siding. Impulsive, impressionable, and restless, he plunges wholeheartedly into the revolution from its very start; he fights with reckless courage in the ranks of the Red Army at the front, wins a decoration, and soon becomes a commissar.

After the end of the Civil War, Mitya goes to Moscow. The demobilized soldiers look askance at the growing profusion of goods in the store windows which only yesterday were nothing but shattered glass. In the beginning Mitka is not disturbed by these changes. "With mocking attention, he looked at all of this as the work of his own hands, flattering himself with the secret thought: 'I wanted it, and it appeared; I will not want it and it will go.'" But one day, as he stands by a store window, lightheaded with hunger, looking at the tempting display of tasty delicacies, a woman approaches the store. She is obviously the wife of a NEP man, "elegant and splendid like an Arabian morning." "With simple courtesy," Mitka stretches his hand to open the door for her. But she takes his gesture amiss and strikes his hand. That evening Mitka gets drunk and from then on rapidly begins to roll downhill.

Sinking to "the lower depths," Mitka becomes something of a celebrity and virtually the leader of a gang of thieves.

Here, too, as at the front, his candid and impulsive character wins him many friends. He is joined by his old chum of Red Army days, Sanka Babkin. But Mitka himself is not impressed with his new career as a safecracker. To him, theft is not a profession, but a "persuasion," (as banditry is to Nomakh, the hero of Yesenin's unfinished play). He steals out of protest, but he does not feel that he has broken with his past. "I belong, I'm one of them," he says with feeling to Manka Vyuga (Masha Dolomanova), his childhood friend whom he meets again "at the depths," where she has become "gang queen." "I can still die if necessary," he continues. "But I am not a man to peep through keyholes. Didn't I fight? No, no! Allow a hero not to boast of his heroism."

The allusion to "keyholes" refers simultaneously to two characters in the novel: the chairman of the house committee, Chikilev, a little Soviet pettifogger, about whom "even the pencil feels too disgusted to write," and Mitka's former fellow soldier Atashez, who now occupies an important post in the economic apparatus. Atashez tries to explain to Mitka that the NEP does not mean the end of the revolution, but merely its adoption of "new forms." With his whole direct and impressionable nature Mitka is repelled by these explanations. And the entire background of the novel—the crowded and squalid life in the little apartment in the Blagusha district, with its kindly but scatterbrained café singer Zinka; the Bundyukovs, who love their quiet so much that they prefer to remain childless; the former landowner Manyukin, who earns a livelihood as an entertainer in the Blagusha all-night taverns—all this background merely brings into sharper relief the moving restlessness of the novel's only sincere and honest character —the thief Mitka Vekshin.

But Mitka is not the only hero of the novel. He has an interesting rival in the person of Nikolay Zavarikhin, a young fellow who comes to Moscow from the village in the hope of striking it rich (his trunk is stolen by Manka Vyuga at the station). "Everything was remarkable about him: his great height, as of a man who drew himself up to deliver a blow, the banked fire of his hard, pale-blue eyes, the leather trimming of his fancy felt boots . . . and his gay mittens, so brightly decorated, you'd think their maker was singing a song as he worked, and tracing out its wonderful refrains in color" (these gay and vivid colors mark the verbal mastery of Leonov himself). Nikolka hates the city and yet is drawn to it. He despises the city folk for their easy work and agile hands, but he knows that only the city can give him an opportunity to utilize his extraordinary acquisitive talents. He challengingly presents himself as a "bourgeois," adding: "But now there will be a new breed of bourgeois—without bellies. There won't be anything to stick a knife into." Nikolka's sullen, close-mouthed peasant strength is best expressed in his remark denying the assertion that strong men never cry: "That's rot! A strong man cries when he has nothing to put his strength to."

The writer Firsov, in whose name the narrative is often told, and who represents Leonov himself, remarks that "Mitka and Zavarikhin were spawned in the same hour by the earth, indifferent in her creative rage. The first goes down, the second up. When their paths cross, there are catastrophes, revulsion, and hatred. The first will die a death cruel and splendid; the second will make a three-time fool of death. Both are right: the first, in his honesty and will; the second, in his strength. And both are harbingers of the awakened millions."

Official criticism did not wait for the appearance of the last chapters of the novel (it ran serially for several months in the magazine *Krasnaya Nov*); it descended upon Leonov for exaggerating "the mud-faced danger" supposedly emerging from the NEP-time village. Obligingly, Leonov altered his original intention in mid-course: Mitka does not die, but leaves Moscow for the remote provinces where he becomes a lumberjack, thus breaking his ties with the criminal underworld. Zavarikhin's subsequent fate is indicated in passing in the early pages of the novel: by his large-scale trading in hemp, Nikolka will ultimately win glory for his peasant name not only at home, but also abroad. But we are told about this outside the framework of the story itself; at the end of the novel Zavarikhin is still a small-time owner of a stall in a dark corner of the market place.

The changes made by Leonov in the course of writing the novel as a result of critical attacks are obvious even to the naked eye. However, the reasons for his sense of failure with this work are much more complex, and expressions of dissatisfaction crop up in many places in the novel. What is the source of Leonov's feeling that the novel, on which he has "expended almost all of himself," is in some sense a failure? Some clues to this may be found in his comments on his alter ego, the writer Firsov: "Not loving the things he had to write about in those years, Firsov was afraid of touching Mitka, who appeared to him as a dark, subterranean force, a flame which, once it has broken through, subsides and flares again, momentarily changing form and color. . . . Firsov did not love Mitka enough to tell the truth about him, about the reasons why, in the end, he dropped out of the life he had won by dint of so much suffering and effort."

These lines help us to understand Leonov's sense of creative failure in connection with *The Thief*. Leonov the artist was unquestionably aware of the moods of disappointment with the results of the revolution which existed in Soviet society. During the years when he was writing the novel, disillusionment with the NEP caused many suicides among the young men who had fought in the Civil War and had been fired with the ideas of Wartime Communism. These suicides included the gifted trade-union leader Yury Lutovinov, the proletarian poets Kuznetsov and Khvastunov, and the brilliant peasant poet Sergey Yesenin.

Another conflict emerged and became widespread in the village: awakened by the revolution, the peasant youth was longing to spread its wings, but it felt hamstrung by the duality of the government's policy. Leonov himself was more in sympathy with Mitka than with Zavarikhin; but— like his alter ego Firsov—he *did not love him enough* to tell the whole truth and defend him from the attacks of his critics.

Among the failures of *The Thief* one must include the image of Mitka's youthful love, Masha Dolomanova, who later, through her husband, the thief Aggey, became the "gang queen," Manka Vyuga. In some of her traits she is kin to Dostoyevsky's Grushenka in *The Brothers Karamazov*. Dostoyevsky's influence may be traced in many pages of *The Thief*, particularly in the portrait of the former landowner Manyukin, who, from the writer's many oblique hints, appears to be Mitka's real father. It is felt also in the picture of Mitka's loyal friend Sanka Babkin, and especially of the latter's wife, Xenia.

Despite its flaws, however, *The Thief* is a novel of great scope, with a well-developed plot. Among the writer's most successful moment there is the meeting between Mitka and his sister Tanya, who left the parental roof before him and joined a circus where, thanks to the devotion of Pugel, her instructor, she became a celebrity as an aerialist. Her love affair with Nikolka Zavarikhin and her early death during a circus performance are particularly poignant.

The Thief had a most extraordinary history. At the end of 1959 the novel, which had not been reprinted since the middle of the 1930s, was issued in a new edition. From the preface to this edition the reader learns that *The Thief* has undergone a radical revision, which took Leonov two years to accomplish. In a brief note to the new edition, Leonov says the following:

"The author has reread the book written more than thirty years ago, with pen in hand. To intervene in a work of such long standing is as difficult as stepping for a second time into the same creek. But it is always possible to follow the dried-up bed, listening to the crunching of the pebbles underfoot and looking without fear into the hollows that are no longer filled with water."

In this brief preface every word is a riddle. Why was it necessary to "intervene" in a work written more than thirty years ago? The very comparison of the novel to a "creek" is unconvincing (*The Thief* was not a creek, but a wide river). And how did the water vanish from this "creek"?

A comparison of the two versions reveals that, in revising the novel, the author sought to strip both leading characters of all the traits which had elicited the reader's sympathy—sometimes against the author's will. Leonov achieved this by whittling down the importance and attractiveness of the images of Mitka and Zavarikhin. The digression in which Leonov indirectly admits his failure "to love Mitka enough" is also deleted. In its place we find the harsh and disapproving lines: "Approximately by the middle of the book, we graphically see the futility of Firsov's attempts . . . to save the image of Vekshin, which until recently still held his sympathy—even if somewhat shaken—but which is now *almost hateful to him*" (italics mine—V.A.).

The devaluation of Zavarikhin is still more drastic. He is depicted as a coarse and cynical man, ready to trample down the lives of even those who are near to him for the sake of his interests, as he has done with his fiancée, Tanya Vekshina. The new edition has also been purged of the intimation that Zavarikhin would win renown both at home and abroad through successful trade: he now ends in a concentration camp. In the earlier version Zavarikhin fell in love at first sight with Manka Vyuga, who stole his trunk at the station when he first arrived in Moscow, but he never saw her again, and never looked for her. In the new version he sometimes thinks of her after "a grueling day in the camp." And he never learns that Manka Vyuga also "suffered, revenged herself, and fell, again and again, until at last she came to rot away her days quite near" the place of his own exile.

The *Literary Gazette* (February 7, 1960) published some interesting comment on the new version of *The Thief*:

"Once upon a time, the twenty-three-year-old Leonov, back from the southern front in the Civil War, was struck by the contrasts of NEP-time Moscow. He thought about many problems that seemed insoluble to him at the time —problems connected with the future of his generation, with the search for a place in life. . . ."

But the present version of the novel, according to the *Literary Gazette*, "is a condensation of certain thoughts which have stirred Leonov over three decades; it is a debate of the firmly convinced and experienced writer with his own younger and wavering self."

To the present-day Leonov, the entire 1927 version is a gross political error, and he spares neither effort nor his heroes in order to "correct" his novel. And so, the large river of his earlier narrative has, in fact, dwindled in the later edition to a "dried-up creek."

Having failed, in the latter 1920s, to create a "hero of the epoch" in the images of Mitka Vekshin and Nikolka Zavarikhin, Leonov did not abandon hope that he would still succeed in finding him. He shifted his attention to another milieu, whose active elements devoted themselves to work in the first Five-Year Plan for the industrialization of the country.

Sot (1929) was the first major literary work dealing with the industrialization theme. The idea of building a cellulose-paper combine in the North originates with the chairman of the Province Executive Committee, Potyomkin, who spent his youth, until his army days, as a lumber floater, and who was later a worker in a paper-manufacturing plant. The abundance of forests and available men, and the paper shortage in the country lead Potyomkin to the idea of building a paper factory. As he dreams of it, he becomes more and more enthusiastic and, together with some "knowledgeable people" in the region, he develops a plan for a mighty combine. In his mind's eye Potyomkin already sees an island of industry in the midst of a vast peasant ocean. Thanks to his persistence, Potyomkin succeeds in obtaining approval for his project from the center.

Of course, the novel's interest does not lie in the history of this construction project, but in the men depicted in it. For the first time, the reader of the late 1920s was offered a work reflecting, not the lives and feelings of individuals, but the epoch in the totality of its components. The center of the narrative is held by Uvadyev, one of the leaders of the project and an ex-foreman of a paper factory. After the end of the Civil War his life was spent in responsible but uninteresting work. Uvadyev's credo is simple and direct: "In our age it is necessary to think big: in terms of dozens of factories, thousands of hectares,[3] millions of people. . . ." The workers on the new project, "Sot-Stroy," to which Uvadyev is now assigned, dislike their new chief. One of them says to him: "You have no understanding of a workingman, you are a hard master!"

The young engineer Favorov is closest to Uvadyev in his outlook. He sees the current period as a parallel to the days of Peter the Great, who also used "the whip, and drove in endless piles to drain the wide expanses of the Russian swamp." In brief, the novel presents a generation of men who are "economic workers, co-operators, men of living experience, practical men of the American type." At the other pole, rarely looked at, are the workers and peasants and, even further, the monks who are living out their days in the woods.

There is little communication among most of Leonov's characters in *Sot*. Uvadyev finds it difficult to speak a common language even with his own mother. A worker's widow and a worker herself, Varvara Uvadyeva sharply criticizes the way of life enjoyed by her son and the other "commissars." Accustomed to poverty, she is angered "at even the slightest evidence of comfortable living." She leaves her son, goes to live somewhere in a cellar, and finds a job as a switch operator on a streetcar line. "I refuse to be a flunkey. I may be a fool, but I'll be my own fool!" To escape loneliness, Varvara marries an elderly man who earns his livelihood by selling portraits of "the leaders" in the market place.

In *Sot*, as in *The Thief*, Leonov paints a graphic picture of the life and moods of the Moscow back streets, where Varvara goes to live with her husband. The motley population of the district consists of workers, erstwhile ladies who are now selling sweets in the market, and petty "NEP-

[3] A Russian land measure.

men." All these people are united in their hatred of the powers that be.

Leonov does not succeed in presenting Uvadyev as the "hero of the epoch." Against his wish, the artist in him shows his central character as a stony hulk in whose vicinity no living thing can grow: his wife Natalya leaves him; his affair with a young girl, the daughter of an engineer employed on the project, ends in failure. Uvadyev escapes from his personal disasters into work, leaving Moscow for the construction site.

The novel also offers a striking picture of life in the remote northern province and the small town of Makarikha, around which the new construction is developed. The reader is astonished by the persistence of the old social forms. A locomobile sent from the center makes its appearance in the town square. A group of peasants examines the machine with curiosity, and a conversation ensues which is reminiscent of the opening pages of Gogol's *Dead Souls*. " 'Look at all those tubes!' one of the peasants exclaimed, yawning solely from excess of feeling. The peasant eye was teased and tempted by the lubricating tubes which fairly seemed to beg for transfer to the home-brew apparatus. 'Come a second revolution, and we'll have to take it all apart again; you can get ruptured on the job!' added another, not without enthusiasm."

Leonov does not minimize the antagonism between the government and the working people. Once, when a dam bursts on the project and the workers toil on its repair without sparing themselves, Uvadyev wants to praise one of them, who plunged into the work with particular disregard of himself. He says to the worker: "But you are really one of ours!" In reply he hears the sullen and intractable: "I'm nobody's, I am my own. You think you rule me? You like the voiceless ones; they lick your boots, but keep a rope for you in a dark corner."

Acute need fills the peasants' hearts with bitterness. Observing the endless cases of iron and nails arriving at the construction site, a peasant says to his fellow villagers: "They'll build for you! I carted cases from the station the other day. . . . Iron and iron, pure-blooded iron, peasants! And we must plead like beggars for a nail or a horseshoe." Suffering from shortages of the barest essentials, the peasants do not conceal their disapproval of the "squandering waste" attending the construction project.

For all his loyalty to the regime, Leonov did not want to conceal that, under the conditions which developed by the late 1920s, "socialist construction" did not further the consolidation of the country, but, on the contrary, hastened the process of class differentiation in the new society.

In his tireless search for a dynamic and positive hero epitomizing the period of construction, Leonov stumbled upon a large theme which for many years became his central preoccupation. It was the theme of *fathers and sons*. Though not, of course, new in Russian literature, the theme was highly interesting in its new interpretation: for the first time in Russian literature, the writer—himself a young man at the time—gave his sympathy, not to youth, but to the "old men." This was particularly apparent in the novel *Skutarevsky* (1932) and in *The Road to the Ocean* (1935).

Along with novels and shorter works Leonov has written a number of plays: *The Orchards of Polovchansk* (1936–38), *The Wolf* (1938), *An Ordinary Man* (1940–43), and others. I shall forego analysis of these plays, since Leonov is at his weakest as a dramatist. His plays remind one of icebergs, nine-tenths of which are submerged under water. Many of the decisive events in the lives of most of the characters seem to have taken place before the opening of the play and quite outside its framework. The only exception is *The Invasion*, written in 1942.

Hitler's attack on the Soviet Union in June of 1941 and the defeats sustained by the Red Army for almost two years were a great shock to Russia, and most of all to the upper strata of Soviet society; the latter turned out to be the least prepared for these defeats. A detailed characterization of these moods will be found in Chapter 16, devoted to literary developments during and after the Second World War. No writer in the Soviet Union failed to reflect this bitter period in his work. Like others, Leonov was deeply shaken, and responded with his play *The Invasion*.

The action of the play unfolds in a small provincial town on the eve of its surrender to the Germans. The center of action is the family of Doctor Talanov. The old doctor has decided not to leave his native town, feeling that its people will have even more need of his help during the occupation than in peacetime. Just before the arrival of the Germans, the doctor's errant son, Fyodor, returns home after imprisonment. Fyodor has had a stormy youth: he killed the woman he loved, was sent to prison, then to a concentration camp. Since he has never written them from the camp, the doctor and the rest of the family fear Fyodor. During his years in the concentration camp he may have grown hardhearted. He might even go over to the Germans.

While the doctor is talking with his son, the chairman of the Executive Committee, Andrey Kolesnikov (the fiancé of Talanov's daughter Olga), calls on him and tries to convince him to evacuate. As Andrey enters, Fyodor manages to slip behind a screen. Kolesnikov confides to the doctor that he will also remain in the city for underground work. Fyodor inadvertently turns over a chair and comes out of his hiding place. He offers to help Kolesnikov, but the latter refuses, distrusting him. There is an exchange of caustic words. Kolesnikov gives the impression of a man who has lost his bearings. After he leaves, Fyodor says to his father: "I am not an artilleryman, Father, but *this gun isn't working any more*" (italics mine—V.A.).

On the day when the Germans arrive, Fyodor disappears, intensifying still further the apprehensions of his family. In the occupied city the Germans live as if they were sitting atop a volcano: every day some German soldiers and officers are killed. The assassinations are attributed to Andrey Kolesnikov, but the Germans fail to capture him. All the greater is the astonishment of the Talanov family when the mysterious partisan, captured by the Germans and brought to their home, turns out to be Fyodor and not Kolesnikov. Afterward Fyodor is taken to the prison cellar, where he meets other Soviet partisans. Threatened with death before a firing squad, he is asked by the other prisoners why he posed as Kolesnikov and showed such heroism. Sullen and sparing of words, he replies: "I prolonged your lives . . . and I ask for no receipt." Fyodor is shot, and several hours later the city is retaken by Soviet troops.

For a full appreciation of Leonov's play, we must return to Mitka Vekshin, whom Leonov did not "love enough" to tell the whole truth about him. The emotions which Leonov experienced during the bitter war years helped him, more than fifteen years later, to give just due to Mitka and the other young people who had been critical of the Soviet regime, and whose true worth Leonov had failed to see.

The boldness and unexpectedness of Leonov's reorientation is brought into sharp relief by the fact that Soviet critics and the theater directors who produced the play refused for a long time to reconcile themselves to the idea that the hero of the play was not the Communist Andrey, but an erstwhile concentration-camp prisoner.

The short novel *The Taking of Velikoshumsk* is so fragmented that it can scarcely be called a novel. This is somewhat—but not altogether—camouflaged by the fact that three of its protagonists bear the same name, Litovchenko: the tank-corps general who arrives to inspect the front; the young driver of the famous "203" tank, who plays an important role in the story; and the elderly peasant woman into whose house the general comes to warm himself.

The background of the story is formed by the roads of the Soviet advance, described with remarkable vividness. Like "splinters in the river of war," the returning people and cattle flowed along these roads: "lean cows with sorrowful Biblical eyes pulled ramshackle carts, and old men walked alongside, helping the beasts to reach home. Small flocks of peasant children, often four of them under a single piece of sacking, looked with uncomplaining smiles at their mothers who trudged along with tightly drawn lips, with nothing to rely on in the world except their own hands, now hanging limply down their sides. . . ." And all around the caravans returning to their own ruins lapped "the bitter sea of peasant trouble."

The rather weakly delineated plot of the novel is balanced by the history of the famed "203" tank, whose crew is proud of its military biography. This crew consists of the tank commander Sobolkov, whose wife and children are left behind in distant Altay, and who has won the respect and love of his men by his comradely warmth and courage; the tank's gunner, the merry, hard-drinking Obryadin, about whom the radioman Dybok says: "You're a friend to the whole honest world, Obryadin, but you'd be a king among loafers!" The tank driver, after the death of his predecessor, is the young Vasya Litovchenko. All of them are linked by the bonds of love for one another and for their tank. After the last and most violent encounter with the enemy, only Vasya and Dybok remain alive, and Dybok swears eternal devotion to his friend.

The underlying meanings of the conversation between General Litovchenko and his old schoolteacher Mitrofan Platonovich Kulkov are highly significant. Like Leonov, Litovchenko did not find his teacher among the living, but saw him in a dream. The teacher and the general sat silently in this dream, and "there was a profound question in the old man's silence: how will history repay for the irredeemable human suffering caused by the war?"

Litovchenko is deeply stirred by Kulkov's question. He feels as if he were "at a lesson, thirty years ago." And he begins to tell the old man about the coming material blessings to be brought by the still incompletely realized program, and about the "sage from Gori" (i.e., Stalin). But the humanist teacher, unreceptive to high-flown rhetoric, is not to be placated by future perspectives. To all of Litovchenko's arguments about a shining future, Kulkov replies: "To seek friends in the future is the fate of loneliness."

The Soviet general's dispute with his own conscience ends as abruptly as it began, but it throws a new light on the question that arises in the minds of Soviet people along the roads of the advance: what "price" will the Soviet government set on the country's unprecedented feats of self-sacrifice, how will it reward the people of our time, dressed "in the tattered army coats of death"?

After the publication of *The Taking of Velikoshumsk,* Leonov was silent for almost ten years. It was not until the end of 1953 that he came forward with a new novel, *The Russian Forest,* and, a year later, with the play *Golden Carriage.* These works (especially the play) contribute little that is new to the writer's extensive literary "economy," and the new novel is artistically weaker than many of Leonov's previous works.

The literary portrait of Leonov cannot be completed without at least a passing glance at the question of Dostoyevsky's influence upon his work. This influence was mentioned in the discussion of *The Thief.* It is especially evident in Leonov's treatment of his heroines, including Nastya (*The Badgers*), Masha Dolomanova, and Xenia, Sanka's wife (*The Thief*), Liza Pokhvistneva (*The Road to the Ocean*), and others. It may be felt, further, in Leonov's language, although his style is richer and more vivid. Like Dostoyevsky, Leonov makes wide use of the wealth of suffixes and prefixes in the Russian language to lend the desired shading to what, for one reason or another, he does not want to say directly and openly.

Nevertheless, I would question the view of some Russian critics abroad that, were Leonov free in his creative work, he would have become a "Soviet Dostoyevsky." Dostoyevsky's central concern was with ethical and religious problems, which determined the entire character of his work. Leonov is alien to moral, religious, and philosophical preoccupations. He is an accomplished artist, who perceives the world through images. But his spiritual and emotional world is devoid of that intensity with which Dostoyevsky's works were so profoundly charged.

13 MIKHAIL PRISHVIN (1873-1954)

Among the writers of the older generation who had won their literary fame before the revolution of 1917, but had later become an organic part of Soviet literature, we must name, first and foremost, the late Mikhail Prishvin.

In his autobiography, written for the anthology *Writers* (edited by V. Lidin, Moscow, 1928), Prishvin relates only a few basic facts about his life:

"Out of my childhood, adolescence, and early youth I fashioned a tale which I have not yet altogether finished living, and which gives me great joy. The title of this autobiographical tale is *Kurymushka*. It would be tedious now to talk again about that period. My youth was revolutionary—the customary youth of the Russian intellectual. I belonged to the circle of the archaic Bolshevik, the well-known Vassily Danilovich Ulrikh. After serving a prison term in Riga, I went to Leipzig, where I studied agronomy at the university. Returning to Russia, I engaged in agronomic work for a year and a half. The special literature in this field still retains from that period [1904] a bulky work on *Potatoes in Field and Garden Culture* and several pamphlets and articles. At the same time I devoted myself to the study of folk speech. In 1905 I abandoned forever the profession of an agronomist and went north, where I wrote the book *In the Land of the Unfrightened Birds*."

In this autobiographical sketch Prishvin does not speak of his first story, "Sashok," published in a children's magazine, *Rodnik*, in 1906. We might also have omitted to mention it if the writer had not used its plot again in the story "At the Burnt Stump," which appeared in the magazine *Apollon* in 1910. Later the same plot—about the hunter and dreamer Gusyok—was developed for a third time in the opening part of the long autobiographical epic

The Chain of Kashchey, which began to appear in print in 1923.

Prishvin's first story, "Sashok," went unnoticed by the critics. The writer won recognition only after the publication of his book of sketches *In the Land of the Unfrightened Birds* (1906). This book has its own curious history. When he was still working as an agronomist, Prishvin began to write stories and sketches for children. Soon afterward he went to live in Petersburg. Here he met the future academician and ethnographer N. Onchukov, who advised him to go north to study and record folklore. Prishvin went to Vyg Lake, in the province of Arkhangelsk. When he returned, he brought with him the manuscript of the book of sketches. The book was not merely noticed; it produced a great impression.

Soon afterward the writer Alexey Remizov brought Prishvin into a circle of young decadent writers, who influenced him to some extent. Inwardly, however, they remained alien to him. Among the writers who exerted a lasting influence on him, he mentions only Lermontov, Tyutchev, Aksakov, and Lev Tolstoy.

Prishvin's second book, *The Bun*, utilizes for its plot the famous Russian folk tale about a bun (*Kolobok*). Out of a handful of flour, an old woman bakes a bun and puts it on the window sill. The bun jumps down from the window, rolls across the house and into the street, and begins to wander over the world, becoming a symbol of free and footloose wandering. Prishvin's bun encounters on its way many other folk-tale characters—Marya Morevna, Kashchey the Deathless, Baba-Yaga. *The Bun* begins in the spirit of a fairy tale; written on two levels—fairy tale and autobiography—it is imbued with fine lyricism. In this book Prishvin introduces himself for the first time as a lyrical hero. His goal is to realize his dreams of a new, happy, and beautiful world, where the childhood vision may be reborn within the hero himself in all its unspoiled freshness and integrity. And foremost among Prishvin's dreams is the desire for freedom of thought and for creative freedom.

It was of this book that Alexander Blok said that it was not poetry, but added a moment later: "No, it is poetry, and something else as well." Prishvin refers to this comment in his essay "Baring the Method," in the book *Crane Homeland*. After long reflection on the meaning of Blok's "something," Prishvin came to the conclusion that a sketch or an essay always contains two elements: the writer begins with direct observation of people and nature; some of this he succeeds in condensing into poetic images, the rest is presented as direct material, interwoven with his comments and ideas. Prishvin started out on his literary path by combining elements of the folk tale with original philosophic lyricism. Such a synthesis of two entirely different genres in the essay had never been attempted in Russian literature before.

Among the works published by Prishvin before the revolution of 1917, one must name *Adam and Eve* (1909), *The Black Arab* (1910), *At the Walls of the Unseen City* (1907), *Nikon Starokolenny* (1907), and *The Beast of Krutoyarsk* (1907).

In contrast to other writers, who are loath to offer autobiographical data, Prishvin willingly and even joyously talks about his life. In addition to the brief essay written for the anthology *Writers*, we know of four other autobiographical sketches, each of them containing pages of incomparable freshness and perfection. In "The Hunt after Happiness," (included in the book *Crane Homeland*), the writer tells of the mistake he had made shortly before the revolution in building a house on the plot of land he had inherited from his mother. In the eyes of the peasants Prishvin was a *pomeshchik*, a "landowner." After the revolution, for a time, they did not molest the writer, respecting his mother's memory. Later, however, "strangers" arrived from "other parts," and soon Prishvin received an official order to vacate the premises. At the meeting which passed the resolution to evict him, a friend of the writer attempted to intervene in his behalf: "One day we may raise a monument to him, as we did to Pushkin." But others cried: "There you are! That's why we should throw him out now, so that we wouldn't have to bother raising monuments afterward."

In his essay "Baring the Method," Prishvin tells in detail how he arrived at his own literary genre and how it was, generally, that he chose such a "slow road to literature, through ethnography, by horsecart, as it were":

"I came to literature at an age when a man no longer has any need to strike a pose, and without any thought of gaining a position in society. . . . I began to write in the era of superfluous people, of Chekhov characters. The absence of a way of life in which an artist's personality develops thoughtlessly, like a flower, was about to condemn me also to impotent meditation about the problem of moral reconciliation of life with one's childhood vision. . . ."

Prishvin first described how he overcame this "impotent meditation" in his *Adam and Eve* (1909), in which he made use of the Biblical legend of the two Adams. According to this legend, the second Adam came into the world long after the first had sinned and suffered exile from Paradise, after he had multiplied, and his children had populated the earth. This second Adam became *the Landless Adam*; he took up the work of cultivating a narrow strip of land. The *ocherk* or "sketch" form developed by Prishvin was just such a "narrow strip of land." And one of the most characteristic qualities of his sketch is its rich suggestiveness, its wealth of "subtextual" content.

The introductory chapter of Prishvin's autobiographical prose epic *The Chain of Kashchey*[1] sheds a good deal of light on Prishvin, the writer. In this chapter—"The Rabbit" —Prishvin describes a walk he took one autumn day, which led him past the country house where he had spent his

[1] Kashchey is one of the most frequently recurring images in Russian folklore. The embodiment of the power of darkness and evil, he never appears as his true self, but conceals himself in a variety of objects and creatures, most often in an egg. In order to destroy him, it is first necessary to find his hiding place. Kashchey entangles life in a chain of evil, and it is this chain that the hero of Prishvin's novel is seeking to break.

childhood. As he looked at the house and the surrounding landscape, Prishvin was struck by the picture of "triple dying": everything around seemed to be dying—the house, the day, and the year, with its golden falling leaves. And in the midst of this, at the end of a long avenue strewn with maple leaves, on the ivied terrace, sat a rabbit. At first the presence of this rabbit seemed to the writer almost a deliberate mockery. He was at that time struggling with the idea of a novel in which he hoped to describe the house and the years of his youth spent in it. Many of the pictures were already formed in his mind, but he still had no central hero. And he asked himself: "Can it be that my beloved native land will not provide me with a hero? I thought of the many remarkable men born on this land. There, not too far away, lay the fields once plowed by Tolstoy; here were the woods where Turgenev had hunted; here Gogol had come to seek advice from the extraordinary old monk Amvrosy. How many great men had sprung from this black-earth region, but they seemed, indeed, to have come and gone like spirits, while the land was left all the poorer—exhausted, gutted with clay ravines, covered with dwellings unworthy of man, resembling heaps of manure."

It occurred to the writer that some little old peasant, who had done nothing in his lifetime beyond the humble planting of orchards in the ravines to hold down the soil, was perhaps a worthier hero for his novel than many of the great men who had left this land. Presently another idea came to Prishvin: it was not necessary to have a hero; the novel could do very well without him—"he can simply come out, like the rabbit, to sit for a few moments on the terrace, and the most grandiose events will follow."

When he reached this conclusion, Prishvin ceased to torment himself and began to write a story, told in the first person by his alter ego, Alpatov, whose childhood nickname was Kurymushka, a local expression meaning "Little Rabbit." *Kurymushka* was first published as a children's book. At the same time Prishvin began his major novel,

The Chain of Kashchey, the separate parts of which he called "links."

The Chain of Kashchey was conceived as a cycle of *povesti* or "tales," linked by the events in the life of his principal character, Mikhail Alpatov, beginning with the period of Czar Alexander II and ending with the overthrow of Nicholas II. In a certain sense *The Chain* is a parallel to Gorky's *Klim Samgin*, and it helps us, to some extent, to see where Gorky had sinned in his work against the pre-revolutionary intelligentsia.

Prishvin is right, of course, in saying that *The Chain of Kashchey* grew out of sketches and essays. It is reminiscent of an antique patch-quilt, in which a multitude of pieces are sewn into one large fabric. It is not by chance that the narrative abounds in lyrical digressions addressed to the contemporary reader. Each digression is rich in allusions, which heighten the modern reader's interest in the tale of the distant past. Thus, in "The Green Door" (the sixth link), the author says that, in the days of Alpatov's youth, "there was a law for men of conscience in our land, which said: 'one cannot live like this.' The prison cell seemed the only possible dwelling for the man of conscience, a temporary ordeal to be suffered until the day of the world catastrophe, after which it would become permissible to live well, because the terrible inequality would then be a thing of the past."

In another passage of this link the writer speaks again to the contemporary reader, explaining:

"My friend, this reference to our age gives me still greater courage to yield to my imagination, for I have become convinced that our fathers have not transmitted to their children any ready-made forms of marriage; that, in these revolutionary times, mothers have bartered their daughters' dowries for bread; and in this emptiness of life, Alpatov's dreams are real and will find their own interpreters."

The first link of the epic—"Azure Beavers"—describes Alpatov's early childhood and his father's death. Kurymushka's father, a man of ready enthusiasms, has reduced his family to financial ruin. When he dies, he leaves his wife, Marya Ivanovna, and their five children without means. Fortunately, Marya Ivanovna, like the writer's mother, is a descendant of an old merchant family and possesses considerable business acumen, which helps her to cope with her difficult situation.

Feeling the approach of the end, his father calls Kurymushka and gives him a slip of paper with a drawing of some strange "azure beavers"—as if trying to bequeath to him the gift of imagination and the hunger for the "unknown." The leitmotiv of this first link is the dream of something extraordinary, a dream intensified by the meeting with Marya Morevna, the fairy-tale maiden. To Kurymushka, this maiden is reincarnated in the young daughter of the general from whom his parents had bought their estate. Like a true little knight errant, Kurymushka is fired with the idea of saving Marya Morevna from captivity in the land of the evil wizard Kashchey. And, in his imagination, Kashchey is the old man he heard about in a conversation among adults, who had spoken of some old man who "arranged things" for young women.

The second link—"The Little Cain"—describes the shattering of illusion, the first failure, complicated by an episode first sketched by Prishvin in *The Bun*. This theme —the search for a forgotten or still unknown land—plays an important part in Prishvin's work. The second link, like the sketch "The Hunt after Happiness," relates how Kurymushka attempts with several schoolmates to escape to a certain mysterious country called "Asia." On the third day the fugitives are captured by a district policeman. The young adventurers are the butt of many jokes, and a little ditty is composed for the occasion: "They went to Asia, and came to the gymnasium." All of Kurymushka's life seems to flow through two irreconcilable worlds: the childish world, full of mysteries, illusions, and dreams, and the frightening world of adults who hide their secrets from children. The childish world is inhabited by oppressed children and hapless paupers like the penniless dreamer and passionate hunter Gusyok, whom we first met in the guise of Sashok in Prishvin's earliest published story (1906).

When Kurymushka discovers for himself the terrifying world of adults, he is filled with animosity toward it. The longing to free himself of the dreadful "chain of Kashchey" is born and grows stronger in the young hero under the impact of this menacing dark world, governed by "adults."

Prishvin describes Alpatov's youth in the third link; and Kurymushka's return to his mother and his desire to continue his education in the fourth.

The fifth link—"State Criminal"—tells about the birth of his great love, for Ina Rostovtseva, whom Alpatov meets during his imprisonment for revolutionary activity. At that time a number of young women who sympathized with the revolutionary movement posed as sisters or fiancées of prisoners without families in order to obtain permission to visit them in prison. Ina becomes Alpatov's "prison fiancée," but he falls in love with her in earnest, and searches for her all over Petersburg after his release.

Most of the links of the second part of the *Chain* are devoted to Alpatov's love for Ina, his search for her, their brief meetings, their friendship and alienation, and his final break with her. This theme of the great love which remains unfulfilled became the central theme of many of Prishvin's later works, particularly of his book *Ginseng* (1933), his remarkable cycle of sketches *Undressed Spring* (1940), and *Facelia* (1940).

Among the links of the second part of *The Chain of Kashchey*, the sixth—"The Green Door"—is especially important for insight into Prishvin's creative world. Against the background of his search for the elusive beloved, the writer sketches in his impressions of prewar Germany and his reflections on the great and little truth of ordinary people. While he describes the German worker Schwarz and his peasant wife with warmth and respect, Alpatov finds that many people of their circle aspire to little more than honest service to that "brief truth" which in Russia is called the philistine way of life. But it is also in Germany that Alpatov becomes aware of his own inconsonance with the world of his revolutionary comrades. He makes this discovery during one of his visits to the Dresden Art Gallery, where he often comes to admire the Sistine Madonna. One day he meets at the gallery his friend and comrade Nesgovorov. A short, but intensely charged dialogue follows. The blunt and direct Nesgovorov, who has no interest in art and no understanding of it, asks:

"What has happened to you? Why are you sitting here, among the bourgeoisie, all dressed up and staring at the Madonna like an owl?"

Alpatov tries to explain why the Sistine Madonna moves him so deeply (her face reminds him of a Russian reaper he once saw in a field). But his words fail to reach Nesgovorov. With perhaps a deliberate exaggeration of his rejection of art, Nesgovorov says that his one wish as he looks at the Madonna is to hide under one of the seats until evening, when the guards go home, and then destroy the picture. He is convinced that the visitors to the gallery are "idlers," who find in the Madonna "an escape, a blessed refuge to help them forget their obligations to mankind." Alpatov replies that he could "kill" any man who destroyed the Madonna. Nesgovorov reminds Alpatov once more that revolutionaries are "midwives" who must cut "the umbilical cord that ties people to God." And Alpatov feels more poignantly than ever that he can never accept Nesgovorov's blunt and simple philosophy.

In the seventh link ("The Young Faust") Prishvin describes his hero's life at the German university, his study of German philosophy, and his encounters with other Russian students abroad, who are shown in a number of fascinating portraits, some of them reminiscent of the heroes of Dostoyevsky's *The Possessed*. This link also indicates the direction of Alpatov's future work. With the diploma of "Torfmeister," he plans to return to Russia and devote himself to draining its many swamps.

The final links of *The Chain of Kashchey* deal with the developing relationship between Alpatov and Ina. But the brief episodes of friendship alternate with new periods of alienation. Soon after his return to Petersburg, Alpatov comes to the conclusion that his great love does not evoke a genuine response in Ina, a young woman of another, privileged world, and they part. With his diploma as Torfmeister, Alpatov-Prishvin soon finds work in the provinces. His life there, illuminated by his inner experiences and meditations, provides material for the cycle of sketches collected in the book *Crane Homeland* (1929), which, in a way, is a sequel to *The Chain of Kashchey*. Significantly, it is subtitled "The Story of an Unsuccessful Love."

To collect material for this book Prishvin made a number of visits in the course of several summers to the Dubny district and Moscow Polesye. The stories of his meetings with the local residents, his reflections on life, and his descriptions of nature, astonishing in their perfection, place *Crane Homeland* and *Berendey's Kingdom* among the finest achievements of the newest Russian literature. There is, perhaps, no other writer with such an ear for folk speech, with such talent for seizing and conveying the sly uniqueness of the man of the people. Prishvin never strove for sensational material or striking plots. He merely gathered what lay in the path of his many wanderings, with gun in hand, over the forests, swamps, and fields of the wide expanses of central Russia. Yet, seen through the prism of the writer's "loving attention," the trifles gathered in this way became transformed into glittering jewels of enchanting beauty.

Here are a few illustrations. One day the writer hears about a chief of militia in an out-of-the-way village, with the incredible name of Schopenhauer. Prishvin takes a trip to the village and finds Schopenhauer, no longer a chief of militia, but a pensioned invalid. Making his acquaintance, Prishvin soon learns the secret of his name. His former name was Aslenkov. As a private in World War I, Aslenkov was wounded and taken prisoner. In the German hospital he was under the care of a nurse called Luiza Schopenhauer. Returning to Russia after the revolution, Aslenkov found all his relatives leaning toward the old way of life; one of them had even become a kulak. But Aslenkov himself sympathized with the revolution and joined the Communist Party. And so he wanted to shake off "all the Aslenkov dust" from his feet. When he learned that it was now possible to change one's name, he recalled Luiza Schopenhauer. To him, she remained an incarnation of all that was brightest and most beautiful in life, and he decided to adopt her name. Of course, he knew nothing of the existence of a famous German philosopher of that name, or of the remoteness of his philosophy from that of Karl Marx.

Prishvin seems to be most fascinated by episodes and encounters in which the old and new in the life of the people are fantastically intertwined. Describing a geological excursion into the depths of the Pereyaslavl district (*Secrets of the Earth*), Prishvin draws a remarkable portrait of Father Filimon, a former priest now working as a ferryman on Pleshcheev Lake. At first Father Filimon continued even after the revolution to perform the ritual duties of a priest at the ancient little church in his village. Soon the deacon and the caretaker left, and the priest took over their work as well. Meantime, his family suffered great hardship, and his wife went to work in a factory. But it was not until he lost the last member of his flock that Father Filimon locked up the church and became a ferryman, soon developing a great love for the lake. And the local people coined a new expression for ferrying across the lake: they called it "crossing with the priest."

Despite the folk character of his topics and language, Prishvin had no illusions about the speedy acceptance of his works by the people. "The best I can hope for," he wrote in *Crane Homeland*, "is the popular success of some love ditty of my composition. But *Crane Homeland* and *Berendey's Kingdom* would evoke nothing but mockery. . . . *Crane Homeland* will come here many years later, and then only in fragments, included in some schoolbooks. . . ."

The same idea is wonderfully illustrated in the incident with the writer's little friend, the shepherd boy Vanyushka.

Vanyushka did not read the story Prishvin gave him. He began it, but it bored him and he says, as if to justify himself: "If you were writing the truth! But I'll bet you made it all up yourself. . . ." And Vanyushka boasts that he can write a better story. When Prishvin asks him to tell it, the boy's story, about a night on the swamp, turns out to consist of but a dozen words: "It's night. There is a huge, huge bush by the water. I sit under the bush, and the ducklings keep going—swee, swee, swee." The writer remarks that the story is very short, but Vanyushka is undaunted: "Why short? They kept on with their 'swee, swee' all night long. . . ." After this conversation Prishvin reflects for a long time "about the great creative power and sense of freedom" inherent in every living being and vividly expressed in Vanyushka's rebuff to the writer and the boy's own story.

In the early days of the war Prishvin wrote two cycles of sketches, *Undressed Spring* (first published in the magazine *Oktyabr*, April–May 1940) and *Facelia* (published in *Novy Mir*, September 1940), and collected fragments of his "Writer's Diary" in a book under the title of *The Spring of the World*. In all these works we find the same Prishvin, with an undiminished feeling for the truth of life and the truth of art, telling many stories of his encounters with people, often with matchless artistry. One of these stories tells of the writer's encounter with a coachman, a man of heroic proportions, called Pcholka, or Little Bee.

"We saw before us a giant with a long blond beard, sitting in the coachman's seat of an ancient sleigh, such as one rarely sees today. There was a pride in the giant's carriage that seemed to flow from an exuberance of strength and freedom, as if he were not a mere driver, but the unchallenged master of the entire Volga region. Maxim Gorky had this quality, and another, too, a great singer, also born on the Volga. It was as if they drew it from the Volga herself. She spreads in flood, but these men are ready to spread with their whole souls, paying no more attention to trifles than to the dust under their feet."

Prishvin began a conversation with Pcholka, in which some nearby fishermen joined in. When the writer used the word "fine-pored," a small man, with a gray, sharp, and clever face, who also turned out to be a fisherman, remarked to him that he was speaking to "dark, ignorant men of Nekrasov's[2] day; to them, a simple word like 'fine-pored' is less intelligible than Chinese." To Prishvin's astonishment, another member of the group turned to the skeptical citizen, crying out: "You're pretty small-holed yourself!"

It is not easy to be an independent writer in a country held in the rigid grip of a dictatorship. Prishvin did not always succeed in retaining his independence. It is enough to recall his resignation from the literary group Pereval at a time when it was under fire from the official critics. But in his work itself, Prishvin succeeded better than many of his contemporaries in remaining free and independent—a writer with his own creative "meridian."

A wealth of material on this problem may be found in the writer's *Literary Diary*, which he kept for fifty years. Some of the entries were used by the writer himself during his lifetime, in works like *Undressed Spring, Facelia, The Storeroom of the Sun* (1945) and *The Eyes of the Earth* (1945–46). But most of the *Diary* began to appear posthumously. Some of Prishvin's ideas about the nature of creativeness are closely akin to the thinking of Boris Pasternak in *Doctor Zhivago*. "I have left far behind me," remarks Prishvin in one of his entries, "any proud attempts to govern my creative work as if it were a mechanism. But I have made a thorough study of the conditions under which I can produce sound works: the first of these is the integrity of my individuality. And so, recognition and protection of the conditions necessary for maintaining this integrity have become my guiding principles in relation to creative work. I do not direct my creative activity as if it were a mechanism, but I conduct myself in such a way as to assure that durable works will come out of me."

---

[2] The reference is to N. A. Nekrasov, the nineteenth-century poet.

Mikhail Prishvin

During the celebration of Prishvin's seventy-fifth birthday in 1948, the writer confessed in an interview with a reporter for the *Literary Gazette* that he had not the slightest desire for the fame of a "master" or "singer"; what he wished most of all was to be a "contemporary." In one of his diary entries in 1952 (published after his death), Prishvin dwells on this theme in greater detail:

"I look at some people and think of how they follow time and will pass, with all that is temporary. But contemporary men are those who are the masters of time. Thus, Shakespeare is far more contemporary to us than N., who watches the trend of the time so closely that yesterday he argued for plays without conflicts, but today he has heard something new, and now is all for conflict. . . ."

And, as we review his extensive and uniquely original literary heritage, we see that Prishvin truly succeeded in being a "contemporary" writer in the most dramatic epoch of Russia's history. But what renders him "contemporary" is not so much his lyrical comments and descriptions, as the images of ordinary people he has recorded in his work, with their spiritual wealth, independence, and profound sense of innate freedom. Truly, Prishvin was not only the singer of the "land of unfrightened birds." In the years of Russia's deepest bondage, he was able to portray the *unfrightened soul of the man of the people*.

14 ALEXEY TOLSTOY (1883-1945)

Alexey Tolstoy grew up and began to realize his spiritual identity on the threshold of the twentieth century, at a time when the old way of life was breaking up and a new, industrial Russia was just beginning to emerge. He was brought up in the family of his stepfather, on a small estate in Samara Province. His mother, a Turgenev by birth and a distant relation of the famous writer, was a woman of considerable cultural interests and herself a writer, mainly of children's books. His stepfather was also a cultivated man, and the family spent many long winter evenings over books, often listening to the stepfather read aloud from the works of Nekrasov, Turgenev, Tolstoy, and Pushkin. The little Tolstoy knew of no other books for a long time, and it was only later, at school, that he "discovered" and became a passionate reader of Jules Verne, Mayne Reid, and Fenimore Cooper.

Tolstoy's mother cherished the hope that her son would become a writer. When the boy was ten, she suggested that he write a story. For several days the child labored over a story about a boy named Stepka, but the results were so disappointing that his mother never repeated her suggestion. Tolstoy also tried to write poetry, with equally small success.

On graduating from the *realschule* in 1901, Tolstoy left for Petersburg, where he enrolled at the Technological Institute and lived the usual student life of the early twentieth century: he became actively interested in politics and took part in the famous demonstration outside the Kazan Cathedral in 1903. When the higher educational institutions in Russia were temporarily closed, Tolstoy went to Dresden, to study at the Polytechnicum. At this time he made another attempt at writing poetry. On his return from abroad he showed the poems to his mother, but she reluctantly repeated her earlier comment that they were weak.

Nevertheless, these poetic experiments gave Tolstoy an opportunity to make the acquaintance of the leading symbolist poets of the turn of the century—Vyacheslav Ivanov, Konstantin Balmont, Andrey Bely. In the spring of 1907 Tolstoy published his first book of verse. The verse was "decadent" and imitative. During this period Tolstoy also made his first attempts at prose (*A Magpie's Tales*), but they failed to satisfy him. It was not until 1910 that he published his story "A Week in Turenevo," which was later included in the book *Beyond the Volga*, describing the life of the latter-day descendants of the Russian landed nobility (the book was subsequently reissued under the title *Under the Old Lindens*).

In 1913 Tolstoy wrote his first dramatic work, the comedy *The Violators*, also dealing with the disintegration of the gentry's way of life. After that he often wrote for the theater, producing more than twenty plays. However, they are not typical of his work as a whole, and, with the exception of *Ivan the Terrible*, are largely forgotten. But even this work falls short of the literary level of Tolstoy's fiction.

The First World War temporarily interrupted Tolstoy's work as a writer. He became a war correspondent for the Moscow newspaper *Russkiye Vedomosti* and went to the front. There, writes Tolstoy in his autobiography, "I learned to see real life, and I took part in it, throwing off the tightly buttoned black frock-coat of the symbolists. I came face to face with the Russian people." Some of his articles and sketches of that period are helpful toward a better understanding of Tolstoy. Especially interesting is the story "An Ordinary Man" (included in the collection *War Days*). One night an officer making the rounds of his front-line sector accidentally overhears a conversation between some peasant soldiers. The private Anikin is explaining to the younger men the meaning of the world conflict:

"You must understand it, men. Doesn't our strength lie in our people? It does. Yet they're all fools—they've lost all notion of their own selves. You ask them: 'Where do you live?' 'In Russia.' 'And what's it like, this Russia?' 'Don't know.' All he knows, the numbskull, is his village, his mother, and his dad. That's why the devil has stirred up the German: 'Get at them, go on, they have no understanding of themselves.' It's no joking matter now. The German's trying to take over our whole country. That's why we are now getting a bit clearer in our minds."

During the early years of Tolstoy's career as a writer, he acquired a firm reputation as the chronicler of the dying landed gentry. And yet, along with his interest in morals and manners, Tolstoy had early developed a taste for ideology, for "large principles." And in the story "An Ordinary Man" the soldier Anikin voices Tolstoy's own idea: out of the fire and blood of the world conflagration will come a renascence of the Russian national state. The human material for this new national integration, Tolstoy felt, lay in the vast reserves of ordinary, inconspicuous Russian people, kept down by officials, ambitious money-makers, and sharp "operators" of every kind.

Tolstoy enthusiastically welcomed the February revolution, but in the Communist "October" he saw the collapse of all his cherished ideas. He emigrated to Europe, but did not remain there long. He missed Russia, and already in the autumn of 1921 he joined the *émigré* group which, with its organ *Nakanune* (On the Eve), published in Berlin, was in the nature of a springboard for the return home. In terms of literary work Tolstoy's Berlin period (1921–23) was quite productive. It was during those years that he wrote his novel *Aelita*, the story "Black Friday," and other works.

On his return to Soviet Russia in 1923 Tolstoy wrote the novel *The Adventures of Nevzorov, or Ibikus*, and a short novel, *Azure Cities*. In the former he "exposes" and "indicts" both the "philistine" at home who does not accept the October revolution and the *émigrés* who fled it. This tendentious book would not deserve any mention if Tolstoy had not captured in it a good many traits of the demoralized and disintegrating milieu in which he had himself lived when he shared the arduous odyssey of the *émigré*.

Azure Cities (1925) is written in quite a different psychological key. Its hero is the young Communist Buzheninov. Desperately ill with typhus during the Civil War, he dreams of the marvelous azure cities which he and his comrades will build after their victory. He survives the illness and, after the war, enters the polytechnicum. Later, his health undermined by his strenuous work over the plans for an "azure city," Buzheninov decides to go for a rest to his native town in the provinces, which he had not seen for many years. The first impressions of his childhood home shock him with the hopeless persistence of its poverty. Among the old familiar figures, the only new one is the militiaman, whom the angry market women, still engaged in private trade, have nicknamed "the bullfinch." Everything in the town remains the same, the monotonous flow of its dreary existence broken only by the faint whistle of trains rushing by in the distance. And yet, there are new elements too. The old narrow life of the little man has become more shifty and cunning; the old tavern is graced by a new sign, "Renaissance"; the tavern-keeper's son has become a commerical agent, fawning at the strong and oppressing the weak—a carrion bird.

"Yes, yes, Comrade Khotyaintsev," Buzheninov says to a Communist acquaintance, "the hooves of our days are silenced. The great years are dead. Happy are those who rot underground." And nothing can help, except perhaps a "devastating explosion." Buzheninov ends tragically: he sets fire to the town after hanging his plan for an "azure city" on a telegraph post, and surrenders himself to the authorities. Tolstoy's own parting words to Buzheninov are spoken by Khotyaintsev:

"It seems that life does not forgive rapt dreamers and visionaries who turn away from it. It clutches at them, rudely jabbing them in the side: 'Wake up, peel your eyes, get off your high horse.' . . . Life, like a baleful, bloated shrew, hates superficiality. The whole point is to master her and seat her, nice and proper, at the head of the table." A similar mood permeates the somewhat less vivid story "The Viper."

The process of reconciliation and acceptance of the Soviet regime by Tolstoy during the NEP period was typical for a substantial portion of the old technical intelligentsia which had not emigrated abroad but remained in Russia. At a later stage these moods, which were treated with suspicion by the official publicists of the '20s, served as the basis for a somewhat primitive Soviet patriotism. The beginnings of future Soviet patriotism found their first clear expression in Tolstoy's novel *The Hyperboloid of the Engineer Garin* (1925). The young Soviet scientist, Khlynov, sent to Germany for graduate study under Professor Wolf, says to the latter, "After all, we are a good people. Nobody has loved us yet. . . ." But a time will come "when America will try to grab us by the throat," and then the Germans will see for themselves "what splendid fellows in the helmets of ancient Russian heroes will rise up along the Eastern borders." The agent of the Criminal Investigation Office, Shelga, and his little assistant Vanka Gusev are similarly portrayed in the novel as Soviet patriots.

However, for all their diversity of theme, these early works could not have assured Tolstoy a permanent place in the history of modern Russian literature. He won this place with his *Peter I* and the trilogy *The Road to Calvary*.

Both works have a rather complex history. In his autobiography Tolstoy explains his interest in the period and the person of Peter I in the following passage: "It was, perhaps, with the artist's instinct rather than consciously that I sought in this theme a clue to an understanding of the Russian people and Russian polity. I was greatly helped in my studies by the late historian V. V. Kallash. He introduced me to the archives and documents of the Secret Office and the Preobrazhensky Department, recording the so-called 'Word and Deed' affairs.[1] The riches of the Russian language were opened before me in all their brilliance, genius, and power. I grasped at last the secret of the structure of the literary phrase: its form is determined by the inner state of the narrator, which leads to movement, gesture, and, finally, verbal expression, speech, in which the choice of words and their arrangement are coincident with the gesture."

The first version of the future three-volume novel—*Peter's Day*—was written while Tolstoy was still abroad. Emotionally, it differs sharply from the later, final text. This is how Tolstoy saw "Peter's mission" in *Peter's Day*: "The royal city was being built at the edge of the land, on swamps, at the very border of the German realm. The people did not know who needed it, they did not know for the sake of what future ordeals they were compelled to shed their sweat and blood and perish by the thousands." Those who ventured to ask questions or to express their discontent "were taken, hands and feet in irons, to the Secret Office or the Preobrazhensky Department; and those who were simply beheaded were the fortunate ones. . . . And so it was that Peter, squatting in swamp and wilderness, consolidated the state and remade the land by his sole dread will. . . ." The country swarmed with commissars, informers, spies; carts loaded with convicts jolted over its roads; "the land was gripped with fear and trepidation. Cities and villages stood abandoned, their inhabitants fleeing to the Don, the Volga, to the Bryansk, Murom, and Perm forests." Pondering on Peter's plans and thoughts, Tolstoy seemed to ask: "But wait, was Peter really concerned with the good of Russia?"

In this first version of *Peter I*, Tolstoy replied to the question in the negative: "It was not a strong and festive Russia that entered the family of great nations" as a result

---

[1] The reference here is to Peter's secret police and the dreaded phrase "Word and Deed," pronounced by its agents when they broke into a home to arrest their victim. The archives contained testimony of people under torture, with its inevitable terse expressiveness.

of Peter's efforts. Instead, "pulled in by the hair, bloody and frenzied with fear and despair, she appeared before her new relations wretched and inferior—as a slave. And from then on, however formidable the roar of Russian guns, the great country, stretching from the Vistula to the Chinese Wall, remained enslaved and humbled in the eyes of the whole world. And the burden of that day, and of all the days, past and future, fell as a leaden weight upon the shoulders of him [i.e., Peter] who had taken upon himself a load too great for any man—to be sole arbiter of the destinies of all."

But the tragedy of Russia was not confined to her appearance before the world as a "slave." Peter's policies engendered within the country a deep passivity that found expression in a multitude of negative phenomena: sloth, bureaucracy, indifference.

Later, the same problem was to be discussed in *The Road to Calvary* by Tolstoy's favorite hero, the engineer Ivan Telegin: "How stupidly and ineptly everything is done in our country, and the devil alone knows what a reputation we Russians have. It is a pity and a shame. Just think —a most gifted people, an enormously rich country, and what is the face we present? An insolent government clerk's! Instead of life—paper and ink. . . . We started this official scribbling under Peter the Great, and we can't stop to this day."

This assessment of Peter's "work" coincided with that of the best historian of the Petrine era, Professor V. Klyuchevsky, who wrote that "Peter's reform was a struggle of the autocracy against the people, against its stubborn backwardness. Peter hoped to awaken initiative and activity in the enslaved society by the sheer intimidation of power, and to bring European science and popular enlightenment to Russia over the heads of the slave-owning gentry. . . . But to attempt a combination of tyranny and freedom, enlightenment and slavery is the political equivalent of squaring the circle; it is a puzzle we have tried to solve since Peter's day, and it still remains unsolved."

In the first and second parts of his epic novel *Peter I*,

embracing Russian life at the end of the seventeenth and the first quarter of the eighteenth centuries, Tolstoy departed sharply from his initial view of "Peter's mission." The writer attempts to mitigate the darker aspects of the age. In his earlier descriptions of the inhuman working conditions in the factories of the day, or of Peter's cruelty, Tolstoy's sympathies had been with the Czar's victims. In the second version of the novel he closes his eyes to these facts.

The history of Peter's reign in Russia is embodied in an entire gallery of characters. Some, like Khovansky, Shaklovity, and Mstislavsky, represent the old, reactionary boyar strata which, under the leadership of the Czar's own sister Sofia, resisted Peter. But Peter depended in his work on younger forces. He never hesitated to recruit his assistants from among the common people. Foremost among these were Menshikov, the son of a groom, who had sold rabbit pies in the market, and Brovkin, a former boyar's serf who became a rich merchant with Peter's help. Brovkin's daughter Sanka is already a woman of the new era. Along with Sanka, we are shown a number of her contemporaries, who had been trained and educated abroad.

Close to these new elements also is the group of boyars, more intelligent and farsighted than the rest, who actively supported Peter's reforms. These included Pyotr Tolstoy; the first Russian Field Marshal, Boris Sheremetyev; and others. Tolstoy also shows us foreigners who took an active part in Russian life in Peter's day—men like Jacob Bruce and Patrick Gordon.

Another group consists of characters in which Tolstoy embodied the masses of the people, who carried on their backs all the burdens, both of wars and of the vast construction of new cities, harbors, and factories. Such are Fedka, nicknamed "Wash-Yourself-in-Mud," Andrey Golikov, and others.

Especially symptomatic of Tolstoy's evolution is his attitude toward "Peter's fledglings," his favorites and protégés, "the homeless, clever men who wanted change." Tolstoy's talent and his intimate knowledge of another—contemporary—dramatic epoch, help the writer to achieve brilliant insight into the most secret nooks of the social psychology of Peter's "new people." Here is Sanka Brovkina, yesterday an unknown serf hauling manure, today a lady of the court and Peter's favorite. Her husband complains that Sanka has got entirely out of hand—they even sleep apart now. Instead of quieting down and getting herself with child, she reads all night, studies politesse, and seethes with unquenchable longings.

The reader is also shown a whole gallery of "trading men" raised up by Peter, his "backbone strength"—all the Bazhenins, Demidovs, and Sveshnikovs who are ready, for the honor of being mentioned "by name and patronymic" in the Czar's edict, to supply him with vast sums for his construction projects. Tolstoy does not conceal these men's faults, their greed, their contempt for the weak, their egotism. But at the same time he seems to admire them, as if saying: indeed, they are a band of cunning rogues; but could Peter have budged this "cursed land," could he have gotten the upper hand over the arrogant boyars' resistance to change without their help?

Tolstoy's books quickly won great popularity among the strata which had risen from social limbo during the Five-Year Plan period and were filled with avid longing to live well. *Peter I* became emotionally something of a bible to the up-and-coming men of the time, whose social optimism echoed the optimism of Peter's protégés. These "new men" had not been conscious of any links with Russia's past, but Tolstoy seemed to have taken them by the hand and led them through the chambers of history, encouraging them with a broad gesture: keep your head high, you have predecessors; and just as they represented progress in their day, so you do in ours. The secret purpose of Tolstoy's novel was, of course, to justify Stalin by the analogy of Peter.

Tolstoy himself gave this a broader rationale. In his autobiographical sketch *My Road* (1943) he wrote that the theme of Peter I attracted him by the "abundance of the 'unkempt' and richly creative energy of a period in which the Russian character was revealed with such extraordinary vividness." There were several periods in Russian history, he felt, when the Russian national character had thus revealed itself: "Four epochs claim my attention and demand expression for the same reasons: the epochs of Ivan the Terrible, Peter, the Civil War of 1918–20, and the present one—unprecedented in sweep and significance. . . . To fathom the secret of the Russian character, of its greatness, it is necessary to acquire a thorough and profound knowledge of its past—of our history, its pivotal moments, the tragic and creative epochs when the Russian character was taking shape."

Tolstoy had planned to write a third volume of his epic novel. "The two published parts of *Peter I*," he wrote in *My Road*, "are merely an introduction to the third novel, the most significant of the three both in content and picturesqueness, embracing the events from the conquest of Narva [1703] until Peter's death." This novel was never completed, although individual chapters appeared in the magazine *Novy Mir* in 1944, while Tolstoy was still alive, and in the January issue of 1945.

In the interval between the second and third volumes of *Peter I*, Tolstoy began a dramatic trilogy, *Ivan the Terrible*, permeated with similar moods. The first part of the trilogy appeared in print and was produced on the stage in 1941.

It is, perhaps, not accidental, either, that *Peter I* was written in part at the same time as the trilogy *The Road to Calvary*. The first volume of the trilogy—the novel *Sisters* —was written in 1919, while Tolstoy was still living abroad. He worked on the subsequent volumes, *Nineteen-Eighteen* and *A Gloomy Morning*, after his return to the Soviet Union.

This trilogy shows the revolution through the prism of the minds of people belonging to the bourgeois and landowning intelligentsia, socially akin to Tolstoy. The narrative centers on the lives of the two Bulavin sisters—Katya and Dasha—and their friends, and later husbands, Ivan Telegin and Vadim Roshchin. The action of the novel takes place during World War I, the February revolution, the October days, the uprising of the Left-wing Socialist-Revolutionaries, the Makhno episode, and the Civil War. With a confident hand, and at the same time with great inner warmth, the writer leads his heroes through all the exigencies of the dramatic and complex popular revolution. In the scope of its events and characters *The Road to Calvary* has no equal in Soviet literature. At first Tolstoy's heroes, and particularly Vadim Roshchin, were bitter enemies of the October revolution, and Dasha, Telegin's wife, was at one time involved in the Savinkov plot. To explain Dasha's action, Tolstoy wrote: "In those days the human will was moved by inspiration rather than calm reflection. Swept by the hurricane of events, human life tossed like a stormy ocean, and everyone thought of himself as the savior of the foundering ship."

In this epic novel Tolstoy achieved the cherished ambition of many Soviet "Fellow-Traveling" writers—to create an "honest-to-goodness" biography of Soviet people. The first attempt in this direction was made by Mikhail Bulgakov in his novel *The Days of the Turbins*. But no one except Tolstoy succeeded in bringing his heroes to the point of complete acceptance of Soviet reality without violence either to the plot or to their characters. Tolstoy attempted to sum up the meaning of this difficult road in the epigraph to the second part of the trilogy: "Thrice drowned in water, thrice washed in blood, thrice boiled in lye. We are now purer than pure."

This epigraph is the leitmotiv of the epic, the key to the soul of the older generation of Soviet intelligentsia of the 1930s. In composition this group was an amalgam of remnants of the old, pre-revolutionary intelligentsia and the new, which had grown up during the revolutionary years but had retained close ties with the old. A part of the pre-revolutionary intelligentsia, long reconciled to the Soviet regime, had in its youth sympathized with or belonged to various socialist and liberal parties and fought for Russia's democratic development. Those were deeds and events of a distant past, but in the waking hours of night such people were still nagged by the worm of reminiscence and stirred by a sense of guilt. And the source of the guilt was the knowledge that life in contemporary Russia was impossible without an often ignoble compromise with one's conscience. By his trilogy *The Road to Calvary* Tolstoy liberated this intelligentsia from such disturbing feelings. He loudly proclaimed to it, for the whole country to hear: you are "purer than pure," and your actions, even when bad, are merely the "costs" of the great period of change in Russian history. He invited his heroes to stop tormenting themselves with the old "accursed questions."

Tolstoy attached many hopes to the victory in World War II; he spoke of them in his article "On the Historic Frontier" (*Literature and Art*, October 23, 1943):

"Our people and the rest of the world look at us, Soviet writers, with impatient expectation. The next word is up to you, novelists, poets, and dramatists. What the readers expect of us is not a mere reflection, not a picture of facts, but elucidation of their meaning and a creative look into the future. They expect us to be a step ahead of today. They expect flights of prophetic creative imagination, as inspired with genius as the profound and radiant soul of the victorious people. They expect, not a line here and there, not hints and glimpses, but the whole *new Adam*. . . . We are at a turning point, just as the Russian writers were in 1917–20, on the eve of the tumultuous literary development of the revolutionary quarter-of-a-century that followed. Our literary habits and techniques, the methods we employed before the Patriotic War, are obviously poorly suited to the present day. We must search for new ways. The instruments with which we tilled the Soviet land in peacetime are not quite useful in the terrible, heroic, and naked epoch in which we live today."

For his two prose epics and his faith that Soviet writers would create the "new Adam" after the war, the official literary spokesmen paid high homage to Tolstoy as they escorted him to the grave. In the magazine *Novy Mir*, Alexander Drozdov called him "the center of our solar system" and a "marshal of Soviet literature."

Tolstoy traveled a long way from the *Old Lindens* of the landed estates on the Volga to unconditional acceptance of Stalin's dictatorship. The chief trouble with the old Russia, as he saw it, had been the inept government apparatus which suppressed all manifestations of the people's talents.

At first Tolstoy had hoped that the ordeals of World War I would lead to a national revival of Russia. But when, instead, the people threw down their arms and the October revolution began, Tolstoy, together with his readers, emigrated abroad. But he did not remain there long. His close and concentrated effort to understand the meaning of events is evidenced in the first part of the future trilogy *The Road to Calvary*, with its expressive epigraph from *The Tale of Igor's Host*, "O, Russian Land!"

Returning to Russia and observing attentively the life around him, Tolstoy grasped intuitively and with "an artist's boldness" that the October revolution contained within itself not only a social utopia alien and hostile to him, but also enormous lodes, whole "Himalayas" of a will to national life. Almost physically, with his skin, as it were, he sensed the new reader, "with young, laughing eyes." This new reader, who had just destroyed the foundations of the old life, was still without a culture—but culture, after all, was something to be acquired in time.

In his novel *Nineteen-Eighteen* Tolstoy repeatedly returns to the idea of a new national consolidation, born of the revolution: "Who had expected that Great Russia, cut off from all seas and from the grain-producing provinces, from coal and oil, hungry, poverty-striken, typhoid-ridden, would still refuse to yield, that she would, gritting her teeth, again and again send her sons into frightful battles? Only a year ago the people abandoned the front, and the country seemed to have turned into a lawless anarchic swamp. But in reality it was not so: tremendous cohesive forces were emerging in the land."

The beginning of the Five-Year Plans did not shake Tolstoy's feelings, but further strengthened them. He regarded the industrialization of the country as a new push toward national consolidation and responded to it "as an artist" with the novel *Peter I*. In this new work Tolstoy, without concealing Peter's ruthlessness, tells the reader that without such methods of terror Peter could not have crushed the boyar opposition and budged the "cursed land" from dead center.

The parallel between the Petrine epoch and Soviet life during the Five-Year Plans was in the air at the time, but no one except Tolstoy had ventured to develop it on so vast a canvas. From then on, Tolstoy's popularity began to grow, and he himself came to "accept" everything, becoming one of the chief spokesmen of official literature.

Nor was Tolstoy daunted by the Moscow trials of 1936–38. In 1937 he published his story "Bread," eulogizing Stalin's military genius during the defense of Tsaritsyn. Tolstoy himself regarded this story as a necessary link between the second and third parts of *The Road to Calvary*. The most sensational aspect of the story was not so much the glorification of Stalin, as the depiction of Trotsky as the evil genius of the Russian revolution. It was easy for Tolstoy to do this: he was now hitting back, as it were, for his initial fear of "October" as the beginning of a "world social revolution." Shocking in its crude falsification of facts, the writer's picture of Trotsky and his associates during the Brest-Litovsk negotiations fairly seethes with hatred of these leaders of October. According to Tolstoy, they wanted to "blow up Soviet Russia so that the whole world would explode from the monstrous detonation." "But, of course," he adds, "the world itself was nothing to them but the same arena for personal adventure and the play of ambition. Provocation and betrayal were their methods."

In sharp contrast to the images of Trotsky and the Leftwing leaders of "October" are those of Lenin and Stalin. True, Stalin's role in the story is almost nominal; he is always shown in the company of Lenin, either pensively silent or agreeing with him. "Lenin," writes Tolstoy, "depended upon the creative forces of the masses for the victory and success of the revolution, and retained his optimism through all misfortunes, sufferings, and ordeals. He pointed out that the revolution had already called into being a new type of Russian. He asserted, passionately and prophetically, that the history of Russia was the history of a great people, and that her future was great and boundless."

This story, which appeared at the height of the terror and brutal repressions against virtually the entire leadership of the October revolution, certainly enhanced Tolstoy's prestige in official circles, but stunned his fellow writers and the reading public with amazement. No other leading Soviet writer had ever reached such "Himalayas" of slander in his works.

Tolstoy was bold and consistent. Having sensed, with his "artist's impudence" (his own words, in the "Message to Young Writers," 1938), the consolidation of national tendencies in the course of the revolution, Tolstoy no longer drew a line at anything. After completing "Bread" he began the third part of *The Road to Calvary—A Gloomy Morning*. As time went on, the writer became progressively kinder in his treatment of the rank-and-file heroes of the Civil War on both sides—all those "honest, simple and trusting, heavy-handed Russian people." Together with Captain Roshchin, who had by now re-evaluated his past, Tolstoy looked fondly at the young workers of the time, with their naïve belief that they were taking part in "the world revolution." As for "Father Makhno" and his associates in the anarchic peasant movement which opposed both the Reds and the Whites, Tolstoy described them with a virtually Repin-like splash of color.

Tolstoy died relatively early, in the full flower of his talent. But his ideological development was complete; there was no further place for him to go. And, in a sense, death was kind to him, coming at the height of his fame.

After the war, and particularly after Stalin's death, interest in Tolstoy visibly began to decline, and the only works out of his immense literary legacy that are still alive and are likely to remain alive are *Peter I* and *The Road to Calvary*.

15 MIKHAIL SHOLOKHOV (1905–   )

With his talent and his manner of writing, Mikhail Alexandrovich Sholokhov is perhaps the last heir to Russia's rich epic tradition. His epic sweep won him great popularity in the young Soviet society, which had launched a lively discussion in the middle 1920s about the problems of cultural heritage and "learning from the classics."

Sholokhov has told us about himself and his life in a short autobiography prefacing the second collection of his stories, *The Azure Steppe* (Moscow, 1926). He was born in 1905 in the Cossack village of Veshenskaya, in the former Donets district. His father stemmed from the peasants of Ryazan province and frequently changed his occupation: he was, among other things, a cattle trader, a farmer on land purchased from the Cossacks, and a salesman in a store. His mother, who was half-Cossack, half-peasant, learned to read and write when her husband took the little Sholokhov to the nearby town to attend the gymnasium. She wanted to be able to write to her son without her husband's help. Sholokhov's studies at the gymnasium lasted only until 1918. After 1920 he worked and "roamed" all over the Don region. He worked in the food industry, "chased" the armed bands which raided city and village in the region until they were finally routed in 1922, and was "chased" by them.

He began to write in 1923 and published his first book, *Don Tales*, in 1925. The following year he added a number of new stories to the collection and reissued it under the title *The Azure Steppe*. The stories deal with episodes of the Civil War. When the book appeared, its author was only twenty years old. The reader is immediately impressed with the vividness of language in the descriptions of the local landscape, the diversity of speech of the various characters, the lively dialogue. Here is a short example: "Night came from the steppe, deepening all colors, and the sun had barely set when a star appeared, as if suspended over the well, twinkling, shy, and timid like a bride at the first visit of the prospective bridegroom" ("Mortal Enemy"). In these stories we frequently encounter the first silhouettes of many of the future characters of *The Quiet Don*. Thus, in the story "Bigamist," the woman Anna is easily recognizable as an early sketch for Aksinya, and her husband, Alexander, as Aksinya's husband, Stepan Astakhov.

Already in these early stories one feels how confining the short-story form is to Sholokhov's epic talent. It took him more than ten years to write the novel *The Quiet Don*. The first volume appeared in 1928, the second in 1929, the third in 1933, and the fourth and last in 1940. In literary quality and scope this work has no equal in Soviet literature.

Interesting details concerning Sholokhov's first steps in literature are related by Isaac Lezhnev in his monograph on Sholokhov (1948). The literary community's first response to Sholokhov was unfriendly. Some critics even accused the writer of "kulak ideology." Even worse, there were rumors, whispered at first, but later published openly in the press, that the real author of *The Quiet Don* was not Sholokhov, but "some White officer who was killed in the Civil War."

The honors for discovering Sholokhov's literary talent belong to A. S. Serafimovich, also of Cossack origin. When the author sent the first volume of *The Quiet Don* to the magazine *Oktyabr* in 1927, the editors' response was cool. Nevertheless, after some hesitation, the novel was turned over to Serafimovich for comment. As he read it, the older writer felt at once that he was in the presence of a "literary masterpiece." He reiterated this opinion later in a review published in *Pravda* in 1928. Serafimovich compared Sholokhov with "a young yellow-billed eaglet who has suddenly spread out his huge wings." "His characters," said Serafimovich, "are not painted, not written. They are not paper figures, but tumble out of the pages in a living, gleaming crowd, each with his own nose, his own wrinkles, his own eyes, and his own speech...."

In some way the characters of Sholokhov's epic are reminiscent of the heroes of Tolstoy's *War and Peace*. The reader of *War and Peace* forgets that the author shows only the upper strata of the early nineteenth-century society. Tolstoy's heroes are the embodiment, the expression of the nation, and the reader responds to them as if they were his own, his kin, near and dear to him. The same is true of *The Quiet Don*. The reader easily accepts the novel's characters; he shares the joys and sorrows of the lame Cossack Panteley Melekhov and his wife Ilyinishna; he takes part in all the details of their family existence, and from the very first lines becomes fond of the family's general favorite, the younger son Grigory, and his little sister Dunyashka, with her "pathetic and naïve mixture of childhood and blossoming youth." Only writers who feel organically linked with the people in periods when great national problems are in the process of solution are capable of painting their characters with such loving attention.

But Tolstoy also comes to mind for another, less direct reason. In his article "A Few Words about My Book *War and Peace*" (1868)[1] Tolstoy wrote: "I know the things that are thought to constitute the character of the time and that are not found in my novel: the horrors of serfdom, the immuring of wives in walls, the whipping of grown sons.... But I do not regard this picture of the time, which persists in our imagination, as true, and I did not wish to convey it...."

When Sholokhov wrote *The Quiet Don*, he was also fighting against the traditional image of the Cossacks, who were so dear to his heart. This is pointed out by I. Lezhnev, a famous Soviet critic known for his independence of judgment: "From his youngest days, from the very beginning of his creative career, Sholokhov was inspired

[1] *Complete Works*, Vol. XVI, p. 53.

with the passionate desire to refute the prevalent fiction about the Cossacks, to eradicate 'down to its very roots' the cloyingly false official rhetoric about the Civil War in the Don region. By his entire work Sholokhov seems to be saying to an invisible opponent that his picture of the Don region and its people, of their life and customs is wrong: 'When you speak of a Cossack, you have in mind the White, forgetting about the Red and completely ignoring the fact that a considerable proportion of the working Cossack population belonged to the Greens [who rejected both Whites and Reds]. . . . You see only cruelty, crudity, and ignorance, but have you ever suspected the high humanity and tenderness often concealed under the outer rudeness? . . . Have you ever guessed how contradictory and painful was the average Cossack's road to the revolution, if he was gifted, intelligent, sincere, and desperately sought the truth?'"

The Quiet Don is a great river, flowing not through a peaceful region, but through a land aflame with war and revolution. Ordinary people are compelled to solve the great problems of a crucial epoch, and they solve them slowly, thinking hard, in the sweat of their brows, vacillating, anguished, yet solving them after all. Such is the political pathos which carries this epic novel through its fifteen hundred pages. And this is why the novel has awakened such a fervent response among contemporary readers.

The contents of *The Quiet Don* are algebraically expressed in several lines of an old Cossack song, which the author used as an epigraph for his novel:

Oh, how should I, the quiet Don, not flow so turbidly?
From out the depths of the quiet Don the cold springs leap,
Amidstream of the quiet Don the white fish churn. . . .

The confusion and drama of the epoch are set off from the very first by the passionate intensity of the personal life of the novel's main character, the young Cossack Grigory Melekhov. His first love is awakened by a married woman, a neighbor's wife, Aksinya Astakhova. Life had early inflicted brutality on Aksinya: when she was fifteen years old, she was raped by her father. His own family avenged her by killing him. Later Aksinya was married to a man from another village. But her husband discovered that Aksinya was not a virgin and beat her savagely for this "insult." Aksinya withdrew into herself.

When she becomes aware of Grigory's feelings, Aksinya avoids him at first, but the gentle and persistent Grigory finally wins her affection. With all the passion of her broken, trampled, unexpended feelings, Aksinya falls in love with the tender, "animal-like" young man. She asks him to leave his family and the village and settle somewhere else with her. But Grigory delays decision: how can he leave the farm? Their liaison is soon discovered by the village. Aksinya's husband is away in the army. But his service is soon over; he returns and once more begins to torment his wife. The older Melekhov hears about Grigory's infatuation and decides to cure his son by getting him married. Although the family is not wealthy, it is respected by the villagers, and the vain and ambitious old man, Panteleymon Melekhov, decides to go with a matchmaker to the rich Cossack, Miron Korshunov. Korshunov's daughter, Natalya, falls in love with Grigory at first sight. Pretty and sincere, she awakens something akin to sympathy and affection in Grigory, who still longs for Aksinya.

But their marriage is not a success. Reserved and awkward in her caresses, Natalya only stirs up Grigory's unhealing wound, his desire for Aksinya. Soon he renews his relationship with Aksinya and both leave the village, hiring out as farm laborers at the estate of the landowner Listnitsky. All efforts of the old Melekhov to persuade Grigory to return to his family are vain. Natalya has no alternative but to return to her parents' home. Once, when her longing becomes unbearable, she secretly sends Grigory a letter, asking how she is to live; can she hope that he would return to her one day? Grigory replies: "Live alone," and Natalya tries to kill herself by cutting her throat with a scythe. For many months she hovers between life and death. In the meantime Aksinya gives birth to Grigory's daughter.

War breaks into this tense situation. "Over the arteries of the land, its railways, Russia, convulsed, began to drive gray-coated blood to her western frontiers."

Both of the Melekhov sons are in the army. The elder, Pyotr, a calm, even-tempered man, is soon promoted to officer rank. Grigory is his equal in courage. But while Pyotr accepts the war as something inevitable and derives satisfaction from his promotion for good service, Grigory is depressed over the daily mass killings. It even seems to him at times that he will never be the same after the war, that he will never be able to caress a child. An important role in Grigory's inner life at this troubled time is played by the soldier Garanzha, who sympathizes with the revolutionaries, and whom Grigory meets in a hospital. Garanzha opens Grigory's eyes to the meaning of the war: the only people interested in it are the "masters." After his conversations with Garanzha, Grigory feels as if he had been blind for years, and has suddenly gained sight.

Meantime, life in the village also changes. Aksinya's daughter dies. The son of the landowner for whom Aksinya works takes advantage of Grigory's absence and becomes her lover. When Grigory returns on furlough and learns about it, he breaks with Aksinya, beats up his rival, and returns to his father's house, where he is awaited by the gentle Natalya. As he approaches the village, as he sees his house in the distance, Grigory poignantly feels "his own, his Cossack, national spirit, imbibed with his mother's milk, loved throughout his lifetime, taking the upper hand over the greater human truth" which was revealed to him by Garanzha.

The second volume of *The Quiet Don* is almost entirely devoted to the revolution as it was reflected in the life of the Cossacks. Somewhat surprisingly, the author halts to deal here with the separatist moods which emerged among the Cossacks (especially among the officers) under the impact of Russia's military defeats and the revolution. These moods had evidently stirred Sholokhov himself in his youth. This communicates itself through the warmth of his portrait of the young Cossack officer Atarshchikov, who is enamored of the glorious Cossack past. It also makes itself felt in the care with which the author presents the ideas of another officer, Izvarin, who tries to win Grigory to his viewpoint. Izvarin argues that the way of the Cossacks has never coincided with that of Russia, and that it certainly does not coincide with it at the moment. Izvarin ascribes the growing pro-Bolshevik sympathies among Cossack soldiers to the Bolshevik promises to end the war. He is convinced that as soon as the war is over, the paths of the Cossacks and the Bolsheviks will diverge again and forever. Although a great deal in Izvarin's arguments is not clear to Grigory, some of them elicit a response, and this will make itself felt later on.

The figures of the Communists—Shtokman, Bunchuk, Lagutin, and Valet—are the weakest in the novel. They are unconvincing schematic clichés instead of living men. As soon as Sholokhov turns to them, he begins to be hounded by failure; even his usually fluid and elastic phrases become dry and unwieldy. This is all the more striking since, in depicting Communists, Sholokhov sincerely tries to enlist the reader's sympathies. Sholokhov the Communist does his utmost to paint sympathetic party members, but Sholokhov the artist rejects all these efforts.

The reason for this failure may lie in the fact that the Communists were outsiders among the Cossacks. With all his innermost peasant-Cossack instinct, Sholokhov placed little value on the radicalism and revolutionary fervor of people who had nothing to lose by the revolution. This is graphically expressed in one of the scenes. Some of the Cossacks, including Grigory, have come back from the war as "Reds." When the Civil War breaks out, the local Communist, Valet, urges the Cossacks to leave the village before the Whites occupy it, and to join the Red detachments. Although Grigory and the other Cossacks are to some extent in sympathy with Valet, they are reluctant to leave the village and their farms. And Grigory cries out to Valet with irritation:

"'Stop babbling! It's different for you: you've nothing before you, and nothing behind you—it's easy for you to pick up and go. But we have to think it over carefully....' His black, suddenly angry eyes glittered and, baring his strong, closely-set teeth, he cried: 'It's easy for you to wag your tongue, you scum! You were always a rolling stone: you own nothing but the jacket on your back...!'"

The events in Soviet Russia during the first Five-Year Plan compelled Sholokhov to interrupt his epic novel for a time. In 1932, instead of the third volume of *The Quiet Don*, he published another novel, *Virgin Soil Upturned*, mirroring the collectivization in the Don region.

As a work of art, *Virgin Soil Upturned* is weaker than *The Quiet Don*. It paints a picture of the collectivization in the village of Gremyachy Log. Its action unfolds in the same locale as that of *The Quiet Don*—in Sholokhov's native region.

The first collective farms—voluntary peasant communes and *artels* ("cooperatives")—sprang up in the very first years following the revolution. But their number increased slowly, and the peasant masses obviously showed no desire to part with their individual farms. In 1929 the government launched the campaign of compulsory collectivization. It was attended by the "liquidation of the kulaks," prosperous peasants whose properties were confiscated and who were deported with their families to Siberia and the far north. Under the pretext of the "anti-kulak drive," similar measures were applied on a mass scale to all who resisted collectivization. These measures provoked peasant uprisings in various parts of the country, which were put down with merciless brutality. Especially bloody were the uprisings in regions inhabited by a prosperous peasantry, as in the Ukraine, North Caucasus, the Don region, Siberia, and the Volga region. This frightened the government. In 1930 Stalin published his famous article "Dizziness from Success," in which he sought to shift the responsibility for the horrors of the collectivization from the shoulders of the party to those of overzealous "collectivizers." However, the collectivization policy remained in force, if in somewhat tempered form.

The first literary works dealing with the progress of the collectivization provided no inkling of the true character of events, presenting as they did a picture in which the majority of the peasantry favored the collectives, with only the surviving remnants of the Whites and the kulaks opposing them. Sholokhov was the first writer to convey the truly tragic quality of the radical change that was being wrought in the life of the peasants. True, Sholokhov also made use of the current clichés about the intrigues of Whites and kulaks. But he succeeded in raising an edge of the curtain over the thoughts and feelings of rank-and-file peasant Cossacks, and showed that the poor peasants were also frequently afraid of joining the collective farms and supported the kulaks.

The Communist Sholokhov accepted the idea that the collectivization was a progressive measure, but the artist suffered the events together with the Cossack masses. The central figures of the book are not, however, the peasant Cossacks, who oppose the collectivization, and not even the resolute Maidannikov, who chooses to follow the Communists, but the local Communists in charge of the collectivization and the worker Davydov, who was sent to the village from the center. A Leningrad worker and former sailor, Davydov is one of the "twenty-five-thousanders" mobilized by the Communist Party from among workers for assignment to villages, to help the local authorities. The local Communists vividly drawn by Sholokhov include the secretary of the party cell, Makar Nagulnov, a hero of the Civil War who dreams of "world socialist revolution," and the chairman of the village Soviet, Andrey Razmetnov. The latter belongs to the category of Communists whose "nerves" sometimes give way. When Davydov assigns him to "de-kulak" a large family with many children, he cries out that he was not trained by the party "to make war on children."

In his portraits of the Cossacks, Sholokhov succeeded best with those of the opponents of collectivization. The image of Titok Borodin is particularly vivid. During the Civil War, Titok fought on the side of the Reds. After the war he plunged into farming with a will, and "took hold" of his land so energetically that he began to prosper. His village neighbors cautiously advised him not to overdo it, or else—heaven forbid—he might find himself classed as a kulak. But Titok refused to heed them, arguing that he had been "nothing" before the war, and had fought in order to become "everything." Didn't the new national hymn say just that?

When Makar Nagulnov's resolution to "liquidate the kulak" Titok is passed at a meeting of the poorest peasants of the village, the meeting falls into uneasy silence. Razmetnov explains to Davydov, who is unfamiliar with local conditions, that the case of Titok is complicated: "this hurts to the quick, it draws blood." The affair ends tragically for Titok: his property is confiscated, and he is sent to the Cheka with the rest of the kulaks. When he is already sitting in the cart, with his hands tied, Titok cries to Nagulnov: "Remember, our paths will cross! You've trampled me down, but my turn will come! Whatever comes, I'll get you!"

The appearance of *Virgin Soil Upturned* in 1932 produced a literary sensation reminiscent of the one created two years earlier in the villages by Stalin's article "Dizziness from Success."

Sholokhov the artist understands the organic character of the peasant resistance to collectivization. Sholokhov the Communist attempts to explain this resistance by the rigidity of the peasant psyche and the peasantry's natural reaction to the errors and "excesses" of the local authorities. These errors must be carefully corrected at the next stage. Such is the political philosophy of the novel, defended by the worker Davydov and, through him, by the author himself. This makes it understandable why Sholokhov could not choose as his central figure a rank-and-file Cossack who is sincerely working for the kolkhoz system. And the novel as a whole fails to keep the promise of the title: there is no virgin soil upturned here—only huge chunks of earth torn out of the land as by a bombshell.

Only the first part of *Virgin Soil Upturned* appeared in 1932. Sholokhov had long since completed the second part of the novel as well. In 1936 the editors of *Novy Mir* (the journal which published the first part) announced that the manuscript of part two was returned to Sholokhov for revision. But it took almost a quarter of a century before the second part of the novel finally saw the light of day.

After responding to the dramatic events of the early 1930s with his *Virgin Soil Upturned*, Sholokhov returned to his cherished work, *The Quiet Don*.

In terms of literary quality the third and fourth volumes of this epic novel are the writer's crowning achievements. Both volumes deal with the Civil War in the Don region. At the beginning of the revolution Grigory Melekhov and many of the other Cossacks of his generation were drawn to the Bolsheviks. Although he had been promoted to officer rank at the end of the world war, he instinctively shunned his fellow officers. The regular Cossack officers also avoided their new colleagues, promoted from the ranks during the war. The atrocities committed by the Bolsheviks, which, in the eyes of the justice-loving Grigory, were in no way different from those of the Whites, cooled his ardor. He was more and more disturbed over the entire course of the complicated struggle in which it was so difficult to discover which side represented truth and justice. Imperceptibly to himself, the young Melekhov became filled with resentment against the Bolsheviks: "They had broken into his life, taken him from the land! He saw that similar feelings were taking hold of the other Cossacks. . . . And, looking at the uncollected sheaves of wheat, at the uncut corn trampled by horses' hooves, at the empty threshing floors, each man recalled his own land, on which the women groaned in exhausting toil, and his heart turned hard with rage."

The words of the officer Izvarin began to bear fruit. It seemed to Grigory and to other Cossacks that the best solution would be to secede from the rest of Russia: the Russian peasants need land—"let them fight! On the Don we have land aplenty," and hence there is no reason for fighting. All that is needed is to drive out the Bolsheviks from the Don as quickly as possible.

When the Cossack Ivan Alexeyevich, who is in sympathy with the Reds, tries to prove to Grigory that the Soviet government is a government of the working people, Grigory answers angrily: "But this government of yours, whatever you say, is a rotten government. And you praise it like a mother who says: 'He's snotty, but he's ours.' You'd better tell me straight out, and then we'll talk no more about it: what does it give us, the Cossacks?" To all of the arguments of Ivan Alexeyevich, Grigory has one answer: "To us Cossacks this government brings nothing but ruin. . . . Communists, generals—they're nothing but the same yoke." Grigory even remains indifferent to the argument to which, in his lifelong search for "justice," he has always been especially responsive. Ivan Alexeyevich assures him that the Soviet government would bring about social equality. But Grigory no longer believes in it: "That's what the Bolsheviks used to say to fool the ignorant. They've spilled out a sackful of fine words, and people rushed to them like fish to bait! And where has this equality gone to? Take the Red Army. They passed through the village: the platoon commander in good calf boots, and 'Vanyok,' the plain soldier, in rag leggings. I saw the commissar—decked out in leather from head to foot, leather trousers, leather jacket, while the next man hasn't enough leather even for shoes. And that is only after a year of their government; what will become of equality when they really take hold?"

Sholokhov succeeded particularly well in showing the segment of the Civil War which is known in the history of the revolution as the struggle of the Don Cossacks for independence. In depicting this struggle Sholokhov broke with the official legend which painted all movements against the Soviet regime as counterrevolutionary attempts to restore the old order. His excellent knowledge of the history and life of the Don Cossacks served Sholokhov well, and he showed convincingly that the roots of the separatist movement were by no means nourished solely by restorationist moods. The decisive role in the Cossacks' struggle against the Soviet regime was played by the democratic traditions of the Cossacks, who were more prosperous, more independent, and more civilized than the mass of the Russian peasantry.

With all the fervor of youth Grigory plunges into the Civil War. He is now in command of an entire Cossack division, and the old Panteley is proud of his son. Grigory's fame spreads far and wide over the Cossack villages. And only rarely in the welter of bloody days and restless nights does some fragment of the distant peaceful past flash through Grigory's memory: "the wide steppe, the summer roads, a peasant cart, his father in the driver's seat, the bullocks, fields covered with golden bristle after the grain was harvested, the black scattering of rooks along the road. . . ." Among the memories of a life that now seems gone forever, Aksinya's image rises up at moments and scalds Grigory with the old passion. " 'My love! My unforgettable darling!' he whispered, drawing away with distaste from the chance woman sleeping next to him."

It gradually becomes clear to the participants in the separatist movement that the Cossacks cannot hope to hold out in the ever-spreading struggle. Their leaders once more begin negotiations and form an alliance with the Whites. Like the rest of the rank-and-file Cossacks, Grigory is distrustful of these "allies." Nor does he expect any good from the officers. Halting in transit in his native village, Grigory speaks of his doubts to Natalya: "Life's gone all wrong, and perhaps it's my fault too. . . . Perhaps we ought to make peace with the Reds. . . . But how? Who can bring us together with the Soviet government? How can our mutual grievances be settled?"

The events of the Civil War also hold the central place in the fourth volume of *The Quiet Don*, the first part of which appeared in 1937, and the concluding part not until 1940.

Inwardly divided, "roaming like a blizzard in the steppe,"

Grigory is not only unable to find his way through the maze of political problems, but is equally split in his personal life, still torn between his wife Natalya and Aksinya. The longing for Aksinya wins again, and she herself tells Natalya about the resumption of their relations. This happens just as events in the country take a sharp turn for the worse. The Whites and, with them, the Cossacks, suffer defeat after defeat. When she learns that Grigory has again returned to Aksinya, Natalya goes to the village midwife for an abortion and dies of the resulting hemorrhage.

Notified of the misfortune, Grigory rushes home, but by the time he arrives Natalya is dead. The White Army at this time begins its panic retreat to the Black Sea. Old Panteley, mobilized into the fight against the Bolsheviks, also dies. At first, Grigory joins in the retreat. But he contracts typhus on the way, and during his illness he begins to think a great deal about the meaning of the events about him. Once, as he lies ill, he hears an old song, struck up in the steppe by the retreating Cossacks. "The centuries-old song . . . lived on and dominated the black steppe. In simple words the song spoke about the free Cossack forebears who had fearlessly fought down the Czar's hosts, who had 'plagued' merchants, boyars, and army commanders. . . . Gloomily, the Cossacks listened to this song." Grigory feels deeply shaken by it, his throat contracts with a spasm. A decision gradually comes to him: he's had enough of wandering about to unknown destinations, he will not follow the Whites to foreign lands. Come what may, he will remain in his native Don region. . . .

Still gloomier is the final part of the novel. Its landscape is bare, lonely, and harsh. Grigory has been with the Whites and with the Reds, and is "sick of both revolution and counterrevolution." He is "terribly weary at heart." "It's no joking matter," he says angrily, "eight years without getting off the horse! Even at night there is nothing but dreams of all this fine life: either you're killing, or you're being killed!" He has one longing now—to return home, to his land; he hungers for the plow. His village has long been in the hands of the Reds; there is a Revolutionary Committee there. And although its chairman, Mikhail Koshevoy, is Grigory's brother-in-law, he does not trust Grigory and refuses to give him credit for his loyal service with the Reds at the time when he believed and followed them. Nor is the Revolutionary Committee satisfied with Grigory's offer to serve a prison term for his participation in the separatist Cossack uprising. To the sincere and hot-tempered Grigory this distrust is like a blow of the whip to a high-strung horse. The horse rears up once more, and Grigory joins the bandits. Here he is stricken with a new misfortune. After anguished hesitation caused by Natalya's death, Grigory has once more returned to Aksinya. But as she flees with him, Aksinya is shot and dies. The bands are routed. In the final pages we see Grigory, mortally tired, indifferent to everything, wandering toward his native house. He is met by Mishatka, his son, who will complete to his father the melancholy tale about the end of the once-populous Melekhov household. . . .

Ending on such a tragic note, the novel provoked a heated discussion in Soviet literary circles. I have already mentioned that *The Quiet Don* attracted immediate attention with its very first volume. Throughout the years, the interest in the novel never slackened. True, most of the critics were convinced that sooner or later Grigory Melekhov would become a Bolshevik, and that the entire novel would be a new, Soviet version of Erckmann-Chatrian's once-sensational *History of a Peasant*; that it would create the portrait of a peasant who had gone through the revolution, who supported it and was happy with its results. This is why the first reviews of the fourth volume were filled with unconcealed disappointment: "Reading the final pages of Sholokhov's latest book," wrote Osip Cherny in the *Literary Gazette*, "it is difficult to shake off the impression that the printers mixed up the title sheets, and that in reality the whole of *The Quiet Don*, including the fourth volume, was written long before the *Virgin Soil Upturned*." Some critics had even publicly repented of their early affection for Grigory Melekhov, explaining that their sympathies had been nothing but "an advance payment to the future kolkhoz member."

Two works devoted to *The Quiet Don*—one by I. Lezhnev, the other by B. Emelyanov—are of particular interest.

In his essay "Two Souls" (*Molodaya Guardia*, No. 10, 1940) I. Lezhnev gives due tribute to the mind and talent of Sholokhov, "a great Russian writer." But, he says, as the reader yields to the enchantment of Sholokhov's images, he must occasionally rein in his feelings. He hears the whisper of cold reason: "What delusion is this? Think carefully: can you, should you love these people? After all, Grigory Melekhov is our enemy, and yet you've allowed yourself to become so emotional, you've so lost control of yourself that you're ready to kiss him."

B. Emelyanov's approach in his article "About *The Quiet Don* and Its Critics" (*Literaturny Kritik*, Nos. 11–12, 1940) is more profound. The center of the debate, the point around which all the views and hypotheses of the critics revolve, is the question: "Is *The Quiet Don* a tragic work, and is Grigory Melekhov the hero of a tragedy?" Emelyanov says at the outset that this is not a question of form or literary genre, but a "cardinal" question, essential both for an understanding of the critics' position and for clarification of the novel's meaning. Emelyanov himself concludes that "Sholokhov was the first of our writers to show the 'tragic element' in the revolution and the Civil War. He was the first to convey the sense of the enormous complexity of the road by which the mind of the masses must travel toward an understanding of the objective course of history." The critics who deny this "tragic element" in *The Quiet Don*, he says, are making a mistake.

To illustrate his point, Emelyanov cites Aeschylus' tragedy *The Persians*, presented in Athens several years after the Greek victory at Salamis. The action of the tragedy unfolds in Asia Minor, in the Persian capital. Aeschylus showed on the stage the camp of the defeated, the Persian wives and mothers weeping for their dead, and

Xerxes himself, King of Persia and enemy of Athens, in the midst of mourning and misfortune. The audience could not but sympathize with the conquered, but this, says Emelyanov, in no way diminished their sense of victory. "The critics do not understand," says Emelyanov, "that the nobly sorrowful tone of Sholokhov's tale, the melancholy and exalted end of his epic, confirms the sense of victory all the more strongly, the more tragic it is."

The direct responses of readers and listeners to Sholokhov's novel were collected by I. Lezhnev in his essay "Two Souls" (in the magazine *The Young Guard*, No. 10, 1940). The last part of *The Quiet Don* was broadcast over the radio. Listeners sent in a great number of enthusiastic letters. Workers and village teachers expressed in these letters their admiration for the novel and its principal hero, Grigory. A woman worker employed in a Moscow factory wrote that, although the broadcasts took place at a late hour, she sacrificed time from her short sleep, but did not miss a single broadcast. Even children often refused to go to bed, anxious to hear what happened to Grigory. A woman worker from another factory compared *The Quiet Don* with *War and Peace*, adding that the former was even nearer to her heart than Tolstoy's epic, because everything in it was "our own."

The Quiet Don is unquestionably Sholokhov's most successful work. Had the writer adhered to the stock formula of a "happy ending," he would have violated his integrity not only as an artist, but as an eyewitness of the great popular revolution. It is precisely because Grigory Melekhov had "from the very beginning, from 1917," sought passionately for the right way and was unable to find it, and so had wandered all his life "like a drunken man," floated helplessly "like dung in an ice-hole," that he will bring intact to future generations the whole shaken soul of the people, which felt dissatisfied with the results of the revolution.

To conclude this discussion about *The Quiet Don*, it must be added that a new and revised version of the novel appeared in 1955. The revisions introduced by Sholokhov in the new edition were essentially stylistic in character; he eliminated a large number of provincialisms which abounded in the first edition. But there were also a number of political revisions in the text in the spirit of the current official tenets. These changes diminish to some extent the artistic value of the work. I shall cite but two examples. In Chapter Thirteen of the first volume of the original edition, we read that, along with a variety of adventurers and scoundrels who had come to the Supreme Headquarters in Mogilev at the outbreak of the February revolution (March, according to the European calendar), there were also people "who sincerely wanted to help Kornilov to raise the old Russia, which had fallen in February, back to her feet." In the new edition (Vol. 2) "people who sincerely wanted to help" are not mentioned at all; instead, the author enumerates "manufacturers and bankers." "There were other 'visitors' too—representatives of the Anglo-French imperialists," who "urged Kornilov to hurry with his action against the revolutionary people." The additions to the Fourteenth Chapter are of a similar character, enlarging on the activities of the "imperialist circles of England, America, and France."

During the war years Sholokhov began to write a new novel, *They Fought for the Homeland*. Its first chapters appeared in *Pravda* in 1943 and 1944. The first part of the novel was published in 1955; the second was merely announced. In this work Sholokhov centered his attention on a number of portraits of soldiers. Its action takes place in the Don steppe, against the background of Cossack farms. The final chapter of the first part describes the retreat of the Soviet Army to the left bank of the Don. At the cost of heavy losses the regiment halts the German advance.

This first published part of the novel (according to Sholokhov's own admission, he thinks and writes "slowly") is inferior to *The Quiet Don* in literary quality, but it will nevertheless take a firm place in the literature of the war period. With great skill the author reveals the inner world not only of his heroes but also of the lesser characters who play only a modest role in the novel. I shall confine myself to a single illustration. The heavily bleeding Zvyagintsev is dragged on a tarpaulin stretcher by the nurse who picked him up. "He saw bending over him the pale face of an unknown girl, freckled even under its thick coat of suntan, a faded cap over her tangled shock of fiery-red curls. The face was obviously homely—an ordinary, plain, snub-nosed Russian face, but such deep and sincere tenderness and anxiety shone through the roughened features of this face, such ageless feminine warmth glowed in the mild gray eyes, that it seemed to Zvyagintsev that those eyes were as necessary, good, and indispensable as life itself, as the endless blue sky spreading over him, with its wide bank of fleecy clouds. . . ."

In certain measure the appearance of the second part of *Virgin Soil Upturned* was sensational even in Sholokhov's literary biography. As has been said above, in 1936 the editors of *Novy Mir* returned the manuscript of the second part to Sholokhov "for revision." The first chapters of this part began to appear only in 1955. Then followed another interruption. The interruptions and delays in the publication of the second part gave rise to many rumors. On February 12, 1960, the concluding chapters of the novel finally appeared in *Pravda*, and after that the novel was published in book form.

Commenting on the appearance of the second part of *Virgin Soil Upturned*, Harrison Salisbury published an article in the New York *Times* of February 18, under the title, "Sholokhov's Hero Dies a New Death." In this article the long-time Moscow correspondent of the New York newspaper told about the rumors which had long been current in Moscow in connection with Sholokhov's novel. Sholokhov had ended his novel on a tragic note: its principal hero, Davydov, died during the "great" purge of the middle 1930s. Such an ending was obviously at odds with the present demands of "socialist realism." When Khrushchev visited Sholokhov in Veshenskaya Stanitsa before his trip to the United States and invited the writer to accompany him to America, there were new rumors, alleging that Khrushchev had succeeded in persuading him to change the end of his novel and save Davydov from death in prison.

In the final version of the novel both Davydov and his friend Makar Nagulnov die one night when they break into the house of the kolkhoz property manager Ostrovnoy, who is hiding two diversionist plotters—the former Cossack officer Polovtsev and his aide Lyatievsky. The latter also dies, while Polovtsev manages to escape. But he is soon arrested somewhere near Tashkent. The novel ends with the disclosure of a wide counterrevolutionary conspiracy in the Don region, the arrest of all the plotters, and their trial. In this version the reader's interest in Davydov recedes to the background. And if the tormented image of Grigory Melekhov wakened in the reader grave reflections about the tragic meaning of the great popular revolution, the crime-fiction ending of *Virgin Soil Upturned* transforms this novel from a tragedy, as it was originally conceived, into a political melodrama.

In 1955, during the celebration of his fiftieth birthday, Sholokhov said somewhere that people abroad accuse the Soviet writers of writing "according to the party's dictates." In reality, said he, this was not altogether so: "Each of us writes according to the dictates of his heart, but our hearts belong to the party. . . ."

The literary biography of the most prominent Soviet epic writer is testimony to how much better it would have been both for him and for contemporary Soviet literature as a whole if the writers' hearts belonged, not to the party, but to the writers themselves.

16 LITERARY DEVELOPMENTS: WORLD WAR II AND AFTER (1939–62)

THE WAR THEME: "WE HAVE SEEN MUCH SUFFERING"

The future historian of Soviet letters will find that, from its very first days, the Soviet-German war brought about a change both in the themes and subject matter of Soviet literary works, and in their choice of heroes.

The country's younger generation had been brought up to think of the regime created by the revolution and the Communist Party as in some sense unshakable. This was suggested particularly by the literature of the last prewar decade which dealt with war themes. The action of most of these works took place along the Soviet frontiers, and their characters were border guards and G.P.U. workers who repulsed the surprise raids of "arrogant bandits" with unvarying success. In the lives of the younger Soviet generation, these "border units" played a role similar to that of the Maginot Line in France: the life of the Soviet Union flowed on behind their protective wall with a confident sense of security.

But then the war broke out, and all these optimistic notions collapsed at a single stroke. The country suffered not only military defeats, but shattering spiritual blows. "We have seen much suffering on our way, and many reproachful eyes. We have learned to understand and read their message like a book," remarks the late Boris Lavrenyov in his story "The Portrait."

Such passing remarks are encountered in many versions in numberless sketches, stories, and poems. In the poem "You Remember, Alyosha, the Roads of Smolensk?"—dedicated to the poet A. Surkov—Konstantin Simonov writes:

> You know, it seems that, after all, our homeland
> Is not the city house where I spent festive days,
> But all this village soil our grandfathers had trod,
> With the plain crosses of their Russian graves.

The poet confesses that it was the war which brought him face to face with this eternal "village" Russia. The encounter shook Simonov profoundly. He was moved not only by the poverty of the rural regions, but even more by the quiet courage of the simple people, their readiness to endure and resist. He reminds his friend of the peasant hut near Borisov, which they saw when the Red Army was already withdrawing from the area, and the words of the old woman whose husband lay dead in the hut. The woman said to the retreating soldiers: "Go now, my sons, we'll wait for you." "We'll wait for you!" The poet hears these words at night, and it seems to him that he is "followed by their voices," filling him with surging love for his native land and its people. Surkov's answering poem is written in the same key of humility and deep emotion:

> Through smoke-filled nights and graying twilight,
> We carefully bore forward
> The undying flame of faith
> In our Russian, native folk.

The sincerity of these poems is all the more significant if we recall that their authors were not nonpartisan poets, but old party members who had written in an altogether different vein before the war (this is especially true of Surkov), when they had spoken boastfully of marching into Europe with a victorious Red Army.

Similar moods permeated the work of older poets. The best war poem, "Courage," was written by Anna Akhmatova: "We know what lies now on the scales" (*Pravda*, March 8, 1942).

NEW HEROES

Along with the humility, behind which it is easy to discern a sense of guilt before the people, there was another striking feature in the early literature about the war: for twenty years the heroes of most of the Soviet literary works had been Communists. But in the fiction and drama dealing with the Soviet-German war, the heroes were from the very first predominantly ordinary, nonpartisan people of the masses—peasant women, children, townsmen, and villagers. These new heroes were not only non-Communists, but had only yesterday been held under suspicion by the Communist authorities for their far from sympathetic moods, and some of them were even recent inmates of concentration camps.

Against the grim background of the war these heroes were welcomed by the readers with sincere emotion and gratitude. Years later, the poetess Yulia Neyman spoke in her poem "1941" (*Literary Moscow*, No. 2, 1956) of the feelings which prevailed in the country during the first year of war:

The Moscow of those days . . . the sudden onslaught
  of disaster . . .
Uncounted losses, unimaginable griefs.
No, my contemporaries, do not deny it:
It was like torch flame—that immaculate year!
Pretenses crumbled down like plaster,
And by the light of causes laid bare,
The year of camouflage and blackout
Revealed our friends and neighbors as they were.
Casting away all dubious weights and measures—
Questionnaires, length of service, offices and years—
With the full gauge of faith and courage
We measured that by which our lives were pure. . . .

And this is why, recalling the terrible events of that year, "the hours on duty, the roofs and aerostats," Neyman renders with deep truth its fundamental meaning in the spiritual life of the people. For it was then that they experienced "in earnest" and for the first time "the sense of proud citizenship."

Out of the flood of literature of that period, few works survive the test of time. Among them are *The Stories of*

Ivan Sudarev by Alexey Tolstoy, Leonid Leonov's play *Invasion*, Alexander Korneychuk's play *The Front*, and Konstantin Simonov's novel *Days and Nights*.

ALEXEY TOLSTOY: *The Stories of Ivan Sudarev*

The hero of *The Stories of Ivan Sudarev* (*Novy Mir*, September 1942) is a Soviet partisan, fighting alongside his fellow villagers against the German occupants. He explains to his chance companion (in "A Night in the Hayloft") that, in the course of this war, "more ideas have accumulated in the mind than are normally allotted to a man for his natural existence: what our fathers and grandfathers had not thought through, we must now think through in the shortest possible time, sometimes between two volleys. . . . And draw immediate conclusions with the help of arms. . . ."

The same idea is expressed in another of Ivan Sudarev's stories ("How It Began") by the director of a secondary school, Vasily Vasilievich Kozubsky: "We are taking an examination, a great historic test. . . . Will Russia perish under the German onslaught, or will the Germans perish? In their ancient graveyards, our grandfathers have risen from the grave to hear our answer. It is for us to decide. . . . Do you carry our culture within yourself—our honest, wise peasant culture? We are all to blame because we have not cherished, have not guarded it well enough. . . . We Russians are spendthrift. . . . But never mind—Russia is great, solid, and enduring." "Do you know," Vasily Vasilievich asks, "what goodness and virtue lie hidden in the Russian silence? What mercy and compassion, under the cotton kerchief? What capacity for self-sacrifice?"

The most interesting of these stories is "A Strange History." Its hero is the peasant Pyotr Filimonovich Gorshkov, who returned to the village shortly before the outbreak of war, after serving a ten-year sentence in a concentration camp for his hostility toward the kolkhoz system. Knowing this, the Germans ask him to serve as burgomaster and report on the partisans. Gorshkov accepts the appointment, then, making use of his position, he gathers information about the German movements and turns it over to the partisans. In the end the Germans discover his activities and hang him.

LEONOV: *The Invasion*

Essentially similar is Fedya, the hero of Leonid Leonov's play *The Invasion* (*Novy Mir*, August 1942). He, too, returned home from a concentration camp just on the eve of the war, after serving a sentence for killing a woman. The play was dealt with in detail in the chapter on Leonov.

KORNEYCHUK: *The Front*

One of the most successful literary works of the first year of war was *The Front*, a play by the Ukrainian dramatist Alexander Korneychuk, published (a most unusual procedure) in *Pravda* (August 24–27, 1942). The action of the play unfolds during the first weeks of the war, with their series of defeats, and it deals with the effort to overcome the profound crisis undermining the strength of the Red Army as a whole. The commander of the front is Ivan Gorlov, a Civil War hero who boasts that he "learned how to fight in battles, not in academies." The writer shows him as a vain man who has sunk into spiritual sloth and who tries to cover up his ignorance by the argument that the most important quality in a general is personal courage; all the rest, he says, will come of itself.

Ivan Gorlov has surrounded himself with friends and comrades of Civil War days, who are linked by a tacit system of mutual support. Any young commander, no matter how talented, is regarded as an interloper, since he did not fight in the Civil War, and Gorlov's associates try to keep him from the more responsible posts. One of these talented commanders in the play is the young Major General Ognyov. His relations with Gorlov are presented in the play with utmost candor. Neither man conceals his critical attitude toward the other. But the opposition to Gorlov is not confined to Ognyov and several other young officers. Ivan Gorlov is also opposed by some of his old Civil War comrades, as well as his own son, Lieutenant of the Guards Sergey Gorlov. Another critic is his brother, Miron Gorlov, a factory director who has come from the rear to study German airplanes.

Observing Ivan's methods of command and gathering some data from other commanders, Miron comes to the conclusion that his brother's general approach is seriously wrong. Miron believes that it is essential "to declare war upon ignoramuses and ignorance in military matters." War cannot be won by "courage" alone. Such an attitude reminds Miron of certain trust directors, who persisted in boasting of their work-calloused hands, loud voices, and ability to swear, but knew nothing of technology and refused to learn. They bragged of their "proletarian origins, but would not go to school." It was a good thing, he says, that the Central Committee of the party "took a sharp turn" and swept them out of their posts.

The reader guesses at the outcome of the play long before the final scenes. Orders come from Moscow, removing Ivan Gorlov from command of the front and appointing Ognyov in his place.

The appearance of Korneychuk's play reflected the tense situation which developed both in the rear and at the front as a result of the heavy losses sustained by the Red Army. Nevertheless, the fact that such sharp criticism of the leadership was permitted produced an enormous impression both on the wide reading public and on the political workers at the front.

SIMONOV: *Days and Nights*

The early moods engendered in the country by the unsuccessful conduct of the war were also expressed in Konstantin Simonov's *Days and Nights* (*Znamya*, September–December 1943, and January–February 1944). The novel, depicting the struggle for Stalingrad, was one of the best Soviet works not only on Stalingrad, but on the war as such.

Generally, Soviet fiction of the period abounded in works devoted to individual cities—Leningrad, Moscow, Stalingrad, Sevastopol, and others.

The reader's attention is held immediately by the opening lines of Simonov's book: "The woman sat leaning exhaustedly against the clay wall of the barn, and in a voice flat with fatigue described how Stalingrad burned down. The day was dry and dusty. The breeze rolled yellow puffs of dust along the ground. The woman's feet were scorched and bare; as she spoke, she gathered up the warm dust against them with her hand, as if trying to assuage the pain."

Captain Saburov, who has just arrived with a fresh unit of reinforcements for the Stalingrad fighters, listens to her story. Saburov, twenty-nine years old, has fought since the beginning of the war. He was severely wounded at Voronezh, saw many abandoned cities, and heard many stories of fleeing refugees. But his heart contracts as he hears the woman at the barn: there is no reproach in her voice, only despair, and her story is not even about her personal suffering. He looks around at the vast open steppe before them and realizes that retreat is no longer possible. "Where have they driven us?" he whispers, and the few words hold all the anguish he has felt during the past twenty-four hours, staring out upon the steppe from the platform of the railway car.

On arrival in Stalingrad, Saburov is ordered by the division commander to retake three buildings from the Germans, starting that same night. And the entire novel takes place essentially within the confines of a single square and several half-ruined houses. But to Saburov, these three houses, the broken windows, the wrecked apartments, the soldiers, dead and alive, the woman with her three children found hiding in the corner of a cellar—"all this together was Russia, and he, Saburov, was defending it."

The simplicity and inner economy of the narrative prove to be the best means for conveying the unprecedented and heroic. Almost every participant in the defense emerges as a living person. We see the wily "boss" of the division,

Protsenko, and the old army veteran Konyukov, who reverts, in moments of stress, to the vocabulary of the old Czarist army; we see the young nurse Anya Klimenko, who feels deeply that she cannot die, for she "has not yet lived at all, has not seen anything of life." The passages about the love that comes to Anya and Saburov, her "awkward childish kiss," and the apple she receives as a gift from her mother on her "wedding" day are particularly moving. Even the Commissar Vanin, who cannot manage to finish his "political report" and whose associates tease him that he cannot do it because his "writing is so dull," is humanly convincing.

The novel's "simplicity" is deceptive; within it there is scope for the tragic and the humorous, the heroic and the intimate or quietly human, like the little scene in the shelter at night, when Saburov writes letters to the families of those who died in battle.

Simonov's novel *Days and Nights* retained its place throughout the war years as the best work on Stalingrad. Soon after the war, its supremacy was challenged by the novel of the young writer Victor Nekrasov, *In the Trenches of Stalingrad* (*Znamya*, August–September 1946). In content it was similar to Simonov's book, but it presented a wider milieu, dealing not so much with the officers, as with the masses of soldiers and the plain people of the city caught in the midst of war. The official critics were somewhat disturbed by the democratic moods evoked by Nekrasov's novel, and it may have been pressure on their part that led the writer to give up the broader initial title, *Stalingrad*, for the more limited one under which it was published in book form. I shall return to this novel in the chapter devoted to Nekrasov.

The striking change in the fictional heroes of the first two years of the war was especially underscored in the treatment of the Communist hero. While the new heroes, the ordinary rank-and-file people, moved naturally in the poetry and prose of the early part of the war, the infrequent Communist heroes—such as we find in the *Front Line Diaries* by the late V. Stavsky, or in the anthology

The Comsomol in the Battles for the Homeland—are endowed with such a multitude of superhuman qualities that the reader inevitably begins to doubt: were there really such heroes? The Comsomol member Chekalin stared "laughing" into the eyes of his torturers and continued to sing the "Internationale" when the rope was already around his neck. The heroic action of the young Comsomol girl Zoya Kosmodemyanskaya, who was cruelly tortured by the Germans to force her to betray the names of her partisan friends, became very early the subject of many songs and poems. But their authors seemed to vie with one another in inventing details, behind which the living prototype disappeared, until the literary Zoya supplanted the moving image of the valiant girl.

FADEYEV: *The Young Guard*

Among the works of that period which still survive in literature is the novel by the late Alexander Fadeyev, *The Young Guard* (first published in the magazine *Znamya* in 1945). The central roles in the narrative are held by real people, the heroes of Krasnodon, a town in the Donets-Basin: the Comsomol member Oleg Koshevoy and his comrades, Ulyana Gromova, Ivan Zemnukhov, Sergey Tulenin, Lubov Shevtsova, and others. These young people, who organized an underground group during the German occupation, were betrayed to the occupants and were almost all executed. One might have expected both the theme and the heroes to be intimately familiar to Fadeyev, author of such novels as *The Rout* and *The Last of the Udege*, whose heroes were young people of the Russian Far East during the early 1920s. And yet, from the very first pages of *The Young Guard*, the author assumed an oddly false tone, making many of his heroes into wooden and stilted poster figures. The only living characters in the book are Fadeyev's contemporaries—the responsible party officials, Shulga, Protsenko, and others—and the parents of the younger underground fighters. The author was also successful in his picture of the background, particularly in the scenes of the Red Army's retreat and the evacuation.

At first the novel was favorably received. But before long, the literary authorities indignantly discovered that Fadeyev's older characters, who had stayed in the town to direct underground work, showed themselves incapable of coping with their task and were often completely helpless. Nor did they have any contact with the underground organization of Oleg Koshevoy. It was suggested to Fadeyev that he rewrite the novel, and this task took several years. As a result, there are three versions of the work: the first, published in 1945 in the magazine *Znamya*; the revised version of 1947; and the final one of 1951. The last contains none of the vivid pictures of the chaotic retreat and evacuation, and shows the responsible party workers, left in the city to coordinate underground activity, firmly and skillfully "directing" the underground youth organization. The literary value of the work, which had many flaws to begin with, suffered still further in the revisions.

As significant as the new heroes were the new "villains" in the literature of the first half of the war: more and more frequently, we encounter among them men and women who would have served as "heroes" a few years earlier and who now failed to meet the test of the time. Typical of these is Tsyplenkov in Boris Gorbatov's *The Family of Taras*. They were the people to whom Yulia Neyman referred when she spoke of those whose "plaster" of pretenses had crumbled and who stood before their contemporaries "as they were."

TVARDOVSKY: *Vasily Tyorkin*

A very special place in Soviet wartime literature is held by Alexander Tvardovsky's long poem *Vasily Tyorkin*. Tyorkin is the Soviet Soldier Schweik. In the tone of good-natured, but roguish humor, Tvardovsky succeeded in voicing, through his hero, not only the griefs and joys, but also the feelings of bitterness of the rank-and-file Soviet soldier. Vasya Tyorkin made his first entrance into literature during the Soviet-Finnish war, when the army newspaper of the Leningrad Military District began to publish verses about a soldier-wit. The newspaper employed a whole brigade of writers, including Tvardovsky, and the verses were by many hands. Someone suggested that the soldier be called Vasya Tyorkin, a name derived from a novel by a pre-revolutionary writer, Boborykin. There were some objections on the ground that Boborykin's hero was a cunning rogue of a merchant, but Tvardovsky liked the name. He tells us about these early incidents in *Novy Mir* (November 1951). Before long, Tvardovsky came into sole possession of the new hero.

Addressing his hero, the poet says:

> I have no right to forget
> What I owe to your fame,
> Where and how you have helped me
> When we met during the war.

In these lines the poet seems to open a door to his own soul. Tvardovsky belongs to the small group of writers and poets (Olga Bergholts, Vladimir Dudintsev, Vera Panova, Vasily Grossman, and others) who were deeply and lastingly moved by the ordeals suffered by the people during the war. While many writers began to forget during the later, victorious period of the war what they had seen of the people's psyche on the roads of retreat, Tvardovsky remained true to his initial feelings. It is not by chance that the last part of the poem, which was completed after the victory, includes an entire chapter about the bereaved soldier who had lost his whole family in the war. And Tvardovsky makes no effort to conceal the fact that he places much more store in his reader, the former frontline soldier, than in all the "clever critics."

> May we sometimes be remembered
> After the third glass of beer
> By a soldier with an empty sleeve.

As the coming victory became more and more apparent, the official publicists raised their voices with increasing insistence on a change in the thematics of war literature. The critics were clearly displeased with works which continued, even after the Soviet armies had taken the offensive, to dwell on the grave sufferings of the period of retreat and defeats. And yet, many writers sensed the power and significance of the themes of the early war period and were not in a hurry to turn their attention to the later, victorious stage. The official critics branded this clinging to earlier themes an "ideological mistake," and urgently demanded that writers "switch over" to more optimistic attitudes. In essence this was a camouflaged debate between two groups inside Soviet society, and the question at stake was the possible defeat, along with the military victory, of the people's hopes for substantial changes after the war.

OVECHKIN: *With Greetings from the Front*

We find a glimpse of these hopes and expectations in Valentin Ovechkin's novella *With Greetings from the Front*, published in the May 1945 issue of the magazine *Oktyabr*. This story is almost without plot: a train is going west, in the direction of the front. One of its passengers is Captain Spivak, returning from home leave after recovery from severe wounds. Before the war Spivak worked in a District Committee in the Poltava region. He is of peasant origin and thoroughly familiar with the life of the kolkhoz village. Now he is lying in an upper berth and listening to the conversation in the railroad car. The other travelers include an army man, a woman teacher (the widow of a major), an old man, an old woman with a little girl, and two war invalids. Each has had a share of wartime grief, each "has been in the close neighborhood of death and has thought a great deal about life." Only two persons in the car are silent—the invalids, one blind, the other without a hand. They became friends while still at the front. Discharged, they first went to the blind man's home, but found none of his family alive. Now they are traveling to the handless man's village.

The teacher talks about her family, which had once been large and closely knit (on holidays, there were eighteen persons at the table!). Now only two people are left—she and her sister. The sister had lost her husband in the war and later remarried. The second husband recently came home a legless invalid. The other passengers had also seen their share of sorrow. The old man lost his three sons at the front. Now he is preparing to bring up his remaining grandsons.

Captain Spivak listens and reflects to himself that, the nearer the end of the war, "the more people think of their personal lives, of their ravaged homes, the difficult tasks of reconstruction ahead. . . . He had heard much talk in the same vein at home in the village from the people he knew."

When he finds his unit at the front, Spivak shares his thoughts with the battalion commander Petrenko, a fellow villager. They discuss the coming postwar life. The human losses, they say, are perhaps felt even more strongly in the village than at the front: here, whatever the situation, a company commander deals with able-bodied men. But in the village, you have to make up a brigade of grandfather Panek, who was decrepit even before the war, the old woman Yavdokha, "a girl of seventy," and some soldiers' wives with ready tongues—say a word to them and you get twenty in return. In addition, you get some youngsters who still ran around without pants before the war. Try and work with such a team!

Petrenko asks about the moods among the peasants, and Spivak answers reflectively that it is difficult to say: you look at some prewar acquaintance, and it's "John, but not the one." And this complicates many problems: "It was easy to agitate for the kolkhozes in the thirties . . . everything was still in the future. But today the same Stakhanovite woman has lost her son and husband in the war, her daughter is in Germany, and she herself is ten years older." And yet, while the people need someone to talk to them warmly, from the heart, many of the local party workers still "live by the memory of prewar conditions. . . ."

The story ends with Captain Spivak and his friend Petrenko deciding to write a letter to their party friends at home, sharing their observations and advice: "We want to see much joy and beauty in the new life on the liberated land after all the horrors of the war. . . ." This letter, signed, "With greetings from the front," is sent by Captain Spivak and his friend Petrenko to the party workers of their native village.

THE AFTERMATH

POSTWAR PURGE

The wide response to this story showed how much its theme meant to contemporary readers. It was discussed in various publications for more than a year. And only the postwar purge of literature, launched at the end of the summer of 1946, put an end to the revealing "conversation" about the story and the problems it raised.

The purge opened with the resolution of the Central Committee of the All-Union Communist Party, of August 14, 1946, "Concerning the Magazines *Zvezda* and *Leningrad*." In this resolution the Central Committee severely criticized "the serious errors" of both magazines in opening their pages to "the vulgar and slanderous attacks by M. Zoshchenko and the poems of A. Akhmatova, devoid of any principles or ideas." At the same time, harsh reprimands were issued to the editors, Sayanov and Likharev, and the oldest Leningrad magazine, *Leningrad*, was closed because it published Alexander Khazin's verse parody, "Onegin's Return to Postwar Leningrad." The wrath of the Central Committee was especially aroused over Zoshchenko's little satire "The Adventures of a Monkey." (The story is summarized in the chapter on Zoshchenko.)

The facts cited in justification of the wave of repressions were strikingly insignificant, which inevitably suggested that the true reasons for the purge lay elsewhere. The harsh meaning of the Central Committee resolution was clarified in the reports of the secretary of the Central Committee, Andrey Zhdanov, at the meeting of Leningrad writers.

In the Central Committee resolution of August 14, we read: "The task of Soviet literature is to help the state to rear our young people correctly, to answer their needs and questions, to bring up the young generation in a spirit of optimism and faith in its cause, to make it unafraid of obstacles and ready to overcome all obstacles." To explain this, Zhdanov said at the meeting of the Leningrad party workers:

"The writer must not hobble along at the tail end of events; it is his duty to march in the front ranks, showing the people the road of its development. . . . Soviet writers and all ideological workers must be in the first line of fire." The writers who avoid this, he said, should be expelled from literature: "We are not obliged to make room in our literature for tastes and habits which have nothing in common with the morality and traits of Soviet people" (*Pravda*, September 21, 1946).

Before long, this entire hastily concocted arsenal of guiding ideas became obligatory for all writers. "Our art is not a museum of historical weapons, but an arsenal meant for war," declared Konstantin Simonov in his speech before the conference of theater workers and dramatists in Moscow, in November of 1946 (*Literary Gazette*, November 23, 1946).

Literature was not the only field subjected to the purge. The resolution of August 14 was soon followed by Central Committee resolutions "On the Repertory of Dramatic Theatres and Measures for Its Improvement" (August 26, 1946) and "On the Motion-Picture Film *A Great Life*" (September 4, 1946). Both resolutions repeated the sequence of ideas enunciated in the earlier one.

The purge initiated by these resolutions lasted until the beginning of 1949. It was attended by an all-out campaign against "adulation of the West," and the list of "adulators" was not confined to Akhmatova and Zoshchenko, damned from the very first, but expanded steadily, with more and more people being accused of sympathies toward the West. Along with the "adulators," anathema was pronounced upon the "cosmopolites," people "without kith or kin." Inevitably, these directives were soon translated into the plots of a number of novels and stories (*University* by Grigory Konovalov, *Three in Gray Coats* and *Zhenya Maslova* by Vladimir Dobrovolsky) and plays (*Another's Shadow* by Konstantin Simonov, *Beketov's Career* by Anatoly Sofronov, and *Great Power* by the late Boris Romashov). Although many of these works were awarded Stalin Prizes, they are all forgotten today.

Among works which have stood the test of time (by writers not dealt with in individual chapters), we may mention the novel by the late Pyotr Pavlenko, *Happiness* (*Znamya*, July–August 1947), and Konstantin Simonov's *Smoke of the Fatherland* (*Novy Mir*, November 1947). Both works contain large doses of the fashionable anti-Westernism and anti-Americanism; nevertheless, they preserve their literary value, and the reader will easily discover between the lines that the official directives enjoyed little popularity within the country.

The action of *Happiness* unfolds at the end of 1944. Its hero, Colonel Alexey Voropayev, comes to the Crimea after partial recovery from severe wounds. He has lost a leg and has been discharged from the army. Now he hopes to restore his health in the Crimea and to send for his son, who remained in Moscow (his wife died during the war). Lack of space makes it impossible to summarize the novel at any length, but it is important to note its clearly expressed anti-Americanism. Voropayev knows English and is assigned to work as a translator at the Yalta Conference between Stalin, Roosevelt, and Churchill. And here we find a sharp picture of the arrogant Soviet chauvinism which dominates the author's thinking and emerges most clearly in Voropayev's talks with the American journalist Harris, and in the conversation between Harris and Shirokogorov, the director of the wine-making Sovkhoz "Pobeda" ("Victory"). Invited to taste some of the Crimean wines made at the "Pobeda," and listening to Shirokogorov's explanations of the special properties of the various kinds of wine, Harris exclaims with unconcealed astonishment: "But, Doctor, how can you occupy yourself with all this 'harmonious' nonsense when your country is in ruins?" Shirokogorov is unabashed: "My dear friend, I am preparing for it the elixir of triumph, the wines of victory, of rest and relaxation. It is impossible to live only in the things of today, for they are most often merely the unfinished business of yesterday. The true present is always in the future." In the course of the conversation, which very nearly ends in a quarrel, Shirokogorov delivers himself of a number of political aphorisms, returning again and again to the idea that "Churchill's England" is America's "kept woman."

KONSTANTIN SIMONOV: *Smoke of the Fatherland*

In Konstantin Simonov's book *Smoke of the Fatherland* the Communist engineer Basargin returns from America to his home town of Pukhovo, in the Smolensk region, after several years' absence. Here he has a wife and a sister who is married to the nonpartisan architect Kondrashev. Basargin brings gifts for everyone, including an electric shaver for Kondrashev, who is enormously impressed and exclaims delightedly that even in such a small thing one can feel "real culture." The remark irritates Basargin. As time goes on, he becomes more and more convinced of Kondrashev's friendly feelings for the Americans. On one occasion Kondrashev's wife asks, "But how about the Negroes?" Her husband mockingly anticipates Basargin's reply, "Why, they hang on every corner." Basargin is especially indignant at Kondrashev's attitude toward the possibility of a new war. Simonov's Kondrashev is not only sharply opposed to a new war, but is perhaps the first character in Soviet literature to advance the idea of peaceful "coexistence": ". . . One system! Two systems! There have been all sorts of systems on earth, and yet people have managed to live and get along somehow with each other." Raising his voice, Kondrashev completes his thought: "There must not be any more war. You understand, must not! It has no right to be. At any price! Because I'll tell you: no matter how good the system, when I'm dead, it's of no use to me." Then, to reinforce his words, Kondrashev tells Basargin that he would say the same thing even in the presence of Stalin himself. It is not difficult to see why the story displeased the official critics.

KONSTANTIN FEDIN: POSTWAR WORKS

Among the works published during the dark years of the postwar purges, it is important to single out Konstantin Fedin's novel *An Extraordinary Summer* (1947–48), although it did not deal with contemporary life. The novel was the second part of a projected trilogy. The action of the first part, *Early Joys*, takes place in 1910–14. The second begins in 1919. After several years as a German prisoner of war, Lieutenant Dibich, who has made several previous attempts to escape, finally returns home. (The third part, *The Bonfire*, was published in 1962.)

Dibich's return home and his passionate desire to grasp the meaning of the events transpiring in Russia at the time are not chance themes: they reflect a major aspect of the creative economy of this interesting and talented writer, and are closely linked with Fedin's own biography. Fedin's childhood and youth were spent in Saratov. After graduation from a commercial secondary school, he entered a commercial college. Shortly before the outbreak of World War I, he went to Germany, where he was accidentally delayed and so found himself a civilian prisoner of war. He earned his livelihood there by giving lessons in Russian and music. In 1919, when he returned to Russia, torn with civil war, he made his way to his native Saratov and enlisted in the Red Army. Soon afterward he began to write. In 1920 he came to Petersburg, where he made the acquaintance of Gorky and joined the Serapion Brotherhood. (He had also planned to write a trilogy about this period, calling it *Gorky among Us*, but its second volume met with the disapproval of the official critics, and the third volume never appeared.)

An Extraordinary Summer, the second part of his other trilogy, also caused Fedin much difficulty. Its action unfolds at the height of the Civil War. The Red Army at that time was under Trotsky's command. But his name had long been banished from the history of the Civil War, and Fedin undertook the difficult task of showing Stalin as a military genius and the hero of the battles for Tsaritsyn (later renamed Stalingrad). Of course, the fact that the novel has withstood the test of time is not due to its falsification of history. What makes it especially interesting is its bold treatment of the problem of creative freedom. The key to the author's philosophic and ethical ideas is given at the very beginning of the novel: "Historical events are attended not only by general agitation, the rise or decline of the human spirit, but invariably also by extraordinary sufferings and privations." Those who understand the meaning of the events suffer as much as those who don't understand it, but they endure their suffering more easily. However, such people are always in a minority. Pyotr Ragozin and Kirill Izvekov, whom the reader knows from *Early Joys*, the first book of the trilogy, belong to this minority. In *An Extraordinary Summer* both are already prominent Communists.

Fedin's ideas about creative work are expressed by the writer Pastukhov, who is making his way, with his family, to his native city in the Volga region. Pastukhov himself is neither White nor Red, and he therefore feels that he is censured by both. Pastukhov's whole spirit revolts against this primitive political arithmetic: "Is the whole world, then, either White or Red? And what can a man do if he is olive-colored?" Pastukhov courageously tries to defend his right to be a free artist. To men like the Communist Izvekov, he explains that an artist by his very nature sympathizes with living, suffering people. Without such sympathy for those who suffer, an artist's work is unthinkable; it becomes cold and rational. And it is precisely this that is at the heart of the writer's basic and tragic conflict with the government: the latter not only questions the artist's right to sympathize with suffering, but demands that he glorify the conquerors and ignore the sacrifice and anguish of millions of people.

There are many flaws in Fedin's novel. Yet, many of the chapters can be read with absorbing interest. His picture of the country aflame with civil war transcends in the scope of his canvas and the eloquence of his language everything else that has been written about it, including even the second part of Alexey Tolstoy's trilogy, *The Road to Calvary*.

Other works written during the tragic years which concluded with Stalin's death in the early part of 1953, such as the novels of Vera Panova and the poems of Alexander Tvardovsky, will be dealt with in the chapters analyzing the work of these writers.

POST-STALIN YEARS

The most important characteristic of the first post-Stalin year was the expectation of significant changes. In this tense expectancy the period of 1953–54 was reminiscent of the first postwar years, 1945–46. At that time the need for "candid conversation" had been stifled by the brutal purge of 1946–49. But as soon as Stalin died, the need reasserted itself. The "conversation" began virtually one month after the dictator's death with an article by the poetess Olga Bergholts, "A Few Words about Lyricism" (*Literary Gazette*, April 16, 1953). But its most striking expression is to be found in the articles by Ehrenburg, "The Writer's Work" (*Znamya*, October 1953), and V. Pomerantsev, "On Sincerity in Literature" (*Novy Mir*, December 1953). Speaking in favor of creative freedom, they urged the idea that a writer's work is similar to giving birth to a child. Ehrenburg wrote: a writer "does not copy and does not describe, he reveals" the meaning of his time. Pomerantsev said that the "boredom" generated by "our books" is the result of their being "manufactured" and "rhetorical." In judging the value of a literary work, he felt, one of the first criteria should be its degree of sincerity.

HOPES OF CHANGE: PANFYOROV

Among the first writers to reflect the general expectation of radical changes was the late Fyodor Panfyorov, in his novel *Mother Volga* (*Znamya*, August–September 1953). The action of the novel begins while Stalin is still alive, but the entire novel is permeated with the moods of the early post-Stalin months. The secretary of the Central Committee of the Communist Party, Muratov, returns from a journey to Siberia, where he met and was favorably impressed by the first secretary of one of the City Committees, Akim Morev. Before long, Morev is summoned to Moscow and told of the Central Committee's decision to appoint him second secretary of the Regional Party Committee in Privolzhsk (fictional name for Stalingrad). Soon after his arrival at the new post, Morev is appointed first secretary, replacing Malinov. Morev is both flattered and disturbed, for he has heard that Malinov had won general acclaim during the war by his courage and initiative. When he cautiously speaks of this to Muratov during a telephone conversation with Moscow, the latter replies drily that Malinov has been recompensed "in full" for past accomplishments, and that, generally, there is no reason for anyone to plume himself on "past services."

Morev quickly discovers why the Central Committee is displeased with Malinov, who is living on "old capital." And he learns that even this "old capital" was won by dubious means. Already during the war Malinov managed to surround himself with a variety of "parasites" who fanned his reputation, stressing everywhere that he was "a man of the people" and eulogizing his special organizational talents. As a result Malinov became so puffed up with pride that he began to refer to his own person as "Himself." Listening to Malinov's cheerleaders, Morev wonders at his failure to realize that these avowedly devoted "cadres" are actually working behind his back for his downfall. Malinov is called to Moscow and never returns to Privolzhsk.

Mother Volga provoked a lively discussion in the press and elsewhere. One of the critics wrote in the *Literary Gazette* (December 8, 1953) that the novel was widely "debated in libraries and whenever people met."

In 1958 *Znamya* published the second part of Panfyorov's novel under a new title, *Reflections* (July, August, October). In 1960 the third part, *In the Name of the Young*, appeared in the magazine *Oktyabr* (July, August). The final installment was published after the author's death. Although weak as literature, these works are interesting in that they reveal a number of factors in postwar kolkhoz life which provoked dissatisfaction among wide strata of kolkhoz peasantry and nearly brought the kolkhoz system to the point of catastrophe. Panfyorov was closely familiar with the life and interests of the local party and economic apparatus in the provinces.

THE THAW: SINCERITY

The "breathing spell" in literature and journalism did not last very long. On January 30, 1954, the *Literary Gazette* published Vitaly Vasilevsky's article "From Wrong Positions," sharply criticizing Pomerantsev. This was a camouflaged official reprimand, and it was understood as such in writing circles. But the new "conversation" had already invaded fiction and poetry. This whole period in the post-Stalin development of Soviet literature became known as "the thaw," after Ilya Ehrenburg's novel of the same title, which elicited a wide response in the country. (*The Thaw* was first published in *Znamya*; its first volume appeared in May 1954, and the second in April 1956.) The action of the first part unfolds in the early months of 1953 and ends during the days of the spring thaw.

Literary Developments: World War II and After

Against the background of the thaw in nature, Ehrenburg writes about "the thaw" in human relations, which began with the softening of the socio-political climate after Stalin's death.

Interestingly, Ehrenburg makes virtually no mention of political events, centering his attention on the human psyche. Something has changed in human relations, people feel less constrained, less frozen, as if they were suddenly permitted to straighten out inwardly. In a characteristic incident the chief designer of a factory, Sokolovsky, learns that the factory director, Zhuravlev, who has always disliked him for his frankness, is planning to destroy him, utilizing the fact that Sokolovsky's former wife and daughter are living abroad. But Sokolovsky suddenly feels: no, "the times are different," Zhuravlev no longer can harm him.

The new moods express themselves most clearly in the discussions of Ehrenburg's heroes about art. Two of the novel's characters are artists: Volodya Pukhov, who adapts himself to official demands, and Saburov, an independent artist and Volodya's former schoolmate. When Volodya arrives in his native town, he finds Saburov living in great poverty. He asks Saburov with a trace of irony: "So you're still trying to argue with the time?" Yes, Saburov disdained success and chose to preserve his independence. In reply to Saburov's ideas, Volodya remarks that, nowadays, Raphael himself would not be admitted to the artists' union, and that, generally, not everybody can work "for the twenty-first century" as Saburov does. To justify his own subservience, Volodya argues that "after all, everybody is dodging, maneuvering, lying . . . some more, some less cleverly." But in the end Volodya is humbled: one day he visits Saburov and, deeply shaken by the inner depth and truth of his friend's work, he confesses his envy.

ATTEMPTS TO CURB THE NEW

The ever more frequent manifestations of "liberalism" and "revisionism" (that is, attempts to re-evaluate and revise the old party positions concerning the direction of literature) began to alarm the literary authorities. In an attempt to strengthen the shaken authority of the party leaders in the field of literature, a meeting of the party organization of the Moscow writers was called early in June 1954.[1] At the meeting Alexey Surkov severely criticized V. Pomerantsev's article "On Sincerity in Literature" and Fyodor Abramov's article "On Kolkhoz Literature" (*Novy Mir*, April 1954). In this article, Abramov had discussed in considerable detail Semyon Babaevsky's *Cavalier of the Gold Star* and *Light over the Land*, and Galina Nikolaeva's *Harvest*. All three novels, awarded Stalin Prizes in the latter part of the 1940s, were heavily slanted, and Surkov could not forgive Abramov for exposing this. He was equally severe with the young critic, Mark Shcheglov (now dead) who criticized Leonov's *The Russian Forest* (*Novy Mir*, May 1954). Ehrenburg's novel, *The Thaw*, also drew Surkov's censure.

The Moscow writers' meeting was only the beginning of the attempt to turn literature back into the old channel. In early August there was a meeting of the enlarged presidium of the executive of the Writers' Union to discuss "The Errors of the Magazine *Novy Mir*." A resolution was passed, and "organizational conclusions" were duly drawn: Tvardovsky was removed from his post as editor-in-chief and replaced by Konstantin Simonov.

It is easy to imagine the spirit of the subsequent preparations for the Second All-Union Writers' Congress, scheduled for mid-December 1954. True, during the preliminary campaign a rather strong opposition group emerged among the writers, led by Valentin Ovechkin and Grigory

[1] A report of this meeting appeared in the *Literary Gazette* on June 15, 1954.

Medynsky, but its chances of a victory at the congress were small. On the whole the congress, with its stress on strengthened party direction, its election of a new executive with Alexey Surkov as first secretary, and its proclamation of "Socialist realism" (which was often forgotten by writers during the period of "liberalism") as the solely approved literary method, was an attempt to turn back the clock. But time was the ally of those who opposed the old practices.

THE THAW PERSISTS: NEKRASOV, DUDINTSEV

Among works which elicited a warm response among readers, and which answered their need to examine and understand postwar life, we must name Victor Nekrasov's novel *In the Native City* (*Novy Mir*, October–November 1954). Its theme is the homecoming of men who had fought at the front. This novel, remarkable in many respects, as well as certain other works on the same theme, will be discussed in detail in the chapter on Nekrasov.

Another novel which stirred wide circles of readers and which, indeed, became a sensation, was Vladimir Dudintsev's *Not by Bread Alone* (*Novy Mir*, August–November 1956). As in the case of Ehrenburg's *The Thaw*, the extraordinary success of Dudintsev's novel was by no means caused by its literary qualities; as a work of literature, it does not rise above the level of mediocrity. I shall discuss the novel at greater length in the chapter on Dudintsev. Here, it can merely be pointed out that the reader's attention was captured by the intransigence of Dudintsev's principal hero, the talented inventor Lopatkin, in his struggle against the bureaucratic system, and by the author's warm sympathy for his hero. Dudintsev succeeded in exposing the very essence of the bureaucratic system, which holds in its tentacles not only scoundrels, but often basically decent and intelligent people.

At first Dudintsev's novel enjoyed overwhelming success. The *Literary Gazette* of October 27, 1956, reports on a meeting at the Central House of Literature, devoted to a discussion of the novel. Vsevolod Ivanov, who opened the meeting, said that the overflow crowd reminded him of his younger days, when Soviet literature was being born, and of the meetings at the Polytechnical Museum, "the forum of this new literature." Ivanov and other speakers felt that Dudintsev's novel continued in the "traditions of Gogol," in that it depicted "an ordinary little man, battered by a succession of misfortunes, but stubbornly and selflessly working for the good of society. The novel is imbued with love of mankind, with genuine respect for the rank-and-file man."

Soon, however, the literary leadership discerned quite different elements in the novel and reversed its judgment. In the article "Literature Serves the People" (*Literary Gazette*, December 15, 1956) the editors wrote: "V. Dudintsev's novel *Not by Bread Alone* provoked heated discussions and impressed many readers by its passionately critical picture of Drozdov. But, although the book possesses certain merits, its positive elements are drowned out under the interminable sufferings of the individual inventor, who is presented as some sort of a martyr. The writer lacks a true, broad perspective on life. . . ." The novel was assigned to the category of works written "in the spirit of depressive nihilism." Before long, it was condemned in even sharper terms, and Soviet publications virtually closed their doors to the author.

DENUNCIATION OF THE "CULT OF PERSONALITY"

In literature the year 1956 seemed in many respects to herald the changes which had been linked so hopefully to Stalin's death. These changes were connected with the struggle at the top echelons of the party—a struggle that prompted Khrushchev to deliver his special report at the Twentieth Congress of the Communist Party in February 1956, in which he exposed and denounced the monstrous reign of terror under Stalin. Although this speech had been delivered before a closed session of the Congress, the news of it spread quickly throughout the Soviet Union.

The effects of Khrushchev's denunciation of the Stalinist "cult of personality" were so far-reaching that he and his closest associates felt impelled to take steps to curb their impact.

Nevertheless, this denunciation exerted a great positive influence on literary life in 1956, and it is small wonder that the sum of that year's achievements was richer and more significant than those of previous years. True, the forces of reaction succeeded in hemming in those who began to seek greater creative freedom on the basis of Khrushchev's speech. Nevertheless, something new began to force its way into literature, and it found particularly forceful reflection in the anthology *Literary Moscow*, Number 2, which appeared in 1956.

Another important factor was the emergence into the arena of public life of new generations and, hence, of new literary talent and ideas.

THE YOUNG GENERATION

The young generation first declared itself in an article by Yevgeny Yevtushenko, "About Two Poetic Generations" (*Literary Gazette*, January 25, 1955): "The sense of generation is essential for the beginning as a poetic passport." The "poetic passport" of the new generation was the fact that they were all children during World War II; they were born in the late 1920s and the early 1930s. Yevtushenko himself was born in 1933. From his earliest childhood he was accustomed to *live within himself*, to judge people not by their words, but by their deeds. The young literary generation, which made its entry on the scene in the middle 1950s, seeks also to be the voice of its younger contemporaries, the youth of the early '60s, born in the late '30s and early '40s. The most characteristic trait of the young poets of the 1950s and early '60s is their need to *be themselves*. In his poem "Who Has Not Advised Me?" Yevgeny Vinokurov (a contemporary of Yevtushenko) writes:

The more I listened to my mentors,
The more I longed to be myself.
(*Literary Gazette*, January 12, 1960)

Vinokurov is echoed by the young poetess Rimma Kazakova:

... Be your own self, just as you are.
Do not fear getting lost in life. If
You are where life is, then, in generous return,
Life is where you are. Live! March forward! Good luck!
(*Yunost*, July 1960)

The self-definition of the younger generation takes place, as was often the case in Russian life both before and after the revolution, within the framework of a debate between *fathers and sons*. True, the literary leadership and the representatives of the older generation avoid admitting the presence of the problem of "fathers and sons" in Soviet life, insisting that this problem is characteristic only of "bourgeois" society. However, this debate between two generations has now become so sharp that both "fathers" and "sons" more and more frequently speak out on the theme. "You snotnose brat! Wipe your nose first!" shouts the enraged director of an agricultural school to the young Comsomol organizer Klavdia, who presses the demands of two fellow students. "When you were soiling your diapers in the crib, I was already building the country!" And he remains deaf to the cautious urging of the representative of the Administration of Labor Reserves who is present at this scene that it is wrong to "set up the older generation as against the young." (See "Two Days," a story by I. Metter, in the magazine *Moskva*, June 1960.)

Still more symptomatic was the admission of Leonid Sobolev, chairman of the Writers' Congress in May 1959, that the discussion about contemporaneity "disturbs" and "irritates" some representatives of the older generation of writers because they "really find it difficult to enter fully into the new life" (*Literary Gazette*, May 28, 1959).

Also pertinent is the article by A. Makarov, "Serious Life" (*Znamya*, January 1961). Reviewing the literary output of the past year, the critic notes the appearance of many new writers. These newcomers are not only young themselves, but they write about young heroes who have experienced neither the revolution, nor the Civil War, nor the collectivization. Indeed, even "the Great Patriotic War has barely touched their lives. To them all this is the past, belonging to their fathers or even grandfathers." This feeling that the revolution and the subsequent stages of its development are things that "belong to the grandfathers" is expressed in highly cynical terms by Tyoma, the grandson of the old Chekist Kirpichev, in L. Zorin's sensational play *Guests* (*Theatre*, February 1954). The young man complains to his friend Nika that his father had inveigled him and the family, on their way to the Caucasus, into stopping over at his grandfather's. "My old man," says Tyoma, "has his quirks. Suddenly it hits him: let's visit grandfather! The best route in the world. Such fun! I've studied all I want about the period of War Communism back at school."

The critic Makarov hopes that the younger writers who, unlike their older colleagues, know the world of their heroes "from within," will succeed in creating vital images of their contemporaries. And though to Makarov himself the appearance of such new literary images might be a melancholy reminder that he, too, has reached the age when a man recalls Pushkin's lines, "And our own grandsons, one fine day, will crowd us out of the way," he is ready to "make room."

FATHERS AND SONS

As we read the works of the younger writers, we soon discover that the conflict between fathers and sons involves in large measure the feeling on the part of the young that their fathers have by no means assured them "an easy life." At almost every step they see problems and difficulties resulting from the mistakes of the fathers. Makarov admits this with considerable courage: "That which presented insurmountable difficulties to us is to them easier than easy. And that which came easily to us, they can attain only by dint of incredible persistence." "The vistas are the same, but are the years?" Makarov asks himself, and answers: "No, the years are different indeed!"

In Natalya Davydova's novel *The Engineer Izotov's Love* (*Novy Mir*, January–March 1960), the aunt of Lena and Alexey, as well as her friends, were "reared by the epoch" and consider themselves "fighters for justice." But, despite affection for their elders, the young Izotovs refer to them among themselves simply as "brawlers" and "intriguers." The younger members of the Izotov family criticize them for the simplicity with which they had approached the most complex problems of love and marriage: "They fell in love and got together, fell out of love and broke up." A similar criticism is voiced by the young worker Victor Zaitsev in V. Kozhevnikov's novel *Be Acquainted, Baluyev!* (*Znamya*, April–May 1960). Zaitsev says to Baluyev: "At our age you were holding public discussions about free love, and Lunarcharsky and some other old Bolsheviks even made speeches about it. But you never thought of the results. . . ." And the young people of today have had to face these often tragic "results." No wonder so many of the newer writers' stories deal with situations in which the free-and-easy attitudes of the fathers toward their responsibilities deprived the sons of normal family life.

Equally tragic in its results was the harshness of the fathers in official circles toward other people, especially those who had the boldness to entertain opinions of their own.

A NEW MOTTO: SINCERITY AND HONESTY

Sincerity and honesty with oneself are the traits which characterize many of the younger writers' heroes. This is true of Andrey, the younger son of Professor Averin in Victor Rozov's play *Good Luck* (*Theatre*, March 1955), and Zhenya Shulzhenko in Alexander Volodin's play *Factory Girl* (*Theatre*, September 1956). It is also true of the heroes of the novel *Colleagues*, by the young writer Vasily Aksyonov (*Yunost*, June–July 1960) and of many of the young heroes of S. Sartakov's *Don't Give Up the Queen* (*Oktyabr*, December 1960). These qualities are also stressed by the young critic Stanislav Rassadin in his article "Men of the Sixties" (*Yunost*, December 1960).

Sincerity and honesty with oneself go hand in hand in the young heroes with loyalty in friendship, as in G. Belenky's story "You Are Not Alone" (*Moskva*, November 1960), I. Gerasimov's "Fellows of Your Own Age" (*Molodaya Gvardia*, June 1960), and others. The critic V. Frolov aptly characterized the young writers when he said that many of them write "with a look into the heart" (*Oktyabr*, October 1959).

However, despite the wide preoccupation with the theme of youth in the fiction and drama of recent years, no writer has succeeded in creating a typical image of the young contemporary with even a remote degree of the artistic vitality inherent in Griboyedov's Chatsky, Pushkin's Yevgeny Onegin, or Lermontov's Pechorin. But though it lacks literary stature, the portrait is revealing. As we scan the features of the young Soviet citizen today, we cannot help recalling Captain Spivak's letter in V. Ovechkin's *With Greetings from the Front*. Captain Spivak together with his friend Petrenko wrote to their party comrades: "We want to see much joy and beauty in the new life on the liberated land after all the horrors of the war. If this beauty cannot be created at once on the sites of the demolished orchards and burnt villages, let it exist in relations among people and in their heroic labor. . . . We want a great deal. We have spilled much blood on this land, and we expect much of the future life."

Soviet youth is opposed to war, and its better elements are inspired with the idea of consolidating moral values. This is the crux of its debate with the Soviet fathers.

17 KONSTANTIN PAUSTOVSKY
(1892–   )

Clarity and softness—these two dissimilar qualities are characteristic of Paustovsky's talent. On the eve of 1939 Paustovsky replied to a questionnaire of the *Literary Gazette* with a brief statement of his literary credo. He recalled a winter evening in a seaside town, when "dusk like antique silver hung over the sea," many years ago, when Paustovsky was very young. He had been fond then of visiting a bookseller he knew; the shop, he said, smelled of old books and prints—"a smell reminiscent of carnations." That evening the bookseller spoke about an old engraving of Mozart's portrait, explaining that it was made with a "diamond needle." The remark reminded Paustovsky of a forgotten story: somewhere in Canada, in a small town, there lived a man who studied the shape of snow crystals; he photographed thousands of snowflakes—melting on "the warm face of a child," settling in the stone folds of a statue in a square. And all of this, thought Paustovsky—the old engravings made with a diamond needle, and the snowflakes—is brought by the literary artist into his work, which must combine the engraver's precision with loving attention to the snowflake melting on a child's face.

Paustovsky's character as a writer is reflected in his face; he looks out of his photograph with keen eyes, and his features are striking in their combination of clear energy with a trace of dreaminess. The Paustovsky family stems from Zaporozhye Cossacks, with an admixture of Turkish and Polish blood. The writer's father was a railroad statistician who died of cancer of the larynx when the writer was in the seventh year of school. It was only much later that Paustovsky understood that his father had been essentially a poet by nature, as was his grandfather, Maxim Grigorievich. It was not by chance that Paustovsky remarked in the first part of his *Story of My Life* that it was partly to his grandfather that he owed his "excessive impressionability and romanticism." "They turned my youth," he wrote, "into a series of clashes with reality. I suffered through this, but I knew that my grandfather was right; a life based on sobriety and common sense may be good, but to me it would be depressing and fruitless."

Of his grandfather's stories the future writer remembered most vividly the tale of the itinerant singer Ostap, who had started life as a village blacksmith. One day two riders, a young woman and an officer, came to Ostap's smithy. The woman asked Ostap to shoe her horse. Struck by her beauty, he offered to hammer out for her a metal rose with the finest leaves and thorns. The woman promised to return for the rose within a week. As he helped her to mount her horse, Ostap, unable to restrain his feelings, kissed her hand. For this, the officer slashed Ostap's face with his whip, so that blood spurted from his eye. Despite his injured eye, Ostap forged the promised rose. The woman came for it at the appointed time. She told him that she had broken with the officer, who had been her fiancé. Although the young woman had fallen in love with Ostap, she could not bring herself to link her life with his, and left for Petersburg. Soon after that Ostap went blind in one eye; he had to abandon his blacksmith's trade and became a wandering lyre singer. He decided to walk to faraway Petersburg, to get another glimpse of his love. But when he reached the capital, he learned that she was dead. He searched out her grave, and was deeply moved to discover his metal rose on her gravestone.

This theme is echoed in Paustovsky's story "Precious Dust," included in *The Golden Rose*, a unique semi-autobiographical book about the writer's work. In this story Shamet, a refuse collector, falls in love with the beautiful Suzy and decides to give her a gift—a golden rose. He gathers the gold by sifting the dust he collects in a jewelry workshop for two years. The grains of gold are smelted, but when the rose is ready and Shamet goes to bring it to Suzy, he finds that she has gone to America, leaving no one her address. Shamet soon dies of grief. To Paustovsky, "the golden rose" is the symbol of the writer's work: the literary artist accumulates in his memory a multitude of the minutest impressions, which are later fused into a nugget. Out of this nugget is made "the golden rose"— the novel, story, or poem.

Paustovsky's youth passed under difficult conditions. When he finished secondary school, his father was no longer alive. He was obliged to help the family by giving lessons while still at school, and later as a university student. In 1914 the family lived in Moscow, and two of his older brothers went into the army. As the youngest, Konstantin Paustovsky was exempted from military service and continued his education. In his free time he liked to sit for hours in Moscow taverns, where "one could order a cup of tea for five kopeks and spend all day amid the din of voices and clanking cups and the tinny rumble of the orchestrion 'machine.'" "The taverns were the Moscow gathering places," he wrote later in his brief autobiography (1958). "Whom have I not met there? Cab drivers, saintly halfwits, peasants of the Moscow environs, workers from the Presnya and Simonovskaya Sloboda, peddlers, milk-sellers, gypsies, seamstresses, artisans, students, prostitutes, and bearded recruits. And the talk I have heard, greedily memorizing every apt and colorful word! Already then I had made the decision to abandon for a time the writing of my nebulous stories and 'go into life,' in order 'to learn everything, to feel everything and understand everything.' Without this experience of life all roads to becoming a writer were closed. This I understood."

In some aspects of his work Paustovsky is reminiscent of Alexander Grin, the romantic novelist who died in the early 1930s. During his lifetime Grin was stubbornly ignored by the literary critics as a writer inconsonant with the epoch. Grin won wide popularity among the Soviet readers, over the heads of the critics, as it were. He was a dreamer, who spent his life in the nonexistent country of

"Grinlandia," defending the right to dream and fantasy, and fighting for the miracle of human goodness with the consistency and devotion of a knight errant. Official recognition came to him only during the Soviet-German war, when Grin's novel *Scarlet Sails* was made into a ballet.

The plot of *Scarlet Sails* is woven of the finest gossamer, gleaming with rainbow colors in a ray of sunlight: the little girl Assol, daughter of the sailor Longren, meets a sorcerer in the woods, who tells her a story about a prince who will come for her. Assol believes the story and begins to wait. Two beings seem to live in Assol—the daughter of a sailor, who makes toys for her, and another, "a living poem, with all the wonders of its harmonies and images, with the mystery of the kinship of words, in all their interplay of light and shadow." Assol's waiting is not in vain— her prince comes.

Akin to this story is Paustovsky's "The Steel Ring," about the girl Varyusha, from the village of Mokhovoye. An old soldier makes her a gift of a magical steel ring. The ring, he promises, will bring Varyusha great joy. But as she runs home through the forest, the ring slips off her finger and disappears in the snow. All through the winter Varyusha grieves and looks for it. Then one day, when the snow begins to melt, she finds it, gleaming on the sodden earth below. She puts it on and begins to wait for the promise to come true. Awaking early next morning, she walks to the edge of the woods. The silence is so deep that she hears the faint tinkling of tiny bells. The girl bends down to the snowdrops; the ringing comes from them, as if a "tinklebug" had crept into their calyx "and was striking a silver spider-web with its foot." In the pine-top, a woodpecker taps five times: Varyusha understands; it means that the hour is five in the morning. At this moment someone invisible walks past her, silently spreading the branches, and all at once Varyusha is filled with joy: it was spring that walked by. . . .

Paustovsky wrote an excellent essay about Alexander Grin, published in the anthology *Year XXII, Book 15*, in 1939. He also devoted to Grin a short chapter, "The Teller of Tales," in his *Black Sea*. In a few pages Paustovsky sketched the literary portrait of this "austere teller of tales" who rejected all compromise with the current age, which had betrayed his expectations. Grin spent his life in overnight lodging houses, in underpaid heavy labor beyond his strength, often half-hungry and destitute. He worked at a variety of trades—as a sailor, stevedore, bathhouse attendant, beggar, and prospector for gold. "His eyes remained naïve and pure as a dreamy boy's. He did not notice his surroundings and lived on gay, bright cloud-banks. . . . Grin's romanticism was simple, joyous, sparkling. It wakened in people a desire for change and variety, for a life full of danger and a 'high sense of nobility,' a life such as those lived by explorers, navigators, and travelers. . . ." When Paustovsky came to Old Crimea, he visited the house where Grin once lived. The simple and severe room was decorated with a single print on the wall—a portrait of Edgar Allan Poe.

It was his own romanticism that won Paustovsky a large and admiring public among the youth of the 1930s. But, in contrast to Grin, Paustovsky unfolds his tales not in some mysterious Grinland, but in Russia—in the U.S.S.R. This brings Paustovsky closer to his readers and has greatly contributed to the growth of his popularity.

Some interesting testimony to his popularity is found in the small book by Sergey Lvov (1956), *Konstantin Paustovsky*. "To my generation," writes Lvov, "which is now at the age of thirty or thirty-five, Paustovsky's books form one of the most vivid memories of our childhood and youth. Our geography teachers will confirm how eagerly we welcomed questions about the eastern coast of the Caspian or the Rion Plain. We could describe these regions as though we had been there ourselves. We had never seen them. We simply knew almost by heart Paustovsky's *Kara-Bugaz* and *Colchis*. . . ."

Sergey Lvov also recalls the expedition organized by the Children's Literary Studio of the Moscow House of Pioneers in 1937; the participants were to sail several hundred kilometers in rowboats along the Desna. The children's enthusiasm knew no bounds when they learned that the expedition was to be led by Paustovsky: "To the younger ones among us this seemed as fabulous as if they had been told that they would spend three weeks with Jules Verne."

We may recall a chapter from Paustovsky's autobiography, which tells about the remarkable old geography teacher Cherpunov. On his desk the teacher often displayed bottles of water with exciting inscriptions: "Water from the Nile," "Water from the Limpopo River," "Water from the Mediterranean Sea." There were many such bottles—with water from the Dead Sea, the Amazon, the Thames, and Lake Michigan. One bottle seemed in no way different from the others, but the childish imagination was kindled and the students begged Cherpunov to let them taste the water of the Dead Sea, to see for themselves whether it was really so salty. Cherpunov never permitted them to open the bottles. Later, some skeptics said that the water in all the bottles came from the faucet. Yet thanks to Cherpunov's device, geography became the children's favorite subject, and they easily remembered the difficult names for the rest of their lives.

In contrast to Grin, passionately absorbed in the world of his images and ignoring both his environment and his own fate (*Scarlet Sails* was written in 1919 in Petrograd, when Grin, not yet recovered from typhus, was spending his nights in icy abandoned houses!), Paustovsky was able to retain contact with the life of his readers, especially his younger readers. Few Soviet writers can vie with Paustovsky's warm insight into the child's soul or his ability to convey it. I shall cite only one example, from the story "Deep in Russia."

Speaking about village boys, the author says: "I knew them through and through. From many years of experience with them, I can safely say that these restless and noisy fellow citizens of ours possess a certain truly remarkable quality. A physicist might define it as 'omni-permeability.' These boys are 'omni-permeable,' or, more exactly, 'omni-penetrating,' or, to use an old ponderous word, 'ubiquitous.'" It seems to the author that, should he find himself on the North Pole, he would inevitably find there "a sniffling boy with a fishing rod, watching for cod at the ice-hole."

More than anyone else, the boys of the village near Beaver Canal loved two men: the apothecary for whom they gathered medicinal herbs, and the old rag-picker nicknamed "Util." This Util appeared in the village once a month. Wearily limping after his lean nag, he cried mournfully: "Rags, old rubbers, horns, hooves!" At the familiar cry, boys and girls came pouring from all the village yards, running and stumbling, pulling along their younger brothers and sisters, and clutching old sacks, worn-down rope slippers, broken cow-horns, and other trash. In exchange for all this, Util gave them new toys. Despite his forbidding appearance, he was a kindly man and accepted everything the children brought. Only once did he reject a child's offering, when a small girl brought the "crumbling leggings of her father's boots." The girl "seemed to shrink, drawing her head into her shoulders, and slowly walked away from the cart toward her house, like a whipped puppy." The children surrounding Util suddenly stood quiet, with wrinkled foreheads; someone snorted loudly through his nose. Old Util began to roll a cigarette, seemingly oblivious of both the weeping girl and the silent children. Finally, he burst out angrily: "Don't you understand? I am doing government business. Don't bring me trash. Bring me things that can be put to further production. See?" But the reference to the government's interests produced no effect on the children; they remained silent. In the end Util could bear it no longer and told them to bring the girl back, grumbling at the quiet children: "Ganged up around me, glaring like I was a murderer!" "The little flock of children dashed like sparrows to the girl's house. . . ." They brought her, flushed and timid. Util took the leggings and gave her in exchange the brightest doll from his cart.

Looking at Util, Paustovsky thought to himself that there was no occupation in the world less attractive than rag collecting. Yet Util had managed to turn it into something that brought joy to the kolkhoz children—and only because his rude exterior concealed a kind heart and a warm imagination, which he was able to put to work even in his "miserable trade."

Paustovsky's popularity owes a great deal to his skill in constructing absorbing plots. In the early days of the revolution many young writers, especially the members of the Serapion Brotherhood, gave considerable thought to the current crisis in literature. Especially persistent in his efforts to find a way out was the late Lev Lunts, who wrote that Russian prose "has ceased to 'move,' it 'lies inert,' nothing happens in it, nothing takes place; its characters either talk or feel, but they do not act. . . . It must inevitably die of lack of circulation, of bed-sores, of dropsy." The only solution, as Lunts saw it, was in plot, and since the tradition of the plot belonged to the West, he urged young writers to learn from Sterne, Stevenson, Dumas, and Conan Doyle.

Paustovsky's plots sometimes remind one of the notes, scarcely legible, faded from dampness and water, which characters in adventure stories used to find in sealed bottles cast up by the sea. In his *Black Sea*, Paustovsky himself recalls such bottles, remarking that even city urchins no longer believe in them today. "And yet," the writer adds, "it is not by chance that they have come to mind. These stories are a gift from the sea. It cast them out upon my threshold, as it had once cast out bottles, along with glittering sunlight, red seaweeds, and medusas."

The search for a combination of the fantastic and the real led Paustovsky to fashion his own unique form of a long tale in which the past re-echoes in the present, creating a sense of continuity from generation to generation. This effect is attained by an interesting method: the tale, or novel, is constructed of a series of seemingly independent and almost complete fragments, which are unified by a common theme and by the unexpectedly revealed connection, across decades, between the characters.

The first of Paustovsky's works in this form was *Kara-Bugaz* (1932). It was also his first great success, which brought him into the ranks of the most popular Soviet writers. The book opens with a letter written in 1847 by a hydrographer, Lieutenant Zherebkov, to his old schoolfellow, describing the mysterious phenomena which attended the voyage of the corvette *Volga* along the eastern coast of the Caspian Sea. Zherebkov had been sent by the Hydrographic Department on an expedition to describe and measure the Caspian coast, and during the voyage he encountered a number of strange phenomena. The extraordinary heaviness of the water and air near and in the Kara-Bugaz Bay, which astonished him, was due to the presence of fumes of Glauber's salt. As was discovered later, Kara-Bugaz is something of a natural factory of Glauber's salt—the largest in the world. Its exploitation, however, began only just before World War I. Paustovsky related afterward that he had been inspired to write the tale of Kara-Bugaz by a meeting with the geologist Natsky, one of the explorers of Kara-Bugaz Bay. Natsky (who appears in the book as Shatsky) was seriously ill at the time of their meeting, and lived in retirement at the home of his sister, a railroad physician. Before beginning the book Paustovsky visited Kara-Bugaz himself and read everything he could find about the bay.

From the very first pages this long tale captures the reader's interest (especially that of the young reader) by its aura of somber mystery. The bay and the surrounding desert seem sunk in heavy, leaden sleep. The leaden weight of the air and the incomprehensible density of the water, together with the strangely morbid manifestations in people visiting this region, oppress the explorers.

Then—without any apparent connection—the author shifts the action to the Civil War period, when a tragic incident takes place on the Caspian Sea, at the mouth of Kara-Bugaz Bay. A group of Reds, taken from Petrovsk by the Whites before surrendering the city, is put ashore, abandoned to virtually certain death, on the dread Black

Island, which is almost entirely bare of vegetation and without fresh water. The few persons who survive are rescued by the meteorologist Remizov, who works in the vicinity of Kara-Bugaz. Remizov is the son of the friend to whom Zherebkov had addressed his letter in the opening pages of the book. Among those saved by Remizov is the geologist Shatsky and a woman, an Armenian teacher whom Shatsky later marries. Both remain with Remizov, to assist him in exploring Kara-Bugaz. Ten years later the author visits them in Makhach-Kala (in reality, it was in Livny) to question them about Kara-Bugaz. The tale continues with the history of the exploitation of the natural wealth of Kara-Bugaz.

The same method—which might be described as the method of relaying the narrative from generation to generation—is used in the construction of *Tale of the North* (1939) and *Tale of the Woods* (1948). The former opens in Mariengamna, on the Aland Islands (which then belonged to Russia), near the mouth of the Gulf of Bothnia, midway between Finland and Sweden. The year is 1826, immediately after the Decembrist uprising in Petersburg. A wounded officer, who had taken part in the uprising, and a sailor who accompanies and supports him, are trying to make their way on foot over the ice and across the Aland Islands to Sweden. The fugitives are arrested, and a series of dramatic events ensues. The book ends in the early 1930s, in Leningrad, where the great-grandsons of the participants in the events at Mariengamna more than a century earlier meet and unexpectedly identify one another.

As the *Tale of the Woods* opens, Tchaikovsky is shown in the early 1890s, living in a remote forest and working on a new symphony. An adolescent girl, Fenya, the daughter of the forester, often brings him wild berries. But when she hears him playing the piano, she does not venture to intrude and sits down on the step outside, listening, charmed by his music. The predatory felling of the woods which begins nearby disturbs Tchaikovsky, and he leaves for Moscow. The book ends during the years of World

War II, and the link with the past is embodied in the person of the laboratory technician at the forest station, Maria Timofeyevna, the daughter of the young girl who more than half a century earlier had listened in enchantment to Tchaikovsky's music.

Traces of this method of linking generations can also be found in Paustovsky's shorter novels, *The Fate of Charles Lonceville* (1931), *Colchis* (1934), and *Black Sea* (1935), and even in the short stories, in which his talent found its fullest expression. In "The Telegram" the aged daughter of a famous artist recalls during the last weeks of her life a journey with her father to Paris, and Victor Hugo's funeral, which they attended. In "Cordon 273"[1] the author lives deep in the forest belt of central Russia. "On the wall there is an engraving—a portrait of Garibaldi —with his signature, yellowed by time. How did it get here? I think of the former owner of this country house, an artist, long-dead, who had lived for many years in Paris, visited Turgenev in France, was acquainted with Viardot and, evidently, knew Garibaldi."

Somewhat apart, in Paustovsky's own admission, is his long autobiography, *The Story of My Life*. The first part of it, *Distant Years*, appeared in the latter half of 1945 in the magazine *Novy Mir*, but was not published in book form until 1947. The second part, *Restless Youth*, dealing with the period of World War I, appeared in 1955; the third, *The Beginning of an Unknown Age*, devoted to the first years of the revolution, was published in 1956; the fourth, *The Time of Great Expectations*, appeared in the magazine *Oktyabr* in 1959; the fifth, *Move to the South*, was printed in the same magazine in 1960, bringing the narrative up to 1923. This is by no means the end of the long and absorbing autobiographical epic. "I must write several more books to bring the action to the present day," wrote Paustovsky in a brief autobiographical note.

The initial text of the first part of the autobiography, as it appeared in *Novy Mir*, contains an interesting

[1] "Cordon" is the technical designation for a forest district.

episode, which for some reason disappeared from the subsequent editions:

"My father never went to church. Only once did he take me to the Cathedral of St. Sofia in Kiev, to a sumptuous service, rich with the glitter of gold and solemn chanting. This was in the evening of December 31, 1899, when a mass was celebrated in honor of the advent of a new century, the twentieth. That evening a straight, thick snow was falling on the city, the street lights burned dimly, and my father was telling me that the new century would bring with it freedom and happiness, that I must believe in this and be a liberal and honest man, and, if fate grants me talent, then I must become a writer."

This was how Paustovsky's remarkable father spoke to his seven-year-old son. The entire work is written in the lyrical pastel tones so characteristic of Paustovsky.

Despite the author's complete loyalty to the regime, official authorities kept the third part of his autobiography from magazine publication, which usually precedes book publication in the Soviet Union, so that it first appeared only in Paustovsky's *Collected Works* in 1957. The critics reproached Paustovsky for the "chamber character" of his autobiography. The critic of the *Literary Gazette* wrote about *Restless Youth* on September 3, 1955:

"Many different people, destinies and events pass before us in *Restless Youth*. But why is it that the broader and farther the narrative flows, the more cities flash before us, the more human faces we see, the stronger becomes the feeling that the horizons are narrowing down in this work, that its boundaries are becoming ever tighter?"

The critic recalls the autobiographies of other writers—Herzen's *My Past and Thoughts*, Gorky's autobiographical stories, and, most of all, Korolenko's *A History of My Contemporary*. In contrast to the latter, he says, Paustovsky's *The Story of My Life* did not become a new *History of My Contemporary*; "it is only a story of private encounters in a private life." This, according to the critic, is the result of Paustovsky's refusal, in distinction to Korolenko, to sacrifice "the beautiful and vivid lines of artistic truth" for the sake of "complete historical truth."

For forty years now the official Soviet critics have forced writers to sacrifice "artistic truth" in the name of an ephemeral "historical truth." In the name of this "historical truth" it is permissible to deviate from reality and to purvey falsehood. But postwar, and particularly post-Stalin, Russia has faced the writer with the demand, not loud but insistent, precisely for the long-suppressed "artistic truth," for truth about the life of ordinary people, their thoughts and dreams, their personal, actual, rather than "historical," life. And Soviet readers accept *The Story of My Life* as the story of a contemporary, alive in our "Unknown Age."

Also somewhat apart from the rest of Paustovsky's rich contribution to literature is his *Golden Rose*, mentioned earlier in this chapter. Its subtitle is "A Book about the Writer's Work." In a short preface to this book the author says that, soon after he began it, he realized that its theme is "inexhaustible." But if he should succeed at least in small measure in giving the reader some conception of the essence of a writer's work, he would feel that he has fulfilled his duty to literature. The book is written in an outwardly fragmentary form, but with passionate inner concentration. One of the sketches in the *Golden Rose*, dealing with the rag collector Zhan Shamet, was discussed earlier in this chapter. Especially valuable among Paustovsky's notes and ideas is the sketch "Lightning," describing the birth of a creative idea in the artist, the collection, or, to be more accurate, the selection of the material for the work, the gathering of verbal jewels that go into its making. There is much tender insight in the writer's words about his native, "diamond," language and about Russian nature. Often, the most seemingly dull technical terms come alive under Paustovsky's touch, transformed into warmly gleaming gems. Take a dry term like "forest landmark," used to describe the posts at the crossings of narrow forest paths. Here is what Paustovsky writes about them: "Around these posts there is always a sandy mound, overgrown with dryish grass and wild strawberries. The mound is formed of the sand dug up from the hole where the post was set. On the planed upper part of the post there are some burnt-in figures—the number of the forest district. Almost always, you see butterflies with folded wings warming themselves on these posts, and ants busily running up and down. It is warmer near the posts than in the woods (or does it only seem so?). And you sit down beside them for a rest, leaning your back against them, listening to the low hum of the treetops, looking up at the sky. . . . In the sky and the clouds there is the same noonday peace as in the woods, as in the dry cup of the bluebell bending over the rich soil, as in your heart. . . ."

Paustovsky's books are populated with vast numbers of people, both those who have become a part of history, and simple, ordinary men and women. We meet in his pages Pushkin, Lermontov, Kiprensky, Tchaikovsky, Levitan, Mozart, and Hans Andersen. We find masterfully sketched portraits of modern writers, from the late Arkady Gaydar, with whom the writer had once walked the length and breadth of the remote and desolate Meshchorsky region, down to the literary youth of the 1920s (the so-called Southern-Russian literary school), including Isaac Babel, Eduard Bagritsky, Semyon Gekht, Valentin Katayev, Yury Olesha, and others whom Paustovsky met in Odessa against the background of the Civil War and utter chaos. It was there too that Paustovsky met Bunin shortly before the latter's emigration from Russia.

But most of all, Paustovsky's works are peopled with ordinary folk, lovers of their native regions like the tar-sprayer Vassily and his grandson Tisha, who later becomes the chairman of the local Executive Committee. Although Paustovsky tries to be impartial toward the people he describes, it is easy to see that his warmest feelings are for the "adventurers," like his uncle Yuzya and his father, who had taught throughout his lifetime that man does not live "by bread alone."

His tireless attention to the details of the life of ordinary people and the nature of his country brings him into close kinship with his older contemporary, Prishvin. Both came into Russian literature after its greatest masterworks had already been created, both went through a long period of torment in search of a theme. And both were helped by the apocryphal folk legend about the two Adams. Like the second comer, the Landless Adam, they toiled on a narrow strip of land. But from this narrow strip, both writers have gathered a rich harvest.

18 VERA PANOVA (1905–   )

Vera Panova belongs to that group of writers on whom the first tragic period of the Soviet-German war left a profound and ineradicable imprint. This group, which is small but very popular with postwar Soviet readers, also includes Alexander Tvardovsky, the poetess Olga Bergholts, Valentin Ovechkin, Victor Nekrasov, Vladimir Dudintsev, and Vasily Grossman. It is characterized by the belief, first formulated by Ovechkin in his story *With Greetings from the Front* (1945), that, after the war, people would expect to hear some "friendly, heart-to-heart talk."

Vera Panova was born in 1905 in Rostov on the Don. Her father, who was an assistant bookkeeper in a bank, was drowned in the Don when she was five. Her childhood was spent in poverty. After her father's death, her mother worked as a saleswoman. Vera Panova never received a good formal education, but from her earliest years she was an avid reader, especially of poetry, at which she tried her hand at an early age. In 1922 she began to work for the Rostov newspapers, first as an apprentice, and later as a staff member. She learned newspaper work by practical experience, serving in turn as an assistant to the district organizer of labor correspondents, a reporter, and an essayist. She traveled a great deal in the Northern Caucasus, visiting factories, Cossack *stanitsas*, and mountain villages.

In 1933 she began to write plays (*Ilya Kosogor*, *In Old Moscow*, and others). Although the two plays named won prizes, Panova felt that "the dramatic form confined" her, and, by her own admission, she was unable to fit into its strict framework all that she wanted to say. It seemed to her, even then, that she might work with greater freedom in the novel or story form.

In 1944, when she was working for radio and the local newspaper in the city of Molotov (formerly Perm) in the Urals, she wrote a story, "The Pirozhkov Family," about a family of workers. It was published in the anthology *Prikamye*. Soon after that she began her novel *Kruzhilikha*. This work was interrupted when the Molotov branch of the Writers' Union assigned her to a military hospital train to help its personnel write a pamphlet about its work during the war years. Panova went to the front on this train and took part in two long runs. These trips resulted in the novel *Traveling Companions* (*Znamya*, 1946).

Although this novel is virtually plotless, it won immediate favor with readers. The first thing that impresses one in it is the "subtext," the tone, warmed by the writer's breath. Many characters, many human destinies pass before the reader's eyes, but none of them strains his attention; yet each, thanks to the author's keen-eyed sympathy, is memorable.

The central figure in *Traveling Companions* is the political commissar Danilov. Before the war he was a director of some institution and could easily have obtained an exemption from the draft; but he refused to make use of his privileges and had been assigned to the task of organizing the hospital train. Despite Danilov's importance in the book, Panova does not allow him to overshadow the rest of the train personnel. In fact, he seems to have interested her less than some of the others, and certain aspects of his character remain unclear to the reader.

Of peasant origin, Danilov was an adolescent when the revolution broke out. Soon afterward he joined the Comsomol. His parents, people of the old school, did not interfere with their son's political activity. They felt that they had done what was most important: they had taught him their ideas of what was good and what was evil; beyond that they allowed him complete freedom.

Panova relates only one incident of Danilov's youth—his unrequited love for the local schoolteacher. Danilov "ailed" with this love for a long time but in the end married a village girl, Dusia, who touched his feelings by her love for him. But he never loved her, and his domestic life was unhappy; he loved only his son, because he saw "himself" in him.

The war has somewhat softened the reserved and withdrawn Danilov. Panova conveys this with a few simple strokes. Returning home from the war, Danilov enters the house with the key he found in the old "hiding place." Everything is the same, but bears the stamp of poverty, which Dusia has endured with quiet courage. He is struck by the oilcloth on the table, worn at the corners; when he was leaving for the army it was new. Also, the ink spots on it. Who made them? And suddenly he understands: it is his son, his son who has "grown up and writes in ink." Danilov closes his eyes, and when he opens them again, "they are wet." He meets his returning wife and son on the steps. They go into the kitchen. In the light, Danilov sees his son's happy face and the face of his wife, grown older. "Weary and repentant," he asks her tenderly, "Well, tell me how you managed. . . ."

Panova is very successful in portraying simple, ordinary people. The attendant, "Uncle Sasha," was a conductor before the war. His family—mother, wife, widowed sister, two daughters, and a little niece—had lived in the town of Luga. For the sake of brevity, Uncle Sasha referred to them as "my six women." When the Germans were approaching Luga, he evacuated his "women," but they all perished during a bombardment. Uncle Sasha broke down and spent six months in a psychiatric hospital. After he recovered he took the job of stove attendant on the hospital train. He is a quiet, kindly man, but since his illness, he has never been able to stay idle; his hands begin to shake, and then he takes up the sock he is knitting. He learned this at the hospital. Uncle Sasha likes to sing. Most of his songs are old: "My Bonfire Glows in the Dark," "Oleg," "The Fire of Moscow Raged and Burned." The wounded men love his songs, and Uncle Sasha travels, always carrying his own stool from car to car, entertaining the wounded with his songs.

Another example of Panova's gift for portraiture is Lena

Ogorodnikova. She was an infant when the revolution broke out. Her mother was a rag-picker, who frequently got drunk. Lena never knew her father, but from her mother's conversations with her friends, Lena gathered that he was a "scoundrel." She did not know what the word meant, and decided that it was a nickname. When Lena was six, her mother sent her to the orphanage, instructing her to say that she had no parents. From then on she lived at the orphanage. She grew up a fine person, but not a happy one. Only once, shortly before the war, when she met and married a man she loved, had she had a glimpse of happiness. After her husband was mobilized, she lived solely on dreams of the coming reunion. But when they met, he confessed that, while in the army, he had fallen in love with someone else. He told her that he had thought a great deal about it, and had come to the conclusion that he and Lena had come together too quickly, that it had been "intoxication," not love. And when they parted, it had passed. "'Mine did not,' said Lena, ashen-lipped. . . ."

Panova's short novel is particularly enchanting because of its simplicity and honesty. For many years, the Soviet literary critics had assured their readers that since the revolution the Russian people had changed beyond recognition, that new men and women had grown up with a special, higher Soviet morality, not to be compared to the old. Panova, shaken by the tragic experiences of the war years, rejected such claims by simply and directly drawing her characters and their motivations in purely human rather than political terms.

The latter 1940s are very important years in Panova's literary career. After the appearance of *Traveling Companions* she returned to her work on the novel *Kruzhilikha*. It appeared a year later (in *Znamya*, November and December, 1947). While it is broader than the earlier work in scope and number of characters, this breadth is achieved at the expense of some of the characters.

The action of the novel unfolds in a large industrial enterprise which may have had as its prototype the factory suburb of the city of Molotov—Motovilikha. The novel opens with a description of early morning: the sun rises; a slow, solemn factory whistle summons thousands of local workers to the morning shift. The heroes of the novel are all characterized by a certain duality: one part seems to exist on the surface, like a superstructure; the other is subliminal, supplementing, and often denying, the "superstructure." These heroes sometimes seem to be details of a large canvas which is still without a central design. The mighty whistle which gathers this multitude of people at the factory can silence their voices in the daytime, but it has no power over the complex flow of their inner lives. Perhaps this is why Panova is so fond of nighttime in the workers' settlement: "night spies on dreams and eavesdrops on conversations." The writer joins night in listening in on these conversations, tenderly saying to her heroes: "Good night, good people!"

The plot of the novel is simple: against the background of this vast enterprise, the writer dwells in detail on the destinies of several characters. Since 1942, Kruzhilikha has been directed by General Listopad. On first acquaintance he produces a dual impression. The reader meets him on the way to the maternity hospital where he is taking his wife Klavdia. Listopad is in a great hurry, since he must also be in time for a meeting of the city's party leadership on "production problems." Listopad knows that he will be criticized with particular zeal by the secretary of the Factory Committee, Uzdechkin. And, indeed, Uzdechkin attacks him not only for overstepping his authority, but also for "directorial autocracy." Listening to Uzdechkin, Listopad feels irritated: doesn't Uzdechkin know that he can easily get him out of the way by returning him to factory work?

The first impression is that Listopad is one of those hard, energetic "bosses" of industry long familiar to readers of the numerous industrial novels of the 1930s. But this impression turns out to be wrong, and the writer herself hastens to stress it. As he reflects on Uzdechkin's charges, Listopad admits that many of them are just.

In the evening after the meeting Listopad longs to telephone the hospital, but he has been told not to call before morning. In the morning he is called to the hospital: the labor pains had never begun, and Klavdia has died in her sleep, together with the child. The doctors attribute her death to the dystrophy which Klavdia, a native of Leningrad, had suffered in the early part of the war. Klavdia has left a diary, written in shorthand. Listopad asks an experienced stenographer to decode it. In these notes Klavdia mentally addresses one of her friends. To her alone she has confided her secret thoughts and feelings. Klavdia was not happy with Listopad, who was always at the factory and came home only to sleep. Finding her in tears one night and learning the reason, he promised to come home earlier. But the promise was only half kept. That same evening he invited one of the factory officials and sat with him till late into the night. When he finally came to Klavdia's room, he immediately fell into a heavy sleep.

Listopad does not remain alone very long. He falls in love with Nonna Sergeevna Yelnikova, a young engineer who works with the chief designer of the factory. She returns his love, but it is not likely that they will be happy together. The story of Nonna's life is also complex, although her childhood was happy. She grew up in normal and cultivated surroundings in Moscow, where her father held a good position. At sixteen, however, Nonna became infatuated with a man who turned out to be an empty braggart. She soon discovered this, but the incident left her with deep scars; it was only when she immersed herself completely in her studies that she succeeded in overcoming her disappointment.

Uzdechkin is also full of inner cleavages. In contrast to the confident and successful Listopad, Uzdechkin is a typical failure. Before the war and the mobilization, he also worked at Kruzhilikha. He returned, severely wounded. How he longed for home! In the midst of his family, among his comrades, all his wounds would heal! But for the time being, they heal too slowly. And no wonder. Uzdechkin's wife, Nyura, who had volunteered for the front as a nurse, was killed. There remain two little daughters, Nyura's adolescent brother Tolya, and the old mother-in-law. While Nyura was alive, the house was managed by the mother-in-law, but after her daughter's death the old woman seemed to give up suddenly; she became intensely religious and lost all interest in the home. The entire burden of work falls upon Uzdechkin. When he comes home from the factory, he cleans up, cooks, and does the laundry. In addition, his relations with Tolya become increasingly strained.

Uzdechkin's job is to represent the basic party mass, and this explains his hostility toward Listopad. But in areas where he does not feel controlled by the director, he himself behaves like a petty bureaucrat. He worries about refurbishing the "House of Culture" connected with the factory, but he never troubles to look in on the "Youthtown" where the adolescents who work at the factory live. And the youngsters continue to suffer from dampness and filth. The writer does not spare Uzdechkin, suggesting that the roots of his antagonism toward Listopad lie in his envy of his successful superior.

Panova's manner in dealing with her heroes is seen in most vivid relief in the chapter "At Night": the settlement is asleep, the houses are quiet, the people are in bed, each seeing "his own dreams." Panova tells about a meeting between Listopad and Uzdechkin under cover of the dark night. Inspired by his love for Nonna, Listopad decides to make peace with Uzdechkin and pays him a surprise visit late in the evening. Uzdechkin has just put the children to bed, and is doing the laundry. Two "truths" clash head on during this nocturnal rendezvous: the truth of the successful and energetic Listopad, and the truth of the little man, who does his work quietly, "without fanfare." And here Uzdechkin is the victor. He takes the offensive at once: he does not dispute that Listopad contributes importantly to the factory, but he receives "much joy" in return, so that for him "it is a profitable deal." Listopad protests against such a formulation. But Uzdechkin is undaunted, criticizing, almost as though in Panova's own voice, Listopad's attitude toward the factory workers: "a human being," he says, "is not a book, to be read at one sitting; you look at him and imagine stories." In contrast to Listopad, he gets virtually nothing for his work, and yet Kruzhilikha is everything to him.

As interesting as the novel itself is the controversy it aroused. Many of the participants in this debate reproached Panova, as it were, for not guiding the reader in separating the "sheep" from the "goats." This point of view was expressed most clearly by the literary critic A. Ivich: "But why is Panova so merciless toward good people that she turns a searchlight on all their faults, compelling us repeatedly to change our attitude toward her heroes, and in the end leaving us baffled. Why is she so kind toward bad people that she turns her searchlight on their smallest virtues?" (*Literary Gazette*, December 24, 1947).

The debate about *Kruzhilikha* was especially heated at the combined meeting of the Prose and Criticism Sections of the Soviet Writers' Union (*Literary Gazette*, January 17, 1948). The report on the meeting notes that it had been a long time since a meeting of the Writers' Union had divided so sharply in its opinions. Panova also had fervent supporters, grateful to her for not offering the reader ready-made appraisals. The author of the report is especially irked because some of the speakers at the meeting turned the novel to advantage "for propaganda in favor of the nonpartisan approach in literature, a viewpoint rather strange in our day and age...."

In essence, the debate around *Kruzhilikha* is not new. It is the old debate about freedom for the artist.

The short novel *Bright Shore* (*Zvezda*, September 1949) has all the faults and virtues of Panova's earlier works. Its action occurs in a large sovkhoz. *Bright Shore* is the first of Panova's works set during the postwar years. Its principal heroes remain the same—the "little people," as they are designated by Soviet critics. But even when the writer portrays responsible workers, she is interested less in their official positions and occupations than in what they "live by."

One such responsible personage in *Bright Shore* is Dmitry Korneevich Korostelev, recently returned from the war. Before the war he worked as a veterinary technician; now he is the director of a large sovkhoz. Korostelev's spiritual image is revealed by Panova in the very first lines of the novel: "On the way to the District Committee, Korostelev stepped in, as he put it, to 'give hell to' his chauffeur, Tosya Almazova." Her husband has just returned from war, and she has been absent from work for five days, taking an unauthorized "vacation." But hearing Tosya's happy laughter, which makes her throat "swell up like a pigeon's," and seeing her glittering eyes, Korostelev finds himself unable to "give her hell." He feels only a secret sadness: here he is, young and not worse-looking than others, and yet he is alone. At the end of the story Korostelev, like Tosya, succeeds in finding a personal life—he falls in love with Marina, a young teacher and the widowed mother of Seryozha. The reader will meet Korostelev again in Panova's novelette *Seryozha*, subtitled, "Several Stories from the Life of a Very Small Boy," written in 1955.

Among Panova's works of the 1950s the widest response was elicited by the novel *Seasons of the Year* (*Znamya*, November–December 1953) and the short novel *A Sentimental Story* (*Novy Mir*, October–November 1958).

The title *Seasons of the Year* is somewhat flat and does not remotely indicate the contents of the novel. The action takes place in Ensk, a town in the Urals. Central to the narrative are two families: Dorofeya and Leonid Kuprianov with their children, and Stepan and Nadezhda Bortashevich with theirs. When the novel opens, the children of both families are already grown, and Dorofeya's elder son, Gennady, has had time not only to get married, but also to get divorced from his wife, Larisa, a student. Both families occupy important places in the city of Ensk. Dorofeya is Deputy Chairman of the City Executive Committee, and although her husband, a railroad machinist, has not followed a public career, he is universally respected. Stepan Bortashevich is the director of the City Trade Office (*Gortorg*). In comparison with the Kuprianovs, the Bortasheviches live in luxury, in an excellent apartment, with rugs, expensive furniture, and two servants. The Kuprianovs live much more modestly, but they own their pleasant little house.

Both families had humble beginnings. Leonid Kuprianov had fallen in love with Dorofeya, a young peasant girl, at first sight, and she, in turn, gave him her lifetime's devotion. After their marriage they lived for a time in an old railroad car near the station, sharing it with another couple, the Tsytsarkins. But this couple lived a strangely disordered existence, very different from that of the Kuprianovs. During the NEP period Tsytsarkin began to speculate and finally wound up in a concentration camp; his wife Margo went to work as a servant with the Bortashevich family.

Stepan Bortashevich's origins were equally modest; after the Civil War, during the NEP, he found work at a perfume trust. A good organizer, he soon began to move up the service ladder; he was considerably helped in this by his future second wife, Nadya. The daughter of a tailor, she had "made herself a career" with the aid of her good looks and taste. She was now a "private secretary." The naïve and uncouth Stepan Bortashevich soon fell completely under her influence, divorced his devoted first wife, Tonya, and married Nadya. But Nadya had played a fatal role in Stepan's life. She loved luxury and was not excessively scrupulous. During the NEP years Bortashevich, as a Communist, had to content himself with the *part-maximum*,[1] but Nadya persuaded him to "borrow," with the aid of the bookkeeper, from the trust in order to furnish their first apartment. Bortashevich resisted at first, then yielded, intending to return the money before long.

After that his life went according to the old proverb, "If a single claw is caught, the bird is finished." The bookkeeper covered up the operations with Bortashevich's connivance, sending innocent people to face court trial and

[1] The maximum earnings which the party permitted its members to receive at the time.

prison. Before the first of these "cases" Bortashevich was badly frightened, but the persons accused of embezzlement "unprotestingly confessed to all the charges, without implicating anyone." This reassured him, and the bookkeeper became progressively bolder in resorting to such "lightning deflectors." In the end, however, Bortashevich is caught; about to be arrested, he locks the doors of his study and shoots himself. His daughter Katya, a student, and his adolescent son, Seryozha, are deeply shaken by the tragedy. Their mother tries to save some of the family valuables, hiding them in a volume of Lermontov, but during the search Katya turns them over to the investigating official. The mother leaves home and children in a rage, and goes to Rostov.

Less dramatic is the episode which occurs in the Kuprianov family. Dorofeya Kuprianova has spoiled her favorite older son, Gennady, from his earliest childhood, and he grows up a cold egoist, concerned only with the satisfaction of his whims. In the end he becomes involved with a gang of thieves, and it is only with great difficulty that he escapes trial, thanks in large measure to Dorofeya's irreproachable reputation.

Seasons of the Year encountered rather severe criticism, not for its literary faults (and these are quite evident, especially in the first part, dealing with Dorofeya's career), but because Panova devoted so much space to the portrayal of Gennady and to his connection with the gang. Panova had put her finger on an open wound. As one reads Soviet postwar fiction, one is struck by the fact that almost every family, including those of the most prominent officials, has its "lawbreaker," a candidate for prison or a graduate of some penal institution (*And So We're Home*, by Zhanna Gauzner, *The Prosecutor's Daughter*, by the late Yury Yanovsky, and *Honor*, by G. Medynsky, to mention only a few examples).

Until recently, writers were afraid to touch upon this aspect of Soviet life. Not only has Panova ventured to write about it, but, by her manner of dealing with this sore problem, she urges her readers, while condemning lawbreakers, to be kinder to their families, instead of subjecting them to the ostracism which was the prevalent response before the war and which still persists today.

Panova's inner world and character is revealed in her novel *A Sentimental Story*, which also helps to broaden the reader's insight into the 1920s. The hero of the novel, Sevastyanov, is returning after a thirty-year absence to the town in the steppes of southern Russia where he had spent his youth. Avidly gazing out the window as the train slows down for a moment at a way-station, he catches sight of a small yellow house, beds of pumpkins and cabbages, and wash drying on a line. And he feels as if someone had suddenly called to him, "Hey, there, take a look, have you forgotten?" With a start he sees himself as he was years earlier—young, smiling, striding with wind-blown hair to meet the train.

How far away the morning when he walked up the iron stairs, and they rattled under his feet "like heavenly thunder!" Together with this staircase, his memory revives the faces of his comrades and the Easter carnival at which he had played the part of some English lord. Who was it? Curzon? Chamberlain? It must have been Chamberlain, for "we had scores with him too; even our matchboxes bore the inscription, 'Our answer to Chamberlain.'" (But Shura Sevastyanov fails to recall one detail: the matches rarely kindled!)

Sevastyanov also recalls a distant spring when three Easters coincided: the Russian, the Jewish, and that of the Comsomol. To celebrate the Jewish Easter, he and a horde of friends had burst in upon Syomka Gorodnitsky. Syomka's was a "bourgeois" home: the table was laid with a snow-white cloth, and the napkins at each place-setting stood rolled up like "fancy little snowdrifts." The forks and knives were heavy, adorned with monograms. The guests were treated with hearty hospitality by Syomka's father and stepmother, while Syomka's face expressed helpless despair: "I didn't choose my father. I did not cook the fish. This woman with her little mustache has nothing to do with me. And, generally, I will hang myself."

The "deeds and days" of those latter-day descendants of Turgenev's Bazarov pass through Sevastyanov's mind. All of them were "atheists," and during that same spring they were busy making straw images of "gods" and "priests" and publicly burning the effigies. Most of them had a difficult time at home, and perhaps this was why their friendship was so close and warm.

These Comsomol youths spent their free time at the youth club, where they organized debates on the most diverse topics, including the problem of whether it was proper for a Comsomol member to eat *kulichi* (traditional Easter cakes). The conclusion was that it was improper. But this did not prevent either Shura Sevastyanov or his comrades from eating them the very next day both at home and at the homes of friends. Putting them away with relish, Shura did not feel himself a "hypocrite"; like his friends, he was simply constantly hungry, and tasty food was a great rarity in their lives. The young people also debated whether it was "ethical to dress well." One of the members of this Comsomol group, Little Zoyka (she was given this nickname to distinguish her from her namesake, known as Big Zoyka), "hammered her little fist on the palm of her hand and cried passionately, 'It's inadmissible, inadmissible!'" And yet everyone knew that she was an only daughter, that her father, a railroad conductor, earned a good salary, and that her mother dreamed of dressing her "like a doll." But little Zoyka would never submit to this.

Shura Sevastyanov and his friend Syoma Gorodnitsky finally left their parents and took up lodgings together. They lived a half-hungry existence until Sevastyanov had a stroke of luck: he found a job with the newspaper *Hammer and Sickle*. The story of his work in the editorial office and his first attempts at writing an article glow with the warmth of memories that bear obvious traces of autobiography. It forms one of the best passages in Panova's book.

In an interview with the correspondent of the *Literary Gazette* (October 3, 1959) Panova remarked about *A Sentimental Story*: "Yes, it contains much that is autobiographical, much that belongs to my own experience, but, of course, there is also invention. But this is a rare instance when I can name exactly the actual prototypes of many of my heroes. *A Sentimental Story* was by no means conceived as a historical novel, although it deals with the 1920s. . . ."

Panova also spoke in this interview about her future literary plans (she was working on a new novel, *The Streets of Leningrad*) and expressed her ideas about the importance of truthfulness in art, both in big and small things, in the general conception and the details.

"Sometimes," said Panova, "you read a novel, and you don't believe the author on the second page, on the tenth, on the seventeenth. And if there is suddenly a flash of truth on the hundredth page, you suspect even that, for it is buried under all that falsehood. Nothing that compromises artistic truth can be tolerated in art."

Among the new writers who came upon the scene after the war there are some who are more talented than Panova. Her voice is not loud, but she wins the hearts of her readers, not by sharp postulation of contemporary problems, and not even by beauty of style, but by the special warmth of her intonation. Her literary voice is very much like herself, as she appears in numerous photographs. In these portraits we see a woman in her middle years looking at us with small, transparent, very animated eyes. The mobility and even nervousness of the face is revealed by the asymmetry of the eyebrows. The attractive lines of the mouth are enhanced by the soft oval of the chin. But best of all in the face is the smile—a smile kind to the point of shyness. This smile is felt in her work as well, and it endears Panova to her readers.

19 ALEXANDER TVARDOVSKY
(1910–   )

Although the various poetic trends and schools which flourished during the early years of the revolution, such as the Acmeists, Futurists, Constructivists, and others, have long since disappeared from the literary scene, and poets of diverse tonalities merge today into the general chorus of contemporary Soviet poetry, there is one voice that retains its individual character within this uniform chorus: it is the voice of the poets of peasant origin. Regardless of the content of their poems or the degree of their talent, the ear will always catch in their works a special musical and lyrical instrumentation.

Among the latest generation of contemporary poets of peasant origin, the most talented is Alexander Tvardovsky. A native of the Smolensk region, he entered literature in the beginning of the latter 1930s with his long poem *The Land of Muravia*, which was immediately noticed by the critics.

Tvardovsky's life was not especially eventful. He was born in 1910 on a farm bought by his father on installments through the Peasant Land Bank. The land was not fertile—all swamps and mounds—but his father, the son of a landless soldier and a blacksmith by trade, loved the "estate" which he had acquired by dint of many years of hard labor. And he transmitted this love for his small scrap of land to his children. Life was difficult, and holidays were rare. The father was a newcomer to the region. Their name had a non-Russian sound, and the villagers often added to it the Polish designation "Pan." The poet's father was a man of considerable native gifts and relatively well-read. During the winter evenings he read aloud to his family. From his earliest years the future poet knew Pushkin's

Poltava and *Dubrovsky*, Gogol's *Taras Bulba*, and the poetry of Lermontov, Nekrasov, and Nikitin. He also knew a great deal by heart, particularly Yershov's fairy tale in verse, *The Little Humpbacked Horse*. His mother was a sensitive woman. In his autobiography Tvardovsky recalls that she was moved to tears by the sound of a shepherd's pipe in the distance beyond the farmland, or the sight of a lonely tree. Tvardovsky began to compose verses before he learned to read and write. He was inspired to this by a distant kinsman of his mother's. Of his first childish efforts, Tvardovsky remembers only a fragment of a poem suggested by Pushkin's "Werewolf."

At the age of thirteen Tvardovsky showed his poems to a young teacher, who criticized them severely, telling him that poems must be written as unintelligibly as possible. For several years, Tvardovsky trained himself to write "unintelligible" poems. His first published poem was "A New Hut," which appeared in the newspaper *Smolensk Village*. Collecting his poems, Tvardovsky decided to show them to another peasant poet of the Smolensk province, Mikhail Isakovsky. The latter helped him generously, and Tvardovsky acknowledges his influence, saying that he is the only Soviet poet whose effect upon him was "beneficial."

Tvardovsky's education was interrupted on completion of the village school. As a boy of eighteen, he went to Smolensk, but his efforts to find literary work did not succeed. Nor was he able to get any other work. In the winter of 1930, after a visit to Moscow, Tvardovsky returned to his native village and began work on *The Land of Muravia*. This period was of utmost importance in his literary life: those were the dramatic years of collectivization. To Tvardovsky, this time was as meaningful as the October revolution and the Civil War had been to the older generation. It was also during this period that he entered a Pedagogical Institute with the help of a party official; but he did not finish his studies at the Institute, completing his education later at the Institute of History, Philosophy, and Literature in Moscow.

The Land of Muravia was written in two years (1934–

36), and met a favorable reception among the critics. Along with the poem Tvardovsky also published a book of verse, *Village Chronicle*. In 1939 he was mobilized and took part in the march into Western Belorussia and the war with Finland. In the latter he was a member of a "writers' brigade," which collectively composed verses about "Vasya Tyorkin." In the early part of the German-Soviet war Tvardovsky began to work independently on *A Book about a Soldier*—a long poem about *Vasily Tyorkin*; and, almost simultaneously, on a new poem, *A House by the Roadside*. Of his postwar works we may note *Vista beyond Vista*, begun in 1952 but completed only in 1960.

Nor can the poet's prose be ignored. Most significant among his prose works is the book of sketches *Homeland and Strange Land* (1947). Tvardovsky spends considerable time also on his work as an editor and on participation in writers' conferences and congresses. He has twice been editor-in-chief of one of the most widely read literary magazines, *Novy Mir*. After having served in this post since 1949, he was dismissed in September 1954, for publishing articles by V. Pomerantzev, F. Abramov, and M. Shcheglov.[1] His second appointment as editor-in-chief of *Novy Mir* came in July 1958.

The Land of Muravia, which immediately brought Tvardovsky into the front ranks of contemporary Soviet poets, is the story of the individual peasant Nikita Morgunok, who refuses to join the kolkhoz, liquidates his holding, and goes forth to search for the legendary land of Muravia, where there are no communes and no kolkhozes. As Tvardovsky relates in his autobiography, the idea for the poem was suggested to him by the late Alexander Fadeyev. Its title was derived from Panfyorov's novel *Bruski*, in which a peasant who opposes the collectivization talks about "the land of Muravia."

Morgunok's fruitless search for the legendary Muravia is

[1] V. Pomerantzev's "On Sincerity in Literature," Abramov's article on people in postwar kolkhozes, and Shcheglov's critical analysis of Leonov's *The Russian Forest* displeased the authorities and led to Tvardovsky's dismissal.

described with great force and sympathy for the hero. The passage in which he mentally appeals to Stalin is especially moving. Let the kolkhoz justify itself some day, he says to Stalin, and let life become "truly fine and happy."

> But now, as I say, I have
> A personal request.
> I, Nikita Morgunok,
> I ask you, Comrade Stalin,
> In the meantime, for a while,
> To let me and my little farm . . . be.
>
> And tell them: well, say, such and such—
> They shouldn't vex and hound me—
> Tell them that one queer duck was left,
> Just one in the whole wide land. . . .

But, perhaps because such "queer ducks"—opponents of collectivization like Morgunok—were numerous throughout the country, Tvardovsky had to make his hero recognize in the end, in the kolkhoz he comes to after much wandering, the very land of Muravia which he had sought so vainly and so long.

Despite certain shortcomings of his poem and the quite obvious influence of the nineteenth-century poet Nekrasov, Tvardovsky's talent was immediately recognized. Among the articles and essays devoted to Tvardovsky, the most substantial is N. Vilyam-Vilmont's "Notes on the Poetry of A. Tvardovsky" (*Znamya*, November–December 1946). Notwithstanding the similarity between Tvardovsky and Nekrasov both in form and theme, Vilyam-Vilmont traces Tvardovsky's search for a democratic poetic style to Pushkin and his "Tale about a Priest and His Laborer Balda." The poet, he suggests, has also been influenced by the English ballad. This is evident in some of the rhythms and intonations of *The Land of Muravia*. English ballads have been known in Russia, in translation, for a long time, and it is quite possible that Tvardovsky was acquainted with them. Culture, says Vilyam-Vilmont, is after all like "a game with a ring, which rolls around the world and is warmed by the hands of all peoples." He illustrates this with a story heard from Tvardovsky himself: the poet recalled how, as a barefoot village boy, he had often listened to a landless farm laborer recite the wonderful adventures of a certain eccentric and his loyal friend. Following the heavy plow, this poor laborer without house or land repeated with strange emotion the unfamiliar, but all the more enchanting, name of another man of the people (a foreign people): "Sancho Panza." It was only much later that Tvardovsky himself made the acquaintance of Cervantes, the creator of *Don Quixote*.

Tvardovsky gained still wider popularity after the publication of his second long poem, about the soldier *Vasily Tyorkin*. This work is truly a folk poem; it was not only written for the people at war, but was created in collaboration with the people, in their coarse gray army coats. In his spiritual make-up Tyorkin is a close kin to Nikita Morgunok, though younger: both are embodiments of the average Russian, from the very heart of the popular mass. And what links them most is the author's feeling toward them. Tvardovsky is fond of Morgunok, although his hero is almost a candidate for penal exile. This is precisely why the poet is obliged to conceal his deep sympathy for Morgunok behind jests and humor. Tyorkin, however, can be loved openly, and the author himself admits that this poem is especially dear to him.

Tvardovsky belongs to the group of writers—unfortunately, all too small—on whom the ordeals endured by the people in wartime left a profound and ineradicable impression. At the end of the poem, completed after the war, the author introduces an entire chapter about a lonely soldier who had lost his family in the war. Returning to his native village and learning of the deaths of all his kin, the soldier

> Sat down weeping at the edge of a dry ditch.
> His mouth trembling bitterly, like a child's,
> A spoon in his right hand,
> A slice of bread in his left.

And Tvardovsky makes a fervent appeal to the readers—to remember, on the bright day of victory and after, this soldier's "holy tears." . . .

Almost simultaneously with his work on *Vasily Tyorkin*, Tvardovsky began his poem *A House by the Roadside*. It was begun, as the poet says in the introduction, in that bitter year

> When in the frozen winter
> War stood at the gates
> Of our beleaguered capital.

This poem—a companion piece to *Vasily Tyorkin*—depicts the wartime fate of a woman, a soldier's wife. Tvardovsky first envisaged *A House by the Roadside* and his heroes, Andrey and Anna Sivtsov, during the days when Soviet troops were in retreat from the Smolensk region. He carried his thoughts of this house as he followed Tyorkin throughout the war, across the border, and into "foreign lands." And one day, "on the way, in a strange land," Tvardovsky chanced upon such a "house," made by a soldier's wife, a prisoner of war:

> That house, without a roof, without a corner
> Yet warm as a dwelling place,
> Your woman managed to preserve
> A thousand miles from home.

This "house"—a cart with some scant belongings—was pulled by a woman surrounded by a flock of children and carrying the youngest in her arms. And every soldier's heart "grew warm" at this sight.

The theme of the poem is simple and tragic. On a fine summer day the peasant Andrey Sivtsov is mowing hay, repeating to himself the old folk refrain:

> Mow, my scythe, while the dew is out;
> The dew is gone, and we go home.

Everything gladdens Andrey on this early morning; the work hums in his hands, when suddenly

> The ancient voice of war
> Howls through the land.

There is no time for preparations or long good-bys: Andrey bids his wife to take care of the children, but much is left unsaid. Should she

> Stay here? Run somewhere else, into the world?

And in the meantime, war comes ever closer, on the heels of the "dusty troops, retreating, rolling back." This war is much more difficult than any in the past. In former wars the men went somewhere far; this time a man goes off to war, but the war itself comes to his home. Fate grants Anna only one meeting with Andrey. When his unit is surrounded and the men are ordered to make their way across the front, he manages to get home for a night. Anna presses him with questions: what is the news, and what is she to do? But there is little that Andrey can tell her. The answers come soon enough. The village is occupied by the Germans, and Anna is taken away to Germany. Far from home, in a foreign land, lying on straw in a barrack, Anna gives birth to a boy and names him Andrey, after the father. Despite the hunger and the difficult conditions, the child lives. People help in any way they can. An old man on his deathbed bequeaths Andreyka his cherished warm vest.

And then the war is over. The ex-soldier Andrey Sivtsov finds his way back to his native village, climbs up a hill, but cannot see his house or yard; the place where his home had been is thickly overgrown with nettles. His fellow villagers who have survived or recently returned from evacuation try not to see the crippled soldier "choking on his grief." But life must go on. Andrey decides to build a new house, hurrying, as though its completion must bring his Anyuta home. One day, to drive away his sorrow, Andrey goes out into the field, to help the others with their mowing. As he swings his scythe, he remembers the old refrain, "Mow, my scythe, while the dew is out." The same refrain runs through the mind of Anyuta as she wanders home over road and highway. The reader knows she is trudging back with her "house" on wheels, but Andrey does not know it. And nobody can tell whether she finally will reach her goal.

In some of its intonations and details this poem is akin to *Homeland and Strange Land*, Tvardovsky's most important prose work (*Znamya*, November 1947), devoted to the early period of the war. On June 22, 1941, Tvardovsky was in a village near Moscow, where he planned to spend his summer vacation. News of the war was brought to him by his little daughter, who had been playing outside. The poet ran out into the street to verify it. Several empty manure carts stood idle by the barn, and near them some peasants and peasant women sat on a pile of straw. One look at them told Tvardovsky that all questions were superfluous. "They sat in silence and replied to my greeting as quietly, austerely, and sparingly as if they were in the presence of the dead. The grim realization of the disaster, clear from the very first, irreparable and affecting each and every one, had stricken them mute, plunged them into a state of dazed torpor." But even they, "with their inbred, profoundly personal recognition of the misfortune that had come upon them," could not yet at the moment imagine its full extent or foresee that the enemy would soon invade their own village.

Tvardovsky tells us that he jotted down his first impressions of those days in a notebook which he later lost. But he retains to this day a vivid image of the picture he saw from the window of the Moscow-Kiev train in the Ukraine: he saw a vast field, solidly covered with the bundles, valises, household goods, and carts of thousands of fleeing refugees. This "refugee misfortune" hummed with a thousand voices, speaking of agitation and anxiety, but most of all, of heavy, sorrowing weariness. At the sight of the train, many of the refugees rushed toward it, and it seemed that they might push it off the rails. Violating the stern but necessary rules, Tvardovsky and his companions pulled into their car a woman with two children. She turned out to be a resident of Minsk, the wife of an officer.

Settling in a corner, she tried her best to conceal her weariness and troubles. In time, the poet forgot her story. But he remembered "the main thing": her "selfless readiness to endure, her determination to keep her spirit, not to depress or frighten anyone with her own grief," which revealed to him the full "greatness of the heroism that our women and mothers were to show in this war."

Of the impressions recorded by Tvardovsky in his lost notebook, he also recalls an autumn night in the steppe. A military unit, which had retreated almost a thousand versts, encamped for the night in the steppe. And suddenly one soldier started a simple Russian song, a song that everyone could join in. It did not say a word about the war, but spoke about life, about love, about the native Russian fields and woods, about the joys and sorrows of bygone village life. The song said nothing about the Germans or the great disaster in the land; modest and simple, it inspired one with faith that the bitter calamity would pass, that good things were yet to come, that "the mother will embrace her son, the soldier raise in his arms the child grown bigger in his absence."

There is great charm in the poet's quick sketches of the Russian landscape. His notes are almost devoid of chronology; the date of an incident or event is indicated only by a few brief introductory words.

Vividly impressed with all the stories he heard in the course of the war, Tvardovsky had thought for a time of collecting everything he remembered into a book—an anthology, as it were, of wartime folklore. Evidently, the plan was never carried out. The harsh reception met by his book *Homeland and Strange Land*, which reflected too clearly for official comfort the panic, suffering, and confusion of the early period of the war, compelled the poet to retire for a time into silence. From the end of the 1940s to the early 1950s Tvardovsky published only his *Poems from My Notebook*, among them such moving poems as "Two Lines," "I Was Killed at Rzhev," and "About a Starling." Unlike the poem "About a Starling," which glows with a sly, warm smile, most of the poems in the book are melancholy, full of sorrowful thoughts:

> Can it be true that somewhere far away
> Our wives have grown older in our absence,
> Our children taller, while we were away?

The pensive sadness of these poems is crowned by the closing poem in the book: "Years have gone by. Trees, once destroyed, came back to life with unexpected force. . . . The war is over. And you, you are still weeping, Mother. . . ."

In recent years Tvardovsky has worked on a long poem, *Vista beyond Vista*. Its first chapters appeared in *Novy Mir* in June 1953, but the poet first conceived it in 1950 when, with a group of other writers, he was sent to the Far East, to observe at close range the Korean War, which had just broken out, and to see the new construction projects on the Angara River. This poem, completed only in 1960, is one of the poet's most successful works. As fine as its main theme are the lyrical digressions, in which the poet describes his childhood in his native Zagorye, where his father's smithy served the village as a substitute for "club and newspaper and science academy." What topics were not discussed by its frequenters? God and the Evil One, generals and Czars, the teachings of Leo Tolstoy and oppressive taxes . . .

Side by side with its lyrical digressions, the poem breathes of contemporary life. Distant railroad journeys are always evocative of a special romanticism both in prerevolutionary and in modern Russian literature. Removed from the routine of their daily lives, people who did not know each other the day before quickly develop intimacy in the railway car and pass the time in sincere and heartfelt talk. Tvardovsky soon came to know his fellow travelers, but could not long conceal his own identity. And he was obliged to answer not only for his own faults, but also for the sins of contemporary Soviet literature at large.

His fellow passengers reproach the writers for "not reflecting life." Oftentimes, these writers acquaint themselves with life during so-called "creative missions." A writer comes to a construction project, "takes a few breaths" of the dust, "pokes a stick into the concrete," then goes home and scribbles away at a novel. And in the book that results everything seems to look "like the real thing," but "the whole is so indigestible that you want to howl aloud."

Listening to this impartial criticism, Tvardovsky is both grieved and compelled to admit that, after all, this just rebuke is far more pleasing to him than "the cold smoke of lies" offered by his professional colleagues. At this point the voice of a passenger from an upper berth breaks into the conversation. This passenger is no ordinary man—he is the collective image of the editor, a product of the poet's fantasy—and the conversation between them is fictional, but extremely characteristic and instructive.

The "editor" admits that he was tempted for some time to break into Tvardovsky's conversation, but it was "entertaining" to listen to the writer who had imagined himself free for the moment of editorial supervision. It was amusing to see how "bold" the poet had suddenly become. Tvardovsky protests against the editor's taunt, but the latter explains in a mocking tone that he is, after all, an editor of a very special kind, created . . . by the fear of the poet himself. And this is why it is so easy for him to edit the poet's writings:

> "You are doing
> All my work for me.
> . . . .
> And I am pleased with you,
> I'm overjoyed, believe me. . . ."

Tvardovsky refuses to surrender: "You can catch me only when I am downcast, in weak moments." "You're not reality, you're only a bad dream." The fictional dialogue ends on an optimistic note:

> And meantime all the traveling crowd,
> Filling the corridor as if it were a meeting hall,
> Stood listening with avid ears
> To our heated, long dispute.

Among the other episodes in the poem, we must also note the chapter "A Childhood Friend," devoted to a meeting on the way with a childhood friend, returning from a concentration camp, where he had been sent, a victim of a false denunciation, during the frightful years of the latter 1930s.

> Both friendship's duty, conscience, and honor
> Command me to record
> The tale of one man's destiny,
> Which crossed the journey of my heart....

It is not easy for the poet to recall this story, but the duty must be discharged, for the man in question is an old friend, "my better contemporary," with whom the author had in childhood herded cows in the field, with whom he had gone to school and joined the Comsomol.

It is especially difficult to pay this "debt of friendship" because, as the poet says:

> ... I know: in many ways
> His was the greater integrity and strength....

Had the times been different, the poet could have been proud of his friendship with this man; but fate and circumstance decreed that, for many years,

> This friendship was regarded as a fault
> That anyone could throw at me....

Now, during his journey to the Far East, Tvardovsky meets his friend at Taishet Station, returning to Moscow after seventeen years in a concentration camp. And the first feeling that "scalds" Tvardovsky is "an ignominious shock of fear."

It must be added that this chapter would scarcely have appeared in print if it were not for Khrushchev's speech at the 20th Congress of the Communist Party in February 1956, indicting Stalin's "cult of personality." This indictment inspired many writers and poets at the time to tell about similar feelings on meeting friends of their youth

(Margarita Aliger in her poem "Rightness" [*Oktyabr*, November 1956]; Ehrenburg in the second part of his novel *The Thaw*; N. Ivanter in her novel *August Again* [*Novy Mir*, August–September 1959], and others). Tvardovsky achieves a significant compromise: neither he nor his contemporaries can simply "forget" their fateful errors, connected with their active participation in the Stalin "personality cult":

> We can't hide anywhere
> From our own memory.
> And then, indeed, it is not meet
> For us to reassure ourselves: "perhaps
> It will die out, vanish—as if it never was." . . .

Tvardovsky does not deny that Stalin's megalomania in his last years had grown to such proportions that he spoke of himself "in the third person." However, he finds some justification for himself and his contemporaries in the fact that to them Stalin was "the organizer of the victory."

This confession defines Tvardovsky's place in present-day Soviet literature. A new generation has already sprung up which has not experienced either the war or the "cult of personality" that dominated a long period in the history of Soviet society. Tvardovsky has sufficient courage neither to fawn at this younger generation, nor to arrogate for himself the role of "a teacher of life." He will be remembered as an important poet, who was able, in his country's grim and fateful years, to retain some features of independence and to invest his great talent as a folk poet in a number of works which will remain a living part of Russian literature.

20 VALENTIN OVECHKIN (1904–   )

Valentin Ovechkin's life prompts reflection on a characteristic trait of contemporary Soviet writers. Before the revolution, people became writers in Russia, as in the rest of the world, by vocation, in response to an irresistible urge to write. Numerous biographies and autobiographies show that this urge often awakens very early, and the writer always remembers the moment of its awakening. Examples of this among contemporary writers are found in the lives of the late Boris Pilnyak, Yevgeny Zamyatin, and others. The first generation of post-revolutionary writers consisted predominantly of writers by vocation.

But the literary organizations that sprang up after the revolution enthusiastically embraced the idea of rapid training of new literary forces. Campaigns were launched "to bring forward new literary elements." These "elements" were recruited among provincial newspaper reporters, in factory clubs, "committees of the poor" and local party committees. Young *rabkors* and *selkors* (factory and village reporters) were given aid and encouragement (later on, they were sent to literary institutes in Moscow and Leningrad to improve their "literary skills"). Heartened by all this official attention, thousands of young people streamed to the capitals and regional centers, where they became frequenters of literary evenings, conferences, and editorial offices of journals and newspapers.

Needless to say, only a small proportion of the aspirants succeeded in becoming writers. In the course of almost forty years only several hundred managed to make their way into literature as writers, poets, and journalists. Among them we may name the late Ivan Zhiga, author of the interesting series of sketches *The New Workers*; Rodion Akulshin, who came to the United States after World

War II; Alexander Avdeyenko, author of the successful short novel *I Love*; the late Boris Gorbatov, who became especially well-known during the war for his novels, *The Family of Taras* or *The Unvanquished*; and others. These writers are characterized by a good knowledge of life, which often makes up for the literary immaturity of their early literary ventures. Valentin Ovechkin is a member of this group.

He was born in 1904 in Taganrog, the son of an office employee. His literary activity began early, while he was still a member of the Comsomol. His first story ("Saveliev") was published in the newspaper *Bednota* (*The Poor*) in 1927. Other early works appeared in provincial newspapers. Then followed a rather long interval when Ovechkin stopped writing and worked as a chairman of an agricultural commune on the Don, and later in Kuban. In 1934 he became a roving correspondent and sketch writer for the newspaper *Molot* (Hammer) and *Kolkhoznaya Pravda* (both published in Rostov on the Don), and for newspapers published in Armavir and Krasnodar.

Ovechkin's first book, *Kolkhoz Stories*, appeared in Rostov in 1935. The second collection was published in 1938 in Krasnodar. In 1939 his work began to appear in the Moscow magazine *Krasnaya Nov*; this included "Guests in Stukachi," "Praskovya Maximovna," and the sketch "Without Kith or Kin." Praskovya Maximovna is a Stakhanovite, a kolkhoz brigadier. But her portrait is unlike the usual tinseled images of Stakhanovites and shock workers. Ovechkin shows her as a restless and quarrelsome person, fiercely devoted to work. She is not only disliked by the kolkhoz members, but is also feared by the district party members, since she often provokes various "perturbations."

When the war broke out, Ovechkin was mobilized and sent to work as a front-line agitator on the Crimean and Southern fronts, and later to Stalingrad and the Ukraine. In 1945 the May issue of the magazine *Oktyabr* published his long story *With Greetings from the Front*, which elicited a wide response in the press.

His sketch "Without Kith or Kin" is very characteristic of Ovechkin's early work. It is written in the form of conversations with chance people, whom the author met in great numbers as a roving newspaper correspondent. He was especially interested in the so-called *letuny* ("fliers" or "floaters"). The main bulk of these "floaters" consisted of kolkhoz members whom the writer calls "hoparounds." Among them Ovechkin distinguishes two groups. The first is made up of artisans, whom he depicts as greedy and avaricious. Coopers, wheelwrights, or locksmiths, they are eagerly welcomed in any kolkhoz and exploit their position, always trying to choose the richest or the most profitable kolkhozes. A typical artisan "floater" is the cooper Gunkin; in contrast to his friend, the worker Zubov, who usually joins the obviously richest kolkhoz, Gunkin takes care to select a "run-down" one. He feels that it is unprofitable to work for a rich kolkhoz, because it spends too much on building and various "funds." The cunning Gunkin chooses the seemingly poor ones, in which the members are paid more for their workdays.

To the second group, the writer assigns kolkhoz members from among former middling peasants, and he treats them with sympathy. One such "long-distance floater" is Gritsko, who is making his way from his native Ukraine to somewhere in the east. He was driven to leave his kolkhoz by its inefficient chairmen. During ten years of kolkhoz life Gritsko had seen a succession of witless kolkhoz leaders: one was a drunkard, another a demoted Machine-Tractor Station director, the third an impractical builder of castles in the air. This last one demanded that the kolkhoz members send him on a trip to the Volga, whence he planned to bring camels for agricultural work. When the people objected that their stables were not big enough for camels, "Mitka the dreamer" proposed cutting holes in the stable roofs to make room for the camels' humps. "The devil knows what sort of man this Mitka is. You say he's bad? He isn't bad, but he hasn't got sense either," says Gritsko in the conclusion of his story, expressing the timid hope that the kolkhoz members will in the end manage to "throw off" this Mitka.

Ovechkin writes slowly, allowing his stories and sketches a long time to mature in his mind, and he is an excellent master of dialogue. His characters are always alive. His greatest success was won by the story *With Greetings from the Front* (*Oktyabr*, May 1945). Because the response to it was so wide and significant, a brief summary of it was included in Chapter 16 (Literary Developments: World War II and After).

Nevertheless, this work stands apart from the general body of Ovechkin's writings. Almost all the rest of his sketches, stories, and plays are devoted to kolkhoz life and its problems. Ovechkin has succeeded in popularizing the "village theme" in postwar literature and in awakening the interest of a small but active group of young writers in this theme. Some of them, like V. Tendryakov, the agronomist G. Troyepolsky, I. Antonov, S. Voronin, S. Zalygin, T. Zhuravlev, and G. Baklanov, have already won for themselves a loyal circle of readers. S. Zalygin writes about this in his article "Thoughts after a Conference" (*Novy Mir*, January 1956):

"V. Ovechkin has a number of followers. I think that among the very active and quite numerous group of writers, predominantly young, who write about the village, there are many whom Ovechkin has helped to find the way. I myself owe him a great deal. I think that much of my work would not have been written if it were not for his stories."

A new period in Ovechkin's literary career began in 1952, with the appearance of his *District Workadays* (*Novy Mir*, September 1952). Here, the reader first meets Martynov and Borzov, representative of two types of district kolkhoz authorities, and also a new kind of kolkhoz chairman, Demyan Openkin, nicknamed "Demyan the Rich," in distinction to the poet of the early revolutionary period, Demyan Bedny ("Demyan the Poor").

District Workadays deals with the life of an average

district in the central part of the Soviet Union. Its action takes place during the busy season, at harvest time, but the harvest does not proceed as rapidly as it should. For three days heavy rains have halted all work in the fields. Demyan Openkin, chairman of the "Soviet Power" kolkhoz, comes to see Martynov, second secretary of the District Committee. Openkin was nicknamed "Demyan the Rich" not only because his kolkhoz is one of the most prosperous in the region, but also because of his appearance. He is a big, massive man, who cannot pass unnoticed. Openkin's visit to the district office is at the invitation of Martynov, who wants his advice on how to speed the harvesting of grain in the district, almost entirely halted because of the rains. But Openkin has long ago collected his grain, and he has "no experience in harvesting grain in mud." This remark suggests Openkin's smoldering resentment. He also has "business" with Martynov: he is worried that his kolkhoz may, as in former years, be made to bear the brunt of the lag in other kolkhozes and compelled to fill their grain deliveries, as a "loan." Openkin does not mind helping neighbors in trouble, but the existing practice makes him indignant: all the lagging kolkhozes are in debt to his. When he occasionally asks their chairmen when they will start paying, they laugh: "We'll square accounts," they say, "under communism." But Openkin feels that communism cannot be built "until we liquidate this damned sponging!" Everybody should take part in the building, "instead of some doing the work, and others trying to ride into the heavenly kingdom on someone else's back!"

In principle Martynov agrees with Openkin and does not conceal it. He promises that no supplementary plans will be imposed on his kolkhoz. But Openkin does not believe him. If Martynov were the first secretary, he would be calm, but Martynov is only the second, and the real master is the first secretary, Borzov, who is currently away on vacation. Openkin turns out to be a prophet. When Borzov returns from vacation earlier than expected and finds that some of the kolkhozes have not yet made their deliveries to the state, he immediately wants to impose an additional levy on Openkin's kolkhoz. To Martynov's energetic objections, Borzov replies: "We need the grain. Why all this sympathy? He's an old wolf, he'll manage!" Borzov knows only one thing: if the government and the party need grain, it "must be got at any cost."

The relations between the two secretaries become increasingly tense. The nature of their disagreement is easily understood: Martynov sympathizes with the kolkhoz members and feels that, by antagonizing efficient chairmen like Openkin, the government undermines the incentives of the best kolkhoz people in producing. But to Borzov, government orders are the supreme law. Superficially, Borzov gives the impression of a man who is "anxious, busy, and pressing for achievement." In reality he has no interest in the lives of the people and is chiefly concerned about his reputation among his superiors. Martynov's conversation with Borzov's wife confirms the opinion he has formed about him.

But if the life and problems of the kolkhoz village are told in a pungent and absorbing manner in *District Workadays*, the story of the love between Martynov and Borzov's wife is stilted and unconvincing. The reader is told about this love, but it is never artistically realized. There is only one detail of interest: Borzova tells Martynov about the circumstances of her marriage, at the time "when it was fashionable to marry famous Stakhanovite women." She had been a famous tractor driver; she was awarded the Order of Lenin and her picture was published in *Pravda*. After her marriage she continued working for a while, but Borzov became jealous of her; later they bought a little house—Borzov wanted "a cosy home" and "quiet." "And that's how it went."

Ovechkin concludes with these lines: "For the time being, the story has no sequel, since it is being written almost from nature. . . . What decisions the Regional Committee will take concerning this district, how things will develop there, where the personal destinies of the characters introduced in the story will lead them—all this will have to be seen, observed in life. Perhaps it will, indeed, form the content of future chapters."

The major events of 1953—Stalin's death and the September plenum of the Central Committee of the All-Union Communist Party, which adopted a resolution to take energetic steps to counteract locally the catastrophic state of agriculture—helped the writer to continue his narrative, providing material for *At the Front Line* (1953), "In the Same District" (1954), *With One's Own Hands* (1954), and *A Difficult Spring* (1956).

Before proceeding to the contents of these works, it is important to examine Ovechkin's publicistic activity, since it permits a fuller understanding of the writer. Ovechkin took an active part in the preparations for the Second All-Union Writers' Congress in December 1954, and also delivered a speech at the Congress which produced a strong impression on the delegates. His speech was devoted to criticism of the main address by Alexey Surkov, the secretary of the Executive Committee of the Union, who spoke "On the Condition and Tasks of Soviet Literature."

Instead of carefully analyzing the state of Soviet literature and the reasons for the "lowering of criteria," Surkov lumped all the works of the preceding twenty years "into a single pile," and tried to draw up "averages." As a result of this operation, he gave this literature a mark of "good," or even "good plus." Nor was there any real "anxiety" in the speech of Konstantin Simonov, which was "moderately critical, moderately self-critical, moderately bold, and moderately cautious." "All proportions duly observed," as Ovechkin put it. And beyond the two speeches, there remained the "anxiety" of writers about the destinies of literature, and the appearance—especially during the most recent period—of "mediocre, dull-gray little books."

However, in touching upon so grave and painful a problem, Ovechkin himself had to exercise the utmost "caution" in searching out the reasons for these alarming facts. Among these reasons, Ovechkin assigns virtually first place to "the system of awarding Stalin Prizes," which is usually done hastily and without regard for the opinion of the wide reading public. As a result, he says, literature has been "infiltrated" by a number of people who supply only talentless, gray works, works which have no genuine connection with life.

Ovechkin does not level this accusation at the younger writers, the authors of "first books." These are either "recent newspapermen, who have traveled and seen a good deal, or else people with some trade or profession, who have worked and lived, and whose ties with the life of the people have never been broken." At the other end of the scale, there are the "veterans," those who were "the leaders at the time of the First Writers' Congress" (in 1934). Unfortunately, says Ovechkin, "Some of these have prematurely declared themselves old men and gone into retirement." They write very little, and yet they include some of "the greatest masters of the written word."

One might justifiably ask, then, who is to blame for the "lowering of criteria" in literature. Ovechkin puts this blame on some "middle generation," which has produced the "half-baked laureates" who occupy eminent posts in various organs of the Writers' Union. And it is members of this group who frequently accuse Ovechkin of preaching "asceticism and fanaticism" and of virtually urging a renewal of the old "movement into the people." No, says Ovechkin, he has no intention of urging writers to repeat the "going into the people" which took place in the '70s of the last century. Nevertheless, he thinks it might be useful to "move some of the writers from their well-warmed places in Moscow," where they even contrive to live in the same house "on Lavrushensky Lane" or in villas "in Peredelkino." As a result of this alienation from living reality, there are periodic "flounderings from side to side" and the substitution of "tar for varnish, and vice versa." A dispersion of such writers to "the periphery" would, in Ovechkin's view, help to strengthen their "party and civic conscience."

Ovechkin's words, it must be noted, produced a strong impression on the delegates, eliciting "prolonged applause" and finding further support in Sholokhov's speech. Reiterating some of Ovechkin's principal ideas, Sholokhov said that he alone had "brought a little animation" into "the pompous boredom and decorum of the congress."

Still more insight into Ovechkin's spiritual and literary character is provided by his speech at the All-Union Conference of Writers "Dealing with Kolkhoz Themes," held in October 1955. "Lately," said Ovechkin in this speech, "we talk so often about literature on rural themes that some people might become anxious that our entire literature may soon be transformed into a rural, peasant one. But no, our literature is not yet threatened by too much love of the peasant theme. We are threatened by the reverse: the abandonment of village themes, disregard for the most important problems and conflicts of our present-day life, the affairs of our kolkhoz construction."

In this connection Ovechkin drew attention to a certain interesting fact: which of the great pre-revolutionary writers, he asked, had not written about the village? The urbanite Dostoyevsky wrote "The Village of Stepanchikovo." Tolstoy, Turgenev, Nekrasov, Chekhov, Bunin, Gleb Uspensky, and Korolenko wrote about the village. They wrote about it when the village was in a state of dire poverty. Yet today, when its life is much more interesting, and when it involves "the chief of our most difficult and complex problems . . . there are fewer candidates among our writers to devote their attention to the village." Among the older contemporary writers we can name offhand only those who have not dealt with the kolkhoz village. The "old men" (with the sole exception of Sholokhov) have shunned the village theme, leaving it to the young writers. It is especially significant that "interest in the village" is shown by young people of the most diverse occupations, among them many inveterate city dwellers, and that this theme is by no means approached from the viewpoint of "summer visitors" or as a mere "writing assignment." Ovechkin points out that this literary youth "is tackling profoundly and in earnest this area in our literature which, if it cannot altogether be called virgin ground, is certainly ground which has not yet been properly cultivated, which has not been plowed deeply enough or thoroughly enough. . . . The young writers are turning to village themes with boldness and resolution."[1]

It is difficult to distinguish in the works which followed *District Workadays* (*At the Front Line*, 1953, and *With One's Own Hands*, 1954) between that which was prompted by life and that which is the product of Ovechkin's creative imagination. At any rate, in *At the Front Line*, Martynov is already the first secretary. His victory over Borzov was taken from life. This was the time when, following the September plenum of the Communist Party's Central Committee, it was decided to dampen the supervisory zeal of the party officials in the village. The continuation of this line found its reflection also in *With One's Own Hands*. Martynov sends his assistants to the lagging kolkhozes. Among the new characters the reader meets in these stories is the director of the Machine-Tractor Station, Dolgushin. He will play a central part in *A Difficult Spring* (1956). A metallurgical engineer and an old Communist, he approaches his assignment as a party order which must be carried out.

Dolgushin's work is complicated by the fact that he is entirely unfamiliar with agriculture and with the forms of struggle inside the kolkhoz leadership. But he learns about this intra-kolkhoz struggle very quickly from his meetings with the member Artyukhin, who has tried to fight "the bottle-gang which drinks away kolkhoz goods." Artyukhin has paid dearly for his efforts to expose these "crooks." First, they had set fire to the kolkhoz calf-stalls when Artyukhin was in charge of livestock breeding. There was a trial, and Artyukhin was fined many thousands of rubles. Artyukhin did not submit and wrote to Stalin, but his letter was intercepted at the local post office by his enemies, who avenged themselves by cutting the throat of his cow. After a succession of troubles he finally "knuckled down." However, he has not given in com-

[1] This speech was later published in the form of an article, "Kolkhoz Life and Literature," in *Novy Mir*, December 1955.

pletely, and is able to tell Dolgushin a great deal about the practices of the kolkhoz leadership. As a result, some of the kolkhoz members begin to think that it is high time to stop "backing the bad," and to begin "backing the good." Dolgushin likes the idea and calls a public party meeting of the kolkhoz, which ends with the election of a new kolkhoz leadership. But Dolgushin pays a heavy price for his popularity among the kolkhoz peasants: he is severely reprimanded by the district authorities for this meeting.

The second part of *A Difficult Spring* appeared the same year, and some chapters of the third part were published in *Pravda* on August 10 and 15, 1956. Dolgushin's position becomes still more difficult when the first secretary of the District Committee, Martynov, is seriously injured in an automobile accident and must spend several months in the hospital. His temporary substitute Medvedev is a self-seeker and a bureaucrat. He is disliked by the kolkhoz members; Dolgushin also sees through him from the first. But Medvedev cannot be caught "barehanded." He has a protector in the person of the second secretary of the Regional Committee, Maslennikov. Besides, the party officials generally are hostile toward Dolgushin: in five months he has received five reprimands from the regional authorities. Partly responsible for this also is his forthright character. When the second secretary of the Regional Committee, Maslennikov, comes to the Machine-Tractor Station, Dolgushin says to him directly: "One is amazed, on the one hand, if you forgive the expression, at the rotten-soft liberalism toward those who should be kicked out of the party, the scoundrels, the hangers-on . . . , and, on the other, at the energetic bossing around of people who work honestly . . . the crude, inflexible methods of direction." Dolgushin's indignant outburst provokes Maslennikov's anger: "You'd like the District Committee and the Regional Organization to give you no directives of any kind, you want complete freedom of action around here. You'll get no such thing, my dear Comrade Dolgushin!" And Medvedev obsequiously echoes him: "We have directed, and we'll go on directing! Nobody will be allowed to weaken the organizing and directing role of the party!"

Dolgushin's position becomes still more untenable when Martynov himself begins to entertain some doubts about him. Martynov notices that, as Dolgushin's popularity increases, some of the kolkhoz chairmen begin to visit him less frequently at the hospital. When he leaves the hospital, Martynov thinks, he will no longer be the "first man" in the district. He wonders how his future work with Dolgushin will proceed under these circumstances: "Two bears in one lair?" The second part of *A Difficult Spring* concludes with these secret anxieties.

In the chapters published in *Pravda*, Martynov has left the hospital and decides to have a frank talk with Krylov, the first secretary of the Regional Committee. In the course of this conversation Martynov asks him to place on the agenda of the next bureau meeting the question of releasing him from the duties of first secretary of his district. At first Krylov thinks that this request is motivated by Martynov's decision to return to journalism. But Martynov simply feels that Dolgushin will be more useful in the post of first secretary than he is. During their talk Maslennikov enters the room. He bursts out with an extremely unflattering characterization of Dolgushin, calling him a "rude, impudent man" who recognizes no authority.

This attack in turn provokes a sharp retort from Martynov. In essence, he says that the Maslennikovs and Medvedevs feel the tide has turned against them. "These are difficult times for you! The leadership is facing complex problems today. You can't get very far on general orders and shouting. And you don't know how to lead in any other way."

It was necessary to dwell at greater length on Ovechkin's stories because they acquaint the reader with the life of the post-Stalin kolkhoz village and show the intense struggle going on inside the lowest echelons of the party apparatus in the village.

Ovechkin's great popularity among the young writers

must be attributed to the powerful indictment expressed in his works. Martynov's notebook contains two lines from a poem by Nikolay Nekrasov:

> He who lives without sorrow and anger
> Does not love his native land.

Martynov wrote down these lines along with his most cherished thoughts and aspirations. Ovechkin tells us that, in his talk with the secretary of the Regional Committee, Martynov confesses: "It is very difficult to divide one from the other—the criticism of faults from the affirmation of what is good. They are interconnected. For example, I have never managed to write an article about something positive without, at the same time, flying into anger over the bad things that interfere with it. . . ."

This confession of Martynov-Ovechkin mirrors the feelings of many young writers, beginning with Dudintsev and ending with Vasily Aksyonov. And it is for his forthright statement of these feelings that Ovechkin is so widely admired by the young writers of the 1950s and '60s.

21 VICTOR NEKRASOV (1910–   )

Nekrasov's life is somewhat unusual, as we learn from his sketch "First Acquaintance" (*Novy Mir*, July–August 1958). The sketch records his impressions of Paris, where he was able to spend one day on his return journey from Italy in 1957. But Nekrasov was not entirely a stranger in Paris, where he had spent the first four years of his life. His parents were evidently *émigrés* from Czarist Russia. His mother had studied medicine at Lausanne University and later settled in Paris, where she worked in a hospital. The family had apparently returned to Russia at the outbreak of World War I. In Paris the Nekrasovs lived somewhere in the vicinity of Porte d'Orléans, and the boy had often played at the Montsouris Park with two other boys of Russian *émigré* families. Finding himself in Paris forty-two years later, the writer wished to verify his childhood memories and asked his guide to take him to the park. He recognized it at once and walked down its length, turning first to the left, then to the right, into a little street, Rue Rolly, where he had lived at Number 11. He also remembered buying candy in a small shop on the corner; the counter in the shop, as Nekrasov recalled, was so high that he had to rise on tiptoe and stretch his hand to put his coin on it. Everything was exactly as he remembered it, and though the shop was closed at that hour, Nekrasov saw and recognized the counter through the window. "But honestly," he adds, "it was much higher then." "A plague on memory," Nekrasov thought to himself. "Why should it preserve a little candy shop for forty years, when it discards much more important happenings of five, ten, and fifteen years ago?"

Nekrasov drew up the schedule for the single day he was able to spend in Paris with great care: it included a visit to the Louvre and an art exhibition, "From the Impressionists to the Present Day," the Hotel des Invalides, and the Grand Opéra. But in the end Nekrasov disregarded all this, "exchanging the treasures of the Louvre for the Paris streets," and strolling through the French capital all day without any plan. Evidently, he did not regret this.

From the same sketch we learn that Nekrasov had completed his higher education before World War II, graduating as an architect. From another article, "Great and Simple Words" (published in the magazine *Iskusstvo Kino* [Film Art], May 1959), we learn that, as a young man, Nekrasov auditioned as an actor for the Moscow Art Theatre (he appeared before Stanislavsky), but had evidently failed.

Nekrasov was mobilized at the very outbreak of the war and fought in it until the summer of 1944; he was wounded at Lublin and sent to the rear when he recovered, never returning to front-line duty.

In the Trenches of Stalingrad (at first titled *Stalingrad*) appeared in the September and October issues of *Znamya* in 1946. The narrative is in the name of Lieutenant Kerzhentsev, who describes the most difficult period of the war and the retreat, often virtually taking the form of flight, of many army units which lost contact with their command posts. The units stream across the Don region toward the Volga and Stalingrad. In its subject Nekrasov's novel is reminiscent of Simonov's *Days and Nights*, but this resemblance enhances rather than weakens its effect. Much of what Simonov sensed in the battle for Stalingrad with the intuition of an experienced writer and journalist, was learned by Nekrasov and his front-line comrades, much more profoundly, from personal experience. The drama of the unfolding struggle compels the author to forget his original intention of making Kerzhentsev his principal hero. Equal importance is often given to Kerzhentsev's friend Igor, a former student at the Art Institute; the Petty Officer Chumak; Valega, Kerzhentsev's orderly and a native of Altai—sullen and laconic, but a loyal man of sterling quality; and many others. Most of the characters are representatives of the younger Soviet intelligentsia from the provinces, and none of them had foreseen or prepared for the war. "They lived, studied, dreamed their own dreams, when—cr-rash!—and everything flew to pieces: home, family, school, history of architecture, Parthenons." All these became unnecessary; the only important thing now was to take a bridge and join the handful of men defending a certain mound. And Kerzhentsev recalls how, just recently, he sat here by the Volga, near Stalingrad, with a young girl, Lyucya, who was asking him whether he liked Blok's poetry: "Silly girl; she should have asked whether he *had liked* Blok—in the past tense." Yet, he had once liked Blok; but now, Kerzhentsev admits, what he likes most of all is "quiet." When the war ends, he will go to live somewhere on the bank of a quiet river; he will fish in the river, and in the evenings he will drink tea with raspberry jam, while his wife darns his socks nearby. "What could be better?"

Occasionally, between attacks, Kerzhentsev manages to glance into a book. Once he comes across Sergeev-Tsensky's novel *The Sevastopol Ordeal* (dealing with an important episode in the Crimean War of 1854–56); the author spoke of the huge losses of the Russian army: out of four thousand, "not more than a thousand" was left. The book dropped from his hands; Kerzhentsev's unit was only several dozen. As a child, Kerzhentsev liked to leaf through an English magazine of the World War I period. The most frightening thing in it was a picture of the Belgian city of Louvain burning after a German bombardment. But it was nothing when compared to burning Stalingrad: the city burns like the taiga, and only two colors can be seen—"the black silhouette of the city, the red sky and the red Volga." Kerzhentsev suddenly realizes acutely "the helplessness, the impotence of art." No words or pictures could convey his feelings at this moment, feelings shared by his friend Igor. But the two friends conceal their feelings from those around them, especially from Georgy Akimovich, an engineer of the Stalingrad tractor plant, whose duty it is, together with Kerzhentsev and his sappers, to blow up the plant with which his entire youth was linked. Georgy Akimovich is a pessimist, forever arguing with the young army men. He is convinced that "we don't know how to fight." When he is asked what it is to "know how," he answers: "To come all the way from Berlin to the Volga—that's knowing how." The young officers cry belligerently: "It also takes knowledge to retreat from the border to the Volga." This, however, does not assuage the engineer's pessimism. Only a year ago there was still the Ukraine, Kuban, oil; now all that is lost, along with vast territories inhabited by fifty million people. Georgy Akimovich knows that the Russians will fight "to the last soldier"; nevertheless, he feels that "only a miracle can save us."

In contrast to most of his contemporaries, Kerzhentsev is tolerant toward Georgy Akimovich, sensing the sincerity of his pain. He himself frequently thinks about a "miracle." And once indeed the "miracle" is revealed to him. This happens during a night watch. Kerzhentsev steps outside for a smoke. Several soldiers walk by, speaking in undertones; a few sing quietly a song about the Dnieper and about cranes. Then they sit down to rest by the roadside and Kerzhentsev overhears their conversation. A young voice argues fervently: "No, no, Vasya. . . . Don't say anything. . . . You'll never find better land than ours. It's true. . . . Like butter—rich, fat. . . ." The young soldier clicks his tongue in a special way to emphasize his words. "And when the grain comes up, it's over your head. . . ."

Kerzhentsev never sees the speaker, but there are "details" which remain with one for the rest of one's life, "sinking deep into the heart" and growing "into something big and significant and difficult to express." There is something in the soldiers' song heard in the night and in the simple words about the land, "fat as butter," about which Nekrasov says: "I don't even know what to call it. Tolstoy called it the hidden warmth of patriotism. Perhaps that is the truest definition. And this is the miracle so ardently awaited by Georgy Akimovich, a miracle stronger than German organization and their tanks with the black crosses."

In distinction to Simonov, who credits the "miracle" of the Stalingrad victory equally to the soldiers and the higher command, Nekrasov cannot, even at the hour of victory, forget the mistakes of the military leadership, for which the people paid with so many needlessly lost lives. It is not by chance therefore that in his story of the first day of the Stalingrad offensive (described with remarkable force), Nekrasov gives a great deal of space to the tragic conflict between the regiment's chief of staff Abrosimov and the regimental commander Major Borodin. Borodin issues one order, Abrosimov another; when the officers attempt to show Abrosimov that his order is impossible to carry out, he draws his revolver, threatening to shoot those who oppose him. The officers submit, but many people pay with their lives for Abrosimov's mistake. In the subsequent trial Borodin succeeds in proving Abrosimov's error, and the latter is demoted to a private.

It is probably because of this, as well as the general democratic feeling of the novel, that it did not please the literary powers. Their disapproval was quite transparently expressed in an article by Boris Solovyov, published in *Izvestia* on November 29, 1946, in which the critic tried to prove that Nekrasov's novel, though not devoid of literary merit, was merely the testimony of a "participant in a battle" who had no conception of "the strategy of the war as a whole."

Nekrasov's article "Three Encounters," published in *Novy Mir* (December 1959), is exceptionally revealing of the writer's literary approach and his personality. The article is devoted to Valega, Nekrasov's favorite character in his novel. The author met the real Valega not in Stalingrad, but later, in March 1944, when the Soviet troops were already attacking along the Southern Bug. His last meeting with Valega was when the latter visited the wounded Nekrasov in a hospital near Lublin. On first acquaintance Nekrasov was not too favorably impressed with the orderly assigned to him. When asked whether he wished to serve as Nekrasov's orderly, Valega made a gloomy reply, indicating that he was not overjoyed at the prospect. It was only later, when he came to know Valega better, that Nekrasov began to understand him: after fighting throughout the battle of Stalingrad as a sapper, he felt it "humiliating to become a servant." He was in reality just as the writer portrayed him in his novel: sullen, sparing of words, but devoted, fond of work and a master of all trades. When he visited the wounded Nekrasov, his whole bearing expressed disapproval: he felt that no such thing would have happened to his officer if he had been with him at the time. Saying good-by to his visitor, Nekrasov wanted to embrace and kiss him, but Valega disliked all "sentiments": he pressed the writer's sound hand and wished him speedy recovery. Nekrasov never saw him again; after recovering he was sent to the rear and never returned to the front.

The second encounter with Valega—this time imaginary —took place in Moscow in 1946, when Nekrasov was writing his novel *In the Trenches of Stalingrad*. He parted with him again when he delivered the manuscript to the editors of the magazine *Znamya*.

The third "encounter" took place almost ten years later, in Leningrad, in the studio of Lenfilm, for which Nekrasov had written a scenario, *Soldiers*. Nekrasov made a special trip to Stalingrad, visiting the ancient Mamay burial mound and other places where the battle had raged in the autumn of 1942. The film was a difficult one to make, and the most difficult part was that of Valega. At first sight it seemed that Valega had nothing to do in the scenario; his role was very small—only seven short scenes. In five of them Valega was silent, and only two of the scenes called for a few brief words. The writer felt somehow guilty before Valega, but the situation was saved by Yury Solovyov, a graduate of the All-Union State Institute of Cinematography to whom the role of Valega was assigned. The young actor captured the essence of the "living" Valega, never having seen him. He read and reread the scenario many times. The "real" Valega never smiled; he was always busy and never had time "for smiles." In one scene, in which Valega listened to Karnaukhov singing a song, Valega-Solovyov "only swallowed once," as if his throat had contracted with emotion, and then he spoke his first words in the film: when the war was over, he would build a house for himself in the woods—he loved the woods—and the Comrade Lieutenant would visit him for three weeks. "Why three?" asked the lieutenant, and Valega replied: "You won't be able to stay longer, you'll be working." Watching this episode in the film, Nekrasov was moved almost to tears because the incident had occurred in reality. One night in the forest near Kovel, Valega had said in a commanding tone, "And you will visit me for three weeks. . . ."

Yury Solovyov and Valega "became real friends," writes Nekrasov, "and their friendship strengthened mine still further." He goes on to quote a passage from Yury Solovyov's letter, describing the actor's work on the character of Valega, whom he had never seen, under front-line conditions, which he had never known. At first, Solovyov tried to "squeeze himself into" the Valega of the book and the scenario, but nothing came of that. Then he searched for other ways, finding them in relation to his own experience. He borrowed his father's heavyish, somewhat swaying gait (although, in Nekrasov's words, Valega had "the soft, silent tread of a hunter"); Valega's constant frown was taken from a man Solovyov was not even acquainted with —a driver talking to a militiaman after his car was damaged in an accident. . . . To the question, which of the three Valegas Nekrasov likes best, he finds it difficult to reply; he can only say that he is fond of Valega.

By his novel *In the Trenches of Stalingrad*, Nekrasov established himself as a talented writer. In his second novel, *In the Native City*, he refuted with considerable courage the hypocritical assertions of the official publicists that, in contrast to the West, Soviet society has no problem of a so-called "lost generation." This novel appeared in the October and December issues of *Novy Mir* in 1954.

It opens in the last period of World War II. The Ukraine has already been liberated, and Captain Nikolay Mityasov, who is recovering from severe wounds, returns to his native Kiev. The "home-coming," of which Lieutenant Kerzhentsev had dreamed so often in the trenches of Stalingrad, disappoints Mityasov. The house where he had lived before the war with his wife Shura was demolished by bombs. Learning Shura's new address, Mityasov goes there and waits in the communal kitchen for her return. A talkative little boy who lives in the same house tells him that Shura is living with an "Uncle Fedya." Mityasov leaves without seeing his wife. Since his wounds have not yet healed completely, the question of where to live is solved very simply: he goes to the hospital. Considerably more difficult is the problem of what to do next. Its difficulty is emphasized by a chance acquaintance with a former army pilot, Lieutenant Sergey Yeroshik, whom Nikolay meets in a tearoom. Sergey introduces himself as "a man without a profession": he lost a leg in the war, and since nobody needs legless fliers, his "biography is generally finished." Nevertheless, his material situation is not too bad. Sergey "knocks about" from place to place, selling slippers made by a cooperative group of war-invalids in Rostov. Traveling presents no problem: his artificial leg assures him of transportation. Despite Sergey's exaggeratedly easy manner, Mityasov senses in him at once the kindred soul of a front-line man. He asks whether Sergey is married. No, Sergey answers, he never married. And then, Mityasov tells this total stranger the whole story of his former relations with Shura and the intrusion into their marriage of an "Uncle Fedya." Sergey secretly finds Shura's address, visits her, and discovers how this "Uncle Fedya" came into her life. "Uncle Fedya" was a member of the Soviet army which made the first breakthrough into Kiev. Fedya was seriously wounded in the fighting, and, since the hospitals were overcrowded, he was brought to the apartment where Shura lived. She nursed him back to health. Eventually, although Shura was older than

Fedya, the two young people, sharing the same room, were drawn into a more intimate relationship.

Lying in the hospital, Mityasov reads a great deal. He gets his books at the library. The librarian is a pleasant old woman, very reminiscent of the one that appears in Nekrasov's first book, *In the Trenches of Stalingrad*. When he leaves the hospital, Mityasov gets a room in the communal apartment where the old librarian lives with her daughter Valya, who had also served at the front. Mityasov has become very friendly with the old librarian, a typical representative of the pre-revolutionary intelligentsia. He also quickly finds a common language with Valya: it is easy to talk to her, recalling life at the front and the good friends of those days. Valya, on the other hand, is the first to make him understand the meaning of his attachment to this former army life: he discovers that he is drawn to it not so much by the desire to fight, as by fear of postwar civilian life.

Mityasov patches up his relations with Shura and moves in with her, but soon he begins to suffer once more from a sense of emptiness. Deciding to return to school and enter a building institute, he makes his final break with Shura and goes to live in the student dormitory. Almost the entire second half of the novel deals with the life and moods of the young people back from the war. Mityasov, as the senior member of his group, is elected *starosta* or "elder." In his group there are five ex-soldiers. Only one of them, who had gone into the army at the age of seventeen, finds it relatively easy to make himself at home in postwar life. The rest have difficulty in adjusting to the new conditions.

One evening "an unexpected and rather strange" conversation takes place between Mityasov and Khokhryakov, the secretary of the party bureau of the department. Khokhryakov is sitting before the stove, throwing wood into the fire. Mityasov sits down nearby. Several days before this, Mityasov had a sharp quarrel with the dean, in the course of which he slapped the dean. The party bureau decided to propose Mityasov's expulsion from the party at the next general meeting. Khokhryakov voted against it, urging a strong reprimand instead. As they sit before the fire, Mityasov looks up at Khokhryakov and asks: "Why are you all afraid of him?" (referring to the dean). He adds at once that his question is not prompted by injured vanity; he is simply at a loss to understand the fear. Khokhryakov does not answer. After a while he asks whether Mityasov had been in the army during the taking of Berlin. Mityasov replies that he had not; he was severely wounded in 1944 (like Nekrasov himself) and sent to the rear. He had not been in Berlin either, Khokhryakov says quietly. But he heard many people say that the last days of fighting were the hardest—hardest because everyone knew that the war would be over in a matter of days, and nobody wanted to die, not even those who had fought with such courage in Stalingrad and Sevastopol. At the approaches to Berlin even these fearless men began to be afraid and to "hug the ground."

On the following day, when he is alone, Nikolay suddenly thinks, "What if this nostalgia for the front is also a sort of 'hugging of the ground'?"

Nekrasov has tied and untied many "knots" in his novel. Nor did he ignore the conflict between true scientists and people who were merely "making an academic career." This conflict was also dealt with in the novels of V. Dobrovolsky and Yury Trifonov. These earlier writers, however, always wrote with a cautious look over the shoulder at the official critics.

Nekrasov presents this conflict in a new form. Before the war, Captain Chekmen had worked as an instructor in an institute. On his return from the front he obtains an appointment as dean of his old department and soon demonstrates his administrative talents. The fly in his ointment, it appears, is the presence on the faculty of the old Professor Nikoltsev, who is highly popular with the students. Chekmen plots to dismiss him and replace him by one of his war comrades. To justify the dismissal, Chekmen resorts to an argument that was fairly widespread during the early postwar years: he recalls that Nikoltsev spent almost three years under German occupation.

"They say," insinuates Chekmen, "that he refused some job or other that was offered him in the building administration. Maybe it's true. But why did he refuse? Who knows? Who can tell us about it? People who themselves remained under the Germans? Forgive me, but I don't trust such people. And what did he live on? They say he was selling his books. Well, if you pardon me, I don't believe it. . . ."

At this point Mityasov slaps Chekmen. Only three or four years earlier, people involuntarily "hugged the ground" when confronted with such arguments. Stalin's death brought a change in this respect. The extent of the change is evidenced by the sympathy which this slap elicited even among Soviet critics. Thus, in her article "Mityasov and Chekmen" (*Literary Gazette*, March 26, 1955), Yulia Kapusto does not conceal her fervent approval of Nekrasov and his approach to the problems of postwar life. Certainly, she says, the war is over, but "the battle goes on in our own life." It takes courage to fight the enemy at the front, but it takes equal courage to discern "an enemy in a member of the party and its bureau, the former Captain Chekmen, one's own dean at school. . . ."

It scarcely needs saying that this article, which so outspokenly supported Nekrasov's treatment of the slapping incident, was sharply attacked by the official critics. One of them, Nikolay Panov, responded to Nekrasov's novel and Kapusto's comment with an article of his own, under the caustic title "Wingless People" (*Literary Gazette*, April 19, 1955). Nekrasov's principal error, he wrote, was the depiction of Mityasov and Sergey Yeroshik as "positive heroes." Their defense by Yulia Kapusto, he went on, was a "poor service both to the readers and the author."

In this connection we may return again to Nekrasov's article "Great and Simple Words." In it Nekrasov criticized the film *A Poem about the Sea*, made by the late director Alexander Dovzhenko, for the pompous utterances of the leading hero, General Fedorchenko. This general called himself immortal and a "lucky man," characterizing everything he did as "splendid." Nekrasov mentally addressed the general, asking: "Ah, Comrade General, is everything you feel and do really so splendid? Isn't it a bit too early to declare yourself lucky? Haven't you become too much of a gentleman yourself?" Nekrasov gives all his praise to another film, *Two Fyodors*, made by the young director Marlen Khutsiev. He is impressed with the reserved laconicism and sullenness of its principal hero, Fyodor, whom he would have liked to meet. It is said, observes Nekrasov, that there is no "lost generation" in the Soviet Union. But "haven't we had enough young fellows who had learned only two things by the age of seventeen or eighteen—to kill and not to let themselves be killed, and nothing else?" And what could they have felt "when this was no longer necessary?" Nekrasov advises Soviet readers to read Remarque. Despite the flaws in the scenario of the *Two Fyodors*, Nekrasov prefers it to Dovzhenko's film: "Its heroes don't speak much; but when they are silent, I know what they think." Nekrasov recalls a comment on his novel *In the Native City* by a certain "responsible comrade" in the Ministry of Culture who was asked to evaluate the novel with a view to making it into a motion picture. The "responsible comrade" decided that a scenario in which a soldier back from the front "lands his fist on a dean's physiognomy . . . won't do," and that the book was therefore unsuitable for filming.

The most important of Nekrasov's recent works is the novel *Kira Georgievna* (*Novy Mir*, July 1961). Kira is a talented sculptor with a rather complicated life history. At eighteen she met and fell in love with Vadim Kudryavtsev, a student of twenty. They lived together for a year before he was arrested and sent to a concentration camp. From the camp he wrote her that she should consider herself free. The story opens twenty years later, when, after Stalin's death, Vadim returns. Although both Kira and Vadim are now married to others, they resume their relationship. The novel is especially interesting because Nekrasov was the first Soviet writer to look into the inner world of a man who was an innocent victim of Stalinist terror, but who has managed to preserve his integrity and vitality.

Although by age Nekrasov might be classified a member of the middle generation of Soviet writers, he is closer in spirit to the younger writers, and most of all to Dudintsev, whom he resembles in the sincerity and boldness of his approach to the problems of contemporary life.

22 VLADIMIR DUDINTSEV (1918–   )

Vladimir Dudintsev, author of the novel *Not by Bread Alone*, which created such a stir both in the Soviet Union and abroad, belongs to the generation of writers whose early youth was suddenly interrupted by World War II. The biographies of most of these writers are almost unavailable. They were not yet sufficiently well known to be included in the two-volume *Soviet Writers* (Moscow, 1959); on the other hand, they are still far from the age when a man is impelled to glance back and talk about his life. However, Dudintsev's biography is told by the German writer Gerd Ruge, who visited the Soviet Union in the spring of 1958. In Moscow, Ruge met three writers —Alexey Surkov, Ilya Ehrenburg, and Vladimir Dudintsev. These three meetings are described in an article, "A Visit with Soviet Writers," in the September 1958 issue of the German magazine *Der Monat*.

Ruge's impression from his conversation with Dudintsev was that *Not by Bread Alone* was not a chance product and that Dudintsev had evidently foreseen the effect it would produce on Soviet readers. In the course of the long interview Ruge was able to learn a good deal about the writer that casts further light on his work.

Dudintsev, who was born in 1918, began to write seriously when he was only thirteen, but his first poem, for which his father rewarded him with a present, was written at the age of six. His schoolmates and teachers regarded him as a prodigy.

Dudintsev's love for literature came early. Such love often takes the form of infatuation: the reader seems to discover writers and to fall in love with them; after a while the feeling passes, and he finds new objects. In the beginning the young Dudintsev was more interested in form than in content. One of his first infatuations was with Isaac Babel; then came Marcel Proust and Boris Pasternak. Twice he was the captive of Anatole France: as a young boy, and later, as an adult. The American writers Dudintsev admired were Hemingway and Dos Passos. Prerevolutionary Russian literature left him cold at first. He felt that Tolstoy was outdated and Dostoyevsky unreadable. It was not until later, he says, that he understood why he had been repelled by Dostoyevsky. Dostoyevsky is not a writer for the young: his work is too traumatic. Only an adult can appreciate his writing, with its true humanity and suffering born of compassion.

It was only as an adult, also, that Dudintsev came to understand the special character of Russian literature. The Russian, typically, ponders a great deal over his destiny. This has determined his literature as well—its form, its content, and its passionate desire to help suffering man. Its writers look for a sword and find a pen.

Dudintsev was born into an intellectual and musical family; his father was a surveyor who had hoped in his youth to become a singer; his mother had been an opera singer. At a school concert the boy was sought out by a writer for *Pionerskaya Pravda* and invited to contribute to the newspaper. But Dudintsev soon came to feel that "they" were trying to press him into becoming "one of them," and he began to resist. This resistance continued in his adult life. "Six days in the week they scold me," Dudintsev remarked to Ruge, "and on the seventh they sometimes praise me." Dudintsev's first poem was published in 1931. After that his poems and stories began to appear in print. At the age of sixteen he won a prize in a literary contest.

Despite his keen interest in literature, Dudintsev's choice at the university was not literature, but law. Working as a lawyer, he thought, would enable him to gather more material for his writing. During the Soviet-German war he was mobilized, and was wounded in 1942. Upon recovering he was assigned to a military court in Siberia. During the war he wrote very little. When it ended, he went to live in Moscow, where he became a roving correspondent for *Comsomolskaya Pravda*. After his story "A Meeting with a Birch," Dudintsev felt he could no longer write "to order"; he had found his link with the Russian literary tradition, and felt the need to write in such a way as to help people become imbued with "intransigence toward evil, and love of good."

Not by Bread Alone was conceived by Dudintsev in 1950; he spent a long time thinking about its plot, and did not begin to write it until 1955. In 1958 he told Ruge that he was at work on another book, but declined to reveal its subject. Ruge's words about Dudintsev's moral credo are revealing: "Rational thinking," said Dudintsev, "is not enough. We must begin with the ethical, following in Kant's footsteps: 'The starry sky above me, and inner law within me'—but outside the reality of speculative thought. This does not mean that I subscribe wholly to Kantian philosophy."

Toward the end of the interview Dudintsev touched upon the charge, frequently made in the West, that Soviet writers are "primitive." He disagreed, suggesting that this impression might be due in part to poor translations. The translators, he said, often condense phrases, deleting images that seem unnecessary to them. But to the writer images and similes are analogous to musical "overtones" or "short waves"; they help him to convey the nuances of meaning and emotion. In condensing sentences at the expense of such images, the translators impoverish the text of the original.

The forerunner of *Not by Bread Alone* was the story "In Its Place," published in *Novy Mir* in 1953. Its action is laid in the Siberian backwoods, in a phosphorite combine. Its principal heroes are two young workers, Vasya Gazukin and Fedya Gusarov. Vasya loves and values money above all else: "Why the devil are we roasting here? For the sake of what?" But Fedya argues that there are interests in the world "higher than money." Fedya has been known since childhood as a "dreamer," and he lives like a "rolling stone." When he first came to the phosphorite combine, he began to feel that at last his dream of "some significant work" was becoming a reality. He was appointed director of the workers' club. The club at that time was little more than a name: it was still only an unheated barrack, but Fedya envisioned the various groups that would be active in it, the library, and the stage for future dramatic production.

Working at the combine, Fedya has also learned to know love. True, his love is unrequited; the woman engineer, Antonina Sergeevna, loves another. But even this is accepted by Fedya, who has attained the understanding that genuine love is a value in itself; it fears "neither daylight, nor envious judgment." The arguments between Fedya and Vasya Gazukin are illuminating. Vasya has also fallen in love, but he wants to win the girl—by his high output, by his fame as a fast worker. Fedya, on the other hand, says that this only demeans love: the important thing is to be a "real human being." And he cites Giordano Bruno as an example of a real human being: "What do you think," he says to Vasya, "suppose some beauty came and said to Giordano, 'Recant and I'll be yours!'? Do you think he would have given up his theory? For the sake of love? Never. Because such a man does not belong to himself any more. He belongs entirely to his work. . . ." The central idea of the story is expressed in the words of the carpenter Samobayev: "If you want to do good, you must not think about yourself in any way at all."

The action of *Not by Bread Alone* (first published in *Novy Mir*, August, September, and October 1956) unfolds at first in the Siberian province, in the small town of Muzga; later it is carried to Moscow. One of the principal characters of the novel is the director of the local combine, Leonid Ivanovich Drozdov. The novel opens with a description of Drozdov's return to Muzga from Moscow, where he had gone on business related to the combine. He was accompanied by his beautiful young wife, the local schoolteacher, Nadezhda Sergeevna. Both Drozdov and his wife are in excellent spirits. In Moscow, Drozdov was given hints that he was about to be given a post in the capital;

and Nadya is pleased with her purchases. The splendid weather, the sun and snow enhance their mood, and they decided to "take a walk" home from the station.

But from the first pages, the author gives us to understand that his heroes are not simple. At one point Nadya asks Drozdov why they are so lonely, why Drozdov seems to have no friends. Her husband explains: "We are now serious people, many-faceted. The further we go, the more facets. A simple key will no longer fit us." He also says that a friend must be "independent," but the people surrounding them are all his subordinates: "Some are envious, others afraid, some are on guard, others are looking out for benefits. We are in isolation, my dear. Complete isolation. And the higher we move up, the more absolute this isolation will become."

To Nadya, who as a girl had been an avid reader of Jack London, Drozdov seemed to resemble the prospector for gold in London's *Burning Daylight*. She had dreamed of meeting a hero, "a man capable of unifying the energies of thousands of people—capricious, indifferent, touchy, and demanding." In their very first conversation after their wedding Drozdov rejected everything Nadya had been taught from childhood. He told her that all of it was "Nineteenth century. Fine Literature." First you must build a house, and then you can begin to "hang up little pictures and decorative plates." Drozdov regards himself merely as a "hard worker." He feels that he is not only a capable administrator, but also quite an intelligent man. This is expressed, to begin with, in his ability to understand himself. He puts himself in the category of men of the "transitional period." Such people, he says, have many faults, "relics of the past." He is also "ambitious" and cannot imagine how anyone could work without this incentive. He delights in his successes, regarding them as testimony to his ability, but he is clearly aware that in an established Communist society there would be no place for him: "I am all overgrown, encrusted with scale and barnacles." As a *builder* of communism, however, Drozdov feels that he is in his element. Since he is a man of contradictions, he needs "a shell, like a snail." And his "shell" is his "firm will."

In logical argument Drozdov is the invariable winner, but Nadya always defeats him in "the argument of feeling." Although superficially she seems, and considers herself, a happy woman, Nadya is not really happy. As time goes on, she becomes more and more critical of Drozdov. Soon this feeling is reinforced still further. One of the other residents of Muzga is the inventor Dmitry Lopatkin, whom Nadya had known before her marriage and with whom she had even been a little in love. Lopatkin had once taught at the same school with her. When the war broke out, he was mobilized. Afterward he returned to his teaching post, but left it when he developed his design for a new pipe-casting machine.

In the beginning Drozdov was sympathetic to Lopatkin's project, but soon his attitude changed. Lopatkin's design, submitted to the Ministry in Moscow for evaluation, was seriously criticized by the Ministry expert, Professor Avdiev, and his closest aides. The Deputy-Minister, Shutikov, also rejected the design. However, while the blueprints were at the Ministry, one of the Ministry employees had time to examine them; borrowing the basic idea of the new design, he sketched out his own substitute, which met with Avdiev's approval. From then on, Drozdov, being a man who avoided conflict with his superiors, lost interest in Lopatkin's work. Drozdov feels that an idea, if it is a correct one, eventually begins to live independently, "and seeks out the strong man who will assure its fulfillment." In Drozdov's opinion Lopatkin is not such a "strong man"; he is only a "mad eccentric," a "Marsian." Nadya is indignant at her husband's reasoning, although at first, against her own conscience, she echoed some of his judgments concerning Lopatkin.

Despite all failures and obstacles, Lopatkin does not surrender and continues to fight for his project. At first he has only a few supporters, all of them people without any influence. The greatest moral support comes from the worker Syanov, in whose home he lives as a roomer. Without Lopatkin's noticing it Syanov and his wife supplement his meager diet. It is at their house that Nadya Drozdova meets him again, when she comes to ask the mother of her pupil, Sima Syanov, to release the girl from the burden of housework. Lopatkin is also helped by the local English teacher, Valentina Pavlovna, who always manages to obtain for him the expensive Whatman paper he needs in his work. Lopatkin is deeply touched by this Whatman paper; one day he tells Valentina Pavlovna that he will never forget those who believed in him when he had no support whatever from the powers that be.

That Whatman paper becomes the cause of a sharp clash between Nadya and Drozdov. She is indignant when she learns that the combine refuses to issue any paper to Lopatkin. Drozdov tries to defend himself, explaining to his wife that the difficulties arise from the fact that Lopatkin is only "an individual artisan." If he were a member of a "collective," he would not lack either Whatman paper or anything else he might need for his work on the design.

Even Zhanna, whom Lopatkin loves, is critical of him. She returns his love, but is afraid to tie herself to such an obstinate dreamer and failure. Nevertheless, he does not yield and goes to Moscow to try to advance his cause. There Lopatkin's steadfastness and faith win him several allies among the staff of the Bureau of Design. They recognize in him a very important quality, "breakthrough power," which must in the end assure success.

In Moscow, Lopatkin meets and finds encouragement from the former professor Busko, a lonely and rejected inventor like himself. They share quarters and their meager food. He is also aided secretly by Nadya Drozdova, who has just moved to Moscow with her husband. Although at times it seems that Lopatkin's project has a chance of winning, the bureaucratic apparatus is too strong; its members connive to charge Lopatkin with revealing confidential information and succeed in getting him exiled to a remote province. Nevertheless, in the end, with the help of several influential friends of whose existence Lopatkin is almost unaware, he emerges victorious in the unequal struggle.

The success of the novel hastened the advent of the usual "critical workout." Soon after the first voices of praise were heard at a meeting in the Central House of Writers in Moscow, *Pravda*, *Izvestia*, and the magazine *Kommunist* moved their entire arsenal of stock accusations against Dudintsev. The most serious of these was the charge of inordinate admiration for "individualism."

Among the reasons for the novel's tremendous success in the Soviet Union we must cite its complex "subtext." Of considerable importance in this subtext was the bold title *Not by Bread Alone*, taken from the reply of Jesus to the devil's threat to turn bread into stone if Jesus persisted in fighting him.

Very serious criticism was leveled at the novel at the plenary meeting of the Executive of the Moscow Branch of the U.S.S.R. Writers' Union (*Literary Gazette*, March 19, 1957). This meeting was devoted essentially to only two subjects: the "errors" of the second volume of the anthology *Literary Moscow* (1956), and Dudintsev's novel. However, the author was permitted to address the meeting himself. Dudintsev spoke twice, but the report contains only one of his speeches. In the course of it Dudintsev related how he conceived and developed the novel:

"I remember the first days of the Patriotic War. I was lying in a trench, while an aerial battle raged overhead, with 'Messerschmidts' knocking out our planes, which were considerably more numerous. At that moment something began to break inside me, for I had always heard until then that our air force was faster and better than any other.

"It is said that I tend to 'blacken' reality. This is not true. I simply do not want to see a repetition of what I saw then. And I have a right not to want it."

It is enough to read this speech carefully to realize that Dudintsev, far from admitting his "guilt," was in fact on the offensive. This was especially clear in that part of the speech in which the writer expressed his doubt of the possibility of genuine "creative discussions," and described the critic as a man who was "menacingly banging his crutch." "I think," said Dudintsev, "that we might be permitted, like young swimmers, to try some swimming on our own—perhaps we shall not drown! But, alas, I constantly feel upon myself a leash, such as small children are sometimes led on. And it interferes with my swimming. . . ."

It is scarcely necessary to describe the disapproval with which the meeting responded to Dudintsev's speech.

Nevertheless, the extent of Dudintsev's popularity in the Soviet Union may be judged indirectly from Vasily Litvinov's article "Let Us Talk Substantively" (*Literary Gazette*, October 10, 1957). The article was written on the occasion of the founding of the Writers' Union of the R.S.F.S.R. Supporting the need for this Union, the author stresses that the principal function of the new organization should be ideological. It is essential, says he, to intensify the struggle "for the party line in literature," for in recent times the "nihilists" have invaded Soviet literature much too frequently. "For the sake of future books, the comrades in the Urals were compelled to give serious battle to homegrown 'nihilists.' In another city, in the south, it was necessary to check the zealous demagogues set on discovering 'their own Dudintsev'—even inventing him, if need be— just to 'keep up with the center.' . . ."

The main secret of the success of Dudintsev's novel lies in its hero's instransigence in his fight against stultifying bureaucracy and for the right to creative individuality.

However, the period of 1957–59 was not an easy one for Dudintsev. His name disappeared from the pages of the literary journals. This exile lasted until the Third Congress of Soviet Writers in May 1959. Khrushchev's address at this Congress mitigated to some extent the ostracism to which Dudintsev had been subjected.

Khrushchev said in his speech that *Not by Bread Alone* had been recommended to him by Mikoyan, who told him: "Read it, some of the arguments here might have been borrowed directly from you." (This, incidentally, was not altogether prudent of Mikoyan, since Khrushchev had indeed voiced some ideas that seem to echo Drozdov!) Khrushchev read Dudintsev's book with interest, and even confessed that the author "has clearly caught certain negative facts." The only trouble was that he exaggerated "the negative aspects of Soviet Life." Despite this, Khrushchev felt that Dudintsev "has never been our enemy or an opponent of the Soviet regime." In fact, after he read the novel, he had a wish to meet Dudintsev, but somehow "there was never time." Khrushchev's speech, the report of the meeting tells us, was followed by "animation in the hall."

In this connection it would not be amiss to touch briefly on L. Ovalov's novel *Party Assignment*, published in the July 1959 issue of the magazine *Moskva*, which also carried the text of Khrushchev's address at the Third Writers' Congress. The novel contains an interesting episode, which casts some light on the extent of Dudintsev's popularity. The chairman of the Donetsk Sovnarkhoz, Kuznetsov, visits Moscow on official business. The authorities in the capital show no undue haste to satisfy his requests, and Kuznetsov becomes angrier and angrier. Then Prokhorov, the ministry official who is most immediately concerned with the work of the Donetsk Sovnarkhoz, remarks to him: "Another disappointment or two, and you'll begin to talk altogether like Dudintsev." Kuznetsov admits that he does not recall Dudintsev, and asks where he works. Prokhorov replies with astonishment that Dudintsev is not working anywhere; he is the author of a novel that "all Moscow" is talking about. When Kuznetsov asks what the novel is about, he is told: "About me, about you, about bureaucracy." With great difficulty Kuznetsov's personal secretary manages to obtain from a librarian the issues of the magazine which contain the novel. . . . It is doubtful whether Ovalov could have told this story before Khrushchev's speech at the Third Writers' Congress.

At any rate, the attitude toward Dudintsev softened following Khrushchev's speech, and, after a silence of almost three years, his *New Year's Fable* appeared in the January 1960 issue of *Novy Mir*. The action of the fable takes place on a mysterious planet, created by the author's imagination. One side of the planet is never lighted by the sun, but the hours on the planet are checked "by the signals of Moscow time." The theme of the fable is "the tricks time plays on us." An important role in it is played by a mysterious man-sized owl, which only a few people see. The owl is the symbol of time.

The story is told in the first person. On the advice of an academician of his acquaintance, the narrator has trained himself to write down his thoughts. But the woman who heats the stoves in the laboratory where he works uses the papers she finds in his desk to kindle the fire, and his notes "flare like gunpowder." One day the narrator receives a visit from a mysterious owl, and soon he begins to feel some curious changes taking place within him. Formerly, his existence was poisoned by a certain S., a Corresponding Member of the Academy, who once contemptuously labeled a well-known work of his "the fruit of idle fancies." After the owl's appearance the narrator becomes indifferent to his enemy.

One morning the chief of the laboratory staff, who spends his leisure hours studying antiquity, reports an interesting discovery: he has found a stone tablet in his garden bearing the image of an owl and an inscription which he succeeded in deciphering: it consisted of someone's name, followed by the words, "And his age was nine hundred." One of the staff members expresses envy of such longevity, and a discussion ensues about the nature of time. "Time is an enigma," says someone. The chief takes an hourglass from the wall and demonstrates to everyone that "time flows." A moment may be compared to a grain of sand which slips to the bottom of the hourglass, leaving no trace. The personnel manager questions the idea: if the passing moment left no trace, it would mean that "we have no heroic past" and no "sunny future," with which the entire work of the laboratory is concerned. "After all," he says, "we have a certain framework. . . ." Here, the usually most silent staff member, a shaggy eccentric, breaks in to say that "the new, which we are seeking," is almost always found outside the framework of the customary.

The sharply posed problem provokes a debate. The

shaggy eccentric insists that time not only can "fly" or move slowly, but it also can "stand still." He tells of some lotus seeds found in an ancient sepulcher, where they had lain two thousand years. Yet a scientist succeeded in growing plants from those seeds. For the seeds, therefore, time had "stood still." The participants in the discussion fail to see the connection between their chief's discovery and the abstract generalizations of their eccentric colleague. Then he tells them a story.

Several years previously, he says, a hundred-odd well-dressed men met in a Park of Culture. This was a congress of bandits, belonging to a society bound by its own laws. At their congress the bandits passed death sentences on six members who had broken their "laws." Five of these sentences were executed. The sixth man escaped death only because he was imprisoned at the time in some provincial jail. This man was the "president," the leader of the bandits. During his stay in prison he thought and read a great deal, and reached conclusions that surprised even himself. He had always felt that the entire meaning of life consisted in appropriating other people's wealth; now he suddenly understood that things in themselves were of no value, that the greatest values were "spiritual beauty" and the approval, friendship, and love of fellow men. He wrote to his "law-bound" comrades about his discoveries and announced his resignation as their president. He passionately longed to achieve everything he had missed in life. He escaped from prison, changed his appearance beyond recognition, and worked days and nights trying to catch up on what he had missed. In three years he managed to graduate from two institutes. He had conceived a great idea and wanted to make a gift to mankind. The laboratory in which he is working today is occupied with the problem of obtaining a condensation of sunlight strong enough to provide bright sunshine and warmth for the inhabitants of the distant continent on the dark side of their planet that never sees the sun. The shaggy eccentric (who is now recognized by the narrator of the *New Year's Fable* as the former bandit leader) is completely engrossed in this problem. But he feels that his days are numbered. And, indeed, several days after he tells his story in the laboratory, he is found with mortal knife wounds in his body. He dies the same day. Sensing his imminent death, the eccentric bequeaths the narrator his bulb-watch and a letter. These are delivered by a young woman, who loved the late bandit. Shaken by all these events, the narrator visits his old friend, a neuropathologist, who tells him that he has only one year left to live. When he leaves his friend, the narrator looks up at the starry sky and thinks: "Very well, the flesh will die. Let it die. But thought, thought! Will it vanish too?" "I will not vanish," answers his thought in the darkness.

The soul of the dead bandit seems to have entered the narrator's body; he begins to work feverishly. The woman who loved the bandit transfers her feelings to him, certain that her lover has not perished, but is reincarnated in the narrator. Although the work progresses rapidly, the narrator's strength is ebbing visibly. Nevertheless, he manages to bring his task to completion. He is so weak now that he seems to be dying when he hears the first planes taking off for the dark continent with their precious load of condensed warmth and sunshine. And then he suddenly begins to recover his strength. One day he glances at the window sill where the mysterious owl had sat, and sees it is no longer there. Only "far, far away in the pale blue sky a large bird was flying toward the horizon, heavily flapping its wings." A new life begins for the narrator: "the ocean of time" is splashing at his feet. . . .

If we eliminate the story's somewhat ponderous embellishment of fantasy, we can easily discern in it the values that Dudintsev has cherished from his earliest youth: selfless dedication to the good, and even a kinship with the Kantian dictum about the stars, to which he referred in his talk with the German writer Gerd Ruge.

Dudintsev was not broken by the ordeals he had suffered after the publication of his novel. He continues to follow the traditions of pre-revolutionary Russian literature.

23 THREE YOUNG WRITERS: YEVGENY YEVTUSHENKO, YURY NAGIBIN, YURY KAZAKOV

The end of the 1940s and the early 1950s were marked by an unexpected development in Soviet literature. Until then there was a feeling, not only abroad, but also in the Soviet Union, that the young people who had come of age at the end of World War II were entirely the product of Soviet life, and hence less likely to doubt or question the established order. But contrary to all expectation, it was precisely this young generation that showed signs of an awakening social restlessness. Stalin's death and Khrushchev's speech at the closed session of the 20th Congress of the Soviet Communist Party in February 1956, repudiating the Stalinist "cult of personality," further hastened the recognition by Soviet society of a new factor in its life—the younger generation.

YEVGENY YEVTUSHENKO

In literature the advent of this new element was announced by the poet Yevgeny Yevtushenko in his article "On Two Poetic Generations":

"New poets do not appear in literature singly. The idea of any poet is always linked in our minds with a specific poetic generation. . . . The sense of one's generation is a must in the beginning, as a sort of poetic passport. Only the poet who is deeply, organically bound with his own generation can later become the spokesman of moods and feelings common to the entire people. . . ." (*Literary Gazette*, January 25, 1955.)

Yevtushenko recalls the almost simultaneous appearance during the last period of the war, and especially after its end, of new names in the pages of Soviet magazines: Mikhail Lukonin, Semyon Gudzenko, Alexey Nedogonov, and others. "These were very young men, but they had already gone through the war and learned the taste of trouble; at any rate, they were certain they had learned it. . . ." And they were memorable for the "honest pain" which had gone into their writing.

Yevtushenko classifies himself as a member of a still younger generation; the dividing line, as he sees it, is the war and participation in it. Yevtushenko was born in 1933, and was only about eight when the war broke out. The poet Robert Rozhdestvensky, closely akin to him in mood, was born in 1932. Another member of their generation is Yevgeny Vinokurov, who had been old enough to participate briefly in the last phase of the war, but who is nevertheless Yevtushenko's contemporary in his spiritual outlook.

A large place in the initial creative efforts of these writers is occupied by evocations of their childhood. Yevtushenko describes his childhood in the poem "My Grandmother":

> I have recalled, in thoughts about those years,
> How the houses lived in expectation,
> And how the snowstorms of 'forty-one swept over
> The little Winter Station.
> In queues, amid a thick barrage of oaths,
> I froze, exhaling crude tobacco smoke those days.
> It was wartime. Mother
> Was at the front.
> I lived with Grandmother alone.

Yevtushenko's grandmother was a woman of character. The chairman of the local City Soviet, dressed in a worn shawl and men's shoes, she dispersed equally stern judgment to the captured deserter and the grain thief:

And, nailed by her sharp, biting phrase,
They had good reason to shrink on meeting her—
The Communist,
> who secretly attended church,
The drunkard
> bookkeeper of 'Raw Materials Procurement.' . . ."
> > (*Novy Mir*, December 1955)

Yevtushenko's long poem *Winter Station* (*Oktyabr*, No. 10, 1956) became in a sense the manifesto of his generation:

> The more mature we grow, the more outspoken,
> For this we thank our fate.
> And changes in the life around us coincide
> With serious changes in ourselves.

In *Winter Station* the poet admits that, in the course of his twenty years, he has already re-examined a good deal in life, and thought about the things he has said, and those he "should have said, but did not." Feeling the approach of a spiritual crisis, the poet decides to "touch the earth again," to visit his home town, Winter Station, in the province of Irkutsk. The poet's great-grandfather, a Ukrainian peasant of the former Zhitomir province, had been exiled to Siberia for participation in a peasant rebellion. (There is also an allusion to the family's revolutionary traditions in the poem "My Grandmother.") The family struck roots in the new place and never returned to the Ukraine.

His relatives greet the poet warmly. At dinner they shower him with questions. The family philosopher, Uncle Volodya, says that every man is nowadays "like the philosophers": "the people think." The arrest of the Jewish doctors, falsely accused of sabotage, has created a painful impression:

> But now, it seems, the doctors were not guilty?
> Why, then, such an injustice against people?
> It is a scandal in the face of all of Europe. . . .

The poet spends his first night at his parents' home in the hayloft, but does not get much sleep. His younger brother climbs up with him and talks most of the night, now boasting of his "foreign flashlight," now asking whether his older brother has ever really seen a "hillicopter."

The poet's sketches of his encounters with the natives are remarkably expressive—for example, that with a gray-haired railroad worker, who tells Yevtushenko about the change in his nephew since his election to the district committee. Since then, he has been unrecognizable. Formerly a fervent debater, now

> He sits, all green and sweating through discussions,
> Banging his leader's-fist. . . .

Of equal interest is the poet's meeting with a young village lad who has come from one of the nearby kolkhozes to Winter Station to seek justice against the kolkhoz chairman. The young man is firmly resolved, should he fail to get help from the local authorities, to carry his complaint all the way to Irkutsk.

Shortly before his departure the poet steps into the local tearoom, where he meets a Moscow journalist who has come to Winter Station in search of materials, and talks to this visitor about some of the "problems" that trouble him. Yevtushenko's naïveté reminds the older writer of his own past; he had himself dreamed of becoming a writer, but later settled into ordinary newspaper work. To console and justify himself, he says to the poet:

> But what's a writer today?
> He is not the maker,
> He's the guardian of thought.

The day of departure comes. Bidding good-by to his native town, Yevtushenko seems to hear its farewell words:

> Walk through the world with proud head,
> With everything turned forward—heart and eyes,

> And on your face—
> the swishing of wet branches,
> And on your lashes—
> rainstorm and tears.
> Love people—then you'll know them.
> . . . .
> And in hard moments—come back here, to me.

This seemingly modest program—be sincere, love people, be honest with yourself and others, do not look down on those who live "modestly"—came to readers, after decades of bombast and rhetoric, as a blessedly welcome message, and the call to "walk through the world with proud head" struck no dissonance in this context.

The most remarkable feature of the latter 1950s was that Yevtushenko's moods were shared by many other young poets—Robert Rozhdestvensky, Yevgeny Vinokurov, Andrey Vosnesensky, Svetlana Yevseeva, Semyon Sorin, and others. Therefore, analysis of Yevtushenko's work gives insight not only into his own poetic personality, but also into the spirit of an entire sector of the young literary generation of the latter 1950s and early '60s.

It is rather astonishing that, despite Yevtushenko's popularity and the unanimous recognition of his talent, the Soviet literary critics have failed to understand clearly either his political character or the special moods of his lyrical hero. In an article, "Without Clear Positions," a young writer and poet, Vladimir Soloukhin (*Literary Gazette*, April 12, 1958), admits that he personally likes a good deal in Yevtushenko's work, and particularly "his angularity instead of smoothness, his freedom . . . and his youthful mischievousness, and his custom of plucking from life the often unexpected and always the least insipid pieces." Yevtushenko's poetry is characterized by "an aggressive tone; it is militant. He cannot simply write poems—he must be palpably aware of an opponent." All this is attractive to Soloukhin, but he is troubled because Yevtushenko does not always find his "opponent" in prescribed places. Soloukhin would be entirely pleased if

Yevtushenko scourged "bureaucracy," "inertia," "everything that impedes our forward movement." But Yevtushenko refuses to be limited to this. He also finds hidden enemies closer home—among members of the Comsomol and the Communist Party—regarding these as the more dangerous. It is to them that he alludes in his "Consider Me a Communist!" and in the following short poem:

> There are many who dislike me,
> Reproaching me for this and that. . . .
> Their looks of hate and malice
> I feel behind my back.
>
> But I am pleased with all of this,
> And I am proud because
> They cannot break me down
> Or force me to my knees.

Soloukhin is still unhappier over such poems as the following:

> I am hemmed in by boundaries. . . .
> It irks me
>   Not to know Buenos Aires,
>   New York.
> I want to wander to my heart's content
>   in London,
> To speak to everybody,
>   even in broken language.
> . . . .
> I want to ride through Paris in the morning!
> I want an art—
>   as various as myself!

Such declarations evoke anxiety in the politically reliable Soloukhin, and he accuses the poet of excessive "declarativeness" and of seeking and finding enemies much too often not in men of other countries and other ideologies, but in "hostile people supposedly surrounding him in our own socialist home."

It must be said that Yevtushenko does, indeed, find his

enemies "in our own socialist home." This is expressed most fully in the poem "Consider Me a Communist!" (*Yunost*, February 1960), and it is not by chance that this poem is dedicated "To the memory of Mayakovsky." It opens with the recollection that, from his earliest childhood, the poet has considered himself a Communist. He regrets that, being born too late, he did not fight either in the Civil War or in the Patriotic War. Still, in another way he was "not born too late":

> I am happy I can wage
> Against all lies and baseness
> A righteous war! . . .

In this war, which is at the same time Civil and Patriotic, victories are difficult. It is also a war in defense of the revolution, but the enemies here are often "so charming in appearance." And Yevtushenko recalls how similar "charming ones" posed as "genuine" in Mayakovsky's day, and often "branded Soviet people un-Soviet!" Today Mayakovsky is "textbook material."

> But how much water was muddied
> Around him by these goody-goodies!

Yevtushenko cannot forgive these well-intentioned "goody-goodies" for blocking publication of Mayakovsky's "Verses about a Soviet Passport" in the poet's lifetime. But to the present youth, Mayakovsky lives "without quotation marks":

> Huge
>   as the Revolution,
> And, like it, incorruptible!
> With every pulsing vein
> He'll fight forever,
> And to us, the Mayakovskys of today,
> His honesty's bequeathed!

The poem closes with the solemn promise that the poet will be "firm to the end":

I'll not be turned into
A fawning sycophant....

Yevtushenko's admiration of Mayakovsky has helped him to grasp certain characteristic, but unpublicized aspects of Mayakovsky's lyrical essence. These are reflected in his poem "Mayakovsky's Mother":

In an old soft armchair she sits,
    tenderly looking
At her young guests,
    their gaiety,
       their ardor, their debates....

She hospitably urges them to taste her quince jam, which her Volodya had been so fond of. Although as a mother she had always quickly sensed when her son was troubled, much in him was closed to her understanding; "sighing lightly," she would iron his absurd "yellow blouse." To her he had been simply Volodya, who must be fed, for whom she must boil tea and make the bed. She had little knowledge of the man who thundered forth from platforms, but she knew him who, afterward, "dropped his cropped head" upon her knees, "breathing heavily." Now the guests around her tell her that he did not die, that he is with them, that he lives:

They speak of immortality,
    Of such things....
But she, if she could only
    fall upon his breast,
Touch his rough head
    slowly
       with her hand,
And chide him
    because he smokes too much.

It is this Mayakovsky, the Mayakovsky of Yevtushenko's poems, that the present young poets in the Soviet Union are attracted to. And they are not alone in this; the youth of the 1960s, generally, respond with enthusiastic admiration to this image of Mayakovsky, as evidenced in many recent stories and novels. We see it most clearly in Sergey Sartakov's *Don't Give Up the Queen* (*Oktyabr*, December 1960). In this work the young caisson-worker Nicolay Koshich loves Mayakovsky with a love very similar to Yevtushenko's. Koshich is nineteen years old. His favorite poets are those who fight uncompromisingly for truth and do not bow before the authorities. Koshich heatedly defends a poet of working-class origin who is close in mood to Mayakovsky, crying: "If everybody would do as he does, exposing every rottenness, we'd reach communism much sooner!"

Although devotion to Mayakovsky is recorded in the stories of many young writers, it must not be overlooked that his renewed popularity is no more palatable to present-day official critics than it was to the official literary critics of his time. The response to Yevtushenko is strikingly similar. This is apparent, for example, in B. Sarnov's article "If We Forget the 'Hour Hand,'" published in the *Literary Gazette* (June 27 and July 1, 1961). Sarnov, one of the younger critics who came upon the literary scene in the latter '50s, quotes some conversations overheard in literary circles: ". . . 'Say what you may, but there has been no poet in Russia since Yesenin and Mayakovsky to equal Yevtushenko's audience. Announce an evening for him tomorrow, and the hall will be filled to capacity. . . .'" "And who knows," says the critic, "perhaps it will."

The critic is vexed by this popularity, as even the title of his article suggests: certainly, it seems to say, if you forget the slow movement of the "hour hand," you must admit that the present popularity of Yevtushenko and his still younger colleague, the poet Andrey Voznesensky, is great enough; but this by no means guarantees their popularity in the future. Yet, despite his hostility, Sarnov remains sufficiently objective to attribute Yevtushenko's popularity to certain "unsatisfied spiritual needs of the reader." He goes even further, saying that "those who are carried away by the poems of Yevtushenko and Voznesensky are ready to see these two poets virtually as the masters of the thought of their generation. This hypnosis has already been in effect for a considerable time, and those who are under its influence *do not by any means feel that they have been deceived.*" (My italics—V.A.)

In this connection it is interesting to note Sarnov's observation that, soon after the war, poetry presented a sort of "generalized" lyrical hero who was "complacent and extremely pleased with himself." The youngest generation, however, longed for a poetry whose lyrical hero was more closely involved with the special concerns and problems of their immediate experience, a hero to whom one could come "with all of one's dissatisfaction both with oneself and with surrounding life." It was this need that Yevtushenko filled:

> Oh, my contemporary,
>   my loyal friend!
> My fate
>   is bound with yours,
> Let us be openhearted then
> And tell the truth about ourselves,
> Bring our concerns together,
> And tell ourselves and others
> What we can now be no longer,
> And what we now want to be. . . .

Sarnov's principal reproach is that Yevtushenko is too declarative. Declarativeness, however, is characteristic of all young poets who feel that they are closely involved with their time and are expressing not only their personal moods, but also those of their contemporaries. It will suffice to recall such pre-revolutionary poets as Nekrasov, Nadson, and Balmont, and such revolutionary poets as Mayakovsky.

Non-Russian readers may perhaps be puzzled by the new flare-up of enthusiasm for Mayakovsky. These readers should remember that there are two Mayakovskys, very unlike one another: one is the officially edited Mayakovsky, the author of such poems as "It's Good" and "Verses about a Soviet Passport," the Soviet "bard" approved by Stalin; the other is the poet reflected through the prism of the minds and feelings of his Comsomol audience in the provinces. The second Mayakovsky is far more democratic than his officially crowned version. The present youth loves its own, unofficial poet, who is echoed so militantly in Yevtushenko's "Consider Me a Communist!" And this was how Mayakovsky had dreamed of reaching the youth of later generations, "Speaking as the living to the living."

Apart from Mayakovsky the political poet, there is Mayakovsky the lyricist; and similarly, along with civic themes, there are many lyrical themes in Yevtushenko's work. Yet it is in their lyric poems that the difference between the two poets is most evident. Mayakovsky remained "a stutterer" even in his lyrics, while Yevtushenko is softer, more tender, closer to Yesenin. This may be seen in such poems as "Mayakovsky's Mother," so akin in spirit to Yesenin's "Letter to My Mother" ("Still alive, my old one? I am too. I send you my regards!"). Also reminiscent of Yesenin's poem "Kachalov's Dog" ("Give me, Jim, your paw for luck. . . .") is Yevtushenko's "To My Dog" ("His black nose pasted to the glass, He waits and waits. . . .").

The posthumous fate and recent revival of two of the most vivid poets of the early revolutionary years—Mayakovsky and Yesenin—is one key to a better understanding of the spiritual character of the present postwar Soviet youth. Very far from one another in their lifetimes, these poets seem somehow to have come closer today. What has brought them together is the response of Soviet provincial readers. This has benefited both poets, stressing the democratic motifs in their work, and pushing further into the background the tribute they had paid to the officially required "civic spirit."

Yevtushenko is still very young, and it is much too early to attempt general assessment of his work. His name has lately become widely known in the West. His reputation in the West was considerably strengthened by his visit to the United States and appearances early in the summer of 1961 at the Harvard University Russian Research Center, as well as by his poem "Babi Yar" (*Literary Gazette*, September 19, 1961), which created a stir both in the Soviet Union and abroad because it exposed the secret anti-Semites in Soviet society. Babi Yar is a deep ravine on the outskirts of Kiev, where the Germans massacred and buried almost thirty-four thousand Kiev Jews in two days in September 1941. Not only has no monument to the martyrs of Babi Yar been erected there since the war, despite numerous cautious reminders, but even the most timid reference to Babi Yar has invariably provoked hostility and suspicion on the part of the powers that be. Suddenly, the question of Babi Yar was raised with utmost sharpness and directness by Yevtushenko:

> No monuments stand over Babi Yar.
> A steep ravine like a rough headstone.
> I am afraid.
>   Today I am as old
> As the whole Jewish people.
> It seems to me—
>   I am myself a Jew.
> . . . .
> Everything here screams silently,
>   and, taking off my hat
> I feel,
>   I am slowly turning gray.
> And I myself
>   become an endless silent scream
> Over the buried thousands.
> I am
>   every old man murdered here.
> I am
>   every murdered child. . . .

The poem ends with the lines:

> There is no Jewish blood in my blood,
> But I am hated with a scabby hatred
> By all the anti-Semites,
>   like a Jew.
> And therefore
>   I am a true Russian!

The reaction of a certain sector of literary "public opinion" to this poem was depressingly hostile. On September 24, only five days after the appearance of "Babi Yar" in the *Literary Gazette*, the newspaper *Literatura i Zhizn* (Literature and Life), the organ of the Writers' Union of the R.S.F.S.R., published a poem by Alexey Markov, "My Answer." Although it did not name Yevtushenko, its very first lines clearly indicate to whom this "answer" is addressed:

> What sort of a true Russian are you,
> When you've forgotten your own people,
> Your soul has grown as narrow as your trousers,
> And empty as a stairwell.

Markov is careful enough not to deny the fact of the mass shooting in Babi Yar, but he asserts that Babi Yar would have flared up into a world conflagration if "millions of Russian close-cropped kids" had not laid down their lives in the struggle with Hitler. Markov ends his poem by asserting that he is the genuine Russian.

Still sharper was the attack on Yevtushenko by the writer D. Starikov in his article "About a Certain Poem," published in the same newspaper on September 27. In this article Starikov insists that the tragedy at Babi Yar was not a specifically Jewish tragedy, and that people of various nationalities were massacred there. Aware that this deliberately prejudiced interpretation was provoking increasing indignation and puzzlement in Soviet society, the makers of literary policy decided for the time being to tone down the discussion which had flared up around Yevtushenko's poem.

However, vivid testimony to the moods prevailing in wide circles of Soviet society was provided by the meeting, held on Poetry Day, October 8, 1961, before the Mayakovsky Monument in Moscow. At such meetings poets usually read their works to the assembled audience. On this occasion Poetry Day was turned into a genuine demonstration in honor of Yevtushenko. When, in response to the request of the vast audience, Yevtushenko read his poem "Consider Me a Communist!" the listeners broke into a thunderous ovation after the lines, "I will be firm to the end, I'll not be turned into a fawning sycophant."

One of the most significant traits common to most of the younger Soviet poets is their strong sense of individuality. This was well expressed by Yevgeny Vinokurov in his poem "Who Has Not Advised Me?" (*Literary Gazette*, January 12, 1960), in which the poet exclaims:

> The more I listened to my mentors,
> The more I longed to be myself.

YURY NAGIBIN

The arrival of the younger generation of prose writers has been less dramatic. Among them, as among the poets, we must distinguish two groups: the older writers who have returned from the front, such as Victor Nekrasov, Vladimir Dudintsev, Yury Nagibin, and Yury Kazakov; and the very young ones, born in the middle and even late '30s, including Vasily Aksyonov, Yury Kuranov, and Yulian Semyonov.

The most talented among the older group, besides Nekrasov and Dudintsev (dealt with in separate chapters), are Yury Nagibin and Yury Kazakov.

Despite the diversity of themes in Nagibin's works, attesting to the wealth of his observation and impressions, his literary biography can be summed up very quickly. He was born in Moscow in 1920. On graduation from secondary school he entered the scenario department of the Institute of Cinematography. In 1942–43 he was at the front; he was wounded, and later became a war correspondent for the newspaper *Trud* (Labor). He began to write in the 1940s.

In distinction to many writers of his generation, Nagibin made his name as the author of short stories and has remained true to this genre. Diverse though his stories are, they lend themselves to classification. A substantial group deals with the war, and here one easily discerns the influence of wartime folklore. In the story "Vaganov" we find the portrait of a young "soldier-avenger" who is "immune to bullets." Although he is killed in the end, his unit continues to believe that he is still alive and fighting somewhere in Germany, clearing the way by his heroic feats for the advance of the Soviet Army. The rumor that Vaganov is alive "became the truth to his squadron, his brigade; it wanted no other truth, and its anger closed the lips of the uninitiated." The writer himself seems to believe in this legend and rewards his hero with the imperishable love of the girl he had met by chance in a front-line village. Vaganov danced with this girl only one evening, but those who saw them felt at once that the two were "worthy partners" who possessed the true secret of Russian dance, where "the challenge is more vivid than the joining, where enticement leads to withdrawal, a dance alive with struggle, pride, and willful defiance."

Allied to the war stories are those about the destinies of people who have come back from the war, but remain outside the stream of life. Characteristic of these stories is "The Man and the Road" (*Znamya*, December 1958): a five-ton truck is rolling down the road, scattering lumps of mud and snow. The "lobster eyes" of its headlights stare into the distance. It pushes forward, a stranger to everything—to the forest, to the frozen river. It is absorbed in its distant goal, engrossed in its own screeching and grating, its stifling, bitter stench. And there is something in common between this truck and its gloomy driver, Alexey Bychkov. But he was not always so sullen. Before the war he lived in his native village on the Psyol River. His childhood sweetheart, Tosya, also lived there. When they were little, the other children made a song about them, "Ding-dong boom, bride and groom." When they grew older, they were indeed betrothed. Then came the war. Throughout the four years of war, Alexey received letters and snapshots from Tosya; but the last letter seemed to hint at something disquieting with its quotation from a poem. When the war was over at last and Alexey returned home, he learned from his mother that Tosya had married the district agronomist about a year before. Bychkov's first impulse was to thrash his happy rival, but when he saw the thin, puny figure, there seemed to be no place in it where he could "land his fist." One day he met Tosya, but she was pregnant, and he could not raise his hand against her.

But Alexey could no longer remain in his home village. He went off wandering across the land, became a first-rate driver, but took to drink. In taverns he often met men like himself, who had "lost their place in life." One day a woman asks him for a ride, hailing him on the road. She reminds him of Tosya and he allows her to climb into his truck. As they ride along, he begins to tell her the story of how life had "mistreated" him, when suddenly he notices that, lulled by the warmth and motion, she is quietly asleep. But he is not offended. When they reach her village, he asks her in parting, "with hopeful tenderness": "And how will it be with us now?" But the woman does not understand; she merely invites him to drop by at the store where she is working if he should ever pass that way again.

Gloomy and disappointed, Bychkov delivers his load and sets out on the return trip without stopping for a rest. But when he opens the door of the truck, he finds that the woman's scent still lingers. And suddenly he feels: she is not "the right one," but sooner or later, by day or by night, he would at last meet the one he has been waiting for so long.

The largest group of Nagibin's works consists of stories about children ("Komarov," "The Old Turtle," "To School," "Holiday Eve"). A fine example of these is "The Winter Oak" (1953): Anna Vasilievna has the reputation of a good teacher, and she is well-liked by the children. But there are some with whom she can make no headway. One of these is Savushkin, who is always late to school. On this day, too, the class has already begun, but he is still out. By the time he comes, Anna Vasilievna has already explained to the children the meaning of a noun, and they begin to name examples: city, street, window, table. Suddenly Savushkin raises his hand and says: "Winter oak." Anna Vasilievna points out that only the second word in his example is a noun; "winter" is a part of speech they have not come to as yet. But Savushkin persists stubbornly with his "winter oak."

Anna Vasilievna has long intended to visit Savushkin's mother to discuss her son. She decides to make the visit that afternoon. After school she walks home with the boy, who takes her by a "short cut," across the woods. But in the woods there are so many wonderful things that Anna Vasilievna begins to understand the reason for the boy's continual lateness. They come to a clearing, where an oak stands, "huge and majestic as a cathedral." It is the boy's "winter oak." He introduces her to all the residents of the winter oak. Rolling away a hump of snow, he shows her a porcupine, wrapped in a nest of decayed leaves. Then he digs up the snow over another root, revealing a brown toad. Savushkin touches it, but it remains motionless. "Playing dead," the boy laughs. "But just let the sun shine on it, and it will bounce off like a ball!" And he goes on acquainting Anna Vasilievna with the inhabitants of his winter oak. Both are so carried away that, by the time they reach the boy's home, his mother, who works in a hospital, has already gone to work, and Anna Vasilievna turns back home. On the way she thinks that the most marvelous creature in this wood is, perhaps, not the winter oak, but the boy, "the little man in his threadbare felt boots and shabby patched clothes, the son of a soldier who had died for his homeland and a quiet nurse—a wonderful and mysterious citizen of the future." (See also a cycle of stories, "Mitya," in *Molodaya Gvardia*, March 1963.)

In a group by themselves are the stories inspired by the author's fleeting encounters and chance acquaintances. These include "A Pipe," "A Nighttime Guest," "In the Streetcar," "Rocky Rapids," "Get Down, We're Here," "Khazar Ornament," and "A Light in the Window."

Nagibin's latest stories, including "Clear Ponds" (*Znamya*, January 1961) are devoted to childhood memories.

Even a partial survey of Nagibin's work reveals that, though the author is closer in age to the "middle generation," in his whole approach to his themes and plots, which give so large a place to the spiritual lives of his heroes, he is already a citizen of the new region inhabited by the young postwar writers of the 1960s.

YURY KAZAKOV

One section of Konstantin Paustovsky's article "Thoughts, Disputable and Indisputable" (*Literary Gazette*, May 20, 1959), written in connection with the opening of the Third Congress of Soviet Writers, was devoted to the question that troubled many minds at the time: "Do we have a talented, progressive new generation of writers, capable of real and serious work?" To illustrate the existence of such a new generation, he named Yury Kazakov. According to Paustovsky, Kazakov's work is especially moving because of "the truth and strength of his ties with the people."

As with most of the younger writers, Kazakov's biography is not very eventful. Like Nagibin, he was born in Moscow, in 1927; on graduation from secondary school he entered the Gorky Literary Institute, completing his studies there in 1957. But he began to write and publish while still a student. Most of his stories breathe of an incorruptible, often somber strength and solitude. Characteristic of Kazakov's work in this sense is the story "Arcturus, a Hunting Dog" (*Moskva*, August 1957). No one ever learned how the blind hunting dog had come to the small northern town. People said that he had been abandoned by some gypsies passing through. The dog remained in the town: "he did not importune anyone, imposed himself on no one, and obeyed no one. He was free." His mother, a purebred Kostroma hunter, must have given birth to him along with his brothers and sisters in some quiet corner. When the pups' eyes opened, one was discovered to be blind: his eyes were covered by a thick white film. After the litter was weaned, the mother lost all interest in them, and the pups scattered their own ways. The blind dog began a difficult life, which early hardened his body and spirit. He found his food in garbage dumps.

It is difficult to guess what his subsequent fate would have been if man had not intervened. The narrator of the story, who lives at the home of the local doctor, tells us about it. Before the war the doctor had a large family; but his two sons were killed in the war, his daughter had gone to Moscow, and his wife died. The doctor lived alone like a hermit. One day, coming home from work, he noticed a dog, a piece of rope dangling from his neck, huddled beside a log pile, asleep. He took the animal home, washed him with warm water, fed him, and was about to turn him out. But the dog would not leave and settled down on the porch. For a long time the doctor wondered: what did he want that dog for? and what was he to call him? Looking up at the night sky, he saw a bright star on the horizon—Arcturus. He decided to give this name to the dog, who responded at once. Arcturus attached himself to his new master with the most fervent devotion. Waking long before the doctor, he sat patiently in the yard under his bedroom window. His blindness caused him much suffering. Once he frightened a herd of cows returning from pasture. Cows instinctively hate and fear dogs as "dog-wolves." Seeing the dog, the cows scattered in all directions. The enraged bull chased Arcturus and nearly gored him. The shepherds kicked him angrily. Arcturus did not whimper, but his whole being expressed "pain, puzzlement, and hurt."

The third and final phase of his life came when the narrator took him into the woods one day. The instinct of the hunting dog, hitherto dormant, awakened in Arcturus. His lack of vision was compensated by extraordinary keenness of hearing—he heard every whisper for miles around. After his first visit to the woods Arcturus frequently began to disappear, but he always returned. Before long, his fame as a remarkable hunting dog spread through the town and its environs. Visiting hunters offered the doctor large sums of money for Arcturus, but he refused to sell him.

Arcturus comes to a tragic end. One day he disappears and fails to return. The doctor misses him so much that he begins to lose weight. All searching proves fruitless. The children volunteer to look for him, but also without avail. Later the narrator leaves the town. After two years he returns. During a walk to the woods he suddenly comes upon a dog's skeleton near a dead fir tree; he also finds a collar with a rusty buckle. These are the remains of Arcturus, who had evidently impaled himself on a dead fir branch.

Kazakov's stories are memorable for their tightly woven plots and the precision and economy of their verbal pattern. Typical in this respect is the story "A House over a Precipice" (*Znamya*, April 1957), which tells about the young girl Tanya, who lives like a prisoner with her mother, an Old Believer. His encounter with the girl and the story of her life move the author deeply. He is distressed by the persistence and viability of the old ways of life: just think of it, he cries, "we're building power stations, living in the atomic age," and side by side with all this there are still "Old Believers, crosses, locked wells, and ancient rattles of night watchmen!"

His younger colleagues like Kazakov, but the older critics, to quote V. Frolov (cf. "Contemporaneity—a Great Virtue in a Writer," *Oktyabr*, October 1959), "accuse him of every mortal sin: decadence, aestheticism, pessimism." Frolov's remarks may be illustrated by the "Open Letter" of the People's Artist M. Romanov (*Literary Gazette*, September 3, 1959) commenting on Kazakov's story "The Loner" (*Oktyabr*, July 1959). Romanov says that, as he read this story, he wondered, "What is talent for?" He does not accept Kazakov's thesis that "talent is a loner, an outsider," and goes on to a rather interesting remark: "To some of the younger readers, your story may perhaps seem original and new; but I was reminded by it of the now forgotten but once—in the days of my youth, before the revolution of 1917—quite widespread debates in intellectual circles about a mysterious primeval people with an incomprehensible, secret soul." Romanov concludes his letter with the assertion that Kazakov's story left him with "a heavy heart," and voices the hope that the young writer will abandon the "artificial world" of his creation, repudiate "his grotesque, distorted images" and realize that such a story serves an "evil rather than a good purpose," since it "degrades man" and "insults his 'living soul,'" thus breaking "with the humanistic character of our art."

For a full understanding of the hostile bias of the author of this "Open Letter," it is necessary to know Kazakov's story itself. Its hero is a buoy-keeper on a large river. Yegor is a braggart, a drunkard, and an idler. He is fond of swaggering before visitors who come to fish in the river and stop over at his shack. But this unattractive man has one pure gift, one sacred corner in his heart. He possesses a remarkable voice. And at moments when inspiration sways him, such inspiration as Pushkin speaks of in "The Poet," his chance listeners forget "Yegor's rudeness and stupidity, his drunkenness and bragging; they forget their long journey and their fatigue . . . and only the extraordinary voice rings and soars, intoxicating the mind; and one longs to listen endlessly, head resting on the hand, bowed, eyes closed, with bated breath and sweet tears flowing unrestrained!" When the song ends, everybody cries out: "You should be at the Bolshoy! The Bolshoy Theatre is the place for you!" Everyone is happy as on a holiday, and Yegor's glory seems to be at its "zenith." Only Alyonka, who loves him, knows that this is not yet his full glory—"only a quarter of it." His full glory comes when Yegor, as he puts it himself, is "drawn in." At such times he goes out with Alyonka to the steep river-bank and starts the ancient song, "Down the sea, the blue sea," in the "purest tenor," seconded by Alyonka. "And they sing, feeling one thing only—that their hearts will burst, that in a moment they will fall dead on the grass; and they no longer have any need of 'living water'—it is impossible to return to life after such joy, such pain. . . ."

Akin to Yegor is Semyon, the hero of Kazakov's story "Night." It is significant that such stories are not immune against the reproaches of Soviet critics. V. Frolov, in the article quoted earlier, refers to a review by V. Bushin, published in the newspaper *Literatura i Zhizn* (Literature and Life) in 1959, in which the author argued that Kazakov had no talent to speak of, that he was merely "a young littérateur who had published some two dozen stories full of 'literary stuff.'" This comment seemed so unjust to Frolov that he came to Kazakov's defense. Frolov feels that Kazakov is both talented and colorful, and that he can be talked to "seriously," without undue raptures, but also without "mosquito stings." Kazakov's special merit, says Frolov, is that he knows how to write "with a look into the heart."

This ability to write "with a look into the heart" is a trait common to many of the young Soviet writers who have come to the forefront in the latter '50s and early '60s. It is the emotional key not only to the works of Yury Nagibin and Yury Kazakov, but also of Alexander Kleshchenko, Yury Kuranov, and Yulian Semyonov.

There is still another trait typical of the work of the younger generation of Soviet writers. They confine themselves in the choice of subject to their own experience, clearly avoiding any broad approach to contemporary life and problems. Hence the prevalence in current Soviet literature of stories and sketches. The novel, which was the dominant literary form from the middle 1920s to the end of the '40s, has been pushed aside to make room for the novella, short story, and sketch. This inevitably brings to mind the beginnings of Soviet literature, when the pioneers of the new era in Russian letters produced their first stories about post-revolutionary developments, not venturing into broad canvases. Today we are witnessing an analogous situation. But we need only compare the subjects of the young writers of the 1920s with those of Nagibin, Kazakov, and Semyonov to see the wide abyss that separates the stories of the early '20s from those of the '50s and '60s. The literary pioneers of the early '20s hurried to show the details of the new revolutionary life, avoiding a look into the inner lives of their heroes. The younger writers of today center all their attention on man in his unique individuality.

This shift of attention to *man* is a guarantee that these young writers will not yield their birthright to the "old men," that they will continue to insist, as they do today, on being the spokesmen and interpreters of their own time.

24 EPILOGUE

It was clear to everyone who followed Soviet literary developments in recent years that Khrushchev's denunciation of Stalin's "cult of personality" in 1956 heralded the beginning of a new phase in Soviet life and literature. Within the party apparatus there were many people, especially among the older generation, who sought to preserve Stalin's prestige and felt that Khrushchev's revelations weakened the authority of the Communist Party. On the other hand, a very significant trend emerged in the country, particularly among the younger elements, which sought to utilize the situation in order to achieve greater creative freedom. As the voices of these elements became more and more insistent, Khrushchev decided to rein them in, criticizing them in a number of "chats" with writers and other creative artists. His statements were later combined in an article, "For Close Ties between Literature and Art and the Life of the People," published in the magazine *Kommunist* in August 1957.

In this article, Khrushchev accused "certain writers, and some party members among them" of beginning to "lose their footing" and diverging from the correct path. "Such people," he said, "approach the tasks of literature and art in a mistaken, distorted manner. They seem to feel that it is the mission of literature and art to seek out nothing but shortcomings, to speak predominantly about negative aspects of life, about lacks and inadequacies, ignoring everything that is positive." Such moods and attitudes are "counter to Leninist principles concerning the approach of the party and the government to problems of literature and life." Khrushchev warned the writers who "had lost their footing" that "the party leadership has no intention of making concessions" or relaxing its standards for them.

More than that: Khrushchev felt that such writers were trying, under cover of the struggle against Stalin's "cult of personality," to "smuggle into our literature and art bourgeois views alien to the spirit of the Soviet people." Stalin had indeed committed many grave errors, especially during his last years, but he had also done a great deal of good "for our country, and for our party," and hence "we were sincere in our respect for J. V. Stalin when we wept at his coffin." Furthermore, he went on, these errors were not to be blamed on Stalin alone; some of his associates, such as Beria, Malenkov, and others, shared the guilt.

The appearance of this article marked the beginning of a campaign against the "revisionists" along the entire literary front. Konstantin Simonov was removed from the post of editor-in-chief of the magazine *Novy Mir* (for publishing Dudintsev's novel *Not by Bread Alone*). Ehrenburg was harshly criticized for his article, "The Lessons of Stendhal," which appeared in *Foreign Literature* (June 1957). The poets Yevgeny Yevtushenko, Robert Rozhdestvensky, and others were taken to task for "revisionist" sympathies. The struggle was waged so energetically that, by the time the Third Writers' Congress convened in May 1959, it seemed that the "revisionists" had already been crushed.

This feeling was expressed in Khrushchev's speech at the congress. Recalling the various stages of the struggle, Khrushchev remarked: "The fight is now behind us. The spokesmen for revisionist views and moods have suffered a complete ideological rout. The struggle is over, and, as the proverb has it, the 'angels of reconciliation' are now in the air. Today is a time when wounds are in the process of healing . . ." The sense of victory was evident in the entire tone of Khrushchev's speech. Politically, he supported the writers of the "dogmatist" camp, who, as he put it, "demonstrate the life-giving powers of the new and its triumph over the old." At the same time, he was almost "liberal" in his comments on Dudintsev's novel *Not by Bread Alone* (see Chapter 22).

A year later, however, at the "meeting of government and party leaders with representatives of the Soviet intelligentsia," which took place in 1960, Khrushchev was careful to eliminate the faint elements of "liberalism" which had slipped into his speech at the Third Writers' Congress. In revised form, this speech appeared as an article, "Toward New Successes in Literature and Art," in the magazine *Kommunist* in May 1961. The basic thesis of this article was that no "liberalism" could be permitted in regard to those who "got out of step, stumbling over relics of the past, those who lost the way themselves and tried to impede others . . ." It is interesting to note Khrushchev's remark that not everyone had liked the "firmness" shown to those who vacillated and strayed. "It may be asked by what right, properly speaking, we pose and solve problems in this manner." In other words, it may be asked "by what right" the party interferes with literary developments. It is significant that such questions are now being raised, and that Khrushchev finds it necessary to reply to them publicly. In his article he puts the question and gives the answer: "By the right of leadership!" This "right" is also cited in justification of the sharply postulated position of the literary officialdom "concerning the party spirit in literature, party leadership, and creative freedom." He dismisses the reproaches of "our enemies in bourgeois countries" who assert that the demand for the "party spirit" in art "limits creative freedom" as "nonsense." The Soviet writers and artists, he writes, regard the party's ideas as their own, and this constitutes the most "genuine freedom."

It is scarcely necessary to dwell on the fact that the "conservatives" (or "dogmatists"), i.e., the enemies of "liberalism," are by the same token the advocates of "socialist realism"—that special Soviet romanticism which demands that Soviet writers and artists fashion their works with a view to teaching their readers and viewers to take pride in the achievements of the government and the party. The most militant proponents of "socialist realism" among the writers today are Vsevolod Kochetov, author of the novels *The Yershov Brothers* (1958) and *Secretary of the Regional Committee* (1961), and the poet Nikolay Gribachev.

In the summer of 1961 writers were invited to express their views on the draft program of the CPSU, which was to be confirmed at the Twenty-second All-Union Congress of the Communist Party in October 1961. The draft program contained a long section dealing with "the tasks of the party in the field of ideology, upbringing, education and culture." In the new program, the party is set up as the highest criterion in all things, and everything is subordinate to it. The draft program was, of course, adopted unanimously by the Twenty-second Congress. However, the debates on the program, in which several writers (Sholokhov, Korneychuk, Gribachev, Kochetov, and Tvardovsky) had also taken part, clearly revealed the existence of significant disagreements. It is enough to compare Tvardovsky's basic ideas with those of Sholokhov, Kochetov, and Gribachev to see the sharp division between the two literary trends which became evident at the congress.

Within the framework of the established Soviet terminology and the absolute acceptance by both sides of the supreme authority of the Communist Party, these writers' speeches were, in effect, a rather unique dispute concerning creative freedom and artistic truth. Of course, we are dealing here with nascent, but nevertheless fundamentally conflicting tendencies, engaged in ill-concealed struggle. It is, perhaps, even more important that, for the first time since the Central Committee's resolution of April 23, 1932 ("Concerning the Reconstruction of Literary and Artistic Organizations," see Chapter 2), two distinct groupings began to emerge in the literary world: the "liberal" one, centered around the executive board of the Writers' Union of the U.S.S.R. and its organs, *Novy Mir* (whose editor-in-chief is Tvardovsky) and the *Literary Gazette*; and the "dogmatic" one, represented by the executive board of the Writers' Union of R.S.F.S.R., with its magazine *Oktyabr* and its newspaper *Literature and Life*. The two groups have been waging a subterranean struggle, which occasionally breaks through to the surface in public polemics around individual literary works. By the end of 1962, however, all the cards in this struggle were reshuffled: the publication of *Literature and Life* was suspended, giving way, in 1963, to the weekly *Literary Russia*; at the same time, the "liberal" Kosolapov was replaced by Alexander Chakovsky as editor-in-chief of the *Literary Gazette*.

It appears that Khrushchev and the Central Committee of the party had at first decided to remain semi-neutral. Despite the party leadership's unquestionable sympathy with the ideas of Kochetov and Gribachev, it nevertheless did not openly support them at the Twenty-second Congress, realizing that the majority of the delegates sympathized with Tvardovsky's speech. The spokesmen for both tendencies were given recognition: Korneychuk and Kochetov were re-elected (to the Central Committee and the Auditing Commission respectively); Sholokhov was elected to the Central Committee; Tvardovsky and Gribachev were both elected candidate members of the Central Committee.

In his article, "Toward New Successes in Literature and Art," Khrushchev remarked that the "meetings" or "chats" between representatives of the literary and artistic world and leading members of the government and the party were becoming a "good tradition." Significantly, such meetings are usually connected with some current conflict, which remains relatively unknown except within fairly narrow literary circles.

In 1962 there was a number of such meetings of representatives of "the party and the government" with writers, artists, composers, and others. These meetings were preceded by the visit paid by Khrushchev and other party and government leaders on December 1, 1962, to the exhibition of paintings organized by Moscow artists. According to the *Pravda* report of December 2, Khrushchev "expressed a number of basic views about the high mission of Soviet art," condemning the "liberalism" shown by the organizers of the exhibition, who had forgotten that "in the leadership of the arts there must be ideological consistency and adherence to principle, a clear-cut and irreconcilable rejection of any waverings or deviations from the main line of development of our art—the art of a people building communism. . . ." Khrushchev was especially sharp in his criticism of abstract artists: "It is impossible to look at these smeared canvases, devoid of meaning, content, or form, without puzzlement and indignation. These pathological distortions are a contemptible aping of the decadent formalist art of the bourgeois West."

Khrushchev's comments set the tone for the lively discussion concerning the problems of art which continued in the Soviet press throughout December. On December 17 a "meeting" took place between "the leaders of the party and the government and representatives of literature and art." This meeting was addressed by Khrushchev, as well as many writers and artists; the Soviet press, however, did not report the contents of these speeches, publishing only the long programmatic report of Leonid Ilyichev, Secretary of the Central Committee of the Communist Party and chairman of the Committee's Ideological Commission.

Ilyichev's report clearly reveals the situation in Soviet literature at the end of 1962. The compulsory conformism, which held absolute sway under Stalin and which, in somewhat moderated form, remains the basic principle of Communist literary policy today, is fighting to maintain its positions, but it is obviously being forced to retreat under the pressure of contemporary life. From this point of view, Ilyichev's report is of extraordinary importance for the understanding of the present transitional state of Soviet literary policy and Soviet literature.

Echoing Khrushchev, Ilyichev directed his chief thunder at the abstractionists and formalists, indulging in polemics of extreme rudeness. But the central import of his report is the struggle against the increasingly vocal exponents of creative freedom. From Ilyichev's report we learn that Khrushchev has received a letter from "a group of workers in literature and art," expressing their "joy" at the "restoration" by the party of "Lenin's spirit—the spirit of freedom and justice. Architects rejoice over the opportunity to build modern houses; writers welcome the opportunity to write truthful books; composers and theatre workers can breathe more easily. . . ."

After they have thus expressed their loyalty to the party, the authors of the letter cautiously but firmly argue against Khrushchev's comments at the exhibition of paintings by Moscow artists:

"Such an exhibition has become possible only after the Twentieth and Twenty-second Party Congresses. Our appraisals of this or that work shown at the exhibition may differ. But if we all address this letter to you now, it is because we want to say in all sincerity that, unless different artistic tendencies have an opportunity to exist, art is doomed to extinction.

"We see how your words at the exhibition are being interpreted by artists of the only schools which flourished under Stalin, permitting no one else to work, or even to live.

"We are deeply convinced that this was not your intention, and that you are against it. We appeal to you to halt the shift to methods of the past in the field of creative art, methods which are in contradiction with the entire spirit of our time."

Under Soviet conditions, such a letter—and particularly the fact of its publication—is of signal importance. It does not, of course, betoken the end of the enforced conformism, but it is a clear sign of its coming doom. Meantime, Ilyichev spoke of still another collective letter to the Central Committee. "This letter," he indignantly declared, "had even called, among other things, for the 'peaceful coexistence' of all tendencies in art, which smacks of a call for peaceful coexistence in the realm of ideology." The authors of this letter were apparently subjected to considerable pressure, for, as Ilyichev goes on to report, "the comrades who signed it have evidently carefully weighed everything once more, and have decided to withdraw their letter."

Ilyichev then proceeds to defend his position, and unwittingly presents a most revealing picture of the growing unpopularity of the official literary policy and the open protest against it:

"We are told that a situation sometimes develops at

various meetings, during discussions of creative problems, when it is considered embarrassing and old-fashioned to defend the correct party position. One may, so to speak, become known as retrograde and conservative, one may be accused of dogmatism, sectarianism, narrowness, backwardness, Stalinism, and so forth.

"A few days ago, at the conference of motion picture workers, the well-known film director Sergey Gerasimov noted with anxiety that it requires courage today to defend the positions of socialist realism. . . ."

Ilyichev attempts to counter all these developments with the rather unconvincing assertion that "It is the great good fortune of our art that the party . . . determines the tasks and direction of creative work." More than that, "Our party supports the wholesome, life-affirming critical trend in the art of socialist realism." "Critical trend!" This is already a new concept. And Ilyichev cites in this connection the publication, "with the approval of the Central Committee of the CPSU," of Alexander Solzhenitsyn's long story, *One Day in the Life of Ivan Denisovich*, which describes the life of prisoners in a concentration camp in the early 1950s (*Novy Mir*, November 1962). What he ignores, however, is the fact that this story is written in the best humanist and realistic traditions of Russian classical literature, and without a trace of the falseness which is the hallmark of "socialist realism."

The subject of *One Day* has been taboo in Soviet literature until the most recent period, and it is small wonder that its publication required the special "approval of the Central Committee of the CPSU." Tvardovsky, the editor-in-chief of *Novy Mir*, rightly stressed in his short preface to the story that its "material" is "unusual in Soviet literature," and that it carries "an echo of the pathological phenomena in our development connected with the period of the exposed and rejected cult of personality."

The story describes a day in the life of a concentration camp inmate—the peasant Ivan Denisovich Shukhov—from reveille at five o'clock in the morning, when the barrack walls are gray with hoarfrost, to the evening, when Shukhov goes to bed. Shukhov's only crime was that he and his unit had been surrounded and captured by the Germans during the war. He escaped and managed, at the cost of great risk and suffering, to reach the Soviet side. Like many others who had been taken prisoner by the Germans, he was sentenced to ten years in a concentration camp. The story tells about a single day, but Ivan Denisovich must live through "three thousand, six hundred and fifty-three" such days to complete his term. They must be lived in the camp, where the highest law is "the law of the *taiga*[1]"—the arbitrary and merciless law of the jungle. And yet, remarks the author, people "live here too." "These are the ones who perish: the men who lick the soup bowls, who rely on the medical section, who run to the officials to squeal." Despite the inhuman conditions, Shukhov, like some of his other comrades in misfortune, remains a decent, gentle human being, whose ordeal has only added to his stature and dignity.

The publication of Solzhenitsyn's *One Day in the Life of Ivan Denisovich* may indeed prove to have marked a turning point in Soviet literature. It created a sensation in the Soviet Union and produced the general impression that the leaders of official literary policy had been forced to retreat. A return to the full precepts of "socialist realism," which only recently had so insistently been pressed upon the Soviet literary world, now seems no longer possible.

The "meetings" or "conferences" of representatives of "the party and the government" with writers and other members of the so-called "creative intelligentsia," which have become Khrushchev's favorite method of popularizing his directives, continued in 1963. His "meeting" of March 7–8, 1963, was especially important. It was followed, at the end of the month, by a plenary meeting of the Executive Committee of the U.S.S.R. Writers' Union. Like many of his previous utterances, Khrushchev's speech

[1] *taiga*: the trackless forest of the Russian north.

at the beginning of March again concerned itself primarily with the question of the younger generation. Again, as at the conference of December 17, 1962, Khrushchev sharply criticized the work of the sculptor Ernest Neizvestny and the film *The Gate of Ilyich* (*Zastava Ilyicha*), based on a scenario by Khutsiev and Shpalikov. Victor Nekrasov had praised this film in his long essay, "On Either Side of the Ocean" (*Novy Mir*, November–December, 1962):

"Much has already been written about the younger generation, and many films have dealt with it, both here and abroad. Yet I have not found any book or any other film in which the questions before youth are posed with such seriousness, such sharpness, such personal concern . . . questions as: What next? What is the right way? How are mistakes to be avoided? And, generally, how is one to live?"

This appraisal was not to Khrushchev's liking, and he attacked *The Gate of Ilyich* decisively:

"The makers of the picture draw the viewer's attention to the wrong strata of our youth. Our Soviet youth, in its entire life, its labor and its struggle, continues and multiplies the heroic traditions of preceding generations. . . . But here an attempt is made to convince the 'children' that their 'fathers' cannot teach them how to live and that it is useless to ask their advice. In the opinion of the makers of this film, youth must make its own decisions on how to live, without the aid or advice of its elders."

This approach to the youth problem, says Khrushchev, betrays a desire "to turn youth against the older generations, to create a quarrel between them, to bring dissension into the harmonious Soviet family. . . ."

Khrushchev also attacked the young poet Robert Rozhdestvensky for his sharp criticism of the poet Nikolay Gribachev (known for his sympathies toward the so-called "conservatives," Kochetov and Sobolev). In rebuking this attitude, Khrushchev argued that "Soviet youth, brought up by the party, follows the party and regards it as its teacher and leader."

Even these few excerpts from Khrushchev's statements reveal quite clearly what the leaders of "the party and the government" would like Soviet youth to be. They insist that the problem of "fathers and sons" does not, and indeed cannot, exist in the Soviet Union—that it is generally only a "bourgeois" fiction. Nor does Soviet youth, they say, have any desire to set itself apart from the representatives of the older generation or even to entertain "critical" attitudes toward them.

Khrushchev's views and wishes were duly taken into account and became the leading principles at the Fourth Plenum of the Executive Committee of the U.S.S.R. Writers' Union, held at the end of March 1963. All the "sinners" were mentioned by name, and each was criticized by the participants of the plenum. It is nevertheless worth noting that Sholokhov, Leonov, Fedin, Paustovsky, and Akhmatova took no part in the condemnation of the erring writers. The attack on the "dissenters" was opened with the speech of the poet Alexander Prokofiev, who spoke sharply against Yevtushenko and Voznesensky. The speaker also directed his shafts against the young writer Vasily Aksyonov. (Following Aksyonov's *Colleagues*, mentioned earlier, he wrote "A Ticket to the Stars" in 1961 and "Oranges from Morocco," which appeared in the magazine *Yunost* [*Youth*] in January 1963.)

Ehrenburg was also attacked for championing creative freedom, even defending exponents of formalism and abstractionism (though he did not align himself with them). In particular he was criticized for his memoirs, which we shall discuss at greater length below.

Though the speeches of the critics contained all the standard clichés, none of those who criticized the *"frondeurs"* denied their extraordinary popularity among the young. Aksyonov was not present at the plenum. Yevtushenko and Voznesensky attended and were even allowed to speak. As compared to similar speeches during the Stalin era, theirs were not statements of capitulation: nevertheless, they admitted errors. Rozhdestvensky had published an admission of error before the plenum meeting.

A short letter from Aksyonov, written in a similar vein, appeared in the April issue of *Yunost*. The halfhearted character of the recantations which Yevtushenko and Voznesensky offered is obvious from the report of the plenum meeting in the *Literary Gazette* of March 30. The author of the report writes plainly that the first part of Yevtushenko's speech "did not satisfy the meeting." "In his speech," the account continues, "we can clearly discern notes which show that Yevgeny Yevtushenko has not truly realized his mistakes—both in the publication of his *Precocious Autobiography*[2] and in some of his poems."

Among the important events in the life of the Soviet literary community in 1963 one must mention the VIIIth Plenum of the Executive Committee of the R.S.F.S.R. Writers' Union in April and the All-Union Conference of Young Writers, held in Moscow on May 7–11. At the VIIIth Plenum (reported in the weekly *Literaturnaya Rossiya* [*Literary Russia*] on April 5) none of the "dissidents" were in evidence. But the attacks upon them were even now more violent than those made at the December 1962 meeting. The tone of the meeting was set at once by the chairman of the Executive Committee, Leonid Sobolev:

"It has been painful and shameful to learn that there are some among us . . . who have substituted toadying to spiritual philistines, native or foreign, for service to the people . . ."

The guilt, however, said Sobolev, was not with the young alone. "We," "the elders," were also at fault for failing to be sufficiently vigilant, for "nearsightedly encouraging rebelliousness, political cynicism, an ironic attitude toward

[2] The reference is to the poet's *Precocious Autobiography*, available in English translation. It was originally written for the French weekly *L'Express*, and appeared in the issues of February 21 through March 21, 1963. An admission of error was published by Yevtushenko in *Pravda* of March 30. However, since —as the poet himself has said—his poems are usually "autobiographical," *Precocious Autobiography* contains nothing new to those familiar with his work. The only item of particular interest in the autobiography is the poet's story of his first reading of "Babi Yar," which the audience heard "standing."

the things that Communist thought holds sacred." Sobolev went on to say that he had long waited to see when the "offensive" against the *"frondeurs"* would finally begin:

"Truly, we have waited for it, for an offensive along the entire front—in questions of upbringing, religion, morality, the family, in questions of art and of attitudes toward work—a full-scale, well-prepared and irresistible offensive. And it has come; these are its victories. The offensive has smashed the hopes of our ideological enemies to poison our youth with the subtle contagion of supposedly revolutionary courage, to instil, by means of literature, drama and films, the idea of the split between generations, to shake belief in the great cause of the building of communism, to infect our youth with the cynical psychology of beatniks and Broadway boys. . . ."

All the other speeches at the plenum, as well as the editorial in *Literaturnaya Rossiya* of April 5, maintained the same tone. These statements characterize the ideological atmosphere which had been created by the time when the repeatedly postponed Fourth All-Union Conference of Young Writers finally convened.

Despite the extreme care which the arbiters of literary policy lavished on preparations for the Conference of Young Writers, they were not pleased with the results. The truth of the matter is that there was, in fact, no conference of young writers at all. The "appearances" of a conference were maintained only on the first day, which opened with a speech of Konstantin Fedin, First Secretary of the Executive Committee of the U.S.S.R. Writers' Union. Fedin was followed by the First Secretary of the Central Committee of the Comsomol and four writers: Nikolay Rylenkov, who delivered a report on the work of young poets, Anatoly Sofronov and Victor Druzin, who reviewed the prose of young writers, and Alexey Surkov, who spoke about tradition and innovation. None of these figures can be properly classified among the young. At the evening session of the same day the plenum heard speeches by cosmonaut Yury Gagarin and "the eldest"

Ukrainian poet, Pavlo Tychina. It was only after all these addresses that the floor was finally given to the young writers themselves. But the list of speakers did not include any names familiar to the reading public. They were all new and unknown, but neither *Pravda* nor the *Literary Gazette* troubled to report the contents of their speeches. After that the floor was again turned over to speakers representing political organizations: the secretary of the Comsomol in the Ukraine, the chairman of a kolkhoz in the vicinity of Moscow, and a deputy chief of the political administration of the Army and Navy in charge of Comsomol work.

The subsequent work of the conference was conducted in seminars or groups. The *Literary Gazette* reports that there were twenty seminars, and the participants in the conference numbered little over three hundred. Of these, one hundred and seventy belonged to the younger generation; one hundred and fifty were older writers, many of whom were given the task of directing the seminars. Another plenary meeting was called on the fourth and last day of the conference. However, instead of discussing the results of the conference, the meeting heard an essentially political speech by the Secretary of the Central Committee of the Comsomol, Sergey Pavlov, which was followed by short speeches by eleven young writers and poets. Again, neither the general press nor the literary publications carried any reports of these speeches.

The categorical, aggressive tone of Pavlov's address suggested that the vacillations at the top levels of the Communist Party were over, that resumption of the harsh "Zhdanov line" had been decided on, and that the coming "ideological" plenum of the Central Committee of the Communist Party had only to put the seal of its authority on this decision. Very soon, however, it became obvious that the actual situation was far more complex than it had appeared from the sidelines. On May 11 Pavlov's address was published in *Pravda*, and on May 12 *Pravda* carried a long interview given by Alexander Tvardovsky, editor-in-chief of the magazine *Novy Mir* and a well-known member of the so-called "liberal group," to the United Press correspondent in Moscow, Henry Shapiro. This interview was a graphic demonstration of the fact that the struggle around questions of ideology and, specifically, of literary policy continued, and that its outcome was—despite Pavlov's claims—by no means decided.

Tvardovsky accepted many of Khrushchev's basic postulates; he condemned "formalism" and "abstractionism," rejected the idea of "peaceful coexistence" in the realm of ideology, and said that the very idea of a conflict between "fathers and sons" was a "contrived notion." At the same time, while in agreement with these positions, Tvardovsky sought to give a liberal interpretation to the literary policies based on them. To attain this objective, he resorted to a simple and seemingly innocent maneuver: he set up as literary models writers with a strongly pronounced democratic and humanistic approach—an approach that leads the "conservatives" to distrust them. Among these writers, whom Tvardovsky named in his interview, were Yefim Dorosh, Valentin Ovechkin, Vladimir Tendryakov, Yury Bondarev, Gavriil Troyepolsky, Alexander Yashin, and Alexander Solzhenitsyn.

Nor did Tvardovsky neglect the problem of Yevtushenko and Voznesensky. However, he criticized these poets gently, as an older comrade speaking of younger ones, adding: "I hope that there is no need for me to stress that I am saying this only because I wish them well and would like to see them approach their calling with a more serious and responsible attitude." In speaking of the magazine he edits, Tvardovsky said, as though in passing, that *Novy Mir* would publish new works by Vasily Aksyonov, Victor Nekrasov, and Ilya Ehrenburg during the coming year.

Of course, the publication of Tvardovsky's interview in *Pravda* was not insignificant. It may well indicate that the leaders of literary policy realize the purely ephemeral nature of their victory over the "dissenters."

The expanded plenum of the Central Committee of the CPSU—convened on June 18 for the purpose of discussing

Epilogue

"Current Problems in the Ideological Work of the Party" —was to be a most important event in the development of the ideological policies of the party during this period. It was an extremely broad plenum, held with the participation not only of the members of the Central Committee and its candidate members, but also members of the Central Control Commission and a large number of party secretaries from all levels of the party hierarchy, propagandists, agitators, club and library workers, and, of course, representatives of the unions of writers, artists, and theater workers. The "accused" were not invited this time, but their absence did not prevent the plenum from being turned into a virtual court trial, at which highly serious charges were made.

The attack opened with Ilyichev's speech. According to Ilyichev, "the indictment of the cult of personality," necessary in itself and giving rise to beneficent "spring floods," had also brought about the emergence of "scum" to the surface. Young people who "lack sufficient stability" seize upon all sorts of "notions" "served up" to them by the "enemies of socialism." These remarks set the tone of the entire subsequent discussion. The writers and artists were condemned not so much for the literary or even political character of their works as for serving as the "mouthpieces" of enemies, who cleverly gained influence over unstable youth and turned it into an instrument for their own ends. In his closing speech at the plenum, Khrushchev formulated this idea even more crassly. Without naming anyone, he spoke about "our enemies' yes-men," about "ideological henchmen" who help the "class enemies" and "want to spit upon their own people and their people's work," who "try to dip into the garbage pit and depict our citizens in the darkest colors." Accordingly, the resolution adopted by the plenum directly condemned "the preaching of peaceful ideological coexistence" (a label attached by the "conservatives" to all demands for a modicum of creative freedom) as "betrayal of the cause of the workers and peasants."

It seemed that the conservatives had gained a decisive

victory, winning Khrushchev to their side. Nevertheless, their insistent demands to consolidate writers, artists, composers, theater and motion-picture workers and others into one union were not met. Openly prompted by the desire to facilitate party control over the activities of the "creative intelligentsia," these demands, repeated again and again in the early part of 1963, were treated with cautious distrust by the "liberals." It was raised again at the plenum, but was not included in its lengthy resolution. This was interpreted by many people as a clear sign of continuing vacillations in governing circles and in Khrushchev's own mind. And indeed, these vacillations were further betrayed by the fact that the Soviet delegation to the Leningrad Forum of European Writers included such "sinners" as Aksyonov and Ehrenburg.

This unstable equilibrium inside the literary community should be kept in mind as one analyzes the articles of the literary critics and their attitudes toward the works which drew public attention and unsettled the literary authorities. Among these works we must name Ehrenburg's memoirs, *People, Years, Life*, which began to appear serially in *Novy Mir* in 1960 and are still unfinished. At first these memoirs received no comment by the critics. However, as Ehrenburg began to deal with the nineteen-thirties, particularly the latter half of the decade, and as he described the moods during the major Moscow trials and the great purge, he provoked the authorities and Khrushchev himself. The other writer who drew harsh criticism was Victor Nekrasov, who was attacked for his article, "On Both Sides of the Ocean" (*Novy Mir*, November–December 1962). A sharp critical response also greeted Alexander Yashin's "Vologda Wedding" (*Novy Mir*, December 1962). A native of Vologda Province, Yashin had managed to retain his ties with the region of his birth. It is possible that the severity of the critical reception of "Vologda Wedding" also reflected earlier displeasure with Yashin's story "Levers," which appeared in the second volume of *Literary Moscow*, published in 1956 (see Chapter 16, "Literary Developments: World War II and After," p. 271). Though

Epilogue

"Vologda Wedding" is a simple story—a friend of his youth invites Yashin to her wedding and he accepts the invitation, hoping not only to renew old acquaintances, but also to collect folklore materials still to be found in the far north—it was Yashin's observations of life in the contemporary kolkhoz village which angered the critics.

Among those assigned to the camp of the dissidents was Alexander Solzhenitsyn, whose novella, *One Day in the Life of Ivan Denisovich*, made him overnight the most popular writer in the Soviet Union. Since it had appeared in *Novy Mir* with the permission of the Central Committee of the Communist Party and had received favorable comments from many highly placed participants in the "meetings" of late 1962 and early 1963, the "conservatives" did not venture to criticize it openly. They chose instead a roundabout approach. The January issue of *Novy Mir* contained Solzhenitsyn's story, "Matryona's House," which became a convenient target for attack. The action takes place in the summer of 1953, the year when the narrator returned from the dusty, hot desert region where he had lived in exile "to Russia—just anywhere, at random." A teacher by profession, an ex-inmate of a concentration camp, he had small chances of finding work in a big city. Therefore he began from the outset to think in terms of finding a teaching post somewhere in a village, especially since he already at that time sensed that "something was beginning to give."

At length he succeeded in obtaining work in a small village in a remote part of Moscow Province. He found a room in the hut of the kolkhoz peasant Matryona Vasilyevna. A very poor woman, her home houses herself, her roomer, a lame cat, mice, and cockroaches. Matryona suffers from some strange "black disease," which periodically causes her great pain. Despite all the shortcomings of Matryona's quarters, the narrator is captivated by her radiant smile, her truthfulness, kindness, and constant joyous readiness to help others. The story ends with a remarkable passage on Matryona's death:

"Misunderstood and abandoned even by her husband, she had buried six children, but not her warm friendliness. A stranger to her sisters and sisters-in-law, absurd, stupidly working for others without reward, she had not accumulated any possessions by the time she died. A dirty-white goat, a lame cat, rubber plants. We have all lived next to her and never understood that she was, in truth, that righteous soul without which, as the proverb goes, no village can survive. Nor a city, nor the whole wide world."

The work of Yevtushenko, Voznesensky, and Aksyonov is approached with similar distrust—sometimes with open hostility—by the critics of the "Stalinist" camp.

The conservative critics, for example, were displeased by Aksyonov's story "A Ticket to the Stars," because its heroes, while they can by no means be classified as *stilyagas* or *modernyagas* nevertheless refuse to fit into the categories of characters acceptable to official Soviet circles. Yet it was difficult at first to find a suitable pretext for criticism. But before long a solution was found: Aksyonov heroes, the critics decided, resembled the characters in Salinger's *The Catcher in the Rye*. And, of course, it is one thing when you deal with characters in the "bourgeois West," where the protest of seventeen-year-old boys against their environment is appropriate and even progressive, but quite another when such a protest occurs in Soviet life. What is it that Dimka, of "A Ticket to the Stars," rebels, "dares to rebel," against?

Since the publication of "A Ticket to the Stars," every new work by Aksyonov has been virulently attacked. He was harshly criticized for his stories "Halfway to the Moon" and "Papa, Put It Together" (*Novy Mir*, July 1962), and for his "Oranges from Morocco" (*Yunost*, January 1963). The hero of the first story, the chauffeur Kirpichenko, works in a lumbering enterprise in the far north. He has saved up a considerable sum of money, which he intends to spend on a vacation somewhere in the south. He travels a part of the way by plane and falls in love at first sight with the stewardess, Tatyana Victorovna. His feeling is so strong that, instead of continuing south after reaching Moscow, he returns to the point of departure, hoping to meet her again in the plane. However, she is not there, and he begins to fly back and forth in search of her. It is only at the end, when his savings are virtually exhausted, that he sees her again at the airfield where he had originally taken the plane for Moscow.

"Papa, Put It Together" is a story about a young man, Sergey, and his little daughter Olya, whom he takes for a stroll one Sunday. Although it is supposed to be a day of rest, his wife has an important meeting at her institute. Sergey takes Olya to the park. On the way the child, who has just begun to go to school, asks her father to "put together" separate letters into words. At first everything goes well. In the park the father meets an acquaintance, Vyacha Sorokin. It turns out that Olya also knows this "uncle." Afterwards Sergey asks the child where she had met him, and his daughter explains that she and her mother often meet him when her mother goes to work. Sergey is troubled by a vague suspicion. He telephones the institute to ask whether the conference has ended and discovers that there has been no conference that day. But his wife is not at home either. And Sorokin begs off when Sergey invites him to spend the day with them, saying that he must study for examinations. Sergey takes his daughter out again, gives her a ride in a motorboat, and proceeds to the sports stadium. All the while, Olya continues her game, asking "and then what?" And Sergey mumbles sadly, "A soup with a cat. . . ."

"Oranges from Morocco" is less burdened with "problems" than any of Aksyonov's preceding works. Its action takes place somewhere in the Far East. The team of prospectors, working for a cooperative enterprise which its workers have dubbed "Wasted Labor," is searching for oil. They have already drilled in two places, but found nothing. There are many characters: the author allows each to carry the narrative in his own name for a certain period of time. Thus the novella becomes a sort of review of the young people working in the area.

Aksyonov revealed much about himself in a speech delivered at the Forum of European Writers, held in Leningrad in early August 1963. The younger generation, said Aksyonov (*Literary Gazette*, August 27, 1963), is seeking new ways, but its search does not preclude its learning from the classics. Just recently, said Aksyonov, he had reread some of Pushkin's works, and was astonished at how "contemporary" they seemed to him. Soviet literary youth, he went on, follows with interest the new literature of the West. He derived "great pleasure and benefit" from the works of Alberto Moravia, Protalino, and Salinger. Aksyonov and his contemporaries are fond of many of the "angry young men" in England. Aksyonov himself is especially interested in Alan Sillitoe, whose heroes, he said, "are people with whom my characters, of whom I am very fond, could easily find a common language." He also read with great enjoyment the novel of the Spanish writer Juan Goytisola, *The Surf*, as well as the sketches of his journey to southern Spain. Aksyonov did not feel sufficiently competent to offer any conclusions concerning the development of the modern European novel, but he is greatly concerned with two problems—the characters and the plot. He doubts that it is necessary to "break down everything." In order to achieve "mutual understanding with modern man," says Aksyonov (a doctor by training), "the writer must have the same 'blood formula' as his contemporaries, and this is the whole secret of 'mutual understanding. . . .'"

The two camps—"conservative" and "liberal"—in the Soviet writing community clashed sharply at the Leningrad Forum. The forum, as we have said earlier, was held after the June Plenum of the Central Committee, when the "conservatives" were once more in the ascendancy. This affected the very choice of the membership of the Soviet delegation, which did not include Victor Nekrasov, Konstantin Paustovsky, or Alexander Solzhenitsyn. Besides Aksyonov, the only other "erring liberal" to be included in the delegation was Ilya Ehrenburg, chosen simply because he is well known to many of the visiting Western writers.

The principal topic at the forum was the fate of the modern novel, or rather the current crisis of this literary form both in the West and in the Soviet Union. It must be said that Soviet criticism raised the problem of the crisis in the Soviet novel long before this forum.

Perhaps the most interesting study of the crisis in Soviet literature is Vladimir Turbin's small book, *Comrade Time and Comrade Art* (Moscow, 1962). Noting that there are "unforgivably few" new books dealing with the present, Turbin contends that the best works of Soviet art appeared in the 1920s and 1930s. The reason for this, he claims, is that today (i.e., after the war) "art has come face to face with a still unexplained and unique set of objective laws governing the development of the new society. Life impudently overflows the edges of the old ferroconcrete syllogism, which asserts that:

"Evil was the product of class antagonism: there is no class struggle within Soviet society: hence. . . ."

Today, Turbin writes, we must ask, "Hence what?" and "what comes next?"

"Man moves toward a new era," he continues, "weighted down by petty cares and joys, by vexations at work and family problems. The roar of nuclear blasts is drowned out by the nervous ringing of telephones, the chattering of typewriters and the fragile tinkle of glass broken by a child's ball. And it is understandable why this is a time when the history of art seems to grow shallow and our sentimental longing for geniuses remains unfulfilled. The world is entering a period of qualitative changes . . . compared to which the great revolutions of the past were only more or less substantial accumulations. The life that is opening before us has no analogies in the past."

Explaining his feelings about the present age, Turbin adds, "Art is learning. It is learning to grasp the profound significance of the self-evident."

Turbin's book elicited a wide response among literary scholars. However, most of them remained cautious at best. Turbin raises a great number of truly urgent problems in his small book, and he expressed them boldly, without glancing over his shoulder at his colleagues. It seems to him that we are on the eve of a new art, where the closest friend of art will be science, its new central hero the figure of the scientist, and its new muse Urania.

Somewhat simpler is A. Borshchagovsky's interpretation of the causes of the crisis. In his article, "The Quest of Our Young Prose" (*Moskva*, December 1962), Borshchagovsky recalls how the late Mikhail Prishvin came to the editorial office of *Novy Mir* in the summer of 1947. Mopping his wide forehead with a handkerchief, he spoke of meeting a newly married couple on the way. They were carrying their purchases: chairs, a picture, a teapot, and a flowerpot. "Everything was different, meant for different homes, taken from different periods. I don't know how one can write," he added slyly, "no equilibrium has been established. We have no stable way of life."

The roots of the crisis in the Soviet novel are bound with the still unfinished process of the emergence of a new society. In the West, the crisis of the novel is caused by the collapse and disintegration of old norms and traditional modes of life. But whatever the causes, the crisis of the novel, which exists both in the Soviet Union and in the West might have encouraged open discussion. In reality, the opposite was the case. The very fact that all was not well in Soviet fiction led the Soviet writers (especially those of the older generation) to adopt an attitude of watchful distrust, intensifying their mood of so-called "vigilance," which expressed itself in deliberate aggressiveness.

The glaringly open character of this watchful aggressiveness may be seen from the report of Bernard Pingaud, one of the participants in the Leningrad Forum, which appeared in the French *L'Express* (August 22, 1963). Pingaud wrote, "Our first impression was that we had fallen into a trap." While the speeches of the Soviet writers—Sholokhov, Fedin, Leonov, and Simonov—were reported in detail in *Pravda*, those of the foreign guests, with rare exceptions, were generally ignored. The situation was saved by Ehrenburg, who immediately sounded the right note. "During the first days of the meeting," he said (the forum lasted altogether only four days—from August 5 to August 8), "as I listened to some of the speeches, I felt as though I were present at a dialogue between the deaf, in which the participants carry on a lively exchange without hearing one another."

Ehrenburg's entire speech was prompted by a desire to smooth over the rough edges. Without mentioning Fedin, who had spoken contemptuously about Kafka, Proust, and Joyce, Ehrenburg said that he regarded them as "important." "I do not hold them up as a banner, but neither do I make of them targets for shooting practice."

Pingaud reports that Tvardovsky's speech was heard with great attentiveness and "enthusiasm." As editor of the magazine *Novy Mir*, Tvardovsky adopted his own criterion of literary merit: if, in reading a novel, he finds himself involved sympathetically with some of the characters and begins to see others as his "personal enemies," he takes this to mean that "a splendid miracle has taken place—a work of art has come into being." Tvardovsky concluded his speech with an excerpt from one of his poems —his credo as a poet and writer. Tvardovsky will not agree to "delegate his word" to anyone, not even to Leo Tolstoy. "Let Tolstoy be God," but he, Tvardovsky, "answers for himself," and therefore:

"I want to say the things I know best
Of all the world. And say them in my own way . . ."

It is easy to see that, despite all his curtsies to "socialist realism" and his endorsement of the idea that the writer is "enlisted" in the service of the people's interests, Tvardovsky, in these lines, defends creative freedom.

According to their own reports, the Western writers were also impressed by the speeches of two young writers —Vasily Aksyonov and Daniil Granin. Like Aksyonov, Granin does not reject the traditional forms of the novel, but speaks in favor of the search for the new. The modern age, he says, makes "new demands on the novel." It is interesting that these new demands flow out of the new characteristics of our time. Among these, he stresses the growing importance of science (we note here a similarity with the ideas of Vladimir Turbin). Scientific discoveries, following one after another, affect each of us. A new fictional hero emerges in the person of the scientist, who has nothing in common with the image of the individual scientist of earlier periods. Today scientific discoveries are so complex that they demand the intensive collective effort of large groups of scientific workers. Granin has derived a great deal from reading the French aviator and writer, Antoine de Saint-Exupéry, and much was revealed to him in the French writer's works after he had accompanied a group of scientists in a flight "to get the feel of" a thunderstorm. Granin was side by side with these scientists, and yet he felt that they were somewhere far away, that somehow they "lived in the future."

When the meetings of the forum ended, the writers visited Moscow and Yasnaya Polyana. Afterward some of them went, on Khrushchev's invitation, to visit him in Gagra. Ehrenburg, Aksyonov, and Granin were not among those invited, but the "conservatives"—with Leonid Sobolev at the head—were generously represented. Alexander Tvardovsky was the only prominent "liberal" to receive an invitation. The visit concluded, significantly and rather unexpectedly, with a reading by Tvardovsky of his new long poem, *Tyorkin in the Other World* (later published in the August issue of *Novy Mir*). This gesture was characteristic of Khrushchev's cultural policy of balancing between the "conservatives" and the "liberals."

The new poem is in a slyly humorous tone, typical of Tvardovsky. In the beginning of the poem, the author asks the reader to approach his work with an open mind, unlike the critics who tend to hear everywhere "the echoes of forbidden ideas." He says to the reader:

> "Don't look for treachery everywhere,
> Don't try to scare us from behind a bush.
> Forget such things. The time is different —
> Like it or not, it's not the same!"

The poet also apologizes for introducing as the poem's principal character the wartime hero, Vasily Tyorkin. This, too, he says, can be explained; it's not for nothing that people say, "cannons ride into battle backward."

In addition to the poem's sly humor, there is a strong satirical note as well. Just as our world is divided into two sectors—the Soviet and the bourgeois—so in the "other" world. And, of course, the bourgeois sector abounds in all sorts of absurdities and superstitions, while the Soviet is a chip of "our own Soviet" life. "We" have science, "they" have deception and fog. In the "bourgeois other world" the "discipline is weak" and the "foundations are shaky"; "here" the "foundations are inviolate," we have a "firm regime." We have "columns," they have "a mob." And so on, to the smallest details. In "our" other world, we even have newspapers although here they are called the "journals of the dead." Tyorkin is also astonished at the innumerable employees filling a variety of posts. When he asks timidly whether it would be possible to reduce the personnel, he is told that it cannot be done. "In order to reduce the staff," an old "soldier pal" tells him, "it would be necessary to employ a new, special staff. . . . In short, in order to reduce, it is necessary to expand."

In attempting to sum up the characteristic features of the literary developments of the past two years, it is necessary above all to examine the changes in the novel itself. The present-day novel, particularly among writers of the older generation, is coming ever closer in its narrative flow to the memoir form. Such is the character of Konstantin Simonov's trilogy devoted to the war. It began with *Comrades in Arms* (1953). Its second part, *The Living and the Dead* (1960) deals with the most difficult period of the war, connected with the battles in Smolensk Province and near Moscow. Most of its heroes are sustained by their faith in the ultimate victory over Hitler. The third part, *Soldiers Are Not Born*, still uncompleted, appeared in 1963 in the magazine *Znamya*. Another example of the memoir-novel is Konstantin Fedin's novel *The Bonfire* (1962), the concluding part of a large trilogy, the beginning of which, *Early Joys*, appeared in 1943, and the second part, *Extraordinary Summer*, in 1947–48.

Equally close to the memoir in its content is Konstantin Paustovsky's *The Story of My Life*, the sixth part of which is being published in 1964.

There are two other features that we must note in the recent literature: the growing popularity of short stories and novellas, and the increasing role of poetry.

In my chapter on the younger prose writers, I already discussed the most outstanding writers—Yury Kazakov and Yury Nagibin. Vasily Aksyonov also continues to enjoy wide popularity. It was he who coined a new term for the short story and novella—"a little novel" (he used it in his speech at the Leningrad Forum in August 1963). Aksyonov especially admires the talent of Yury Kazakov, whose recent work includes "Adam and Eve" in the August 1962, issue of *Moskva*. Among Nagibin's new works, we must mention his novel, *The Chase* (*Moskva*, 1962).

There are also many new names. Some of the new works which deserve to be mentioned are Yulian Semyonov's "On the Job" (*Yunost*, January–February 1962) and "Petrovka, 38" (*Moskva*, August–September 1963), and R. Zernova's "A City Romance" (*Novy Mir*, August 1962). The latter is reminiscent of Dostoyevsky's *White Nights*. Other memorable works are the stories of Vladimir Voynovich (author of "We Live Here," 1961); in 1963 he published two stories, "I Want to Be Honest" and "A Distance of Half a Kilometer," in the February issue of *Novy Mir*.

Among the new names we must also mention Chingiz Aitmatov, the young Kirghiz writer who received the Lenin Prize for his stories in 1963. His very first story, "Dzhamilya" (1958) attracted the attention of both the critics and a fairly wide circle of readers. His early stories appeared in Kirghiz; now he writes in Russian. Perhaps the most interesting of his stories are "My Little Poplar in a Red Kerchief" (*Druzhba Narodov* [Friendship of Peoples], 1961) and "Mother Field" (*Novy Mir*, May 1963). Chingiz Aitmatov is a romantic writer. His themes seem to have a lively kinship with those of the late Lydia Seyfullina, the author of the once spectacularly successful novel *Virineya* (1924). He has already created his own small but memorable gallery of young Kirghiz women emancipating themselves from the shackles of the old, oppressive way of life.

The successes of the poets are, perhaps, still more apparent than those of the young prose writers. A graphic illustration of this is provided by a description of "Poetry Day" (usually celebrated on December 1) in the newspaper *Literature and Life* of December 2, 1962. On that day a poetry evening was held in the Sports Palace under the chairmanship of the poet Alexey Surkov. The evening was attended by an audience of ten thousand. "The history of poetry," writes the author of the report, "has never known such a tremendous, such a sensitive and honest audience." The evening was opened by an older poet, Nikolay Tikhonov. He was followed by the young poetess Bella Akhmadulina (currently in disfavor with the authorities; her works did not appear in print in 1963). In seconds, a mountain of notes appeared on the chairman's table. They were addressed to different poets, but Andrey Voznesensky, Robert Rozhdestvensky, and Victor Bokov received more notes than any of the others. Many of the notes asked why Yevtushenko was not present (he was visiting Castro in Cuba at the time). The greatest applause was received by Voznesensky, who read a poem addressed to Lenin. Boris Slutsky also won enthusiastic approval for his two poems, *The Master* and *God*. The first is about Stalin: "And my master did not love me . . ."

It would be incorrect to conclude that the works of the youngest poets enjoy the greatest popularity among the younger readers. These poets share their popularity with those of the middle generation (as Boris Slutsky), and those still older who returned from concentration camps and exile after Stalin's death.

Slutsky's recent work includes a moving poem without a title; in it the author asks himself how, "beaten, broken, yet still uncrushed," he can free himself of the weight of past suffering and "unfreeze" his "spiritual Narym."

Among the older-generation poets who have returned from prison, the most famous and admired are the late Nikolay Zabolotsky and Yaroslav Smelyakov.

Zabolotsky began to publish in the late 1920s (his first collection, *Columns*, appeared in 1929). Although his themes at times seem ordinary and commonplace, he somehow gives the reader the sense of being in the presence of a genuine poet, reacting sharply and painfully to the meanness of contemporary life and longing for something noble and beautiful. The dream of the beautiful breaks through most often in brief strokes—in the description of a river, the sky, a melody. Amidst the vulgarity and poverty of daily life, such a stroke seems all the more poignantly to stress the surrounding ugliness of life. Such an attitude could not but bring Zabolotsky to a disastrous end, and his name disappeared from magazines and anthologies for many years.

After his return, Zabolotsky's work revealed many new elements. The sharply pronounced Gogol-like bitterness of his early period had given way to profound contemplativeness. This mood finds particular expression in his posthumous poem, *The Last Poppies Are Dying* (*Znamya*, December 1960). Lamenting the death of nature in autumn, the poet speaks to the man who is wandering down the deserted avenue and asks what has become of his soul; he asks how he dared to let this "beauty, his precious soul" go roaming through the world, to perish at last somewhere in distant parts. Reflecting on the "precariousness of walls," the poet reminds the man that "There is no treason in the world sadder than treason to oneself."

Zabolotsky's experiences shortened his life: after his return, he suffered two heart attacks. Heart disease soon led to his death. He spent his last years in Tarusa, a small town on the Oka River not far from Moscow. The anthology *Tarusa Pages* (*Tarusskiye Stranitsy*, Kaluga, 1961) included ten of his posthumous poems and a short autobiographical sketch.

Yaroslav Smelyakov returned to literature without noise or fanfare. From Yevtushenko's *Autobiography*, the Western reader learns that he had been exiled three times during the Stalin period. During the difficult years when Yevtushenko was expelled from the literary institute for non-payment of tuition fees and, almost simultaneously, from the Comsomol, the younger poet developed a close friendship with Smelyakov and learned about the repressions he had suffered.

Smelyakov does not attempt to keep up with contemporary life. His best poems are devoted to his youth. Among these we may mention *The Marats of Ryazan* (*Novy Mir*, 1961). However, true to his own youth, Smelyakov also seeks closer contact with the young generation. In his article, "The Young Poetry of Our Day" (*Moskva*, December 1962), he describes the railroad journey he took with a transport of young Moscow volunteers on the way to the construction site of a power station in Siberia. The poet shares a compartment with a group of young builders. He tries to engage them in conversation, but feels that he is making no headway: he remains a "half-stranger" to them.

Poetry remains enormously popular in the Soviet Union (see the article by the critic A. Urban, "Poetry in 1962," *Voprosy Literatury* [Problems of Literature], January 1963). Yet it is difficult not to notice—as we have seen in the Fourth Conference of Young Writers in May 1963—that the arbiters of literature have succeeded during the past year or two in separating from the basic sector of young poets a group which has shown itself more pliant than the noisy and recalcitrant tribe represented by Yevtushenko, Vinokurov, Rozhdestvensky, Bulat Okudzhava, Voznesensky and others. The moods and character of this milder new generation of poets are described in Nikolay Tikhonov's article, "The Great Truth of Poetry" (*Comsomolskaya Pravda*, May 12, 1963). Tikhonov had conducted the poetry seminar at the conference, and he tries to bring to the fore two young poetesses—Maya Rumyantseva, from Lipetsk, and Dina Zlobina, from Penza. Both of them have "quiet voices," but, according to Tikhonov, they possess a genuinely lyrical quality. He cites Rumyantseva's poem, *The Loader* (the poetess had once worked for a short period as a loader); in this poem she says that, as she continues to "load" human joys and troubles, she feels "the rebellion of the former loader." But it is precisely this "rebellion" that the reader does not find in the lyrical poems of Rumyantseva and her contemporaries. Indeed, he often finds quite the opposite: they tend to eulogize their country's greatness and achievements.

In the development of drama during the recent period there is a good deal of similarity with that of fiction. Just as it would be erroneous to conclude that nothing of significance has appeared in the field of fiction, so it would be wrong to deny the existence of noteworthy plays on urgent contemporary topics. Yet the "urgent topics" have changed, and the present dramatists are gradually beginning to examine moral and ethical problems, seeking insight into the nature of modern man.

One of the playwrights recently attracting the attention of readers and playgoers is Alexander Arbuzov, author of *Irkutsk Story* (1959). His age and literary experience place him with the older generation of dramatists; he is almost a contemporary of the late Boris Romashov, Afinogenov (author of *Fear*, a play which caused a great stir in the early thirties), and the late Nikolay Pogodin (author of the famous play *The Aristocrats*).

The heroine of *Irkutsk Story* is "bargain Valya," a young woman with a wide but dubious reputation. The young men of her acquaintance think of her as a girl to have fun with, to take to the movies, to flirt with. This opinion is shared by her fellow workers and her friend Victor; indeed, it is what Valya thinks herself. The only one to discern the truth about her heart, with its deep, hidden longing for genuine love is the excavator operator Sergey. Although she does not love him, Valya decides to marry him, and it is only after she becomes his wife that she begins to understand and love him.

The middle generation of playwrights also includes Afanasy Salynsky, author of the fairly well-known play *The Forgotten Friend* (1955). His latest plays are *A Dangerous Companion* and *The Woman Drummer* (1962). In answering a questionnaire of the magazine *Voprosy Literatury* (May 1963), Salynsky described how he wrote the "first pages" of his work. He conceived the idea of *A Dangerous Companion* ten years ago, during a trip to the Yegorshino coal mines in the Urals. These mines are extremely hazardous, methane gas being constantly generated in them. When he learned that mining work is particularly dangerous in that area, Salynsky (himself once a miner) decided to go down into the mines and talk to the men. After some hesitation, the management agreed to allow him to go down. The play is about a miner who betrays duty and friendship in a critical moment.

The idea of *The Woman Drummer* came to Salynsky still earlier, during the war years. The heroine of the play is a member of the Communist Party, ordered to remain in the city under German occupation, to serve as an intelligence agent. After the liberation a rumor spreads among the city residents that the young woman's conduct during the occupation had not been beyond reproach. Yet she carries her evil reputation "with a kind of gay challenge." The plot, of course, is by no means new; it echoes the *Stories of Ivan Sudarev* by Alexey Tolstoy and *Homeland and Strange Land* by Tvardovsky.

The youngest among today's successful playwrights is Alexander Volodin, author of the play *Factory Girl* (1954). Of his more recent plays, we may mention *Five Evenings* (1959) and *My Elder Sister* (1961). In the latter Volodin continues his fight against philistinism and the commonplace narrow-minded conception of goodness, setting up against these the right of man to assert his individuality.

After all the complex and dramatic shifts in the literary policies of the past few years, a return to the precepts of "socialist realism," which only recently had been pressed so insistently upon the Soviet literary world, now seems no longer possible. Such events as the appearance of Solzhenitsyn's *One Day in the Life of Ivan Denisovich*, the publication of Tvardovsky's long poem *Tyorkin in the Other World*, the appearance of Victor Nekrasov and Ilya Ehrenburg once again in *Novy Mir*, and the return of Yevgeny Yevtushenko and Andrey Voznesensky to the literary scene after a period of official disfavor, eloquently attest to the viability of the new. To paraphrase Tvardovsky, something has changed in the very air itself. And this change makes the old formulas obsolete. It demands new approaches, new appraisals and eventually, we hope, new forms of literary expression.

BIBLIOGRAPHY

ANTHOLOGIES

Soviet Literature. An Anthology. George Reavey and M. L. Slonim, eds. London: Wishart & Co., 1933.

Six Soviet Plays. Eugene Lyons, ed. Boston & New York: Houghton Mifflin, 1934; London: Gollancz, 1935.

New Directions in Prose and Poetry. J. Loughlin, ed. Norfolk, Conn.: New Directions, 1941.

Modern Poems from Russia. Gerard Shelley, tr. London: Allen and Unwin, 1942.

A Treasury of Russian Literature. Bernard Guilbert Guerney, ed. & tr. New York: Vanguard, 1943.

The Night of the Summer Solstice and Other Stories of the Russian War. Mark Van Doren, ed. New York: Holt, 1943.

Four Soviet War Plays. London: Hutchinson, 1944.

Soviet War Stories. Mikhail Sholokhov, Boris Gorbatov, Wanda Wassilewska, Konstantin Simonov, F. Panferov. London & New York: Hutchinson, 1944.

Soviet Stories of the Last Decade. Elisaveta Fen, ed. & tr. London: Methuen, 1945.

Seven Soviet Plays. H. W. L. Dana, compiler. New York: Macmillan, 1946.

A Second Book of Russian Verse. C. M. Bowra, ed. London: Macmillan, 1948.

Russian Literature Since the Revolution. Joshua Kunitz, ed. London: Boni and Gaer, 1948.

New Russian Stories. Bernard Guilbert Guerney, ed. & tr. New York: New Directions, 1952.

Russian Poetry, 1917–1955. Jack Lindsay, ed. London: Bodley Head, 1957.

Fourteen Great Short Stories by Soviet Authors. George Reavey, ed. New York: Avon, 1959. Paperback.

Short Stories of Russia Today. Yvonne Kapp, ed., Tatiana Shebunina, tr. Boston: Houghton Mifflin, 1959.

An Anthology of Russian Literature in the Soviet Period from Gorki to Pasternak. Bernard Guilbert Guerney, ed. & tr. New York: Vintage, 1960. Paperback.

The Atlantic, June 1960. Special Issue: The Arts in the Soviet Union.

Masterpieces of the Russian Drama, Vol. II. G. R. Noyes, ed. New York: Dover, 1960. Paperback.

Soviet Short Stories. Avrahm Yarmolinsky, ed. New York: Doubleday-Anchor, 1960. Paperback.

An Anthology of Russian Plays, Vol. II. Franklin D. Reeve, ed. & tr. New York: Vintage, 1961. Paperback.

Modern Soviet Short Stories. George Reavey, ed. & tr. New York: Universal Library, 1961. Paperback.

Year of Protest, 1956. Hugh McLean and Walter Vickery, eds. & trs. New York: Vintage, 1961. Paperback.

An Anthology of Russian Verse, 1812–1960. Avrahm Yarmolinsky, ed. New York: Doubleday-Anchor, 1962. Paperback.

Dissonant Voices in Soviet Literature. Patricia Blake and Max Hayward, eds. New York: Pantheon, 1962.

Great Soviet Short Stories. F. D. Reeve, ed. New York: Dell, 1962. Paperback.

The Penguin Book of Russian Verse. Dimitri Obolensky, ed. London & Baltimore: Penguin Books, 1962. Paperback.

Stories from Modern Russia. C. P. Snow and P. H. Johnson. New York: St. Martin's Press, 1962.

A Treasury of Russian Life and Humor. John Cournos, ed. & intro. New York: Coward-McCann, 1962.

The Russians, Then and Now. Avrahm Yarmolinsky. New York: Macmillan, 1963.

"New Voices in Russian Writing," Max Hayward and Patricia Blake, eds. *Encounter Magazine*, April 1963.

ABRAMOV, FEDOR
- *One Day in the New Life*. Tr. by David Floyd. New York: Praeger, 1963.

AFINOGENOV, ALEXANDER
- *Distant Point*. Tr. by H. Griffith. London: Pushkin Press, 1941.
- *Fear*. Tr. by Charles Malamuth in E. Lyons' *Six Soviet Plays*. Boston & New York: Houghton Mifflin, 1934; London: Gollancz, 1935.

AKHMATOVA, ANNA
    Forty-Seven Love Poems. Tr. by Natalie Duddington. London: Jonathan Cape, 1927.

AVDEYENKO, A.
    I Love. Tr. by A. Wixley. London: Lawrence, 1935; New York: International, 1935.

BABEL, ISAAC
    Benya Krik, The Gangster and Other Stories. Ed. by Avrahm Yarmolinsky. New York: Shocken, 1948.
    Sunset. A play, tr. by Mirra Ginsburg and Raymond Rosenthal in *Noonday* 3. New York: Noonday Press, 1960.
    Collected Stories. Tr. & ed. by Walter Morison, intro. by Lionel Trilling. New York: Criterion, 1955; Meridian, 1960. Paperback.

BLOK, ALEXANDER
    "The Twelve," "The Scythians," and Other Poems, in *An Anthology of Russian Verse, 1812–1960.* Ed. by Avrahm Yarmolinsky. New York: Doubleday-Anchor, 1962. Paperback.
    The Spirit of Music. Tr. by I. Freiman. London: L. Drummond (Essays, Russian Literary Library, No. 5), 1946.

BULGAKOV, M.
    Days of the Turbins. Tr. by E. Lyons in *Six Soviet Plays.* Boston & New York: Houghton Mifflin, 1934; London: Gollancz, 1935.

BUNIN, IVAN
    The Village. Tr. by Isabel F. Hapgood. New York: Knopf, 1923.
    The Gentleman from San Francisco and Other Stories. Tr. by Bernard Guilbert Guerney. New York: Knopf, 1933.
    The Well of Days. Tr. by Gleb Struve & Hamish Miles. London: Leonard & Virginia Woolf at the Hogarth Press, 1933.
    Mitya's Love. Tr. from the French by Madelaine Boyd. New York: Holt, 1926.
    The Dreams of Chang and Other Stories. Tr. by Bernard Guilbert Guerney. New York: Knopf, 1935.
    The Elaghin Affair and Other Stories. Tr. by Bernard Guilbert Guerney. New York: Knopf, 1935.

Dark Avenues and Other Stories. Tr. by Richard Hare. London: Lehmann, 1949.

Memories and Portraits. Tr. by Vera Traill and Robin Chancellor. London: Lehmann, 1951; New York: Doubleday, 1951.

DUDINTSEV, VLADIMIR

Not by Bread Alone. Tr. by Edith Bone. New York: Dutton, 1957.

A New Year's Tale. Tr. by Gabriella Azrael. New York: Dutton, 1960. A Dutton Everyman Paperback.

A New Year's Tale. Tr. by Max Hayward. London: Hutchinson, 1960.

EHRENBURG, ILYA

The Extraordinary Adventures of Julio Jurenito and His Disciples. Tr. by Usick Vanzler. New York: Covici-Friede, 1930; *Julio Jurenito.* Tr. by Anna Bostock, in collaboration with Yvonne Kapp. Philadelphia: Dufour Editions, 1964.

The Stormy Life of Lasik Roitschwantz. A novel, tr. by Leonid Borochowicz & Gertrude Flor. New York: Polyglot Library, 1960.

A Street in Moscow (tr. of *Protochny Alley*). Tr. by Sonia Volochova. New York: Covici-Friede, 1932.

Out of Chaos (tr. of *The Second Day*). Tr. by Alexander Bakshy. New York: Holt, 1934.

The Fall of Paris. Tr. by Gerard Shelley. New York: Knopf, 1943.

The Thaw. Tr. by Manya Harari. Chicago: Regnery, 1955; London: MacGibbon, 1961. (*A Change of Season* includes this work and *The Spring*.)

The Spring. Tr. by Humphrey Higgins. London: MacGibbon, 1961. (Included in *A Change of Season*.)

A Change of Season. New York: Knopf, 1962. (Includes *The Thaw*, tr. by Manya Harari, and *The Spring*, tr. by Humphrey Higgins.)

People and Life, 1891–1921. Tr. by Anna Bostock and Yvonne Kapp. New York: Knopf, 1962. *People and Life*, vols. I, II, and III. London: MacGibbon, 1962–63.

Chekhov, Stendhal and Other Essays. Selected and with an introduction by Harrison E. Salisbury; tr.

by Anna Bostock [and others]. New York: Knopf, 1963.

FEDIN, KONSTANTIN
Early Joys. Tr. by Mrs. G. Kazanina with an introduction by Ernest J. Simmons.

GLADKOV, FYODOR
Cement. Tr. by A. S. Arthur and C. A. Ashleigh. London: Lawrence, 1929; New York: International, 1929.

GORBATOV, BORIS
Taras' Family. Tr. by Elizabeth Donnelly. London, New York: Hutchinson, 1944.

Donbas. Tr. by Bernard Isaacs. Moscow: Foreign Languages Publications, 1953. (Library of Selected Soviet Literature.)

GORKY, MAXIM
Best Short Stories. Ed. by Avrahm Yarmolinsky and Baroness Moura Budberg. New York: Grayson, 1947.

Twenty-Six Men and a Girl. New York: Avon, 1957. Paperback.

Foma Gordeyev. Tr. by Herman Bernstein. New York: Bee De, 1928; tr. by Margaret Wettlin. New York: Dell, 1962. Paperback.

Mother. Tr. by Margaret Wettlin. New York: Collier, 1961. Paperback.

Autobiography of Maxim Gorky: My Childhood. In the World. My Universities. Tr. by Isidor Schneider. New York: Citadel, 1949; Collier, 1962 (with an intro. by Avrahm Yarmolinsky). Paperback.

The Artamonov Business. Tr. by Alec Brown. New York: Pantheon, 1948.

Reminiscences of Tolstoy, Chekhov, and Andreyev. Intro. by Mark Van Doren. New York: Compass Books, 1959. Paperback.

Bystander. Tr. by Bernard Guilbert Guerney. New York: Cape & Smith, 1930.

Seven Plays of Maxim Gorky. Tr. by Alexander Bakshy with Paul S. Nathan. New Haven: Yale University Press; London: H. Milford, Oxford University Press, 1945.

The Lower Depths and Other Plays. Tr. by Alexander Bakshy. New Haven: Yale. Paperback.

GROSSMAN, VASILY

The People Immortal. Tr. by Elizabeth Donnelly. London, New York: Hutchinson, 1943.

Stalingrad Hits Back. Moscow: Foreign Languages Publications, 1942.

IVANOV, VSEVOLOD

Armored Train 14–69. Tr. by Gibson-Cowan and A. T. K. Grant. New York: International, 1933; London: Lawrence, 1933.

The Adventures of a Fakir. New York: Vanguard, 1935.

ILF, I., AND PETROV, E.

The Twelve Chairs. Tr. by Charles Malamuth. New York: Vintage, 1961. Paperback.

The Complete Adventures of Ostap Bender. Including the two novels *The Twelve Chairs* and *The Golden Calf.* Tr. by John H. Richardson. New York: Random House, 1963.

The Little Golden Calf. Tr. by Charles Malamuth. New York: Farrar & Rinehart, 1932; London: Grayson & Grayson, 1932.

The Little Golden America. New York: Farrar & Rinehart, 1937.

KATAYEV, V.

The Embezzlers. Tr. by I. Zarine. London: Benn, 1929; New York: Dial, 1929.

Time, Forward! Tr. by Charles Malamuth. New York: Farrar & Rinehart, 1933.

Lonely White Sail. Tr. by Charles Malamuth. New York: Farrar & Rinehart; London: Allen & Unwin, 1937.

KAVERIN, V.

The Larger View (tr. of *Fulfillment of Desires*). Tr. by E. Swan. New York: Stackpole, 1938; London: Collins, 1938.

Two Captains. Tr. by E. Swan. London: Cassell, 1938; New York: Modern Age, 1942.

KAZAKOV, YURI

Going to Town and Other Stories. Comp. and tr. by Gabriella Azrael. Boston: Houghton Mifflin, 1964.

KORNEYCHUK, ALEXANDER
    The Front. In *Four Soviet War Plays.* London: Hutchinson, 1944.
    The Front. Tr. by Bernard L. Kotem & Zina Voynow. In *Seven Soviet Plays.* New York: 1946. (See ANTHOLOGIES)

LAVRENYOV, BORIS
    Stout Heart, and Other Stories. Tr. by D. L. Fromberg. Moscow: Foreign Languages Publications, 1943.
    The Forty-First. Moscow: Foreign Languages Publications, 1958.

LEONOV, LEONID
    The Badgers. Tr. by Hilda Kazanina. London, New York: Hutchinson, 1947.
    The Thief. Tr. by Hubert Butler. New York: MacVeagh, Dial Press, 1931; Vintage, 1960. Paperback.
    Soviet River (tr. of *Sot*). Tr. by Ivor Montagu & Sergei Nolvandov. New York: MacVeagh, Dial Press, 1932.
    Skutarevsky. Tr. by Alec Brown. London: Dickson & Thompson, 1936; New York: Harcourt, Brace, 1936.
    Road to the Ocean. Tr. by Norbert Guterman. New York: Fischer, 1944.
    Invasion. In *Four Soviet War Plays.* London, 1944. (See ANTHOLOGIES)
    Chariot of Wrath (tr. of *The Taking of Velikoshumsk*). Tr. by Norbert Guterman. New York: Fischer, 1946.

MAYAKOVSKY, VLADIMIR
    The Bedbug and Selected Poetry. Tr. by Max Hayward & George Reavey, ed. by Patricia Blake. New York: Meridian, 1960. Paperback.
    Mayakovsky and His Poetry. Compiled by Herbert Marshall. London: Pilot Press, 1942. Revised edition, 1945.
    Mystery-Bouffe: An Heroic, Epic, and Satiric Representation of Our Epoch. (Second Variant: 1921). Tr. by George Rapall Noyes & Alexander Kaun. In *Masterpieces of the Russian Drama,* compiled by G. R. Noyes. New York: Appleton, 1933.

NAGIBIN, YURY
> *Each for All.* London, New York: Hutchinson, 1945.
> *The Pipe: Stories.* Tr. by Shneerson. Moscow: Foreign Languages Publications, 1958.

NEKRASOV, VICTOR
> *Kira Georgievna.* Tr. by Walter Vickery. New York: Pantheon, 1962.

NIKOLAEVA, GALINA
> *Harvest.* A novel. Moscow: Foreign Languages Publications, 1952. (Library of Selected Soviet Literature.)
> "The Tractor Kolkhoz." In *Two Collective Farms.* Moscow: Foreign Languages Publications, (Sketches of Soviet Life.)

OLESHA, YURY
> *Envy.* Tr. by Anthony Wolfe. London: Leonard & Virginia Woolf, 1936.
> *The Wayward Comrade and the Commissars.* Tr. by Andrew MacAndrew. New York: New American Library, 1960. Paperback.

OVECHKIN, VALENTIN
> *Collective Farm Sidelights.* Moscow: Foreign Languages Publications, 1959.

PANFYOROV, FYODOR
> *Brusski: A Story of Peasant Life in Soviet Russia.* Tr. by Z. Mitrov & J. Tabrisky. London: Lawrence, 1930.

PANOVA, VERA
> *The Factory.* Tr. by Moura Budberg. London: Putnam, 1949.
> *Span of the Year.* Tr. by Moura Budberg. London: Harvill, 1957.
> *A Summer to Remember.* London: Yoseloff, 1962. (Formerly published by Arlington Books in 1959, under the title *Time Walked.*)

PASTERNAK, BORIS
> *Prose and Poems.* Ed. by Stefan Schimanski; intro. by J. M. Cohen; tr. by Beatrice Scott, Robert Payne, & J. M. Cohen. London: Ernest Benn, 1959.
> *The Last Summer.* Tr. with intro. by George Reavey. London: Owen, 1959; New York: Avon. Paperback.

Safe Conduct. Tr. by Beatrice Scott, *et al.* New York: New Directions, 1958; Signet Books, (NAL). Paperback.

Selected Writings. Norfolk, Conn.: J. Laughlin, 1949. (New Directions Series 9.)

Doctor Zhivago. Tr. by Max Hayward & Manya Harari. New York: Pantheon, 1958; Random House, Modern Library; Signet (NAL). Paperback.

I Remember: Sketch for an Autobiography. Tr. with preface and notes by David Magarshack. With an essay on translating Shakespeare, tr. by Manya Harari. New York: Pantheon, 1959; Meridian, 1960. Paperback.

The Poetry of Boris Pasternak, 1917–1959. Selected, ed. & tr. by George Reavey, with three prose pieces by Pasternak. New York: Putnam, 1959; Capricorn, 1960. Paperback.

Poems, 1955–1959. Tr. by Michael Harari. London: Collins & Harvill, 1960.

In the Interlude. Poems 1950–1960. Tr. by Henry Kamen. Oxford University Press, 1962.

Poems. Tr. by Lydia Pasternak Slater. New York: Barnes & Noble, 1964. Paperback.

PAUSTOVSKY, KONSTANTIN

The Golden Rose. Literature in the Making. Tr. by Susanna Rosenberg. Moscow: Foreign Languages Publications, 195–. (Library of Selected Soviet Literature.)

The Black Gulf. Stories. Tr. by E. Schimanskaya. London: Hutchinson, 1946.

The Story of a Life. New York: A. A. Knopf, 1964.

PAVLENKO, PYOTR

Red Planes Fly East. Tr. by Stephen Garry. New York: International, 1938.

Happiness. A novel, tr. by J. Fineberg. Moscow: Foreign Languages Publications, 1950. (Library of Selected Soviet Literature.)

PILNYAK, BORIS

The Naked Year. Tr. by Alec Brown, intro. by Prince D. S. Mirsky. New York: Payson & Clarke, 1928.

The Volga Falls to the Caspian Sea. Tr. by Charles Malamuth. New York: Cosmopolitan Book Corp., 1931.

SHOLOKHOV, MIKHAIL
  Tales of the Don. Tr. by H. C. Stevens. New York: Knopf, 1962.
  The Silent Don. Tr. by Stephen Garry. New York: Knopf, 1942. (Includes *And Quiet Flows the Don* and *The Don Flows Home to the Sea.*)
  And Quiet Flows the Don. Tr. by Stephen Garry. London: Putnam, 1934; New York: Knopf, 1934; Signet (NAL). Paperback.
  The Don Flows Home to the Sea. Tr. by Stephen Garry. London: Putnam, 1940; New York: Signet (NAL). Paperback.
  Virgin Soil Upturned (American title: *Seeds of Tomorrow*). Tr. by Stephen Garry. London: Putnam, 1935; New York: Knopf, 1935.
  Harvest on the Don. Tr. by H. C. Stevens. New York: Knopf, 1960; Signet (NAL), 1962. Paperback.
  Sudba Cheloveka (*Fate of a Man*). New York: Van Nostrand, 1960. Paperback.

SIMONOV, KONSTANTIN
  The Russians. In *Four Soviet War Plays.* Tr. by Gerard Shelley and adapted by Tyrone Guthrie. London: Hutchinson, 1944.
  Days and Nights. Tr. by Joseph Barnes. New York: Simon & Schuster, 1945; Ballantine, 1962. Paperback.
  The Living and the Dead. Tr. by R. Ainsztein. New York: Doubleday, 1962.

SOLZHENITSYN, ALEXANDER
  One Day in the Life of Ivan Denisovich. Tr. by Ralph Parker; New York: Dutton, 1963. Tr. by Ronald Hingley and Max Hayward; New York: Praeger, 1963.
  We Never Make Mistakes. Tr. and with an introduction by Paul W. Blackstock. South Carolina: University of South Carolina Press, 1963.

TOLSTOY, ALEXEY
  The Death Box (tr. of *The Hyperboloid of Engineer Garin*). Tr. by Bernard Guilbert Guerney. London: Methuen, 1937.
  Ordeal: A Trilogy (tr. of *The Road to Calvary*). Tr. by Ivy & Tatiana Litvinova. Moscow: Foreign Lan-

guages Publications, 1953. (Library of Selected Soviet Literature.)

Peter The First. Tr. by Tatiana Shebunina. New York: Macmillan, 1959; Signet (NAL). Paperback.

Daredevils and Other Stories (tr. of *The Stories of Ivan Sudarev*). Tr. by D. L. Fromberg. Moscow: Foreign Languages Publications, 1942.

A Week in Turenevo and Other Stories. Intro. by George Reavey. New York: Evergreen, 1958. Paperback.

TVARDOVSKY, ALEXANDER

Several of Tvardovsky's poems—"To My Critics," "Pioneers," "Death of the Hero" (a fragment from "Vasily Tyorkin")—appeared in a special issue of *The Atlantic*, June 1960.

YEVTUSHENKO, YEVGENY

Selected Poems. Tr. and with an introduction by Robin Milner-Gulland and Peter Levi. New York: Dutton, 1962.

Precocious Autobiography. Tr. by Andrew R. MacAndrew. New York: Dutton, 1963.

ZAMYATIN, YEVGENY

We. Tr. by Gregory Zilboorg. New York: Dutton, 1924; Dutton Everyman Books, 1959. Paperback.

ZOSHCHENKO, MIKHAIL

Nervous People and Other Satires. Ed. by Hugh McLean. New York: Pantheon, 1963.

Scenes from the Bathhouse and Other Stories of Communist Russia. Compiled by Marc Slonim, tr. by Sidney Monas. Ann Arbor: Ann Arbor Paperbacks (University of Michigan), 1962.

The Wonderful Dog and Other Tales. Tr. by Elisaveta Fen. Second edition. London: Methuen, 1942.

INDEX

"About a Certain Poem" (Starikov), 395
"About Mood, Plot, and Language" (Bondarev), 16
"About Myself, about Critics, and about My Work" (Zoshchenko), 112, 118, 123
"About Myself, about Ideology, and a Few Other Things" (Zoshchenko), 114-15
"About Scum" (Mayakovsky), 72
"About the Day and the Age" (Zamyatin), 103-4
"About the Writer's Work" (Ehrenburg), 141
"About This" (Mayakovsky), 77
"About Two Poetic Generations" (Yevtushenko), 297
Above Barriers (Pasternak), 178
Abramov, Fyodor, 294, 333
Acmeists, 331
Adalis, Adelaida, 189
"Adam and Eve" (Aksyonov), 432
Adam and Eve (Prishvin), 224, 225
"Adventures of a Monkey, The" (Zoshchenko), 125-26, 284
Adventures of Nevzorov, or Ibikus (Tolstoy), 238-39
"Aerial Ways" (Pasternak), 179
Afinogenov, Alexander, 48-49, 57, 436
Aitmatov, Chingiz, 432-33
Akhmadulina, Bella, 433
Akhmatova, Anna, 189, 272, 284, 286, 416
Aksyonov, Vasily, 301, 356, 396, 416, 417, 420, 422, 424-26, 429, 430, 432
Akulshin, Rodion, 28, 344
Aliger, Margarita, 56, 343
All-Union Combined Associations of Proletarian Writers (VOAPP), 21, 29-31
All-Union Conference of Proletarian Writers (1925), 29; (1955), 352
All-Union Conference of Young Writers, Fourth (1963), 417, 418, 435
All-Union Congress of Soviet Writers, First (1934), vii, 152, 181, 188, 197-99, 351; Second (1954), 294, 350; Third (1959), vii, 298, 378, 379, 400, 407, 408
"America" (Mayakovsky), 73
Andersen, Hans Christian, 315
Andron the Good for Nothing (Neverov), 39
And So We're Home (Gauzner), 327
Annensky, Innokenty, 189
Another's Shadow (Simonov), 286
Antonov, I., 347
Apollon (magazine), 222
Arbuzov, Alexander, 436
"Arcturus, a Hunting Dog" (Kazakov), 400-2
Aristocrats, The (Pogodin), 47, 436
Armored Train 14-69 (Ivanov), 32, 36, 37
Arosev, Alexander, 27, 200
Artamonov Business, The (Gorky), 5, 7
"Art of the Soviet People" (Katayev), 27
Associations of Proletarian Writers, x, 21, 28-31
"Atlantic Ocean, The" (Mayakovsky), 73
"At the Burnt Stump" (Prishvin), 222
At the Front Line (Ovechkin), 350, 353
At the Top of My Voice (Mayakovsky), 77, 78
At the Walls of the Unseen City (Prishvin), 224
At the World's End (Zamyatin), 99, 158
Attila (Zamyatin), 105, 107, 108, 109, 110
August Again (Ivanter), 343
Autobiography (Pasternak), 178 n, 180-81, 184
Autobiography (Yevtushenko), 435
Avdeyenko, Alexander, 47, 48, 345
Averbakh, Leopold, 29, 30
Averianov, M. V., 83
Azure Book (Zoshchenko), 122
Azure Cities (Tolstoy), 45, 238, 239-40
Azure Steppe, The (Sholokhov), 251-52

Babaevsky, Semyon, 294
Babel, Isaac, ix, x, 7, 29, 32, 39, 143-55, 315, 371
"Babi Yar" (Yevtushenko), 393-95
"Backbone Flute" (Mayakovsky), 177
Badgers, The (Leonov), 39, 203, 206-7, 208, 221
Bagritsky, Eduard, 28, 189, 315
Bakhmetyev, Vladimir, 8
Baklanov, G., 347
Balmont, Konstantin, 177, 237, 392
Balzac, Honoré, 196
Baratashvili, N., 180
Barbusse, Henri, 152
"Bargain Sale" (Mayakovsky), 68
"Baring the Method" (Prishvin), 224, 225
Bast Shoes (Zamoysky), 52
Bathhouse, The (Mayakovsky), 74, 75-76, 77
Baudelaire, Pierre Charles, 68
Be Acquainted, Baluyev! (Kozhevnikov), 300
Beast of Krutoyarsk, The (Prishvin), 224
Bedbug, The (Mayakovsky), 74-75, 76, 77
Bednota (newspaper), 345
Bedny, Demyan, 43, 93 n
Before Sunrise (Zoshchenko), 124-25, 126
"Beginning, The" (Babel), 145-46
Beketov's Career (Sofronov), 286
Belenky, G., 301
Belkin's Tales (Pushkin), 158
Bely, Andrey, xii, 41, 157, 158, 177, 178, 184, 237
Berendey's Kingdom (Prishvin), 231
Bergholts, Olga, 281, 290, 317
Beseda (magazine), 1
Beyond the Volga (Tolstoy), 237
Bezymensky, A., 43
Bibik, Alexey, 8
Birzhevye Vedomosti (newspaper), 128
"Black and White" (Mayakovsky), 73
Black Arab, The (Prishvin), 224
"Black Friday" (Tolstoy), 119-20
"Black Man" (Yesenin), 85
Black Man, The (Olesha), 188, 194, 196-97
Black Sea (Paustovsky), 306, 309, 312
"Black Shawl" (Pushkin), 78
"Blizzard Veils the Sky in Darkness" (Pushkin), 78
Bloch, Jean-Richard, 152

Blok, Alexander, xii, 9-13, 18, 19, 20, 41, 61, 83-84, 100-1, 103, 111, 124, 184, 187, 224
Bogdanov, A., 20-21, 52
Bolshevik (magazine), 125
Bolshoy Dramatic Theatre, 38, 105
Bondarev, Yury, 16, 420
Bonfire, The (Fedin), 288, 431
Book about a Soldier (Tvardovsky), 333
Book for Parents (Makarenko), 57-59
Boris Godunov (Pushkin), 196
Born of the Storm (Ostrovsky), 51
Borshchagovsky, A., 428
"Bread" (Tolstoy), 249, 250
Brecht, Bertolt, 151
Bright Shore (Panova), 324-25
"Broadway" (Mayakovsky), 73
Broken Jug (Kleist), 178, 182
"Brooklyn Bridge" (Mayakovsky), 73
Brothers Karamazov, The (Dostoyevsky), 212
Bruce, Jacob, 243
Bruski (Panfyorov), 39, 45, 54, 55, 333
Budenny, Semyon, 151
Bugrov, 6, 7
Bukharin, N. I., 61-62, 72, 181-82
Bulgakov, Mikhail, 32, 37-39, 45, 246
Bun, The (Prishvin), 223, 228
Bunin, Ivan, 13-17, 315, 352
"Buried Treasure" (Zoshchenko), 116
Burlyuk, David, 62, 65-66
Burning Daylight (London), 374
"Burnt-Out Land, The" (Kluyev), 51, 52
"Buryga" (Leonov), 205
Bushin, V., 404
Byedny, Demyan. *See* Bedny, Demyan
Byely, Andrey. *See* Bely, Andrey
Byelyenky, G. *See* Belenky, G.
Byezymyensky, A. *See* Bezymensky, A.
Bygone Days (Pilnyak), 158

Captain's Daughter, The (Pushkin), 38, 89, 179
Catcher in the Rye, The (Salinger), 424
Catherine II, the Great, 89
Cavalier of the Gold Star (Babaevsky), 294
Cement (Gladkov), 8, 39-40, 44
Cervantes, Miguel de, 335

Index

Chain of Kashchey, The (Prishvin), 223, 225-26, 227-31
Chakovsky, Alexander, 410
Chaliapin, Feodor I., 2
Challenge, The (Bogdanov), 52
Chapayev (Furmanov), 32, 33-35, 150
Chase, The (Nagibin), 432
Chekhov, Anton, 16, 68-69, 111, 203, 352
Cherny, Osip, 265
Cherry Stone, The (Olesha), 188, 194
Childhood (Gorky), 7
"Childhood of Luvers, The" (Pasternak), 179
Chocolate (Tarasov-Rodionov), 44
Chukovsky, Korney, 8
Chumandrin, Mikhail, 42-43
"City Romance, A" (Zernova), 432
Civil War, Bolshevik, 24, 26, 32, 34, 35, 37, 39, 40, 44, 55, 128, 129, 143, 204, 246, 250, 263, 289, 315
"Clear Ponds" (Nagibin), 399
Cloud in Trousers, The (Mayakovsky), 63, 66-67, 70
Cohen, Hermann, 177
Colchis (Paustovsky), 312
Colleagues (Aksyonov), 301, 416
Collected Works (Paustovsky), 313
Collected Works (Yesenin), 91, 94
Collectivization, 51-56
Commissars, The (Libedinsky), 41-42
"Comrade Churygin Has the Floor" (Zamyatin), 105-6
Comrade Kislyakov (Romanov), 46
Comrades in Arms (Simonov), 431
Comrade Time and Comrade Art (Turbin), 427-28
Comsomol in the Battles for the Homeland (anthology), 279
Comsomolskaya Pravda (newspaper), 372, 435
Congress in Defense of Culture (1935), 152-53
"Consider Me a Communist!" (Yevtushenko), 388, 389-90, 393, 396
Conspiracy of Equals, The (Ehrenburg), 134
Conspiracy of Feelings, The (Olesha), 194, 197
"Conspiracy of Noble Minds, A" (Pertsov), 201
Constructivists, 331
Cooper, James Fenimore, 35, 236
"Cordon 273" (Paustovsky), 312

"Courage" (Akhmatova), 272
"Cow, The" (Yesenin), 86
Crane Homeland (Prishvin), 224, 231-33
Crazy Ship, The (Forsh), 95
Critics, Soviet, xi, 15, 16, 50, 57, 70, 77, 87, 103, 110, 125, 156, 182, 201, 253, 265-66, 282, 292, 294, 299, 301, 313-14, 324, 327, 366, 367, 377, 391-92, 404, 432
Cursed Days (Bunin), 13-15

Dangerous Companion, A (Salynsky), 437
Dangerous Connections (Zoshchenko), 123
Davydova, Natalya, 300
Days and Nights (Simonov), 274, 276-78, 358
Days of the Turbins, The (Bulgakov), 38, 246
Dead Souls (Gogol), 216
"Deep in Russia" (Paustovsky), 307
Diary (Blok), 11
Diary of Kostya Ryabtsev, The (Ognyov), viii
Difficult Spring, A (Ovechkin), 350, 353-56
"Distance of Half a Kilometer, A" (Voynovich), 432
District Workadays (Ovechkin), 347-50
Dobrovolsky, Vladimir, 286, 366
Doctor Zhivago (Pasternak), 178 n, 180, 184-87, 234
Dom Iskusstv (journal), 108
Don Quixote (Cervantes), 194, 335
Don Tales (Sholokhov), 251
Don't Give Up the Queen (Sartakov), 301, 391
Dorosh, Yefim, 16, 420
Dos Passos, John, 371
Dostoyevsky, Fyodor Mikhailovich, 3, 16, 98, 212, 221, 230, 352, 371, 432
Dovzhenko, Alexander, 367
Doyle, Conan, 33, 309
"Dragon, The" (Zamyatin), 101-2
Drozdov, Alexander, 247
Druzin, Victor, 418
Dubrovsky (Pushkin), 332
Dudintsev, Vladimir, 281, 295, 317, 356, 370-82, 396, 407
Duncan, Isadora, 84
Dyoma Bayunov (Korobov), 45
"Dzhamilya" (Aitmatov), 432

Early Joys (Fedin), 288, 289, 432
Early Trains (Pasternak), 182

Ehrenburg, Ilya, 30, 45, 47, 49, 127–42, 143 n, 152–53, 290, 292–93, 294, 295, 343, 370, 407, 416, 420, 422, 426, 428–29, 430, 438
Eideman, 172
"Elemental Upheavals and Culture" (Blok), 18
Emelyanov, B., 266–67
"Emelyan Pilyay" (Gorky), 4
End of a Little Man, The (Leonov), 204, 206
Energy (Gladkov), 47, 59
Engineer Izotov's Love (Davydova), 300
Envy (Olesha), 44, 188, 189–93, 198–99, 200, 201
Erckmann-Chatrian, 265
Erdman, Nikolay, ix
Esenin, Sergey. *See* Yesenin, Sergey
Essays on Proletarian Literature (Lvov-Rogachevsky), 43
Eves (Ehrenburg), 130
Express, L' (magazine), 428
Extraordinary Adventures of Julio Jurenito and His Disciples (Ehrenburg), 129–30, 141
Extraordinary Summer, An (Fedin), 288–90, 432
Eyes of the Earth, The (Prishvin), 234

Facelia (Prishvin), 233, 234
Factory Girl (Volodin), 301, 437
Fadeyev, Alexander, xv, 31, 32, 35–36, 184, 279–80, 333
Fairy Tales for Adults (Zamyatin), 103
Falileyev, 204
Fall of Paris, The (Ehrenburg), 137–38, 139, 140, 141
Family of Taras, The (Gorbatov), 280, 345
Fate (Avdeyenko), 47
Fate of Charles Lonceville (Paustovsky), 312
Fear (Afinogenov), 48–49, 436
February revolution, 238, 246
Fedin, Konstantin, x, xv, 12, 13, 16, 19, 21, 23, 24, 45, 288–90, 416, 418, 428, 431–32
Fellow Travelers, 25, 29, 30, 43, 134, 135, 181, 246
"Fellows of Your Own Age" (Gerasimov), 301
Fet, Afanasi A., 9, 16
"Few Words about Lyricism, A" (Bergholts), 290
Fifth Wound, The (Remizov), 158
Fires of Saint Dominic, The (Zamyatin), 105

"First Acquaintance" (Nekrasov), 357
"First Love" (Turgenev), 98
Fisher of Men, The (Zamyatin), 99
Five Evenings (Volodin), 437
Five-Year Plans, 48, 56–59, 61, 80, 118, 123, 134, 135, 169, 199, 214, 248, 249, 258
"Flame" (Blok), 18
Flea, The (Zamyatin), 104, 108
"Flood, The" (Zamyatin), 109
Foma Gordeyev (Gorky), 5–6
Foreign Literature (magazine), 142, 407
Forgotten Friend, The (Salynsky), 437
Forsh, Olga, 95, 168
Forum of European Writers (1963), 426–27, 428–30, 432
France, Anatole, 371
Frank, Waldo, 152
Frolov, V., 301, 402, 404
"From My Literary Notebooks" (Olesha), 188
"From the Secret Notebooks of the Fellow Traveler Zand" (Olesha), 188, 194, 195–96
"From Wrong Positions" (Vasilevsky), 292
Front, The (Korneychuk), 274, 275–76
Front Line Diaries (Stavsky), 278
Frunze, Commander, 163, 165
Furmanov, Dmitry, xii, 31, 32, 33–35, 150
Futurists, 19–20, 62, 331

Gagarin, Yury, 418
Gastev, Alexey, 21–22
Gate of Ilyich, The (Khutsiev and Shpalikov), 415
Gauzner, Zhanna, 327
Gay, John, 151
"Gay Adventure, A" (Zoshchenko), 118–19
Gaydar, Arkady, 315
"Gedali" (Babel), 150, 155
Geese and Swans (Neverov), 39
Gekht, Semyon, 315
Gerasimov, I., 301
Gerasimov, Sergey, 413
"Get Down, We're Here" (Nagibin), 399
Gippius, Zinaida, 12
Gladkov, Fyodor, xv, 8, 39–40, 47, 59
Gleb, 352
Gloomy Morning, A (Tolstoy), 245
God (Slutsky), 433
Gogol, Nikolay V., 16, 98, 100, 158, 205, 216, 332

Index

Golden Carriage (Leonov), 221
Golden Rose, The (Paustovsky), 303, 314
"Golden Woods Have Spoken, The" (Yesenin), 88
Good Luck (Rozov), 300
Gorbatov, Boris, 280, 345
Gorbov, Dmitry, 28, 30
Gordon, Patrick, 243
Gorky, Maxim, xi, 1–9, 13, 16, 20, 36, 37, 39, 66, 87, 90, 109, 124, 144, 145–46, 147, 151, 152, 155, 156, 170, 184, 200, 227, 313
Gorky Among Us (Fedin), x, 12, 19, 21, 289
Gosizdat (State Publishing House), 28
Goytisola, Juan, 426
Grabber, The (Ehrenburg), 45, 131, 133
Gradkov, 44
Granin, Daniil, 429–30
"Great and Simple Words" (Nekrasov), 358, 367–68
Great Power (Romashov), 286
"Great Truth of Poetry, The" (Tikhonov), 435
Gribachev, Nikolay, 408, 409, 410
Griboyedov, Alexander, 301
Grin, Alexander, viii, 7, 304–6, 307
Gronsky, 57
Grossman, Vasily, 281, 317
Gruzdev, Ilya, 24
Gudok (magazine), 188
Gudzenko, Semyon, 384
Guests (Zorin), 59, 299
"Guests in Stukachi" (Ovechkin), 345
Gumilyov, Nikolay, 189

"Halfway to the Moon" (Aksyonov), 424–25
Happiness (Pavlenko), 286–87
Hard Times (Zoshchenko), 115
Harvest (Nikolaeva), 294
Harvest Time (Arosev), 27
"Havana" (Mayakovsky), 73
Heine, Heinrich, 9
Hemingway, Ernest, 202, 371
Henry, O., 110, 111
Hero of Our Times, A (Lermontov), 50
Herzen, Alexander I., 313
History of a Peasant (Erckmann-Chatrian), 265
History of My Contemporary, A (Korolenko), 313
History of Russian Soviet Literature, 172
Hitler, Adolf, 137, 217, 395

Hoffman, E. T. A., 22, 23
"Holiday Eve" (Nagibin), 398
Homeland and Strange Land (Tvardovsky), 333, 338–39, 437
"Homeless Russia" (Yesenin), 87, 94
Honor (Medynsk), 327
"Hooligan, The" (Yesenin), 85
"Hooligan's Confession, A" (Yesenin), 81
House by the Roadside, A (Tvardovsky), 333, 336–38
House of Writers, 13, 23
"House over a Precipice, A" (Kazakov), 402
How Steel Was Tempered (Ostrovsky), 50
Humorous Stories (Zoshchenko), 115
"Hunt after Happiness, The" (Prishvin), 224
Hyperboloid of the Engineer Garin (Tolstoy), 240

"I Am Afraid" (Zamyatin), xii
"I Am the Last of Village Poets" (Yesenin), 81, 88
"If We Forget the 'Hour Hand'" (Sarnov), 391
"I Have One Amusement Left" (Yesenin), 86
Ilf, Ilya, 45, 71
"I Look into the Past" (Olesha), 194
I Love (Avdeyenko), 47, 345
"I Love" (Mayakovsky), 77
"Ilya Isaakovich and Margarita Prokofievna" (Babel), 144
Ilya Kosogor (Panova), 317
Ilyichev, Leonid, 411, 412–13, 421
Ilyin, Yakov, 47, 49
Imaginists, 20, 81, 84
I Myself (Mayakovsky), 62, 63
"In a Small Town" (Pismenny), 60
Inber, Vera, 29
"In Its Place" (Dudintsev), 372–73
In Old Moscow (Panova), 317
In Search of Optimism (Shklovsky), 78
In the Land of the Unfrightened Birds (Prishvin), 222, 223
In the Name of the Young (Panfyorov), 292
In the Native City (Nekrasov), 295, 363–67, 368
"In the Same District" (Ovechkin), 350
"In the Streetcar" (Nagibin), 399
In the Trenches of Stalingrad (Nekrasov), 278, 358–61, 362, 363
"In the World" (Olesha), 201

Invasion, The (Leonov), 217, 218–19, 274, 275
Irkutsk Story (Arbuzov), 436
Iron Flood, The (Serafimovich), 32–33
Isakovsky, Mikhail, 31, 332
Iskusstvo Kino (magazine), 358
"Island, The" (Makarov), 52
Islanders, The (Zamyatin), 99
It's Good (Mayakovsky), 76–77, 392
Ivan and Marya (Pilnyak), 172
Ivanov, Vsevolod, 7, 24, 29, 32, 36–37, 296
Ivanov, Vyacheslav, 189, 237
Ivanov-Razumnik, 99
Ivanter, I., 343
Ivan the Terrible (Tolstoy), 237, 245
Ivich, A., 324
"I Want to Be Honest" (Voynovich), 432
Izvestia (newspaper), 43, 170, 361, 377

"Jackdaws" (Yesenin), 83
Jammes, Francis, 68
Joyce, James, 429

"Kachalov's Dog" (Yesenin), 393
Kafka, Franz, 429
Kalita, Ivan, 9
Kallash, V. V., 240
Kalyaev (assassin), 204
Kamerny Theatre, 178
Kara-Bugaz (Paustovsky), 310–11
Karavayeva, Anna, 28
Karpov, M., 52
Katayev, Ivan, x, 27–28, 30
Katayev, Valentin, 29, 47, 54, 189, 315
Kaufman, Rosa, 175
Kaverin, Venyamin, 24
Kazakov, Yury, 396, 400–5, 432
Kazakova, Rimma, 298
"Khazar Ornament" (Nagibin), 399
Khazin, Alexander, 284
Khodasevich, Vladislav, 178
Khrushchev, Nikita, 269–70, 296–97, 342, 378–79, 383, 406–7, 408, 410–11, 412, 414–16, 421, 422, 430
Khutsiev, Marlen, 368
Kiprensky, 315
Kira Georgievna (Nekrasov), 368–69
Kirillov, Vladimir, vii, 43, 96
Kirov, 50
Kirsanov, Semyon, 189
Kleist, Heinrich, 178, 182
Kleshchenko, Alexander, 404

Klim Samgin (Gorky), 156, 184, 227
Kluyev, Nikolay, ix, 51–52, 83, 95, 189
Klychkov, Sergey, vii
Klychkov, Vsevolod, 408, 409, 410, 415
Kolkhoznaya Pravda (newspaper), 345
Kolkhoz Stories (Ovechkin), 345
Koltsov, Alexey, 84
Koltsov, Mikhail, x
"Komarov" (Nagibin), 398
Kommunist (magazine), 406, 408
Konovalov, Grigory, 286
Konstantin Paustovsky (Lvov), 306
Koppelman, 204
Korneychuk, Alexander, 274, 275–76, 409, 410
Korobov, Yakov, 45
Korolenko, Vladimir, 3, 313, 352
Koshevoy, Oleg, 280
Kovyakin's Journal (Leonov), 205, 206
Kozhevnikov, V., 300
Krasnaya Nov (magazine), 24, 25, 26, 57, 91, 165, 169, 210, 345
Kreutzer Sonata, The (Tolstoy), 17
Krick, Benya, 143, 151
Krokodil (magazine), 126
Kronstadt rebellion, 42
Kruzhilkha (Panova), 318, 320–24
Krylov, Ivan, 43
Kulkov, Mitrofan Platonovich, 204
Kuranov, Yury, 396, 404
Kurymushka (Prishvin), 222, 226
Kuznitsa (Smithy), 21, 30

Lady, The (Zoshchenko), 115
"Lament for Yesenin" (Kluyev), 51, 95
Land of Muravia (Tvardovsky), 54, 331, 332–34
Land of Scoundrels, The (Yesenin), 91, 94
Large Conveyor, The (Ilyin), 47, 49
Large Soviet Encyclopedia, 172
Lassalle, Ferdinand, 64
Last of the Mohicans, The (Cooper), 35
Last of the Udege, The (Fadeyev), 35, 279
Last Poppies Are Dying, The (Zabolotsky), 434
Lavrenyov, Boris, 20, 271
LEF (Left Front in Art), 20, 30
Lenin, N., 249–50
Leningrad (magazine), 284

Index

Leonov, Leonid, 20, 39, 45, 47, 203-21, 274, 275, 294, 333 n, 416, 428
Lermontov, Mikhail, 9, 15, 50, 223, 301, 315, 332
Leskov, Nikolay, 16, 99, 104, 158
"Lessons of Stendhal" (Ehrenburg), 142, 407
Letopis (magazine), 7, 144, 145
"Letters from Tula" (Pasternak), 179-80
Letters to the Writer (Zoshchenko), 121
"Letter to My Mother" (Yesenin), 88, 393
"Let Us Talk Substantively" (Litvinov), 378
"Levers" (Yashin), 422
Levin, Boris, 47, 49
Levitan, 315
Lezhnev, Abram, 28
Lezhnev, Isaac, 252, 253-54, 266, 267
Libedinsky, Yury, 29, 41-42
Life and Death of Nikolay Kurbov (Ehrenburg), 127, 131-32
Life of Arseniev, The (Bunin), 15
Life of Matvey Kozhemyakin (Gorky), 5, 7
"Light in the Window, The" (Nagibin), 399
"Lightning" (Paustovsky), 314
Light over the Land (Babaevsky), 294
Likharev, 284
"Lilacs in Bloom" (Zoshchenko), 115
List of Blessings, A (Olesha), 188, 194-95
Literature and Life (newspaper), 247, 395, 404, 409, 410, 433
Literature and Revolution (Trotsky), 62
Literaturnye Zapiski (Literary Notes), 23
"Literary Diaries" (Olesha), 201
Literary Diary (Prishvin), 234
Literary Encyclopedia, 172, 188
"Literary Everydays" (Zoshchenko), 126
Literary Gazette (magazine), 80, 109, 125, 154, 197, 201, 202, 213, 235, 265, 285, 290, 292, 295, 296, 297, 298, 302, 313, 324, 329, 367, 377, 383, 387, 393, 395, 396, 400, 409, 410, 417, 419, 426
Literary Moscow (magazine), 183, 188, 273, 297, 377, 422
Literary Russia (magazine), 410, 417, 418

Little Humpbacked Horse, The (Yershov), 332
Litvinov, Vasily, 378
Living and the Dead, The (Simonov), 431
Loader, The (Rumyantseva), 436
London, Jack, 35, 67, 111, 196, 374
Loneliness (Virta), 55-56
"Loner, The" (Kazakov), 402-3
Losev, A., 59
Love of Jeanne Ney, The (Ehrenburg), 127
Lukashevich, Klavdia, 63
Lukonin, Mikhail, 384
Luna Park Theatre, 66
Lunts, Lev, 23, 24, 309
Lvov, Sergey, 306
Lvov-Rogachevsky, V., 43
Lyeskov, Nikolay. *See* Leskov, Nikolay
"Lyubka the Cossack" (Babel), 154

Machines and Wolves (Pilnyak), 44, 166, 169, 172
Magpie's Tales, A (Tolstoy), 237
Mahogany (Pilnyak), 169-70, 172, 185
"Makar Chudra" (Gorky), 4
Makarenko, A. S., 57-59
Makarov, Ivan, 31, 52, 299-300
Malinovsky, A. A., 20
Malyshkin, Alexander, 28, 59, 158
"Mamma, Rimma, and Alla" (Babel), 144-45
"Mamma and the Evening Murdered by the Germans" (Mayakovsky), 67
"Man" (Gorky), 4
"Man" (Mayakovsky), 67, 177
"Man and the Road, The" (Nagibin), 397-98
Mandelstam, Osip, 29, 141, 189
Mann, Heinrich, 152
Manure (Seyfullina), 39
Marats of Ryazan, The (Smelyakov), 435
Maria (Babel), 154
Mariengof, Anatoly, 81, 84, 87
Markov, Alexey, 395
Marx, Karl, 64, 232
Master, The (Slutsky), 433
"Matryona's House" (Solzhenitsyn), 423-24
Mayakovsky, Vladimir, 1-3, 4, 20, 30, 61-79, 94-95, 124, 177, 178, 184, 194, 390, 391, 393-95
Mayakovsky, His Life and Work (Pertsov), 68
"Mayakovsky's Mother" (Yevtushenko), 390, 393

Medvedev, Seryozha, 65
Medynsky, Grigory, 294-95, 327
"Meeting with a Birch, A" (Dudintsev), 372
Melekhov, Grigory, 266
"Men of the Sixties" (Rassadin), 301
Merezhkovsky, Dmitry, 12
Merry Life, A (Zoshchenko), 115
"Message to Young Writers" (Tolstoy), 250
Metter, I., 298
"Mexico" (Mayakovsky), 73
Meyerhold, Vsevolod, 71
Mikoyan, Anastas, 378
Mister Sinebryukhov (Zoshchenko), 113
Modern Soviet Literature (Timofeyev), ix
Molodaya Gvardiya (magazine), 25, 50, 51, 301, 399
Molot (newspaper), 345
Monat, Der (magazine), 370
Moravia, Alberto, 426
Moryak (newspaper), 153
Moscow Art Theatre, 37, 38, 183, 358
Moscow Association of Proletarian Writers (MAPP), 21, 28-31
Moscow Does Not Believe in Tears (Ehrenburg), 134
Moscow trials (1936-38), 44, 56, 172, 249, 422
Moskva (magazine), 15, 298, 301, 400, 428, 432
Mother, The (Gorky), 6-7
"Mother Field" (Aitmatov), 432
Mother-Stepmother (Pilnyak), 161
Mother Volga (Panfyorov), 291-92
Mountains (Zarubin), 55
Mozart, Wolfgang, 315
Musaguet Publishing House, 178
"My Answer" (Markov), 395
My Childhood (Gladkov), 8
"My Discovery of America" (Mayakovsky), 73
My Elder Sister (Volodin), 437
"My Grandmother" (Yevtushenko), 384-85
"My Little Poplar in a Red Kerchief" (Aitmatov), 432
"My New Translations" (Pasternak), 182
My Past and Thoughts (Herzen), 313
My Road (Tolstoy), 244-45
My Sister, Life (Pasternak), 178
Mystery-Bouffe (Mayakovsky), 70, 71-72
My Universities (Gorky), 7

Nadson, Semyon, 392
Nagibin, Yury, 396-400, 404, 432
Nakanune (On the Eve), 238
Naked Years, The (Pilnyak), 39, 158-60, 162, 166, 172
Na Literaturnom Postu (magazine), 29
Na Postu (magazine), 26, 29
Nasedkin, V., 25
Nashi Dostizheniya (magazine), 27
Natalya Tarpova (Semyonov), 42
Nedogonov, Alexey, 384
Neizvestny, Ernest, 415
Nekrasov, Nikolay A., 234 n, 352, 356
Nekrasov, Victor, 278, 295, 317, 332, 357-69, 392, 396, 415, 420, 422, 426, 438
NEP (New Economic Policy) period, 40, 44-46, 72, 74, 118, 131, 133, 168, 208, 240, 326
Nervous People (Zoshchenko), 115
Netochka Nezvanova (Dostoyevsky), 98
Neverov, Alexander, 31, 39
"New Hut, A" (Tvardovsky), 332
New Workers, The (Zhiga), 344
New Year's Fable (Dudintsev), 379-82
New York Times (newspaper), 269
Neyman, Yulia, 273
Nicholas I, 77
"Night" (Kazakov), 403
"Night" (Mayakovsky), 62
"Nighttime Guest, A" (Nagibin), 399
Nikitin, Ivan, 332
Nikolaeva, Galina, 294
Nikolayev (assassin), 50
Nikon Starkolenny (Prishvin), 224
Nikulin, Lev, 200, 202
Nineteen-Eighteen (Tolstoy), 245, 248
1984 (Orwell), 106
1905 (Pasternak), 179
Ninth Wave, The (Ehrenburg), 139, 140-41
"Noble Malady, A" (Pasternak), 181
Nobel Prize, 15, 174
Nomakh (Yesenin), 91-93, 94
"Not a Day without a Line" (Olesha), 201
Not by Bread Alone (Dudintsev), 295, 370, 372, 373-79, 407
"Notes on Translation of Shakespeare's Tragedies" (Pasternak), 183
Novaya Zhizn (newspaper), 1

Index

Novel Without Lies (Mariengof), 81
Novy LEF (magazine), 70
Novy Mir (magazine), 27, 52, 57, 70, 94, 124, 127, 138–39, 151, 163, 165, 166, 233, 247, 261, 269, 274, 281, 286, 295, 300, 312, 325, 333, 340, 343, 347, 357, 363, 368, 372, 373, 379, 385, 407, 409, 413, 415, 419, 420, 422, 423, 424, 428, 429, 430, 432, 435, 438
Novy Zhurnal (magazine), 105

Ocean of Flax, An (Vityazev), 54
October revolution, 11, 15, 27, 31, 33, 34, 51, 60, 61, 69, 71, 77, 105, 133, 157, 160–61, 162, 171, 172, 238, 248
Odessa Tales (Babel), 151
"Ode to the Revolution" (Mayakovsky), 70
Ognyov, N., viii, 158
Oktyabr (magazine), 25, 44, 124, 233, 252, 282, 292, 343, 345, 347, 385, 391, 402, 409
Okudzhava, Bulat, 435
Okurov Township, The (Gorky), 7
"Old Turtle, The" (Nagibin), 398
"Old Woman Izergil, The" (Gorky), 4
Olesha, Yury, 44, 188–202, 315
On Art and Literature (Shaginyan), vii–ix
Onchukov, N., 223
On Contemporary Literature (Polonsky), 151
One Day in the Life of Ivan Denisovich (Solzhenitsyn), 413–14, 423, 438
"Onegin's Return to Postwar Leningrad" (Khazin), 284
"On Either Side of the Ocean" (Nekrasov), 415, 422
150,000,000 (Mayakovsky), 70–71
One-Storey America (Petrov), 71
"On Kolkhoz Literature" (Abramov), 294
"On Sincerity in Literature" (Pomerantsev), 290, 294, 333 n
"On the Historic Frontier" (Tolstoy), 247
"On the Irtysh" (Ivanov), 36
"On the Job" (Semyonov), 432
"On the Poet's Death" (Pasternak), 61
"On Two Poetic Generations" (Yevtushenko), 383
"Open Letter" (Romanov), 402–3
"Oranges from Morocco" (Aksyonov), 416, 424–25
Orchards of Polovchansk, The (Leonov), 217
Ordinary Man, An (Leonov), 217
"Ordinary Man, An" (Tolstoy), 237–38
"O Russia, spread thy wings" (Koltsov), 84
Orwell, George, 106
Ostrovsky, Nikolay, 16, 50–51
Out among People (Gorky), 7
Ovalov, L., 379
Ovechkin, Valentin, 282–84, 294, 301, 317, 344–56, 420

Paleface Brothers (Zoshchenko), 115
Panfyorov, Fyodor, xv, 31, 39, 45, 54, 55, 291–92, 333
Panov, Nikolay, 367
Panova, Vera, 281, 290
Pantocrator (Yesenin), 85
"Papa, Put It Together" (Aksyonov), 424, 425
"Parting" (Pasternak), 186
Party Assignment (Ovalov), 379
Pasternak, Boris, ix, 61, 65, 78, 174–87, 189, 234, 371
Pasternak, Leonid, 175
"Pauper, The" (Olesha), 198–200
Paustovsky, Konstantin, 16, 153–54, 302–16, 400, 416, 426, 432
Pavlenko, Pyotr, 28, 286
Pavlov, Sergey, 419
Pedagogical Epic, A (Makarenko), 57
People, Years, Life (Ehrenburg), 128, 422
Peredvizhniki group, 112
Pereval group, 24–26
Perevaltsy, 27, 28, 56
Pereverzev, V., 30
Pertsov, Victor, 68, 201
Peter I (Tolstoy), 57, 88, 240–45, 249, 250
Peter I, the Great, 88, 160
Peter III, 89
Peter's Day (Tolstoy), 241
Petrov, Evgeny, 45, 71
"Petrovka, 38" (Semyonov), 432
Petushikhino Breakthrough, The (Leonov), 204, 205
Picasso, Pablo, 14
Pilnyak, Boris, ix, 39, 44, 60, 71, 156–73, 185, 344
Pingaud, Bernard, 428, 429
"Pipe, A" (Nagibin), 399
"Pirozhkov Family, The" (Panova), 318
Pismenny, Alexander, 60
Podyachev, Semyon, viii, 8
Poe, Edgar Allan, 67, 306

Poems (Ehrenburg), 128
Poems from My Notebook (Tvardovsky), 339–40
"Poet, The" (Katayev), 27
"Poet, The" (Pushkin), 403
Pogodin, Nikolay, 47, 436
Polonsky, Vyacheslav, 70, 151
Poltava (Pushkin), 332
Pomerantsev, V., 27, 290–91, 292, 294, 333
Populism, 30, 41, 156
Populist Family, A (magazine), 83
"Portrait, The" (Lavrenyov), 271
Possessed, The (Dostoyevsky), 230
Poultry Maid Agafya (Lukashevich), 63
"Praskovya Maximovna" (Ovechkin), 345
Pravda (newspaper), 26, 43, 252, 268, 269, 272, 275, 285, 354, 355, 377, 410, 417 n, 419, 420, 428
"Prayer for a Star" (Jammes), 68
"Prayer for Russia" (Ehrenburg), 128
"Precious Dust" (Paustovsky), 303–4
Precocious Autobiography (Yevtushenko), 417
Prikamye (anthology), 318
Prince of Homburg (Kleist), 182
Prishvin, Mikhail, 28, 99, 222–35, 428
"Profitable Enterprise, A" (Zoshchenko), 115–16
Prokofiev, Alexander, 416
Proletarskaya Kultura (magazine), 22
Proletcult, the, 20–22, 25, 48
Prosecutor's Daughter, The (Yanovsky), 327
Protalino, 426
Protochny Lane (Ehrenburg), 131, 133
Proust, Marcel, 371, 429
Provincial, The (Zamyatin), 99, 158
Provincial People (Malyshkin), 59
Pugachev (Yesenin), 88, 89–90
Pugavhev, Emelyan, 89
Purges, literary, ix, 26–27, 51–52, 56–57, 126, 284–87, 422. See also Moscow trials
Pushkin, Alexander, 9, 16, 38, 77, 78, 89, 158, 179, 185, 196, 299, 301, 315, 331, 332, 403

"Quarter Century of Soviet Literature" (Tolstoy), xi, 124
"Quest of Our Young Prose" (Borshchagovsky), 428

Quiet Don, The (Sholokhov), 39, 252–58, 261–68

Rablé Factory, The (Chumandrin), 43
Radek, Karl, 172
Radunitsa (Yesenin), 83
Rasputin, Grigory, 105
Rassadin, Stanislav, 301
Rebellion (Serafimovich), 34
Recollections (Bunin), 14, 15, 16
Red Cavalry (Babel), 32, 39, 147–51
Red Roar (Kluyev), 51
Reflections (Panfyorov), 292
Reich, Zinaida, 84
Reid, Mayne, 33, 35, 236
Reminiscences (Gorky), 5–6
"Reminiscences about Blok" (Zamyatin), 100
"Reminiscences about Eduard Bagritsky" (Olesha), 189
Remizov, Alexey, x, 99, 158, 161, 223
Repin, Gorky, Makakovsky, Bryusov (Chukovsky), 8
"Retribution" (Blok), 12
Revolution of 1905, 64, 99
Revolution of 1917, 18–19, 33, 61, 84, 97
"Rightness" (Aliger), 56, 343
Right to Life, The (Romanov), 46
Rilke, Rainer Maria, 175–77
Rimbaud, Arthur, 68
Ripening of Fruits, The (Pilnyak), 169, 171–72
Road to Calvary, The (Tolstoy), 57, 185, 240, 242, 245–47, 248, 249, 250, 290
Road to the Ocean, The (Leonov), 47, 217, 221
"Rocky Rapids" (Nagibin), 399
Romanov, Panteleymon, 45, 46, 402–3
Romashov, Boris, 286, 436
Roschislavsky, Dmitry, 167, 168
Rout, The (Fadeyev), 32, 35–36, 279
Rozhdestvensky, Robert, 384, 387, 407, 416, 435
Rozhdestvensky, Vsevolod, 83
Rozov, Victor, 300
Rublev, Andrey, 171
Ruchyov, Boris, ix
Ruge, Gerd, 370, 371, 372, 382
Rumyantseva, Maya, 435–36
Russian Association of Proletarian Writers (RAPP), 21, 28, 29–31, 48, 57, 108
Russian Forest, The (Leonov), 221, 294, 333 n

Index

Russian Soviet Literature (Timofeyev), 1
Russkiye Vedomosti (newspaper), 237
Russky Sovremennik (magazine), 100, 103
Rylenkov, Nikolay, 418

Sabashnikov, 204
Safe Conduct (Pasternak), 78, 175, 180, 184
Saint-Exupéry, Antoine de, 430
Salinger, J. D., 424, 426
Salisbury, Harrison, 269
Salome, 176
Salynsky, Afanasy, 437
Sarnov, B., 391–92
Sartakov, Sergey, 301, 391
"Sashok" (Prishvin), 222, 223
"Saveliev" (Ovechkin), 345
Sayanov, 284
Scarlet Sails (Grin), viii, 7, 305, 307
Scott, Walter, 33
Scourge of God, The (Zamyatin), 109–10
Scriabin, Alexander, 175
"Scythians, The" (Blok), 11
Seasons of the Year (Panova), 325–27
Second Birth (Pasternak), 180, 181
Second Day, The (Ehrenburg), 47, 49, 135–37
Secretary of the Regional Committee (Kochetov), 408
Secrets of the Earth (Prishvin), 232
Selected Works (Babel), 143, 152
Semyonov, Sergey, 42
Semyonov, Yulian, 396, 404, 432
Sentimental Story (Panova), 325, 328–30
Serafimovich, Alexander, xii, 32–33, 252–53
Serapion Brotherhood, 7, 22–24, 25, 97, 98, 112, 309
Serebrov, A., 203 n
Sergey Alexandrovich, Grand Duke, 204
"Serious Life" (Makarov), 299
Seryozha (Panova), 65, 325
Seyfullina, Lydia, 39, 200, 433
Shaginyan, Marietta, viii–ix, 29
Shakespeare, William, 182–84
Shapiro, Henry, 420
Shcheglov, Mark, 294, 333
Sheremetyev, Boris, 243
Shershenevich, Vadim, 84
Shipovnik Publishing House, 204
Shishova, Zinaida, 189
Shklovsky, Victor, 78, 189

Shock-work Poetry, 22
Sholokhov, Mikhail, 19, 31, 39, 52–53, 251–70, 352, 409, 410, 416, 428
Sillitoe, Alan, 426
Silver Dove (Bely), 158
Simonov, Konstantin, xv, 271–72, 274, 276–78, 285, 286, 287–88, 294, 358, 361, 407, 428, 431
"Sketches" (Bukharin), 62, 72
Skutarevsky (Leonov), 217
"Skyscraper in Cross-Section" (Mayakovsky), 73
Slap in the Face of Public Taste, A (Mayakovsky), 62
Slonimsky, Mikhail, 23, 24
Slutsky, Boris, 433–34
Smell of Life, The (Bezymensky), 43
Smelyakov, Yaroslav, 434, 435
Smoke of the Fatherland (Simonov), 286, 287–88
Smolensk Village (newspaper), 332
Sobolev, Leonid, 415, 417–18, 430
Sofronov, Anatoly, 286, 418
Soldiers (Nekrasov), 362
Soldiers Are Not Born (Simonov), 431
Soloukhin, Vladimir, 387–88
Solovyov, Boris, 361
Solovyov, Vladimir, 9, 187
Solzhenitsyn, Alexander, 413, 420, 423, 426, 438
"Song about a Dog" (Yesenin), 86
"Song about a Falcon" (Gorky), 4
Song about the Great Campaign (Yesenin), 88
"Song of the Stormy Petrel" (Gorky), 4
"Songs of a Drunk" (Yesenin), 85
"Son of a Bitch" (Yesenin), 85
Sorin, Semyon, 387
"Sorokoust" (Yesenin), 81
Sot (Leonov), 47, 214–17
Soviet Writers (anthology), 370
Spacious Earth (Pasternak), 182
"Spain" (Mayakovsky), 73
Spektorsky (Pasternak), 180
Spring, The (Ehrenburg), 142
Spring of the World, The (Prishvin), 233–34
Stalin, Joseph, 108, 109, 163, 168, 244, 249–50, 258, 260, 289, 296–97, 343, 383, 406, 407, 433
Stalin Prizes, 286, 294, 350–51
Stanislavsky, Konstantin, 358
Stanitsa (Stavsky), 52, 54
"Stanzas" (Yesenin), 93
Starikov, D., 395
Stavsky, V., 52, 54, 278
"Steel Ring, The" (Paustovsky), 305

Stendhal, 142
Stern Youth, A (Olesha), 188, 200–1
Storeroom of the Sun, The (Prishvin), 234
Stories (Babel), 151
Stories about Love (Romanov), 46
Stories of Ivan Sudarev (Tolstoy), 274–75, 437
Stories of Nazar Ilyich, The (Zoshchenko), 113
Storm, The (Ehrenburg), 139–40
Stormy Life of Lazik Roitschwantz (Ehrenburg), 132
"Story about the Most Important Thing" (Zamyatin), 102–3
"Story of My Dovecote" (Babel), 146–47
Story of My Life (Paustovsky), 303, 312–14, 432
Strakhov, Nikolay, xi
Streets of Leningrad, The (Panova), 330
"Summer" (Pasternak), 174
Sunset (Babel), 151
Surf, The (Goytisola), 426
Surikov Circle, the, 82–83
Surkov, Alexey A., 143 n, 271, 294, 295, 350, 370, 418
Symbolists, 158

Tabidze, Titsian, 180, 181
Taking of Velikoshumsk, The (Leonov), 204, 219–21
"Tale, The" (Pasternak), 180
Tale of Igor's Host, The (Pilnyak), 171–72, 248
Tale of the North (Paustovsky), 311
"Tale of the Unextinguished Moon, The" (Pilnyak), 162–67
Tale of the Woods (Paustovsky), 311–12
Taras Bulba (Gogol), 332
Tarasov-Rodionov, Alexander, 44
Tarusa Pages (anthology), 434
Tashkent, City of Bread (Neverov), 39
"Tavern Moscow" (Yesenin), 85
Tchaikovsky, Pyotr Ilych, 315
"Telegram, The" (Paustovsky), 312
"Teller of Tales, The" (Paustovsky), 305–6
Tendryakov, Vladimir, 347, 420
Ten Horsepower (Ehrenburg), 134
"Terrible Night, A" (Zoshchenko), 119
Thaw, The (Ehrenburg), 141, 292–93, 294, 295, 343
Theatre (magazine), 299, 300, 301

Theatre and Dramaturgy (magazine), 154
Themes and Variations (Pasternak), 178
There Were Two Comrades (Levin), 47, 49
They Fought for the Homeland (Sholokhov), 268–69
Thief, The (Leonov), 45, 208–14, 221
Third Capital, The (Pilnyak), 156–57, 161, 162, 172
Thirteen Pipes (Ehrenburg), 134
Thirty Days (magazine), 196
"Thoughts, Disputable and Indisputable" (Paustovsky), 400
"Thoughts after a Conference" (Zalygin), 347
"Three Encounters" (Nekrasov), 361–63
Three Fat Men (Olesha), 188, 189, 193–94
Three in Gray Coats (Dobrovolsky), 286
"Ticket to the Stars, A" (Aksyonov), 416, 424
Tikhonov, Nikolay, 24, 29, 433, 435
Time, Forward! (Katayev), 47, 54
Time of Great Expectations, The (Paustovsky), 153
Timofeyev, L. I., ix, 1, 93
Tolstoy, Alexey, xi, 20, 29, 30, 45, 57, 88, 119–20, 124, 168, 185, 236–50, 274–75, 290, 437
Tolstoy, Leo, xi, 15, 16, 17, 41, 98, 155, 176, 178, 184, 202, 223, 253, 352, 371, 429
Tolstoy, Pyotr, 243
"To My Dog" (Yevtushenko), 393
"To Pushkin" (Yesenin), 87
Toroshelidze, 181
"To School" (Nagibin), 398
"To the Pushkin House" (Blok), 13
Town in the Steppe, A (Serafimovich), 32
Transvaal (Fedin), 45
Traveling Companions (Panova), 318–20
Trenyov, Konstantin, 20
Tretyakov, Sergey, 30
Trifonov, Yury, 366
Trotsky, Leon, 25, 62, 249, 289
Troyepolsky, Gavriil, 347, 420
Trud (newspaper), 396
Tsvetaeva, Marina, 178
Turbin, Vladimir, 427–28, 430
Turgenev, Ivan S., 15, 16, 41, 158, 352
Tvardovsky, Alexander, 54, 57, 280–82, 290, 294, 317, 331–43, 409, 410,

Index

Tvardovsky, (cont'd)
  413, 419, 420, 429, 430–31, 437, 438
Tveryak, Alexey, viii
"Twelve, The" (Blok), xii, 11, 19, 61
Twin in the Clouds, The (Pasternak), 177
"Two Chekhovs, The" (Mayakovsky), 68–69
"Two Days" (Metter), 298
"Two Souls" (Lezhnev), 266, 267
Tychina, Pavlo, 419
Tyorkin in the Other World (Tvardovsky), 430, 438
Tyutchev, Fyodor, 9, 187, 223

Ulrikh, Vassily Danilovich, 222
Under the Old Lindens (Tolstoy), 237
Undressed Spring (Prishvin), 233, 234
University (Konovalov), 286
Unsubmissive, The (Karpov), 52
Unvanquished, The (Gorbatov), 345
Urban, A., 435
Uspensky, Gleb I., 352

Vadon, M., 144
"Vaganov" (Nagibin), 397
Valéry, Paul, 175
Vardin, I., 30
Vasilevsky, Vitaly, 292
Vasily Tyorkin (Tvardovsky), 280–82, 333, 335
Velikaya Krinitsa (Babel), 152
Veresayev, V., 20
Verlaine, Paul, 68
Verne, Jules, 33, 236
"Verses about a Soviet Passport" (Mayakovsky), 392
"Verses of a Brawler" (Yesenin), 85
Vesyoly, Artyom, x, 158
"Village, The" (Kluyev), 51
Village Chronicle (Tvardovsky), 333
"Village of Stepanchikovo" (Dostoyevsky), 352
Villon, François, 68, 85, 88, 128
Vilyam-Vilmont, N., 334–35
Vinokurov, Yevgeny, 297–98, 384, 387, 396
Violators, The (Tolstoy), 237
"Viper, The" (Tolstoy), 240
Virgin Soil Upturned (Sholokhov), 52–53, 258–61, 269–70
Virineya (Seyfullina), 39
Virta, Nikolay, 55–56
"Visit with Soviet Writers, A" (Ruge), 370

Vista beyond Vista (Tvardovsky), 57, 333, 340–42
Vityazev, D., 54
Vladimir Ilyich Lenin (Mayakovsky), 76
Vladimir Mayakovsky (Mayakovsky), 66, 177
Volga Flows into the Caspian Sea (Pilnyak), 168, 169–70
Volnitsa (Gladkov), 8
Volnov, Ivan, 8
Volodin, Alexander, 301, 437
"Vologda Wedding" (Yashin), 422–23
Volya Rossii (magazine), 106
Voprosy Literatury (magazine), 437
Voronin, S., 347
Voronsky, Alexander, 24, 26, 30, 91, 166–67
Voynovich, Vladimir, 432
Voznesensky, Andrey, 387, 391, 416, 417, 420, 424, 433, 435, 438

War, The (Ehrenburg), 138
War and Peace (Tolstoy), 253
War Communism, period of, 134
War Days (Tolstoy), 237
"War Is Declared" (Mayakovsky), 67
"Waste of Energy, A" (Gorky), 170
We (Zamyatin), 106–9, 185
Week, The (Libedinsky), 41
"Week in Turenevo, A" (Tolstoy), 237
"We Live Here" (Voynovich), 432
Wells, H. G., 110
"Werewolf" (Pushkin), 332
"We Were in Georgia" (Pasternak), 181
"What the Nightingale Sang About" (Zoshchenko), 118
White Coal, or the Tears of Werther (Ehrenburg), 134, 141
White Guard (Bulgakov), 32, 37, 38
White Nights (Dostoyevsky), 432
Whitman, Walt, 67
"Who Has Not Advised Me?" (Vinokurov), 297–98, 396
Wilson, Woodrow, 71
"Wingless People" (Panov), 367
"Winter Oak, The" (Nagibin), 398–99
Winter Station (Yevtushenko), 385–87
With Greetings from the Front (Ovechkin), 282–84, 301, 317, 345, 347

With One's Own Hands (Ovechkin), 350, 353
Without Cherry Blossoms (Romanov), 46
"Without Clear Positions" (Soloukhin), 387-88
"Without Kith or Kin" (Ovechkin), 345, 346
Without Pausing for a Breath (Ehrenburg), 135, 137
Wolf, The (Leonov), 217
Woman Drummer, The (Salynsky), 437
"Wooden Queen, The" (Leonov), 205
"Word as Weapon, The" (Ehrenburg), 127
World War I, 12, 14, 33, 112-13, 124, 126, 128, 137, 237, 246, 248
World War II, 60, 127, 137, 182, 247, 271, 370, 383
Writer, Art, and Time, The (Fedin), 23
"Writer and Reality, The" (Dorosh), 16
Writers (anthology), 222, 224
"Writer's Notes, A" (Olesha), 188
Writers' Union, vii, 26-27, 31, 56, 103, 125, 294, 318, 324, 351, 377, 378, 395, 409
"Writer's Work, The" (Ehrenburg), 290

Yanovsky, Yury, 327
Yashin, Alexander, 420, 422-23
Yashvili, Paolo, 180, 181
Year XXII, Book 15 (anthology), 305
Yermilov, Vladimir, 29
Yershov Brothers, The (Kochetov), 408
Yesenin, Sergey, 20, 29, 51, 61, 71, 80-96, 124, 184, 209, 393
Yevdokimov, Ivan, 28, 92
Yevseeva, Svetlana, 387

Yevtushenko, Yevgeny, 297, 383-96, 407, 416, 417, 420, 424, 435, 438
"You Are Not Alone" (Belenky), 301
Young Guard, The (Fadeyev), 279-80
Young Man, A (Losev), 59
"Young Poetry of Our Day, The" (Smelyakov), 435
"You Remember, Alyosha, the Roads of Smolensk?" (Simonov), 271-72
Youth Recaptured (Zoshchenko), 113, 122
Yunost (magazine), 298, 301, 416, 417, 424, 432

Zabolotsky, Nikolay, 434
Zalygin, S., 347
Zamoysky, P., 31, 52
Zamyatin, Yevgeny, ix, xii-xiii, 24, 97-111, 124, 158, 185, 344
Zarubin, 55
Zavety (magazine), 99
Zelinsky, Korneny, 94
Zernova, R., 432
Zeromski, Stefan, 87
Zharov, A., 43
Zhdanov, Andrey, 24, 126, 285
Zhenya Maslova (Dobrovolsky), 286
Zhiga, Ivan, 344
Zhuravlev, T., 347
Zlobina, Dina, 435-36
Znamya (magazine), 137, 141, 142, 183, 276, 278, 279, 280, 286, 290, 291, 292, 299, 300, 318, 320, 325, 334, 338, 358, 362, 397, 399, 402, 431, 434
Zorin, Leonid, 59, 299
Zoshchenko, Mikhail, ix, 24, 45, 112-26, 284, 286
Zvezda (newspaper), 51, 83, 125, 284, 324

VERA ALEXANDROVA, born in Russia, has contributed articles on Soviet literature to *The New Leader* and *The Saturday Review*, as well as to French, German, and Russian periodicals. Mrs. Alexandrova's analyses of Soviet cultural and literary developments appear twice a month in the Russian-language publication *Novoye Russkoye Slovo*. Her study, "Control of Soviet Literature in the Post-Stalin Period (1953–56)" was part of Columbia University's research project on the "History of the Communist Party in the Soviet Union."

MIRRA GINSBURG has worked as a translator of Russian for many years, primarily in the fields of fiction, criticism, biography, and the social and political sciences.

DATE DUE

MAR 1 6 1994			
MAY 2 3 1994			
MAY 3 1 1994			
JUL. 2 3 1998			